Windows Server® 2008 R2 Administration

Administration

Instant Reference

Windows Server® 2008 R2 Administration

Instant Reference

Matthew Hester

Chris Henley

Wiley Publishing, Inc.

Acquisitions Editor: Agatha Kim
Development Editor: Kim Beaudet
Technical Editor: Harold Wong
Production Editor: Dassi Zeidel
Copy Editor: Kim Wimpsett
Editorial Manager: Pete Gaughan
Production Manager: Tim Tate
Vice President and Executive Group Publisher: Richard Swadley
Vice President and Publisher: Neil Edde
Book Designer: Maureen Forys, Happenstance Type-O-Rama
Compositor: Craig Johnson, Happenstance Type-O-Rama
Proofreader: Josh Chase, Word One New York
Indexer: Jack Lewis
Project Coordinator, Cover: Lynsey Stanford
Cover Designer: Ryan Sneed
Cover Image: iStockphoto

Copyright © 2010 by Wiley Publishing, Inc., Indianapolis, Indiana

Published simultaneously in Canada

ISBN: 978-0-470-52539-5

For general information on our other products and services or to obtain technical support, please contact our Customer Care Department within the U.S. at (877) 762-2974, outside the U.S. at (317) 572-3993 or fax (317) 572-4002.

Wiley also publishes its books in a variety of electronic formats. Some content that appears in print may not be available in electronic books.

Library of Congress Cataloging-in-Publication Data

Hester, Matthew, 1971-
  Windows server 2008 R2 administration instant reference / Matthew Hester, Chris Henley. — 1st ed.
    p. cm.
  ISBN 978-0-470-52539-5 (pbk.)
  1. Microsoft Windows server. 2. Operating systems (Computers) I. Henley, Chris. II. Title.
  QA76.76.O63H496 2010
  005.4'476—dc22
                                    2009043725

10 9 8 7 6 5 4 3

Dear Reader,

Thank you for choosing *Windows Server 2008 R2 Administration Instant Reference*. This book is part of a family of premium-quality Sybex books, all of which are written by outstanding authors who combine practical experience with a gift for teaching.

Sybex was founded in 1976. More than 30 years later, we're still committed to producing consistently exceptional books. With each of our titles, we're working hard to set a new standard for the industry. From the paper we print on to the authors we work with, our goal is to bring you the best books available.

I hope you see all that reflected in these pages. I'd be very interested to hear your comments and get your feedback on how we're doing. Feel free to let me know what you think about this or any other Sybex book by sending me an email at nedde@wiley.com. If you think you've found a technical error in this book, please visit http://sybex.custhelp.com. Customer feedback is critical to our efforts at Sybex.

Best regards,

Neil Edde
Vice President and Publisher
Sybex, an Imprint of Wiley

*To Deb, for all of your love and support. I could not
have done it without you. It means so much to me that
you are on this journey with me. I love you!*

*To Nicole, Mitchell, and Caitlin for all your patience
when I was in my office writing. You are the best children
a dad could wish for, thank you and I love you guys.*
—Matthew Hester

*To Julie, my best friend, thanks for seeing my potential
and helping me realize it! All that I am I owe to you!*
*To Megan, Nicholas, and Lauren for helping me remember
that all things have been done in the wisdom of him who knoweth
all things. It is my pleasure to be your father!*
—Chris Henley

Acknowledgments

I would like to thank my friend and mentor Kerrie Meyler for guiding me through the process of writing and providing much needed happy hours and awesome advice. Thanks, Kerrie, for everything. I would also like to acknowledge Harold Wong for making sure Chris and I wrote the best book possible and for keeping us on the straight and narrow. I would also like to thank all the wonderful editors and staff at Sybex, thank you for giving Chris and I the chance. Lastly, and most important, I want to acknowledge one of the best coauthors I could ask for, Chris Henley. Thanks for doing this project with me, and I look forward to more from H&H productions.

—Matthew Hester

I would also like to acknowledge the efforts of Harold Wong for his technical suggestions and experience, which have been significant contributions to this work. The production team at Sybex deserves a huge thank you for taking a chance on me and bringing me patiently through the process of getting this book to the presses. Thank you! I also would like to acknowledge the efforts of Matt Hester—a great coauthor, mentor, peer, and friend. Thanks for a great opportunity to work together! I look forward to many more successful projects together!

—Chris Henley

About the Authors

Matt Hester is a seasoned Information Technology Professional Evangelist for Microsoft and has been involved in the IT Pro community for more than 15 years. In his role at Microsoft, Matt has presented to audiences nationally and internationally as large as 5,000 people and as small as 10. Prior to joining Microsoft, Matt was a highly successful Microsoft Certified Trainer for more than eight years. Matt has also published several articles for TechNet magazine and runs a successful blog with about 350,000 touches a month. In his spare time, Matt is a movie buff with a massive DVD collection. He also runs marathons and dreams of joining the PGA tour. Matt cites his father as his role model: "The older I get, the smarter he gets." Funny how that works.

Chris Henley is an entertaining and energetic proponent of technology who has worked in IT for more than 15 years. Chris loves to talk about how technology changes people's lives for the better. He believes that with the right vision and the right technology, anything is possible. In addition, Chris has spent the last five years acting as an Information Technology Professional Evangelist for Microsoft specializing in client and server technologies. He loves speaking to audiences of all sizes and says, "There is no other experience that can compare with speaking to a large audience and helping them understand the possibilities that a new piece of technology can avail them." Chris loves to spend time in the outdoors with his wife and three children. Camping, fishing, hiking, skiing, biking, and chocolate are his favorite pastimes.

Contents

PART VI: Server Tuning and Maintenance   493

Chapter 15: Tuning and Monitoring Performance   495

Chapter 16: Keeping Your Servers Up-to-Date   531

Introduction

Administering and maintaining servers can sometimes appear daunting. In fact, a lot of industry studies say a majority of IT resources (such as budget, personnel, and time) are spent just maintaining existing servers and infrastructure. As administrators, we also do not always have the time to learn how new technologies can improve our day-to-day tasks, and we often rely on the status quo the server can provide.

Although this book is not designed to dig deep into the details behind Windows Server and server technologies, it will provide you with a quick and easy reference to many of the tasks you perform daily. This book will also get you quickly up to speed with many of the new features in Windows Server 2008 R2 as well as show you how Windows Server 2008 R2 can improve your daily administrative tasks.

You will notice that the book is organized specifically to help you find information quickly. It is organized into parts that categorize chapters into major topics. Then each chapter deals with a specific subject. At the beginning of each chapter, you will see what the chapter will cover and where you will find it in the pages. This method of organization is designed to assist you in finding the information that you need to solve immediate problems or begin a process as painlessly as possible. Ideally, this book will become part of your everyday tool belt, something that you can pick up whenever you need a quick reference or a reminder.

We hope you enjoy this book.

Who Should Read This Book

This book is designed for anyone who administers a Windows server environment. It is for experienced and new administrators alike. This book is also for administrators looking to learn how to use many of the new enhancements Windows Server 2008 R2 can bring to their existing networks. This book will show administrators how to improve many of the day-to-day tasks of server administration.

This book will provide guidance for many common server tasks, such as setting up Group Policy and backing up and recovering your server. This book will also show you many of the new and improved features built in to Windows Server 2008 R2 to help you improve server administration and management.

How to Contact the Authors

We welcome feedback from you about this book or about books you'd like to see from us in the future. You can reach us by writing to Matt at raid78@msn.com or to Chris at cj.henley@hotmail.com. You can also contact us via our blogs at http://blogs.technet.com/matthewms/ or http://blogs.technet.com/chenley/.

For more information about our work, please visit our websites:

    http://blogs.technet.com/matthewms/
    http://blogs.techent.com/chenley/

Sybex strives to keep you supplied with the latest tools and information you need for your work. Please check its website at www.sybex.com, where we'll post additional content and updates that supplement this book if the need arises. Enter **Microsoft Windows Server 2008 R2 Administration Instant Reference** in the search box (or type the book's ISBN, 978-0-470-52539-5), and click Go to get to the book's update page.

PART I

Getting Started

IN THIS PART ▷

1

Getting Started with Windows Server 2008 R2

IN THIS CHAPTER, YOU WILL LEARN TO:

E very release of Windows Server has offered numerous features and
functionality to assist administrators and companies with their day-to-day tasks. Each new release has offered plenty of new functionality but has
also increased the administrative burden for the servers. Windows 2000
Server laid the foundation for Active Directory. Windows Server 2003
became the first dedicated server platform from Microsoft. Windows
Server 2008 sought to offer flexibility for our servers by providing role-based deployment included streamlined new roles like Server Core.

Windows Server 2008 R2, an incremental release of the operating
system, continues to build upon prior releases of the server platform.
Windows Server 2008 R2 provides many new and increased capabilities
for a powerful server environment. From improvements in Hyper-V with
the addition of live migration to better power management capabilities
to improvements in IIS to features such as DirectAccess designed to work
specifically with Windows 7, Windows Server 2008 R2 has a lot to
offer you.

However, even with the addition of all these capabilities, Windows
Server 2008 R2's true benefits are for administrators and to improve the
day-to-day tasks of administrators.

Before you begin to dig into the day-to-day improvements of admin-istrative tasks, it is important to understand how the server was built so
you can properly administer it. Do you need to install a new server? Do
you perform an in-place upgrade? Do you migrate existing services like
DNS, Active Directory, or printers? These are all vital questions that
need to be answered so you can start to take advantage of the admin-istrative improvements in Windows Server 2008 R2. This chapter will
take a brief look at planning, installing, and upgrading to Windows
Server 2008 R2. You will also learn about installing the migration tools.

Plan for Windows Server 2008 R2

You have probably heard this phrase 1,000 times (well, make this a
1,001): "If you fail to plan, you plan to fail." Having a solid idea what
role the server will play is important to the health of IT as well as your
sanity. Some of the decisions you make during the planning process
can impact the installation phase. If your planning is off, then your
installation will be off. Although fixing most installation problems
can be straightforward, some can become quite complex to fix, if not

completely irreversible. Everyone has done the "FDISK, format, reboot" dance of destruction at least once to fix the wrong decisions.

In this section, you will look at the hardware requirements and recommendations for a Windows Server 2008 R2 server installation. You will also learn about the roles and features that a Windows Server 2008 R2 server can perform. In addition to the resources mentioned in this chapter, Microsoft offers several free tools to assist you in your planning process. These assessment tools are included in the Microsoft Assessment and Planning (MAP) Toolkit:

```
http://technet.microsoft.com/en-us/solutionaccelerators/
dd537566.aspx?SA_CE=NOT-MAPBETA-SITE-TNETWINSVR-20090615
```

Understand Hardware Requirements

Like its predecessors, Windows Server 2008 R2 offers numerous roles and editions of the server operating system. There is one important distinction in this version; it will be released only in *64-bit versions*. This means before you even start, you need to have the proper hardware to support the operating system. This requirement will also dictate upgrade and migration paths. Table 1.1 shows the base hardware requirements for Windows Server 2008 R2.

Table 1.1: Windows Server 2008 R2 Minimum Hardware Requirements

Resource	Requirement
Processor	1.4GHz x64 processor
Memory	512MB RAM
Drive space	10GB
Drive	DVD-ROM
Display and others	Super VGA 800×600 or higher Keyboard and mouse

These are just the bare minimum to get the server up and running. I highly recommend you take a look at Table 1.2 for additional recommendations for processor memory and hard drive space. These will offer a base system with solid performance and flexibility for additional functions.

Table 1.2: Additional Hardware Recommendations

Resource	Recommendation
Processor	2GHz x64 dual-core processor
Memory	4GB RAM
Drive space	100GB

You need to be aware of a few important facts about the requirements. The amount of memory you can put into the server depends on the chosen operating system. If you have chosen Windows Server 2008 R2 Datacenter or Enterprise edition, you can install up to 2TB of RAM. Other versions are limited to 32GB RAM. Additionally, if you have more than 16GB RAM, you will need more hard drive space to support various system functions such as paging. Also, the edition controls the maximum number of processor cores the system can have. The Web and Standard editions are limited to 4, Enterprise edition can have up to 8, and Datacenter edition can have up to 64, and Itanium-based systems can have up to 64 IA64 sockets.

You should always look at the base requirements as the bare minimum to get the server operating system up and running. Generally speaking, these minimum requirements do not take into the account the workload you will be placing on the server. You should always consider the roles and applications that will be loaded on the server. You should consider the recommendations and requirements for those applications as additional resources to those listed in Table 1.1. This will allow you to have servers that will perform satisfactorily and meet your needs, while having a little room to grow.

If the server role you have selected is going to be used for virtualization workloads, ensure you have enough RAM and processor cores to support the Windows Server 2008 R2 operating system as well as the virtual servers running on the server. How many servers, what types of servers, and what types of applications are all factors you need to look carefully at when planning a virtualization server. One last note of concern for a virtualization server: whether you have chosen to use VMware or Hyper-V virtualization technologies, make sure your processor hardware supports hardware-assisted virtualization. Either AMD Virtualization (AMD-V) or Intel Virtualization Technology (Intel VT) will work. These technologies typically also have to be enabled in the

BIOS because they are generally not enabled by default. Enabling the virtualization will normally require a full hard reboot to take effect. Make sure you have enabled these technologies before installing your virtualization technology.

Understand Windows Server 2008 R2 Editions and Roles

Windows Server 2008 R2 is offered in the same editions as in Windows Server 2008, namely, Datacenter, Enterprise, Standard, Itanium-based systems, and Web. One notable difference is that Windows Server 2008 R2 has the next version of Microsoft's Hyper-V technologies included in Windows Server 2008 R2 Standard, Enterprise and Datacenter editions, and does not offer separate editions without Hyper-V. Table 1.3 gives an overview of the Windows Server 2008 R2 editions available.

Table 1.3: Windows Server 2008 R2 Editions

Edition	Overview
Datacenter	Designed for large-scale enterprise applications or virtualization workloads, this edition is really for large scale-up operations.
Enterprise	This edition supports mission-critical applications as well as providing clustering capabilities. This server will fit most of your infrastructure needs.
Standard	This edition supports mission-critical applications and will fit most of your infrastructure needs.
Itanium-based systems	This edition is designed and optimized for large databases and critical line-of-business applications.
Web	This edition is a specifically designed server for website services.

This is just a brief rundown of the systems. For a full comparison, see http://www.microsoft.com/windowsserver2008/en/us/ compare-features.aspx.

Once you have chosen the right edition for your needs, then you need to look at the services the server will provide for your infrastructure. These services come in the form of *roles*. Windows Server 2008 R2, like Windows Server 2008, provides several server roles that can be installed on the server. A role is a set of software features and functions that provides services for your server and infrastructure. Some of these roles also require some additional planning to have a stable and reliable environment.

Table 1.4 describes the server roles.

Table 1.4: Windows Server 2008 R2 Server Roles

Role	Function
Active Directory Certificate Services (AD CS)	Allows for the creation of certificate authorities. This role allows you to host your own Public Key Infrastructure (PKI) on the server.
Active Directory Domain Services (AD DS)	Provides single sign-on (SSO) capabilities for your network and network services. This allows for the creation of objects (users, groups, computers, and so on) for use with network authentication and authorization.
Active Directory Federation Services (AD FS)	Provides single sign-on capabilities across multiple forests and domains. Additionally, this role provides web single sign-on.
Active Directory Lightweight Directory Services (AD LDS)	Commonly referred to as ADAM, is a lightweight version of AD DS. This role allows for the storage of a base directory used for specific applications.
Active Directory Rights Management Services (AD RMS)	Allows you to provide authorization and verification services to users to access protected content.
Application Server	Provides the ability to have high-performance distributed applications (mainly applications that use the .NET Framework).
DHCP Server	Provides automatic TCP/IP address services for your network.
DNS Server	Provides name and service resolution services for TCP/IP networks. This is a core component for AD DS, and it is highly recommended you use this built-in service for your domain controllers.
Fax Server	Allows for basic fax functions to be hosted on the server, such as sending, receiving, and reporting.
File Services	Provides many services for the file system, including replication, managing shares, and faster file searches. This role also provides services for UNIX clients to access files on the server.
Hyper-V	Provides the ability to create, manage, and perform live migration of virtual machines. Virtual machines operate on the host machine and are servers without the hardware.

Table 1.4: Windows Server 2008 R2 Server Roles *(continued)*

Role	Function
Network Policy and Access Services	Provides resources for routing and remote access. This service also provides the framework for Network Access and Protection (NAP) and DirectAccess. Included in this service are two core components: Health Registration Authority and the Host Credential Authorization protocol.
Print and Document Services	Provides the ability for a centralized print server as well as management for printers. This service also installs the necessary Group Policy objects for printer management through Group Policy.
Remote Desktop Services	Provides the ability for your users to access the Remote Desktop Services on your server. These services provide presentation virtualization for your thin clients. Formerly called Terminal Services.
Web Server (IIS)	Provides the core infrastructure for a web server.
Windows Deployment Services	Installs the services for deploying Windows operating systems across the network.
Windows Update Services (WSUS)	Provides the management framework for Microsoft updates. This service allows you to deploy updates in a variety of options across your network.

NOTE   Table 1.4 gives only a brief explanation of all the services available to Windows Server 2008 R2. For more details, please take a look at Chapter 2. You can also get more explanation of the roles at http://technet.microsoft.com/en-us/windowsserver/2008/default.aspx.

One last consideration regarding roles is that they are also dependant on what edition of Windows Server 2008 R2 you have installed. The edition you choose to install will determine which roles are available to the server and will also determine the hardware requirements. Table 1.5 describes the which roles the editions support and the additional hardware considerations. For a full role comparison table, take a look at the Microsoft site at http://www.microsoft.com/windowsserver2008/en/us/compare-roles.aspx.

Table 1.5: Windows Server 2008 R2 Edition Requirements

Edition	Role Considerations	Additional Hardware Considerations
Web edition	As the name implies, this server is designed to be a web server only. It has the ability to install two roles: DNS Server and Web Server.	Limited to 4 processors and up to 32GB of RAM
Standard edition	Contains all the roles listed in Table 1.4, with one exception; Standard edition does not contain the Active Directory Federation Services. Additionally, the following services have limited capabilities: Active Directory Certificate Services, File Services, Network Policy and Access Services, and Remote Desktop Services.	Limited to 4 processors and up to 32GB of RAM
Enterprise edition	Contains all the roles listed in Table 1.4.	Limited to 8 processors and up to 2TB of RAM
Datacenter edition	Contains all the roles listed in Table 1.4.	Limited to 64 processors and up to 2TB of RAM

Understand Server Core

There is also one installation option of the previously mentioned editions worth mentioning: Windows Server 2008 R2 Server Core. Like in Windows Server 2008, Windows Server 2008 R2 Server Core is a very streamlined version of Windows Server. Server Core has limited functionality and runs a subset of the roles provided by Windows Server 2008 R2. Server Core also does not have a GUI. This means all the administration is either done remotely or via a command prompt. This by no means implies that Server Core does not have usefulness in the network. The Server Core role provides a nice addition to your network without the overhead of a traditional server. This lowers the overall maintenance and security risks for the server. Server Core can also reduce the amount of patching that is required to keep the server up-to-date. The server provides support for these nine roles:

- DNS Server
- DHCP Server

- Active Directory Domain Services (AD DS)
- Active Directory Lightweight Directory Services (AD LDS)
- File Services
- Print and Document Services
- Web Server (IIS)
- Active Directory Certificate Services (AD CS)
- Hyper-V

Windows Server 2008 R2 provides several new features to extend the functionality of Server Core. In Windows Server 2008 R2 Server Core, you can also now install the following:

- A subset of the .NET Framework, versions 2.0, 3.0, and 3.5
- PowerShell
- ASP.NET, the same that is included in IIS
- WoW64, required for Active Directory and Active Directory Lightweight Directory Services

Consider Your Licensing Options

When you install Windows Server 2008 R2 into your environment, you have to take into account the licensing. Overall, the licensing model has not really changed for Windows Server 2008 R2 from Windows Server 2008. Every Windows Server 2008 R2 requires two types of licenses. First, you need a server license for the rights to run the operating system, and second, you need a client access license (CAL) to allow your clients to access the server. CALs come in two flavors:

- The *device* CAL allows access for one device for any user.
- The *user* CAL allows access for one user on any device.

Depending on your existing licensing, you may already be covered for Windows Server 2008 R2. In Windows Server 2008 R2, all of your existing CALs for Windows Server 2008 will allow you to access Windows Server 2008 R2. Again, this is very unique to this release.

There are some important licensing considerations when you use virtualization technologies inside your network. If Windows Server 2008 R2 is solely used for virtualization servers, you do not need to have CALs for the host operating system. However, you will still need CALs for the guest operating systems running on the server. There is one last potential licensing benefit for using Hyper-V on Windows Server 2008 R2. Depending on which edition you have chosen, you may not need to purchase server licenses for your virtualized instances of Windows Server 2008 R2. If you are using Windows Server 2008 R2 Enterprise edition, you are allowed to run one virtualized instance of Windows Server 2008 R2 under your server license. If you are using Windows Server 2008 R2 Enterprise edition, you are allowed to run up to four virtualized instances of Windows Server 2008 R2 under your server license. If you are using Windows Server 2008 R2 Datacenter or Itanium editions, you are allowed to run unlimited virtualized instances of Windows Server 2008 R2 under your server license. For more details and specific license questions and pricing, contact your Microsoft reseller.

Install Windows Server 2008 R2

After you have planned your environment, it is now time to install Windows Server 2008 R2. The installation process is fairly straight-forward. This is mainly because of the role-based nature of Windows Server 2008 R2. You will learn more about installing roles in Chapter 2.

Perform a Windows Server 2008 R2 Full Installation

In this section, you will take a step-by-step look at the installation process for a Windows Server 2008 R2 full installation. We'll cover the key decisions you need to be aware of as you install the operating system.

1. Insert the DVD media into the drive, and reboot the system. Upon reboot, you will see the screen shown in Figure 1.1.

Figure 1.1: Selecting your language

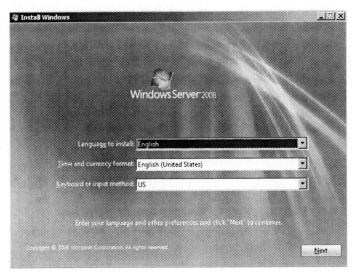

2. Select your chosen language, time/currency, and keyboard
    method, and then click Next. You will see the screen shown in
    Figure 1.2.

Figure 1.2: Starting the installation

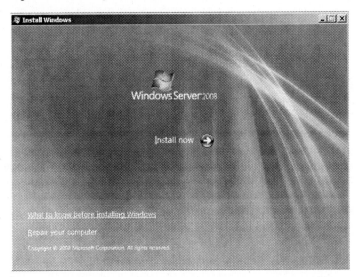

This screen provides the option to install Windows Server 2008 R2 by clicking the Install Now button. There are also two other options to notice. The What To Know Before Installing Windows option provides some last-minute help documentation. The Repair Your Computer option takes you to the repair and diagnostics functions of Windows Server 2008 R2. To continue the installation, click the Install Now button.

3. The next window you see (Figure 1.3) provides you with the choice to install your edition of Windows Server 2008 R2. You can choose to install the full edition of Windows Server 2008 R2 or the Server Core version. Select your version, and click Next.

Figure 1.3: Selecting your Windows Server 2008 R2 version

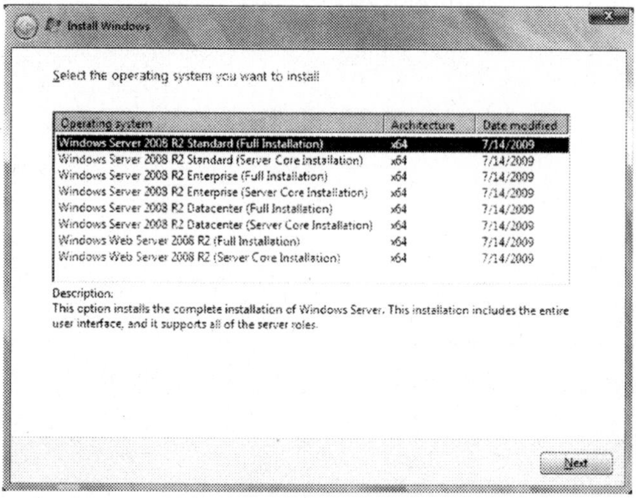

WARNING If you choose Server Core, you will not be able to upgrade to a full version directly without performing a full reinstall of the server. You will, however, have the ability to use migration tools to migrate the server's functions to a full installation of Windows Server 2008 R2.

4. Clicking the Next button will take you to the license agreement screen. This screen, shown in Figure 1.4, allows you to read, print, and agree to the license terms. Select the check box on the bottom

left of the dialog box to agree to the license terms, and click Next to continue.

Figure 1.4: Licensing terms

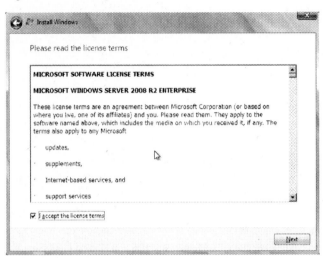

5. The screen shown in Figure 1.5 provides you with the choice between performing an upgrade or custom installation of Windows Server 2008 R2. To perform a new installation, click Custom, and you will be taken to the next step.

Figure 1.5: Upgrading or customizing

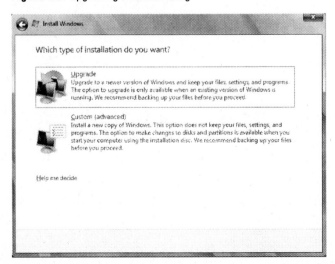

6. The next screen, displayed in Figure 1.6, allows you to choose the location for your Windows Server 2008 R2 installation. This screen also allows you to load drivers for your SCSI hard drives.

    If you are installing on a hard drive connected to a SCSI controller, select Load Driver, and insert the media with the drivers on it. You also have a full set of drive partitioning and formatting options. When you click the drive on which you want to install Windows Server 2008 R2, you are presented with the options to create new partitions or delete, format, or extend existing partitions, as shown in Figure 1.6. Choose the appropriate option, and click Next. If you do not select a partition and the only option you have is unallocated space, then the Windows Server 2008 R2 installation will create a partition on that drive by taking all the unallocated space and formatting it for you automatically with NTFS. Windows Server 2008 R2 will also automatically make a system partition of 200MB in size during this step. The 200MB partition is not assigned a drive and will not be visible in the OS. The partition holds the Windows boot files for the Windows recovery environment (winRE).

Figure 1.6: Selecting a drive and partition

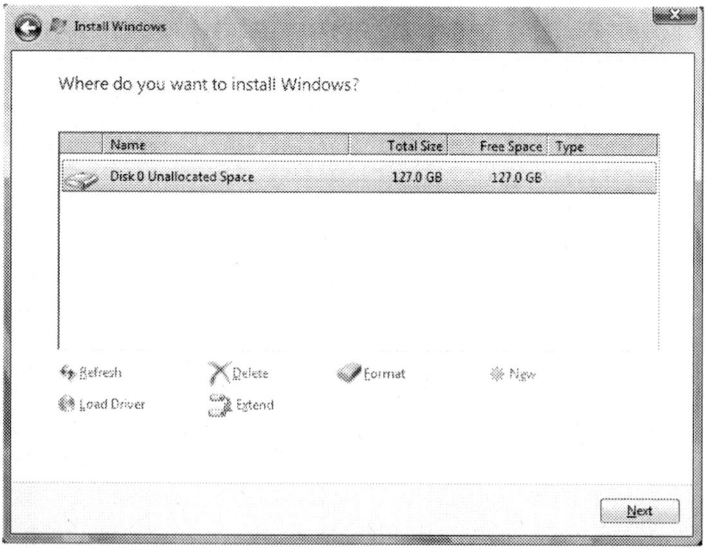

7. When you select your partition, the installation will begin, and you will see a screen similar to Figure 1.7. The system may also reboot several times during this phase of installation.

Figure 1.7: Windows installation progress

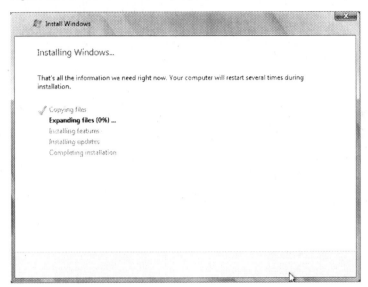

8. After the final system reboot, you will be asked to configure the administrator's password, and you will see screen similar to Figure 1.8.

Figure 1.8: Initial change of password logon

9. After you click OK, you will see a screen similar to Figure 1.9. Now you will set your administrator password. The password needs to be complex. This means the initial password needs to meet the following requirements:

   - Cannot contain the user's account name or parts of the user's full name that exceed two consecutive characters

   - Be at least six characters in length

   - Contain characters from three of the following four categories:

     - English uppercase characters (A through Z)

     - English lowercase characters (a through z)

     - Base 10 digits (0 through 9)

     - Nonalphabetic characters (for example !, $, #, or %)

   There is also an option for you to create a password reset disk. By clicking this option, you can create a recovery disk, which allows you to create a new password for the user ID. You have to create this disk only once, no matter how many times the password for the account changes.

Figure 1.9: Logon window/password reset disk

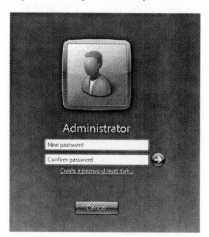

After you have set the password, the Windows Server 2008 R2 installation will complete, and you will see a screen with the initial configuration tasks, as shown in Figure 1.10.

Creating a Password Reset Disk

1. Click the link Create A Password Recovery Disk. This will start the Forgotten Password Wizard.

2. Read the welcome screen, and click Next.

3. Select the drive for the password recovery disk, and click Next.

4. Type in the password for the existing user. If one exists during install, chances are you will leave this field blank and click Next.

5. You will briefly see a progress screen. When the progress reaches 100 percent, click Next.

6. Read the summary screen, and click Finish.

WARNING   Although I hope you should never need the password recovery disk, it is nice to have in case of an emergency. However, it is also very important to keep the disk in a safe and secure location. It is important because anyone who can access the disk can use it to recover the password and therefore gain access to the account.

Figure 1.10: Initial configuration tasks

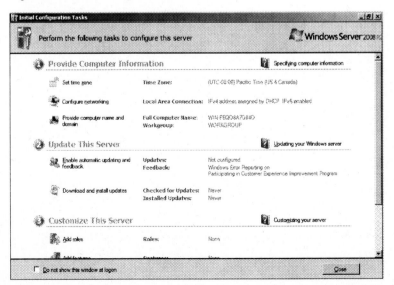

Perform a Windows Server 2008 R2 Server Core Installation

Installing Windows Server 2008 R2 Server Core follows a similar process as the previous steps. The only difference comes in step 3 where you would select Server Core Installation instead of Full Installation for your edition of Windows. You will learn how to add roles in Chapter 2.

Use Sconfig to Configure Your Windows Server 2008 R2 Server Core

After you install Windows Server 2008 R2 Server Core, you need to configure the basics of the server, such as the network settings, computer name, domain membership, and so on. In prior versions of Windows Server, you had to be familiar with the netsh commands in configuring these aspects of Server Core.

Although you can still configure the Server Core installation with netsh commands as you may have done in the past, in Windows Server 2008 R2 Server Core there is a new tool you can leverage called Server Configuration. Server Configuration is a DOS-style menu configuration system providing simple commands to configure your server. This tool allows you to complete these common tasks easily. After you log on to Server Core, type **sconfig**. You will see a screen similar to Figure 1.11.

Figure 1.11: Server Configuration tool

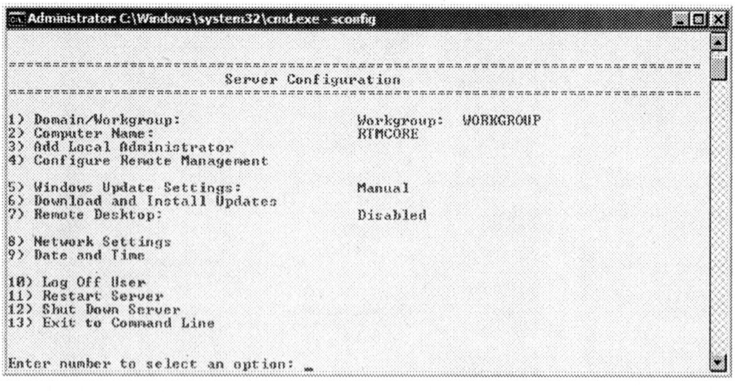

As you can see, this new tool is very easy to follow. For example, after you have launched sconfig, if you want to change the address, you would press the 8 key to configure the settings. Then you just need to follow the menu screens to finish the configuration.

Activating Windows Server Core

When you install Windows Server 2008 R2 in either a full installation or Server Core, you still have to activate the operating system to ensure you have a valid product. Activating will also enable your copy of Windows Server 2008 R2 to function properly. On a full server installation, there is a simple activation wizard located in the Control Panel, named Activate Windows, to take you step-by-step through the process. However, in the Server Core installation of Windows Server 2008 R2, there is no wizard, so you will have to run one of the following two commands to activate it.

If you entered the product key for your Server Core installation during the install process, then run this script:

```
cscript C:\windows\system32\slmgr.vbs -ato
```

If you did not enter the key during the install process, run the following command:

```
cscript C:\windows\system32\slmgr.vbs -ipk <product key>
```

After this command executes successfully, run this to activate Windows:

```
cscript C:\windows\system32\slmgr.vbs -ato
```

Upgrade to Windows Server 2008 R2

Upgrading to Windows Server 2008 R2 can cause you some additional planning and consideration because Windows Server 2008 R2 is released only in 64-bit versions. You cannot upgrade an x86-based system to Windows Server 2008 R2. You can only perform a migration, which I will cover in the next section. Your current operating system and edition will determine the proper path for your upgrade. It is also important to mention when you perform an upgrade, under the covers the process is really an in-place migration. Table 1.6 shows the paths you can take. If your current operating system is not listed, then it is not supported.

Table 1.6: Upgrade Paths

Existing Windows Operating System	Windows Server 2008 R2 Upgrade Options
Windows Server 2003 Standard Edition with Service Pack 2 (SP2) or Windows Server 2003 R2 Standard Edition	Windows Server 2008 R2 Standard, Windows Server 2008 R2 Enterprise
Windows Server 2003 Enterprise Edition with SP2 or Windows Server 2003 R2 Enterprise Edition	Windows Server 2008 R2 Enterprise, Windows Server 2008 R2 Datacenter
Windows Server 2003 Datacenter Edition with SP2 or Windows Server 2003 R2 Datacenter Edition	Windows Server 2008 R2 Datacenter
Server Core installation of Windows Server 2008 Standard with or without SP2	Server Core installation of either Windows Server 2008 R2 Standard or Windows Server 2008 R2 Enterprise
Server Core installation of Windows Server 2008 Enterprise with or without SP2	Server Core installation of either Windows Server 2008 R2 Enterprise or Windows Server 2008 R2 Datacenter
Server Core installation of Windows Server 2008 Datacenter	Server Core installation of Windows Server 2008 R2 Datacenter
Server Core installation of Windows Web Server 2008 with or without SP2	Server Core installation of either Windows Server 2008 R2 Standard or Windows Web Server 2008 R2
Full installation of Windows Server 2008 Standard with or without SP2	Full installation of either Windows Server 2008 R2 Standard or Windows Server 2008 R2 Enterprise
Full installation of Windows Server 2008 Enterprise with or without SP2	Full installation of either Windows Server 2008 R2 Enterprise or Windows Server 2008 R2 Datacenter
Full installation of Windows Server 2008 Datacenter with or without SP2	Full installation of Windows Server 2008 R2 Datacenter
Full installation of Windows Web Server 2008 with or without SP2	Full installation of either Windows Server 2008 R2 Standard or Windows Web Server 2008 R2
Server Core installation of Windows Server 2008 R2 Standard	Server Core installation of either Windows Server 2008 R2 Standard (repair in place) or Windows Server 2008 R2 Enterprise

Table 1.6: Upgrade Paths *(continued)*

Existing Windows Operating System	Windows Server 2008 R2 Upgrade Options
Server Core installation of Windows Server 2008 R2 Enterprise	Server Core installation of either Windows Server 2008 R2 Enterprise (repair in place) or Windows Server 2008 R2 Datacenter
Server Core installation of Windows Server 2008 R2 Datacenter	Server Core installation of Windows Server 2008 R2 Datacenter (repair in place)
Server Core installation of Windows Web Server 2008 R2	Server Core installation of either Windows Web Server 2008 R2 (repair in place) or Windows Server 2008 R2 Standard
Full installation of Windows Server 2008 R2 Standard	Full installation of either Windows Server 2008 R2 Standard (repair in place) or Windows Server 2008 R2 Enterprise
Full installation of Windows Server 2008 R2 Enterprise	Full installation of either Windows Server 2008 R2 Enterprise (repair in place) or Windows Server 2008 R2 Datacenter
Full installation of Windows Server 2008 R2 Datacenter	Full installation of Windows Server 2008 R2 Datacenter (repair in place)
Full installation of Windows Web Server 2008 R2	Full installation of either Windows Web Server 2008 R2 (repair in place) or Windows Server 2008 R2 Standard

Getting Started

PART I

Performing an in-place upgrade is a destructive process in a sense. You are replacing the existing server operating system with the new one, and this is a one-way street, meaning that if the upgrade process goes awry, then you will incur downtime until you resolve the issue and restore your system. Before you perform any upgrade or migration, back up your existing server operating system and data.

1. Insert the DVD media into the drive, which will present you with the screen shown earlier in Figure 1.1.

2. When you click Install Now, you will be presented with a couple of choices on this screen, as shown in Figure 1.12. You can choose to participate in the Microsoft Customer Experience program by selecting I Want To Help Make Windows Installation Better. This program helps Microsoft identify trends for successful and unsuccessful

installations and determine which updates are needed. Choosing to participate is strictly optional. You can learn more about the program by clicking What Information Will Be Sent To Microsoft?

Figure 1.12: Installation updates

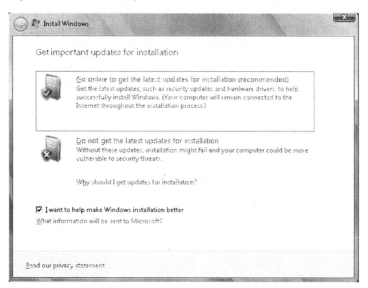

You are also presented with a choice to upgrade your installation files. You should always choose to update installation files; the following are the updates included in this choice:

- Installation updates
- Driver updates
- Windows updates
- Microsoft Windows Malicious Software Removal Tool updates

If you choose to go online and update your installation, you will see a screen similar to Figure 1.13 while downloading the updates. After you're done downloading updates, or if you choose not to update the installation, you will proceed to the next step.

Figure 1.13: Update installation progress

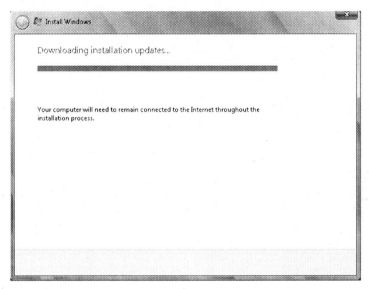

Getting Started

PART I

3. The next step provides you with the choice to install the edition of Windows Server 2008 R2. You can choose to install the full edition of Windows Server 2008 R2 or the Server Core version. Select your version, and click Next.

4. Clicking the Next button will take you to the license agreement screen. This screen allows you to read, print, and agree to the license terms. Select the check box on the bottom left of the dialog box to agree to the license terms, and click Next to continue.

5. The next step provides you the choice between performing an upgrade or custom installation of Windows Server 2008 R2. To proceed to the next step of the upgrade, you need to choose the upgrade option.

6. The Windows Server 2008 R2 installation will perform a compatibility check, and you will see a screen similar to Figure 1.14. The report will be saved to your desktop, and you will see what devices will be affected by the Windows Server 2008 R2 upgrade. Click Next to continue.

Figure 1.14: Compatibility report

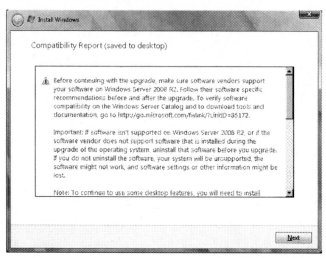

7. The Windows Server 2008 R2 upgrade will continue to the next step, and you will see a screen similar to Figure 1.15. During this phase of installation, all the necessary files, settings, and programs needed for the upgrade will be collected and analyzed. The system may also reboot several times during this phase of installation.

Figure 1.15: Upgrading Windows progress

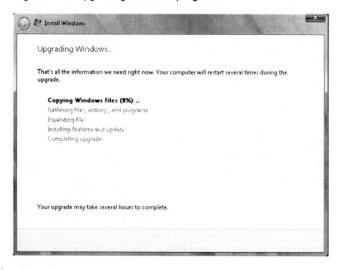

8. After the final system reboot, the upgrade is complete, and you will be presented with a login screen. Log in, and you will finish the upgrade. You can also review the compatibility report again; it is located on the desktop. The file will be called Windows Compatibility Report.htm.

Install Windows Server 2008 R2 Server Unattended

You can also perform an unattended installation of Windows Server 2008 R2. This provides a useful method to rapidly deploy new servers in your environment. Unattended installs are completed by creating an answer file. The answer file is the file containing the main configurations for the Windows Server 2008 R2 installation. Settings can include application configuration, such as configuring the home page in Internet Explorer and controlling the desktop look-and-feel settings. To create an answer file, you first need to install the Windows Automated Installation Kit (WAIK).

Install the WAIK

The WAIK is a flexibility utility tool that allows you to customize your Windows 7 and Windows Server 2008 R2 installs. You can also create the necessary files to assist with configuration and deployments. To run the WAIK, you need to be running either Windows Server 2003 SP1, Windows Vista SP1, Windows Server 2008, Windows 7, or Windows Server 2008 R2.

1. Download the WAIK.iso file from the Microsoft website: http://www.microsoft.com/downloads/details. aspx?familyid=4AD85860-D1F4-42A1-A46C-E039E3D0DB5D&displaylang=en

2. Burn the .iso file to a DVD.

3. Insert the DVD to install the WAIK tools; you should see Figure 1.16.

4. Click Windows AIK Setup to begin the installation.

5. Click Next on the welcome screen.

6. Click Next after you accept the license agreement.

Figure 1.16: Welcome to WAIK.

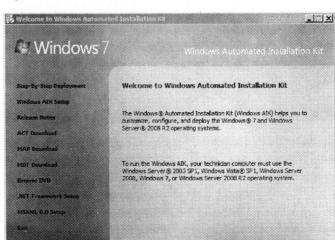

7. Pick a drive and directory to install the tools to. The tools require about 1.2GB of drive space. Then click Next.

8. Click Next to begin to the installation, and click Close on the final screen.

Create an Answer File

After you have installed the WAIK tools, then your next step is to create an answer file. The file contains configuration settings for Windows and provides the settings to your preferred desktop. To create an answer file, you will use the Windows System Image Manager (SIM). Before you create an answer file, you will need to the load the install.wim file from the Windows Server 2008 R2 DVD. The file is located in the sources directory. Copy the file to a local directory, for example c:\source.

1. Start Windows SIM by selecting Start ➤ All Programs ➤ Microsoft Windows AIK. Then click Windows System Image Manager.

2. In Windows SIM, select File ➤ Select Windows Image, and navigate to the directory you copied the install.wim file to.

3. After you select the `install.wim` file you used in step 2, you will be presented with Figure 1.17, where you will choose the edition of Windows Server 2008 R2 for which you are creating the answer file.

Figure 1.17: Windows image selection

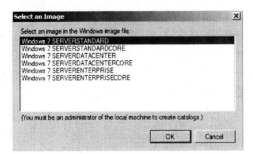

4. After you select the edition, you will be asked to create a catalog file; click Yes. This process can take several minutes.

5. Choose File ➤ Create An Answer File, and your screen will look similar to Figure 1.18.

Figure 1.18: WAIK

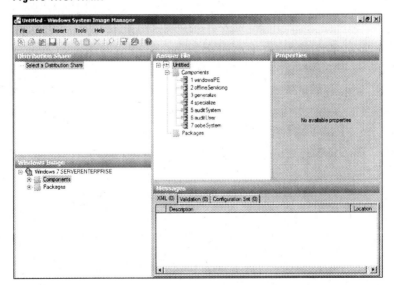

6. You will then need to add and configure the many settings that fit your needs. For more information on configuring the settings, see the help file that comes with WAIK tool set (`waik.chm`).

7. When you are done modifying settings in the answer file, you need to save the file. Select File ➢ Save Answer File. During the save process, the SIM tool will start a validation process. The validation tool will ensure your answer file is correctly formatted and the settings are configured. Before you save, you can also validate the file by selecting Tools ➢ Validate Answer File.

8. Save the answer file with the name `Autounattend.xml`.

Install Windows Server 2008 R2 Unattended

After you have an answer file, then it is time to install Windows. The previous process is good for single-server deployments. However, the WAIK tools also provide resources for many deployment methods. The WAIK tool set provides many tools to quickly deploy multiple servers via a variety of sources. You will learn the DVD method to deploy Windows Server 2008 R2 unattended.

1. Copy your answer file (`Autounattend.xml`) to a disc or USB flash drive (UFD).

2. Insert your UFD and your Windows Server 2008 R2 DVD into the server you want to install.

3. The Windows Server 2008 R2 setup program automatically checks the removable media for a file called `Autounattend.xml`.

4. After the installation is complete, make sure your settings were properly installed.

5. Lastly, you need to reseal the system by running this command:

```
c:\windows\system32\sysprep\sysprep.exe /oobe
/generalize /shutdown
```

Resealing the system will remove hardware-specific and unique system information. This is required if you plan to redeploy the image and properly ready the system for users.

Migrate to Windows Server 2008 R2

Choosing to perform a server migration instead of in-place upgrade has some advantages you should consider. Performing a migration does require two servers; however, this is one of the advantages. On the server you will be migrating to, you will perform a clean install of Windows Server 2008 R2, and clean installations will exhibit more stability than upgraded servers. Migrations also reduce the risk of downtime in your server environment and offer a fallback plan. During migration, the server being migrated is still running, and if the migration fails, you can start all over with the new server without impacting your environment. Lastly, migration allows you to do performance and benchmarking testing prior to fully completing the migration.

Windows Server 2008 R2 migration can be used successfully in these three scenarios:

x86 to x64 scenarios   As mentioned earlier, Windows Server 2008 R2 is available only in 64-bit. Migration is the only method for the x86 hardware.

Virtual server to physical server and physical server to virtual server   If you are looking to virtualization for some of your server components in your current environment, then migration is the way to go. Likewise, if you are looking to move some of your virtual servers to the physical systems, migration offers another great pathway for you.

Core Server to full server and full server to Core Server   As mentioned in Table 1.6, you can perform this type of upgrade only on Windows Server 2008 R2 servers. Migration is the only way to move from a Server Core installation to a full installation of Windows Server 2008 R2. You can also turn a full server into a Server Core through this process. However, make sure your roles on the full server will be supported by Server Core.

Migration can be from x86 or x64 systems and will support the following source operating systems:

- Windows Server 2003
- Windows Server 2003 R2
- Windows Server 2008, full server only
- Windows Server 2008, R2 full server or Server Core

NOTE   Windows 2008 Server Core is not supported for migration since Server Core has no .NET Framework support. Additionally, the system language on both the source and the target have to be the same. For example, if the source server's system language is English and the target server is in Spanish, then the migration tools will not work.

Migration can be performed for the following roles, features, settings, and data:

- Active Directory Domain Services (AD DS)
- DNS
- DHCP
- File Services
- Print Services
- BranchCache
- IP configuration
- Local Users and Groups

Prior to performing the migration, you need to install the Windows Server 2008 R2 migration tools.

Install Windows Server 2008 R2 Migration Tools

The migration tools are new and provide a much improved resource for successfully migrating your environment. You will install the migration tools first on the target Windows Server 2008 R2 server and then on the source server. Prior to installing the migration tools, make sure the source servers meet the system requirements listed in Table 1.7, and verify you are, at the minimum, a member of the Administrators group on the target and source servers.

Table 1.7: Migration Tool System Requirements

Source Server OS	Requirements
Windows Server 2003 or Windows Server 2003 R2	25MB free drive space~LB.NET Framework 2.0~LBWindows PowerShell 1.0 or later
Windows Server 2008 or 2008 R2	23MB free drive space~LBWindows PowerShell or the Server Manager command-line tool (`ServerManagerCmd.exe`)

First you need to install the migration tools on the Windows Server 2008 R2 target server. After the tools are installed on the target server, then you will need to create deployment folders on the target server for the source server. Lastly, to complete the installation, you will need to register the Windows Server migration tools on the source servers. You will see how to install the tools via Server Manager:

1. Open Server Manager (you can also install the tools via PowerShell if you are running Windows Server 2008 R2 Server Core) on the target server, click Features, and then select Add Features. You will see the Add Features Wizard, as shown in Figure 1.19.

Figure 1.19: Add Features Wizard

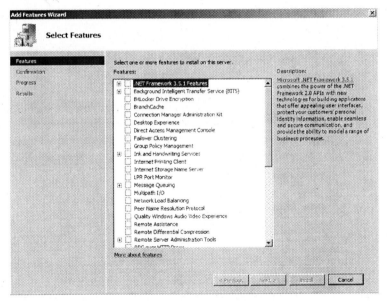

2. You may need to scroll down to select Windows Server Migration Tools. After you select Windows Server Migration Tools, click Next.

3. You will see a screen similar to Figure 1.20. Click Install to install the tools after the installation, review the summary, and then click Close. Additionally, installing the tool set may require you to restart the server, so please plan accordingly.

Figure 1.20: Windows server migration tools confirmation

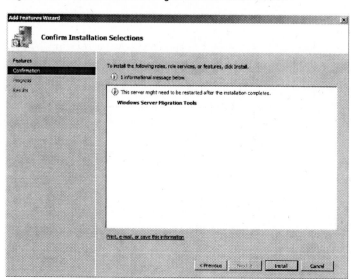

4. After the tools are installed, you need to create the deployment folders on the target computer. To do this, first you need to open an administrator command prompt. Select Start ➤ All Programs ➤ Accessories, right-click Command Prompt, and select Run As Administrator, as shown in Figure 1.21.

Figure 1.21: Selecting Run As Administrator

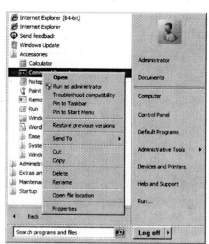

5. Create a deployment folder on the target computer to hold the migration tools; for the following examples, I used `c:\migration`. This folder can also be a network path.

6. In the command prompt window, change to the Server Migration Tools directory. The directory by default is located at `c:\windows\system32\ServerMigrationTools\` (if you installed to the default directory on the C drive). To get there quickly, you can enter the command **cd %windir%\system32\servermigrationtools** and press Enter.

7. Depending on what architecture and operating system your source system is running, you will then need to run one of the following commands. The command will create a directory with the migration tools in it, as in Figure 1.22, which shows a directory created for a 64-bit version of Windows 2003 with the name of SMT_ws03_amd64:

   - If your server is 64-bit Windows Server 2003, type this command and hit Enter:

     ```
     SmigDeploy.exe /package /architecture amd64 /os WS03
     /path c:\migration
     ```

   - If your server is 64-bit Windows Server 2008, type this command and hit Enter:

     ```
     SmigDeploy.exe /package /architecture amd64 /os WS08
     /path c:\migration
     ```

   - If your server is x86 Windows Server 2003, type this command and hit Enter:

     ```
     SmigDeploy.exe /package /architecture X86 /os WS03
     /path c:\migration
     ```

   - If your server is x86 Windows Server 2008, type this command and hit Enter:

     ```
     SmigDeploy.exe /package/ /architecture X86 /os WS08
     /path c:\migration
     ```

Figure 1.22: Windows migration directory

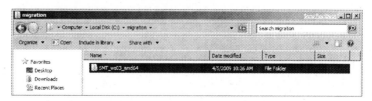

8. Copy the folder created in step 7 to a local directory on the source computer so you can register the tools with the source server.

9. On the source server, open a command prompt. If the server is Windows Server 2003, just run the command. However, if the source server is Windows Server 2008, you will need to run an elevated command prompt. To do that, select Start ➤ All Programs ➤ Accessories, right-click Command Prompt, and select Run As Administrator.

10. Change to the directory you copied the files to in step 8.

11. Type .\Smigdeploy.exe, and hit Enter to register the tools. When this command is complete, you will see a status message, and a Windows PowerShell window will open. You will see a screen similar to Figure 1.23.

Figure 1.23: Windows migration install

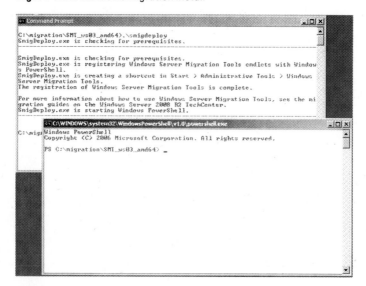

After you install the migration tools, it is then time perform the migration.

Migrate to Windows Server 2008 R2

Regardless of the feature or role you will be migrating to Windows Server 2008 R2, you will follow three general steps after you install Windows Server 2008 R2 on the new target server:

1. Export the settings from the source server to temporary storage.

2. Import the settings to the target server from temporary storage.

3. Transfer any data and shares from the source server to the target server.

In Chapter 2, you will look at migrating specific roles and features.

2

Adding Server Roles and Functionality

IN THIS CHAPTER, YOU WILL LEARN TO:

After you have installed your Windows Server 2008 R2 server, your job has just begun, even though installing the Windows Server 2008 R2 operating system can be a fairly straightforward process. More than likely, you had a purpose in mind for the server. Unlike earlier server operating systems from Microsoft where there were quite a few pre-installed roles and servers, in a Windows Server 2008 R2 installation there are no additional roles or features installed as a part of the base operating system. You have a blank slate for the server in which to create your environment.

As an administrator of a Windows Server 2008 R2 server, you get to choose the roles and features you want to install on the new server installation. Additionally, when you install the needed functionality on the server, Windows Server 2008 R2 will install only the necessary components for the functionality to properly run. This will increase the performance of the server by not installing unnecessary components on the server. This role-based installation methodology has the added benefit of reducing the potential attack surface of your server.

This role-based installation also offers some great flexibility; however, this will add time to your planning process. This also means that when the server operating system first boots up, some things may not work as you expect. This generally is a result of a role or feature that has not been installed yet and not indicative of a bigger problem or server error.

Although there are many roles and services that can be installed on a Windows Server 2008 R2 server, this chapter will focus on just a few. Each role you install on the server can have numerous considerations for installation and planning. The roles selected for this chapter are based on the most common elements in many infrastructures.

Knowing how to properly plan, install, and migrate the roles to Windows Server 2008 R2 are key factors to working with your server. In this chapter, you will learn about planning, installing, and migrating the more common roles you can install on a Windows Server 2008 R2 server. This chapter will discuss both a Windows Server 2008 R2 full installation as well as the Server Core version.

Plan for Windows Server 2008 R2 Roles

Before you can install any roles, you need to plan for the ones you will be installing on the server. Some of the roles will require minimal planning, such as the Fax Server role, but other roles will require a great deal of planning like the Active Directory roles. In this section, we'll cover some of the planning decisions for these common roles:

- Active Directory–related roles
- Hyper-V
- Remote Desktop Services

Plan for Active Directory

One of the most common functions installed on a Windows Server 2008 R2 server is Active Directory (AD). AD governs authentication and access to your network applications and resources. AD provides the directory services that allow you to organize and secure your network infrastructure. Before you begin to plan the AD environment, you need to understand some of the common terminology used in a typical AD deployment:

Forest   This is the main and first logical structure for your directory structure. The forest is the main security boundary and will contain all the objects for your directory, starting with domains. Domains inside a single forest will automatically have a two-way transitive trust with all the other domains in the forest. The forest also defines several things for all the domains in the forest. First, the forest defines the schema for the AD structure. The schema contains the definition and attributes for all the objects in the forest. The schema is extremely important to the AD structure, because it defines the various objects such as the users and groups. It will also define what properties make up those objects; an example of a property would be a last name or phone number. Also, with some enterprise-wide applications, such as email, the schema will get extended to support any new objects or properties needed by the new application. Some applications need to extend the schema to provide the proper objects for the application to function. Second, the forest also contains the replication information for the directory to properly function. Lastly, the forest holds the global catalog, which provides search capabilities for the forest.

Domain   Domains are how you divide the forest into logical units. Domains are created to help control data replication and are instrumental in allowing your directory structure to scale. The domain contains all the security principals (for example, users and groups are stored here) for your organization. The domain also handles the authentication for your network as well and through this provides the base for securing your resources. The domains also helps manage trusts. The domain is also considered one of the main security boundaries for your network. Domains not only allow you to quickly segment resource access for users but also provide a tool to delegate administrative tasks.

Trees   Inside forests you have trees; these are where your domains reside. A tree is where you have domains sharing a common namespace as well as a security context for sharing the many resources located in a domain. Any domains you install underneath the first domain become child domains and get a new DNS name. However, the name inherits the parent domain name. For example, if the parent domain is called admin.com, you install a new child domain called server. The child domain's DNS name would be server.admin.com.

Trusts   Trusts allow the domains to authenticate resources not natively stored in the domain. Trusts can be one-way or two-way. Typically trusts are two-way. For example, if a two-way trust exists between domain A and domain B, users from either domain could log on and be authenticated regardless of physical location. Inside a single tree in a forest, all the domains automatically have a two-way transitive trust between one and another, making the flow of information much easier. You can control and configure the trust relationships to meet your needs. Additionally, when you create a new forest, there is no trust relationship created between the two forests, but you can, however, create one.

Organizational unit (OU)   This provides logical organization to a domain. Without the use of OUs, the domain is just one giant bucket of unorganized objects, making administration a headache. OUs offer the ability to logically organize the objects in your directory. Objects are generally user or group accounts; however, there are several objects you can find in a domain. However, the main objects you will use on a day-to-day basis are users and groups. This organization provides several administrative benefits. Being able to find users and edit properties of a group of users is easier with OUs. You can also delegate administration to the OUs, which allows you to have multiple administrators without having to grant them access to the entire domain. Lastly, OUs are used in the deployment of group policies. Group Policy provides you with the tools to centrally manage and control your clients. Chapter 5 will discuss Group Policy.

User   The user is the account you grant access to log on to your network. This is one of the main objects inside your domain environment.

Group   This is another important AD object. Providing another way to organize your users, groups are an invaluable resource when you're granting secure access to your networks resources, such as file shares, printers, or applications. Groups can have scopes that range from local to the domain to the entire forest.

Domain controller (DC)   This is the main server (or servers) holding your domain objects (users, groups, and so on). The domain controller is also responsible for replication of the directory structure to other DCs as well as for providing support for search capabilities.

Read-only domain controller (RODC)   This is a variation of the domain controller and holds only read-only copies of the directory. Traditional DCs can receive and deliver changes to other DCs in the directory structure, but RODCs can receive only replication updates. Normally these servers are used in branch-office scenarios but could also be used for other reasons such as web applications.

Sites   When you're designing Active Directory domains, OUs, and the many other objects that offer logical containers to help organize your structure, an important physical element of Active Directory is the site. Sites allow you to control the physical structure of your network. Sites help govern three important functions in your environment: replication, authentication, and service location. Sites allow you to define boundaries of your network via IP addresses and subnets, and they give you a mechanism to control traffic. For example, when a user logs on to the network, the site will determine what domain controller will handle the request. The site containing the same IP subnet of the system the user is logging in from will be where the request will be directed. Any domain controllers in the site will then proceed to authenticate the user.

For more information on working with Active Directory, please review the planning guide located here:

```
http://technet.microsoft.com/en-us/library/
cc794908(WS.10).aspx
```

When you start planning your AD structure, you start at the top with the forest and domains. Typically most organizations will have one forest, but it is not uncommon to have more than one forest. For example, you may have a forest for testing and research purposes. This forest is normally logically and physically segmented from the rest of the network. A typical scenario for this type of forest would be when you are testing applications, such as Microsoft Exchange, that extend the schema.

When you install your first domain controller, this becomes the root domain and the beginning of your forest. Server Core cannot be installed as the first domain controller in your forest; the first DC must always be a full install of Windows Server 2008 R2. Additional domain controllers may be installed under the root domain, becoming child domains or installed off the root of the forest, which will become new trees with new namespaces.

The domains are logical units inside the forest that help you organize all the directory objects and define the namespace for the rest of the domains in the forest. You define the DNS namespace for your entire forest when you install the first domain controller in AD; typically this is your company's public-facing DNS name. However, it does not have to be. Remember, these are logical structures, and you can call them whatever best suits the needs of your organization. It is important to note, however, that you should have your DNS name well thought out and planned before you install your first domain controller. Changing your DNS name can have wide-ranging impact not only on your Active Directory forest but on any applications that leverage the directory, such as email or other line-of-business applications.

For example, if your first domain is called corp.com, all the domains installed as part of the parent domains tree will share that namespace of corp.com. Take a look at Figure 2.1 for a quick picture of what a logical structure of Active Directory would look like.

Inside the domain, you create organizational units to further create logical organizational structure for your domain. When you create OUs, there is no right or wrong way to set them up as long as they add efficiency and organization to your directory structure. You may choose to organize the OUs alphabetically by last name, which is the least common way, or align them by business units, which is the most common way. There are any number of other ways, but the main point is that you want to make your life easier as an administrator.

Figure 2.1: Example Active Directory design: triangles represent domains, circles are OUs, and trusts are represented by arrows.

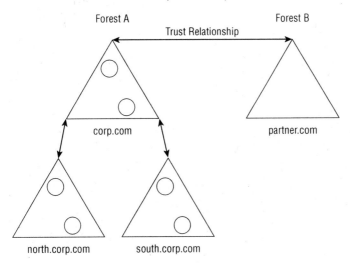

Plan for Hyper-V

Growing in demand is the use of virtualization technologies to leverage underutilized resources to help with server consolidation and flexibility. Windows Server 2008 R2 Hyper-V is built upon the hypervisor technology. Hypervisor allows for virtual systems to access server hardware efficiently. Unlike other virtualization technologies, Hyper-V does not place any third-party drivers in the hypervisor layer. The drivers that are leveraged by the virtualized systems are placed in the parent partition, which is the host operating system. All other virtual machines you install will be placed in child partitions.

Deciding to have your server handle virtualization workloads may seem straightforward, but this role does require additional planning. You need to take a look at what server workloads will be virtualized on the server and what additional hardware resources, if any, will be needed on the server, should you virtualize your open source (Linux) systems. With all of these questions you need to answer, you may be inclined to start looking at your performance logs and application logs to determine workloads. Fortunately, you can take advantage of a resource that Microsoft provides called the Microsoft Assessment and Planning (MAP) Toolkit. You can download this utility from http:// www.microsoft.com/downloads/details.aspx?FamilyID=67240b76-3148-4e49-943d-4d9ea7f77730&displaylang=en.

This tool provides several reporting and analysis functions that you can take advantage of; specifically, to plan for Hyper-V, there is a report that will help you make those server consolidation decisions. The MAP Toolkit will generate both application and server recommendations for your network to determine the most optimal candidates for virtualization. This tool will dramatically reduce the amount of planning time when you are looking at Hyper-V. If you plan correctly, you could have the potential of reducing several of your physical servers to just a few.

Understand Remote Desktop Services

Windows Server 2008 R2 has renamed Terminal Services to Remote Desktop Services (RDS). The functionally of Remote Desktop Services is still very much the same and similar to the functionality of Terminal Services in Windows Server 2008. You can use these services to provide presentation virtualization to your environment. Planning for presentation virtualization follows similar methodologies of server virtualization. In addition to traditional terminal services, RDS provides capabilities for Virtual Desktop Infrastructure (VDI), which allows you to virtualize your desktop infrastructure workload onto servers in your data center. VDI allows you to take your typical desktop applications, data, and even the operating system itself and provide it on your thin clients. The systems those users work on use the Remote Desktop Protocol to connect to the back-end server. When installing RDS, you should consider the proper order for installing these services as compared to the applications you will use on the RDS server. The general rule of thumb is to install these applications after you install RDS so you avoid any potential issues or reinstallations of applications. These applications in most cases will have special installation instructions to make them terminal server friendly.

Another planning consideration is how are you going to allow clients to authenticate against your server and with what level of security. You have two choices:

- Require network-level authentication
- Do not require network-level authentication

This decision can impact the type of clients and the level of security provided by your RDS server. The decision also controls when the authentication of your clients occurs during the logon process. If you choose to require network-level authentication, the user is authenticated before the remote desktop connection is established. This method provides a higher level of security. However, this method also requires your remote desktop clients be using at least version 6.0, and the Windows client needs to support the Credential Security Support Provider (CredSSP) protocol. CredSSP is built into Windows Vista and comes with Service Pack 3 for Windows XP.

If you choose to not require network-level authentication, you will allow any version of the remote desktop client software to connect. However, this will lower the security because the user authentication occurs late in the connection process.

When planning Remote Desktop Services, you need to understand the core services provided by it, as described in Table 2.1.

RDS and Active Directory Services

When planning your RDS server, it is not recommended that you place these services on a server running Active Directory services. There are two reasons for this. First, this can create the potential for security risks on your Active Directory services. Second, depending on the amount of RDS workload present in your environment, the RDS services can degrade your server's performance.

Table 2.1: Remote Desktop Services Functions

Function	Description
Remote Desktop Session Host	This provides two services for the server to host for your environment; this server can host Windows-based applications or a full Windows desktop. This is the core component for RDS.
Remote Desktop Licensing	This server manages and monitors the usage of RDS CALs. CALs are required for connections to the remote desktop server. This server is also a required component when you install RDS.
Remote Desktop Connection Broker	This function is for remote desktop server farms. This service helps load balance the connections to the server.
Remote Desktop Gateway	This allows your users to connect to the remote desktop server over the Internet, without the need to be connected directly to your corporate network.
RemoteApp and Desktop Web Access	This allows your users to connect to the remote workspaces configured on the RDS server via a web browser; this service also provides configuration settings that can be placed on the Start menu of the client computer. The website provides access to applications or desktops you have authorized for web access.
Remote Desktop Virtualization Host	This enables the RDS server to provide desktop virtualization services. This role service will also require the Hyper-V role to be installed on the server.

Required Windows Server 2008 R2 Features for RDS Services

There are two RDS roles, Remote Desktop Gateway and RemoteApp and Desktop Web Access, that will require more services to be installed for the RDS roles to properly function.

If you install the Remote Desktop Gateway service, you will need to install Web Server, Network Policy and Access Services, RPC over HTTP Proxy, and Remote Server Administration Tools.

If you install RemoteApp and Desktop Web Access, you will need to install Web Server and Remote Server Administration Tools.

Understand Windows Server 2008 R2 Features

Windows Server 2008 R2 provides an additional set of functions to the server called *features*. These features were part of Windows Server 2008, but there are also some new features in Windows Server 2008 R2. Some of these features are required for certain roles to function, while other features will add reliability to your server, as in the clustering feature. Some will just add aesthetics, like the desktop experience feature. When planning your server OS, you may need to install some of these features to achieve your desired configuration. In most cases, you will not need to install the necessary features to support a role. Required features will generally be installed when you install the role.

To install a Windows Server 2008 R2 feature, open Server Manager. Table 2.2 provides a quick review of the features.

Table 2.2: Windows Server 2008 R2 Features

Feature	Description
.NET 3.51 Framework	Provides the necessary application programming interfaces for applications to work. The framework is needed for a majority of the roles. On a Windows Server 2008 R2 server, for example, it is required.
Background Intelligence Transfer Service (BITS)	Provides an asynchronous transfer service for files. This can help with the download of files in the background. BITS will also continue a download if interrupted from the point it was interrupted and not start over.
BitLocker Drive Encryption	Provides drive encryption in case the drive is lost or stolen.
BranchCache	Helps reduce bandwidth consumption of clients located in branch-office scenarios. The clients need to be either Windows Server 2008 R2 servers or Windows 7 clients.
Connection Manager Administration Kit	Provides a tool to create Connection Manager profiles for VPN scenarios.
Desktop Experience	Includes common desktop components, such as a media player, visual effects (Windows Aero), and other common desktop applications. Even though these features are installed, they still need to be enabled manually.
Direct Access Management Console	Is the Microsoft Management Console used to manage and configure direct access for Windows 7 clients to a Windows Server 2008 R2 server.

Getting Started

PART I

Table 2.2: Windows Server 2008 R2 Features *(continued)*

Feature	Description
Failover Clustering	Provides failover capabilities by clustering multiple servers together to act as one server.
Group Policy Management	Installs the MMC snap-in so you can manage your Group Policy objects.
Ink and Handwriting Services	Provides support for services typically needed for tablet-style systems. Also includes a useful tool called the Snipping tool, which allows you to create snapshots of Windows screens.
Internet Printing Client	Installs the necessary protocols for printing on the network or Internet.
Internet Storage Name Server	Provides the necessary services for discovering and supporting iSCSI storage area networks.
LPR Port Monitor	Enables the server to print to line printer daemons, which are commonly used on UNIX-based systems.
Message Queuing	Provides messaging support services between applications.
Multipath I/O	Coupled with Device Specific Module (DSM), provides support for multiple data paths to storage devices.
Network Load Balancing	Provides support for TCP/IP to distribute network traffic across multiple servers. This is very useful when your server is providing web services that need to scale as the load increases.
Peer Name Resolution Protocol	Provides name resolution for applications that can register with your computer so other systems can communicate with the applications.
Quality Windows Audio Video Experience (qWave)	Provides a network platform enhancing the quality and reliability of AV applications, such as streaming media capabilities. This feature provides Quality of Service (QoS). Specifically, on Windows Server 2008 R2, it provides rate-of-flow and prioritization services.
Remote Assistance	Provides you and support personnel with the ability to view and share control of a user's desktop that needs support.
Remote Differential Compression	Provides the computation to minimize bandwidth utilization for transfers between two network resources.
Remote Server Administration Tools	Installs tools for remotely managing roles and features on your Windows Server 2008 R2 server. With this feature, you can selectively install the roles or features for which you want to enable remote management.

Table 2.2: Windows Server 2008 R2 Features *(continued)*

Feature	Description
RPC over HTTP Proxy	Used for client applications capable of relaying RPC traffic over HTTP. A common example is Outlook over RPC, which allows Outlook to leverage the HTTP protocol for communication to the email servers.
Simple TCP/IP Services	Provides backward-compatibility support for TCP/IP services and should not be installed unless an application requires any of the functions of a character generator, echo, or other simple services.
SMTP Server	Supports basic email transfer services for email messages and systems.
SNMP Services	Installs agents for monitoring network activity.
Storage Manager for Storage Area Networks	Provides a tool set for centrally managing SANS on Fibre Channel or iSCSI.
Subsystem for UNIX-based Applications	Provides the Windows Server 2008 R2 server to run UNIX-based programs.
Telnet Client	Allows connections to Telnet servers.
Telnet Server	Provides remote command-line administrative capabilities for Telnet client applications.
TFTP Client	Provides read and write capabilities to a remote TFTP server.
Windows Biometric Framework	Installs the necessary support services for fingerprint devices, typically used to log on to the server.
Windows Internal Database	Provides a data store for only Windows roles and features such as AD RMS and WSUS.
Windows PowerShell Integrated Scripting Environment (ISE)	Provides a GUI window to allow you to run PowerShell commands. You can also test and create PowerShell scripts in this new utility.
Windows Process Activation Service	Removes the dependency on HTTP for IIS, allowing other applications to use non-HTTP protocols.
Windows Server Backup Features	Provides backup and recovery tools for Windows Server 2008 R2 for the operating system, applications, and data.
Windows Server Migration Tools	Installs the PowerShell cmdlets for migration; refer to Chapter 1 for how to install this feature.

Getting Started

PART I

Table 2.2: Windows Server 2008 R2 Features *(continued)*

Feature	Description
Windows System Resource Manager	Provides administrator control over how CPU and memory resources are allocated and helps provide reliability to applications.
Windows TIFF Filter	Provides your Windows Server 2008 R2 server with the ability to work with Optical Character Recognition (OCR) files. Specifically for TIFF 6.0 files, this feature will also allow the files to be properly indexed and searched.
Windows Remote Management ISS Extensions	Provides secure communication with local and remote systems using web services.
WINS Server	Is for NetBIOS name resolution for computers and groups on the network, used now primarily in backward-compatibility scenarios.
Wireless LAN Service	Installs the necessary services and configurations for wireless adapters to function properly on your Windows Server 2008 R2 server.
XPS Viewer	Installs the support for XPS documents.

Install Windows Server 2008 R2 Roles

In this section, you will see how to successfully install the roles of a full installation of Windows Server 2008 R2 as well as a Server Core installation. You will learn some of the differences between the two installation methods.

Install Roles on a Windows Server 2008 R2 Full Server Installation

In this section, you'll learn how to install roles on a Windows Server 2008 R2 full server installation. You will go through the installations for Active Directory, Hyper-V, and Remote Desktop Services.

Install the Active Directory Role

As you'll see, you install Active Directory DS by adding the Active Directory DS role via Server Manager. After the role is installed, DCPromo will start. You then use DCPromo to turn the Windows Server 2008 R2 server into a fully functional domain controller. Here are a few important notes you should consider:

- After you install the first domain controller, you should consider installing a second domain controller to give you redundancy. Having a second DC will allow your users to log on in case of a server outage.

- Active Directory will require DNS services. Although you can leverage most existing DNS services, you should seriously consider utilizing Microsoft's DNS. It is made with AD in mind. Additionally, if no DNS server is installed in your network, DNS will be installed as part of the Active Directory installation.

- Installing AD will also install three necessary services required for directory replication:

  - DFS namespaces

  - DFS replication

  - File replication

With this in mind, follow these steps:

1. Open Server Manager.

2. Click Roles in the tree menu on the left.

3. Click Add Roles in the details pane on the right to begin the installation of Active Directory.

4. On the Add Roles Wizard welcome screen, click Next, and you will see Figure 2.2. (You can also select the Skip This Page By Default box on the welcome screen to ignore that page for future role installations.)

5. On the Select Server Roles screen, select Active Directory Domain Services. If you are prompted to add required services, review the services, and click Add Required Services to continue the installation. Then click Next.

Figure 2.2: Selecting server roles

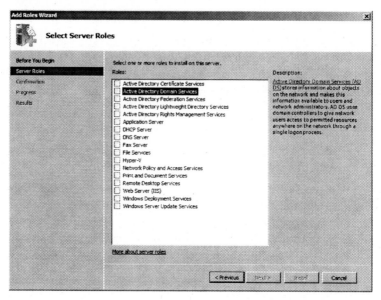

Add Required Features

When you install certain roles and services, you may be required to install features or functions as part of the role installation. When this occurs, you will be presented with a dialog box for adding the required services. For example, when you install Active Directory Domain Services, it requires the installation of the .NET Framework 3.5.1. If the .NET Framework is not installed, you will be prompted to install the services, as shown in Figure 2.3.

Figure 2.3: Adding required features

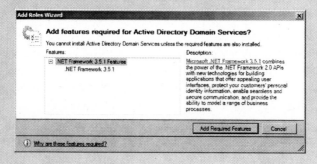

6. On the Active Directory welcome screen, review the information, and click Next.

7. You will be presented with the confirmation screen; click Install to begin the installation of Active Directory.

8. After the role is installed, to finalize the AD installation, you need to run the Active Directory Domain Services Installation Wizard (dcpromo.exe) to finish the installation. On the final screen, there is a link to start the wizard automatically.

Configure Your Existing AD Forest and Domain

If your Windows Server 2008 R2 is joining an existing Active Directory, you need to take a couple of steps to prepare the schema. You need to prepare the forest and the domain before joining the existing forest and domain. When you prepare the forest, you extend the schema to be able to support the new functionality in Windows Server 2008 R2. To prepare the forest, you need to be a member of the Enterprise Admins, Schema Admins, or Domain Admins group on the schema master. To prepare the domain, you need be a member of the Domain Admins group on the infrastructure master. You also need to copy the Adprep tools to the servers to run the commands. To do that, open your Windows Server 2008 R2 DVD, and copy the contents of the \support\adprep folder to both the schema and infrastructure master servers, or run the commands directly from the DVD after you insert it.

To prepare the forest on the schema master, you need to run one of these commands from the adprep directory you copied to the server:

► If you're installing a domain controller from the command prompt, run this command:

    adprep /forestprep

► If you're installing an RODC from the command prompt, run this command:

    adprep /rodcprep

► To prepare the domain on the infrastructure master, from the command prompt, run this command:

    adprep /domainprep /gpprep

9. On the welcome screen, you should click the Use Advanced Mode Installation option to give you the most flexibility and control over the AD installation. However, if you want a default installation of AD, you do not need to select the box. Click Next to proceed.

10. You will see the operating system compatibility screen. This screen discusses the new stronger cryptography used by Windows Server 2008 R2 and how NT 4.0 and older clients are impacted. Review the screen, and click Next to go to the Choose A Deployment Configuration screen.

11. You will be presented with the Choose A Deployment Configuration screen shown in Figure 2.4. Choose the appropriate installation path for your infrastructure, and click Next. (For the purpose of this chapter, you will see a new forest and domain installation)

Figure 2.4: Joining or creating a new domain

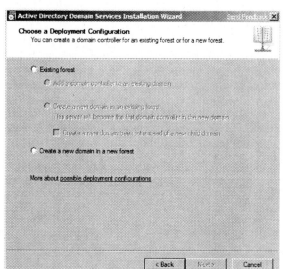

12. Enter the FQDN for your domain, and click Next

13. Enter or verify the NETBIOS name, and click Next.

14. On the Set Forest Functional Level screen, as shown in Figure 2.5, choose the appropriate level of functionality based on your current infrastructure and what operating systems are running your

Active Directory services. For example, if you have Windows 2003 domain controllers, you would most likely set your forest functional level to Windows 2003. Make sure to read the notes and warnings as you choose your functional level because they differ from one functional level to the next. Click Next.

Figure 2.5: Setting the forest functional level

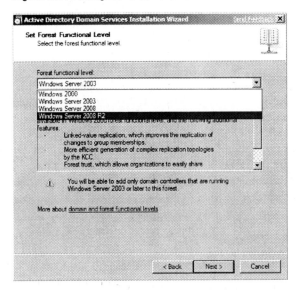

15. On the Additional Domain Controller Options screen, you will be presented with the following choices: to add DNS if no DNS server is found, to run global catalog services, and to turn the server into an RODC. Make the appropriate choice, and click Next. Depending on your existing DNS structure, you may have some additional actions presented in additional dialog boxes.

To Use Built-in DNS or Not

When you first install a new server, you should consider using the built-in DNS provided by Microsoft to support Active Directory services. Microsoft has optimized the DNS server to handle AD services and requests. Although there is nothing wrong with using a third-party DNS server, you need to perform manual configuration to ensure your AD runs properly across the network.

16. On the next screen, you will be asked to choose the installation location for your directory databases, log files, and sysvol folder. Choose the location for the files, and then click Next. It is recommended you separate the database and log files on separate volumes to provide better reliability and performance.

17. Set your Directory Services Restore Mode password, and click Next.

18. On the summary screen, review the settings, and click Next to complete the installation of AD, which will take several minutes to complete. If you are going to be performing future unattended installs of Active Directory, click the Export Settings button to save your settings file for future installs.

19. On the results screen, click Finish, and to finalize the installation of AD, you will have to reboot the server.

Install Hyper-V

Hyper-V allows you to create virtual servers to handle workloads on your server. Virtual servers for all purposes are just like any other server in your infrastructure, and installing the role is straightforward:

1. Open Server Manager.

2. Click Roles in the tree menu on the left.

3. Click Add Roles in the details pane on the right to begin the installation of Hyper-V.

Hyper-V Processor Requirement

If your processor does not support hardware-assisted virtualization, you will see the screen in Figure 2.6. If you get this warning, your current hardware will not be able to run the Hyper-V role.

Figure 2.6: Selecting features

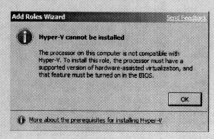

4. On the Add Roles Wizard welcome screen, click Next. (You may not see this screen if you selected Skip This Page By Default during previous role installations.)

5. On the Select Server Roles screen, select Hyper-V. Then click Next.

6. On the Introduction To Hyper-V screen, review the information, which also provides some links to documentation; then click Next.

7. On the Create Virtual Networks screen, as shown in Figure 2.7, review the network adapters and virtual networks that will be created. You can modify your network adapters in Hyper-V Manager after you complete the installation. After you are finished reviewing the settings, click Next.

Getting Started

PART I

Figure 2.7: Creating virtual networks

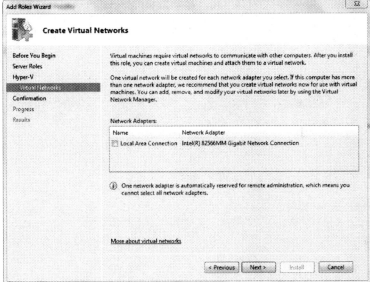

8. Read the summary of the installation screen, and then click Install.

9. After the role installation completes, you will see the installation results windows, which may or may not ask you to restart the server depending on your current server configuration. After you review the results, click Close. If you need restart the server, make sure you save all of your changes before you click Yes to restart the server.

10. If your server required a restart, after the restart completes, you will see the final installation results. Click Close to begin using Hyper-V.

BIOS Hardware-Assisted Virtualization

After you install the Hyper-V role, you may see two error messages, as shown in Figures 2.8 and 2.9. The event IDs for the messages with Hyper-V-Hypervisor as the source are 32 and 41. These error messages are straightforward and generally indicate you have not enabled the hardware-assisted virtualization setting in your server's BIOS for your CPUs. The setting is generally located in the CPU section of your BIOS and in most instances will require you to fully power down the server for the setting on your server to take effect. Consult your server's documentation for the full procedure to enable hardware-assisted BIOS on your particular system.

Figure 2.8: Hyper-V error event ID 32

Figure 2.9: Hyper-V error event ID 41

Install Remote Desktop Services

Remote Desktop Services (RDS) is the newer version of Terminal Services, and it provides you with the ability to handle numerous workloads on the server using the Remote Desktop Protocol (RDP) to handle the requests. In some scenarios, you can use web browser protocols to accomplish these tasks as well.

1. Open Server Manager.

2. Click Roles in the tree menu on the left.

3. Click Add Roles in the details pane on the right to begin the installation of Remote Desktop Services.

4. On the Add Roles Wizard's welcome screen, click Next. (You may not see this screen if you selected Skip This Page By Default earlier.)

5. On the Select Server Roles screen, select Remote Desktop Services. Then click Next.

6. Read the welcome screen, and then click Next.

7. On the Select Role Services screen, you are presented with the roles to install as part of the installation, as shown in Figure 2.10. Refer to the "Planning Remote Desktop Services" section of this chapter for more information on the roles. Select the necessary roles, and then click Next.

Figure 2.10: RDS roles

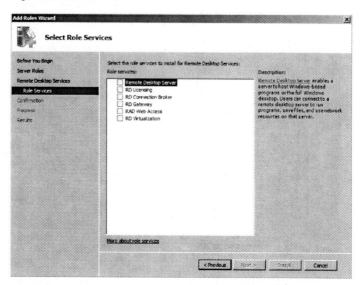

8. Read the note on Uninstall And Reinstall Applications For Compatibility screen, as shown in Figure 2.11. This warning is why it is recommended you install RDS servers prior to installing any applications on the server. Then click Next.

Figure 2.11: Application compatibility warning

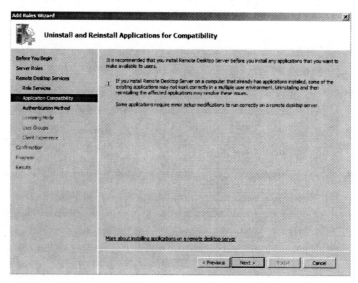

9. On the Specify Authentication Method For Your Server screen, choose the appropriate authentication method for your server, and click Next.

10. Choose the appropriate licensing mode for your RDS setup, as shown in Figure 2.12. This licensing configuration also has to match the configuration for the RDS license server. After you make your selection, click Next.

Figure 2.12: RDS licensing modes

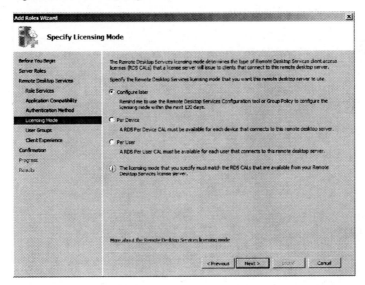

11. On the next screen, you can configure which users or groups can connect to RDS, select the groups, and click Next.

12. On the Configure Client Experience screen, as shown in Figure 2.13, you can select the level of desktop experience for the client. These provide the remote client with a desktop similar to a native Windows experience, which provides features for audio and video playback, audio recording redirection, and desktop composition (features like Windows Aero). Make your selection, and click Next.

Figure 2.13: Configuring the client experience

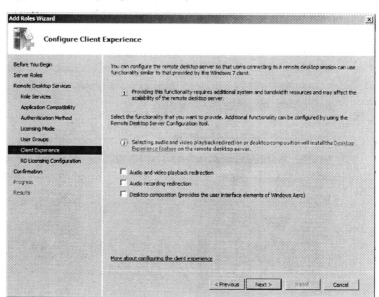

Client Experiences

An important consideration when you configure client experiences for your remote desktop clients is that it can increase the amount of bandwidth and system resources required for your server. This can also impact the scalability of your remote desktop servers. Lastly, if you install either the audio/video playback or the desktop composition, this will require the desktop experience to be installed on the RDS server.

13. If you chose to install the RDS licensing role server, you will be prompted with one last step to configure a discovery scope. The discovery scope allows other licensing servers to automatically find the license server. The scope can be either a workgroup, domain, or forest level. This is not a recommended option, and you should plan on configuring your servers after the installation completes.

14. On the confirmation screen, click Install.

15. Review the results. You may be required to restart the server to complete the installation. When you're ready, click Close to finish the install. On the warning screen, click Yes if you are ready to reboot the server.

16. If your server required a restart, after the restart completes, you will see the final installation results. Click Close to begin using RDS.

Install Roles on a Windows Server 2008 R2 Server Core Installation

As mentioned in Chapter 1, Server Core, like in Windows Server 2008, is a very streamlined version of Windows Server. Server Core has limited functionality and runs a subset of the roles provided by Windows Server 2008 R2. It provides a nice addition to your network without the overhead of a traditional server. This will lower the overall maintenance and security risks for the server. During your installation and planning process, you may determine Server Core servers will be part of your installation. Server Core servers can become an integral part of your environment and provide services similarly to full server installations. For the most part, when you install a role on a Server Core install, the role will function the same as if it was on the full server. Since Server Core does not have a GUI or Server Manager, you need to perform the installation with the command prompt.

Install Active Directory on Windows Server 2008 R2 on Server Core

Installing Active Directory on a Server Core installation can be done either by hand or with an answer file. Either command will start by running DCPromo on the Server Core. If you choose to run the command by hand, you will need to enter all the parameters by hand as part of the dcpromo command. This method can be tricky, and you should consider using an answer file. Creating an answer file is fairly straightforward; all you need to do is create a .txt file with the parameters already entered in the file. To create an answer file, create a new text document and put [DCINSTALL] at the top of the file. Following that, you just need to configure the parameters for the domain join. Table 2.3 describes the parameters.

Table 2.3: Domain Controller Parameters

Parameter	Description and Values
UserName	Username with domain administrative credentials.
UserDomain	Domain of the user.
Password	Password for the user.
ReplicaDomainDNSName	FQDN of the domain to join or create.
Replica or NewDomain	Replica for additional domain controller.~LBNewDomain for a new domain.
DatabasePath	Location of the ntds.dit file; this is a local folder with "" if no value is set. dcrpomo defaults to %systemroot%\ntds.
LogPath	Location of the log files; this is a local folder with "" if no value is set. dcrpomo defaults to %systemroot%\ntds.
SYSVOLPath	Location of the SYSVOL tree; this is a local folder with "" if no value is set. dcrpomo defaults to %systemroot%\SYSVOL.
InstallDNS	Determines whether to install DNS on the domain controller; takes a yes or no value.
ConfirmGC	Determines whether the domain controller will be a global catalog server; takes a yes or no value.
SafeModeAdminPassword	Password for account for Directory Services Restore Mode; make sure the password meets the password requirements for your domain.

Table 2.3: Domain Controller Parameters *(continued)*

Parameter	Description and Values
RebootOnCompletion	Determines whether the server reboots and if you are prompted; takes Yes, No, or NoAndNoPromptEither.
ApplicationPartitionsToReplicate	Specify if you want application partitions to replicate.

Sample Answer File

The answer file shown here would join Server Core to the w2k8r2 .com domain using the administrator account ID with the password of P@ssw0rd. Additionally, this server would not have DNS installed or become a global catalog server, with a recovery password of P@ssw0rd. All the databases would be installed in the default directories, and the server would automatically reboot at the end of the installation.

```
[DCINSTALL]
UserName=administrator
UserDomain=w2k8r2
Password=P@ssw0rd
ReplicaDomainDNSName=w2k8r2.com
ReplicaOrNewDomain=Replica
InstallDNS=no
ConfirmGC=no
SafeModeAdminPassword=P@ssw0rd
RebootOnCompletion=Yes
```

After you create the answer file, you need to drop it on the Server Core and run the dcpromo command with the unattend switch and a path to the answer file. After you run the installation, the passwords will be removed from the answer file. For example, the following command would install the domain controller with the answer file named dcunattend.txt from the root of the C drive:

```
DCPROMO.exe /unattend:c:\ dcunattend.txt
```

During the install, you may see a screen similar to Figure 2.14.

Figure 2.14: Running dcpromo on Core Server

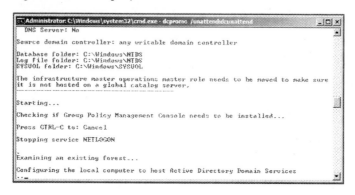

Install Other Roles and Features on Windows Server 2008 R2 Server Core

Installing Active Directory is a unique role installation for Windows Server 2008 R2 Server Core. If you want to install other roles or features on Server Core, you will run the dism command. This is the Deployment Image Servicing and Management tool, which is new to Windows Server 2008 R2. dism will allow you to add and remove roles and features to and from your Server Core installation. Like installing features through Server Manager, if you install a role with dism requiring prerequisite features, you will be prompted to install those features as well. You can also install multiple features at the same time. Although this guide will not list all the roles and features you can install on Server Core, there are a few commands that you need to learn:

- dism /online /get-features will list a state enabled of disabled for the current server installation. This command will also provide you with a list of the features with the appropriate names that can be installed on your Server Core installation.

  dism /online /enable-feature is the base command for installing any new role or feature on the Server Core. You will add the /featurename switch followed by the name of the feature you want to install. For example, to install Hyper-V on the Server Core, your command would look like this:

      dism /online /enable-feature /featurename:Microsoft-Hyper-V

- dism /online/disable-feature is the base command for uninstalling any new role or feature on the Server Core.

Migrate Roles to Windows Server 2008 R2

After you install the migration tools, it is then time to perform the migration. Before beginning any migration of any role of service, you need to make sure you back up your source and destination servers. Regardless of the feature or role you will be migrating to, Windows Server 2008 R2 will follow three general steps after you install Windows Server 2008 R2 on the new target server. First, you will export the settings from the source server to temporary storage. Then, you will import the settings to the target server from the temporary storage. Last, you will transfer any data and shares from the source server to the target server.

Getting Started

PART I

Migrate Active Directory and DNS

You might be wondering why DNS is included in this section; the main reason is that DNS is the name resolution backbone for any Active Directory environment. DNS provides the needed discovery resources for servers, replication, roles, and many other functions inside Active Directory. Before you migrate your Active Directory and DNS structure, be sure to prepare your environment. Make sure your source and destination servers are properly prepared. Preparing the source server is straightforward and can be summed up in one word: *document*. You will want to make sure you take note of the server name, DNS settings, OU information, server roles, Flexible Single Master Operations Roles, and so on. These provide you with the data to help verify that the migration was successful. You also need to consider what role the source server will play after the migration. When the migration completes, the source server will become a member server.

Preparing the destination server takes a little more work. After you install the Windows Server 2008 R2 server, you will need to perform a few steps prior to beginning the migration. One thing you should be aware of is when you install the server, the server name and IP address you assign are temporary and will be replaced later during the migration. The reason behind the replacement of the names is to ensure your client systems will still have the ability to connect to DNS without you needing to reconfigure all the client systems.

When you're ready, you need to join the Windows Server 2008 R2 destination server to the source server's domain by installing the role or running dcpromo. Remember prior to joining the domain to properly prepare your AD environment by running Forestprep and Adprep, mentioned earlier in this chapter. The main reason is to make sure the replication of the directory takes place. This is a big part of the migration, and second part is to migrate DNS and IP settings so the destination server will service the clients on your network.

Active Directory and DNS Migration

When you perform this migration, there will be several times during the process that the server you are migrating from and the server you are migrating to will have their key services turned off, and there will be times the servers will be rebooted. You need to plan for this migration during off-peak hours when your network will be least impacted by the downtime of this migration.

1. Verify what DNS partitions are running on the source and destination servers by running the following command. The destination server should only be enlisted in the same partitions as the source server:

   ```
   dnscmd /EnlistDirectoryPartition
   ```

   If you need to enlist any custom partitions from the source server to the destination server, you may need to run this command on the destination server:

   ```
   dnscmd /EnlistDirectoryPartition <FQDN of partition>
   ```

2. Stop the DNS service on the source server by running the following command. (Or you can stop the service in the services administrative tool.) You need to stop the service to make sure the data is properly migrated.

   ```
   net stop "DNS Server"
   ```

3. You then need to export two registry keys on the source server containing the necessary DNS entries to be migrated:

   ```
   HKEY_LOCAL_MACHINE\SYSTEM\CurrentControlSet\Services\
   DNS\Parameters
   HKEY_LOCAL_MACHINE\SOFTWARE\Microsoft\Windows NT\
   CurrentVersion\DNS Server
   ```

You can either export the keys in regedit, or you can run the following two commands, which will export the keys to windows\ system32\dns on your system drive:

```
regedit /E:A %Windir%\System32\DNS\Dns-Service.REG HKEY_
LOCAL_MACHINE\System\CurrentControlSet\Services\DNS
regedit /E:A %Windir%\System32\DNS\Dns-Software.REG
"HKEY_LOCAL_MACHINE\SOFTWARE\Microsoft\Windows NT\
CurrentVersion\DNS Server"
```

Getting Started

PART I

4. Create a folder called DNS_migrate_system32DNS on a network share or other removable drive; this will be copied to the destination server.

5. Copy all the contents, excluding the samples directory, in the windows\system32\dns directory on the source server, to the DNS_ migrate_system32DNS folder you created in the previous step. You may need to copy additional DNS directories if DNS used custom directories. You can check to see whether you have custom paths by looking at this registry key:

```
HKEY_LOCAL_MACHINE\SYSTEM\CurrentControlSet\Services\
DNS\Parameters\DatabaseDirectory
```

6. Start the DNS service on the source server by running the following command (or do so in the services administrative tool). You need to start the service to provide service on your network until the migration is complete.

```
net start "DNS Server"
```

7. Stop the DNS service on the destination server by running the following command (or using the services administrative tool):

```
net stop "DNS Server"
```

8. Copy all the contents from the directory to the windows\system32\ dns directory on the destination server. Copy and replace any files if prompted.

9. From the DNS directory on the destination server, run both the .reg files created in step 3 to import the registry entries.

10. Start the DNS service on the destination server by running the following command (or using the services administrative tool):

```
net start  "DNS Server"
```

11. After you have started the DNS service, then you need to verify the migration with a command provide by Microsoft called the Convergence Verification Script (CVS). You can download CVS from http://go.microsoft.com/fwlink/?LinkId=135502. After you have downloaded and extracted the command, run the following command. This command will verify the migration:

```
DNSConvergeCheck.cmd <source DNS server>
<destination DNS server> <FQDN of domain>
```

12. The last steps involve you then replacing the IP address and name of the destination server with the IP address and name of the source server. It is important to note that when you rename the computers, this will require a reboot for both the source and destination server. To do this, follow these steps:

   a. Change the source server IP address to another unused IP address on your network.

   b. Change the destination server's IP address to the original address of the source server.

   c. Rename the source server's computer name to an unused name on network. To do this, open the System control panel, choose the Computer Name tab, and rename the system.

   d. Change the destination server's computer name to the original computer name of the source server. To do this, open the System control panel, choose the Computer Name tab, and rename the system.

Migrate DHCP Services

Migrating your DHCP services utilizes one of the Windows Server Migration Tools. This makes this migration more straightforward. Again, before you begin this process, make sure you make the proper backups of your systems. To start this process, you need to do a few things to prepare the destination server and source server:

   ▪ To prepare the destination server, you need to install the DHCP role on the server (although you can also have the migration process install the role as well), make sure you have a enough hard drive space on the server to hold the DHCP databases, and make sure the destination server is a member of the same domain as the source server.

- To prepare the source server, you need to stop the DHCP service and locate the DHCP databases. By default the databases for DHCP are located in the `windows\system32\dhcp` directory. If you are not sure, you can this command to find out the location of the databases:

  ```
  netsh dhcp server show dbproperties
  ```

After you have prepared the source and destination servers, then you can begin the migration:

1. On the destination server, stop the DHCP service. You can do this by going to the services administrative tool and stopping the DHCP server service.

2. Create and share a directory on the source server that you will use for the export and import process. Make sure the administrator ID you are currently logged on with has write permission to the directory. To make the process easier, you should map the drive to the shared directory.

3. On the source server, start the Windows Server Migration Tools. To do that, go to the Start menu, select Administrator Tools, select Windows Server Migration Tools, and click the Windows Server Migration Tools PowerShell shortcut. You could also open a PowerShell session and type the following command:

   ```
   add-pssnapin Microsoft.Windows.ServerManager.Migration
   ```

4. On the source server in the PowerShell window, type the following command to export your DHCP services and configurations:

   ```
   Export-SmigServerSetting —featureID DHCP
   —path <storepath )> —Verbose
   ```

You will also be required to set a password for the export file during this step. When the process is complete, you will see an `srvmig.mig` file in the directory you created in step 2.

After this command is run, your screen should look like Figure 2.15.

Figure 2.15: DHCP export results

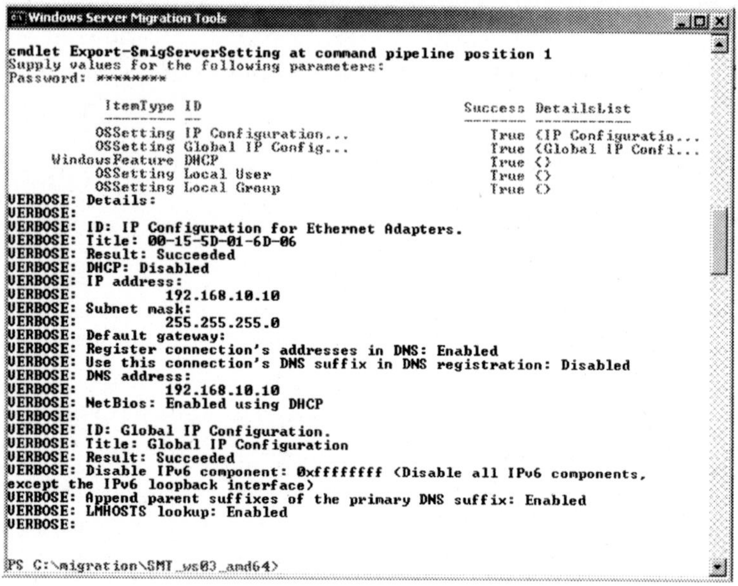

```
Windows Server Migration Tools                                          _|□|×|
cmdlet Export-SmigServerSetting at command pipeline position 1
Supply values for the following parameters:
Password: ********

            ItemType  ID                              Success  DetailsList
            -------   --                              -------  -----------
            OSSetting IP Configuration...             True     (IP Configuratio...
            OSSetting Global IP Config...             True     (Global IP Confi...
       WindowsFeature DHCP                            True     ()
            OSSetting Local User                      True     ()
            OSSetting Local Group                     True     ()
VERBOSE: Details:
VERBOSE:
VERBOSE: ID: IP Configuration for Ethernet Adapters.
VERBOSE: Title: 00-15-5D-01-6D-06
VERBOSE: Result: Succeeded
VERBOSE: DHCP: Disabled
VERBOSE: IP address:
VERBOSE:          192.168.10.10
VERBOSE: Subnet mask:
VERBOSE:          255.255.255.0
VERBOSE: Default gateway:
VERBOSE: Register connection's addresses in DNS: Enabled
VERBOSE: Use this connection's DNS suffix in DNS registration: Disabled
VERBOSE: DNS address:
VERBOSE:          192.168.10.10
VERBOSE: NetBios: Enabled using DHCP
VERBOSE:
VERBOSE: ID: Global IP Configuration.
VERBOSE: Title: Global IP Configuration
VERBOSE: Result: Succeeded
VERBOSE: Disable IPv6 component: 0xffffffff (Disable all IPv6 components,
except the IPv6 loopback interface)
VERBOSE: Append parent suffixes of the primary DNS suffix: Enabled
VERBOSE: LMHOSTS lookup: Enabled
VERBOSE:

PS C:\migration\SMT_ws03_amd64>
```

5. After you verified that the srvmig.mig file is in the directory, you need to unauthorize the DCHP server on the source server. Run the following command:

   ```
   Netsh DHCP delete server <Server FQDN>
   <Server IPAddress>
   ```

6. Import the settings onto the destination server; this is done by running the following command. After this command is run, your screen should look like Figure 2.16.

   ```
   import-SmigServerSetting -featureID DHCP
   -path <storepath )> -Verbose
   ```

7. Start the DHCP service. If you get an error message, make sure the DHCP service is set to Automatic in the Services control panel.

   ```
   Start-Service DHCPServer
   ```

8. The last step is to authorize the DHCP server, and you can do that in the DCHP administrator tool or by running this command:

   ```
   netsh DHCP add server <Server FQDN> <Server IPAddress>
   ```

Figure 2.16: DHCP import results

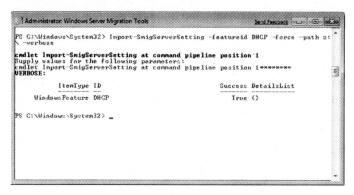

Utilize the Server Migration Tools

As you recall from Chapter 1, the Windows Server Migration Tools can help you accomplish the task of server migration fairly simply; however, make sure you plan the migration process properly. To that end, Microsoft provides several key resources and documents online at the Windows Server 2008 R2 migration website located here:

http://technet.microsoft.com/en-us/library/dd365353.aspx

This site provides key resources for other role migrations, with many planning documents and worksheets.

When you are using the Windows Server Migration Tools, there are really three commands you need to become familiar with to utilize the tool effectively:

Get-SmigServerFeature   This command will display all the roles or features that can be migrated from the source server using the server migration tools. This tool will also display the feature ID names of the services, which are used in the import and export commands. To learn more about this command from the Windows Server Migration Tools, run this command:

    help Get-SmigServerFeature -detailed

Export-SmigServerSetting   This is the root of the command you run on the source server to export whatever feature you have selected to migrate. This command will create the export file srvmig.mig.

To learn more about this command, from the Windows Server Migration Tools, run this command:

```
help Export-SmigServerSetting -detailed
```

Import-SmigServerSetting   This is the root of the command you run on the destination server to import the feature you have selected to migrate. To learn more about this command, run this command from the Windows Server Migration Tools:

```
help Import-SmigServerSetting -detailed
```

3

Automating Administrative Tasks with Windows Server 2008 R2

IN THIS CHAPTER, YOU WILL LEARN TO:

I n Windows Server 2008 R2, learning how to automate everyday tasks can save you a tremendous amount of time and will allow you to spend more time with other administrative tasks. In this chapter, you will get an overview of Windows PowerShell v2. If you are familiar with Windows PowerShell already, then your knowledge will still apply in this version. If you are not familiar with Windows PowerShell, you will learn the basic underpinnings of this extremely powerful and useful tool.

Windows PowerShell is a command-line utility that is built into Windows Server 2008 R2 and allows you to perform virtually all the tasks you can complete in the graphical user interface (GUI). Windows PowerShell is unlike any other scripting tool you may have used with prior versions of Windows Server.

At the core of PowerShell is a very powerful engine providing several key areas for automation. PowerShell is a command-line shell for running basic commands, it's a scripting language for common commands, and it provides the administrative platform for several Microsoft Server–based applications. For example, the Microsoft Exchange 2007 administrative GUI was made entirely from PowerShell. Although in this chapter I will not show you how to build the Exchange interface, you will get an introduction to the PowerShell language.

Windows PowerShell does have a learning curve, but this chapter will get you up and running quickly with this powerful administrative tool.

Learn the Basics of Windows PowerShell v2

In this section, you will learn the basic terminology of Windows PowerShell. You will also take a look at enabling and installing Windows PowerShell v2 on your systems. In addition, you'll learn to start working properly with basic commands.

Understand Windows PowerShell v2 Terminology and Structure

As you begin to learn Windows PowerShell, it is important to start with the terminology and the basic command structure. Learning the basics will allow you to learn the syntax so you can then go on to write your own scripts and commands. The syntax is consistent across the PowerShell engine and allows you to apply what you learn in numerous situations. Microsoft has worked hard with the PowerShell language to allow you to type commands in common-sense language (for the most part), which really allows you to focus on typing what you think.

It is also important to note that PowerShell provides you with another way to administer your common tasks; if you find yourself repeating common tasks, you most likely will be able to create your own PowerShell script to perform the task for you automatically.

The basic building blocks for PowerShell scripts are called *cmdlets* (pronounced "commandlet"). All of the cmdlets you create will be in the common pattern of a verb with a noun. For example, `Get-Service`, `Start-Service`, and `Format-Table` all follow this pattern of verb-noun. In general, when you look at cmdlets, you should be able to figure out the general purpose of what they do based on this naming structure.

You can use the verbs and nouns in many combinations. For the service noun, you can use it with the `Start`, `Stop`, and `Suspend` verbs:

```
Start-Service

Stop-Service

Suspend-Service

Set-Service
```

This pattern is the key to learning the command-line structure. It also provides you with an easy way to find and remember the commands that you use on a regular basis.

You can also add useful functionality to most cmdlets by specifying *parameters* as part of the command-line syntax. For example, if you run `Get-Service`, you will see the status of all the services running on the local server, as shown in Figure 3.1.

If you then add the `-Name` parameter to the `Get-Service` command, you can filter the results to a specific command you are particularly interested in. For instance, you can run the following command to find out the status of the Task Scheduler service, as shown in Figure 3.2.

```
Get-Service -Name Schedule
```

Figure 3.1: Listing services

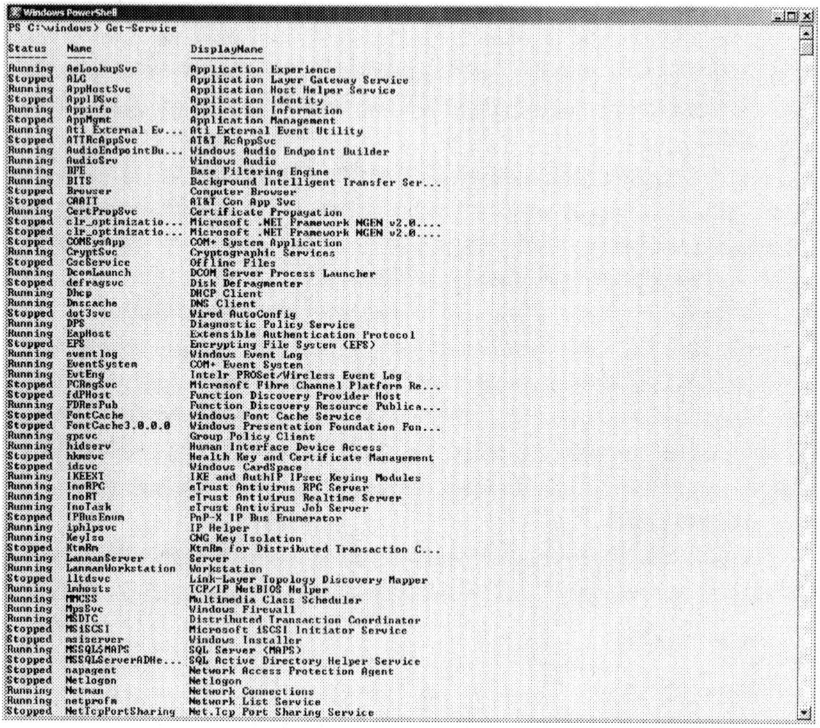

Figure 3.2: Get-Service with -Name parameter

In this command, you see the -Name parameter used to narrow the results of the Get verb.

Additionally, with the use of parameters, PowerShell provides you with the ability to use shortcuts via aliases. For example, the following command is the same command as the `Get-Service -Name Schedule` command you saw earlier:

```
gsv -n Schedule
```

Aliases allow you to abbreviate verb and parameter names for your cmdlets. You can also create your own custom aliases with the `New-Alias` cmdlet. To learn how to do this, run this cmdlet (you will see later in this chapter how to work with other help functions):

```
Get-Help New-Alias
```

However, it is important to note not all cmdlets and parameters have an alias by default. To list the aliases currently on your Windows Server 2008 R2 server, you can run the following command:

```
Get-Alias
```

As you may have noticed, quite a few aliases are built into the system, and some of the aliases may look familiar to you from other command-line shell programs. You may also notice there are a few aliases that have the same cmdlet assigned to them. For example, you may notice these three aliases:

```
cd
chdir
sl
```

They all have the same cmdlet assigned to them, which for this example is `Set-Location`. So, for example, if you typed any of the following commands in PowerShell, you would notice that they would all change your current directory location to `c:\windows`:

```
cd c:\windows
chdir c:\windows
sl c:\windows
Set-Location c:\windows
```

The goal of these aliases is to help ease the transition into learning the PowerShell scripting language.

One last shortcut provided for parameters is that most parameters are positional in nature, meaning you do not always need to use the name of the parameter if you know the proper order for your cmdlet. Although this method can save you typing, this may also create an ounce of confusion if you are not very familiar with the commands you are running. Building on the previous examples, the following command will also show the status of the Task Scheduler; notice there is no '-n' in the command:

```
gsv schedule
```

Functions are another feature of PowerShell you need to be aware of. You can see a list of the currently loaded functions by running this command:

```
Get-Command -Type Function
```

Functions in some cases are a variation of aliases and provide some of the same basics of running commands. However, functions are typically used to extend PowerShell or provide additional abilities to PowerShell. Functions will also provide additional information for your verbs. You will also see some of the functions later in this chapter.

Enable Windows PowerShell v2

Now that you have seen some of the common terms and syntax of installing PowerShell, it is now time to take a look at how to get PowerShell up and running on your Windows Server 2008 R2 server. One of the new changes to Windows Server 2008 R2 is that PowerShell is installed by default. To load the PowerShell interface, select Start ⇨ All Programs ⇨ Accessories ⇨ Windows PowerShell⇨ Windows PowerShell. These will give you the basic PowerShell cmdlets available to you, however, you may not see all the cmdlets you can utilize. Additional cmdlets on your server are available to you when you load the appropriate module(s). To use a module, you will use the import-module cmdlet. For example, when you install the IIS role and the scripting tools for IIS, you get the IIS PowerShell cmdlets. To load the PowerShell modules for IIS you would run this command:

```
Import-Module WebAdministration
```

When you use the import-module cmdlet you have to load each module individually as you need them. The more efficient way to load

PowerShell modules is to utilize one of the built-in administrative tools, which will load all the modules on your server at once. You can find the Windows PowerShell modules in the administrative tools. To load the Windows PowerShell interface, you need to select Start ⇨ Administrative Tools ⇨ Windows PowerShell Modules. When you first run the Windows PowerShell modules, you may see the error message in Figure 3.3.

Figure 3.3: Disabled execution of scripts

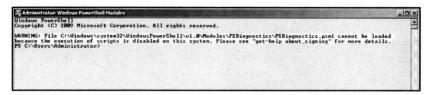

Even though PowerShell is installed on Windows Server 2008 R2 by default, the server does not allow the execution of unsigned scripts. This error message is by design and, fortunately, easy to correct. The cause of the error is most likely because of the restricted execution policy that by default does not allow you to run scripts on your server. The policy is in place to protect your servers from running unauthorized scripts that aren't digitally signed. Digitally signed certificates are all about providing you with the assurance that you are running valid scripts.

Normally when you run scripts locally, these are scripts you have created by hand and are generally scripts you trust. However, whenever you see this message after you have downloaded a script from the Internet or from a friend, you should always take the time to review those scripts. Although it is common to allow locally unsigned scripts to run, you should never enable the remote execution of unsigned certificates. You want to ensure that you do not accidently infect your own servers.

To enable your server to run local unsigned scripts while preventing remote scripts, you need to change the execution policy. After your first install of Windows Server 2008 R2 and when you are initializing the Windows PowerShell modules, you will need to turn this policy off. To do this, follow these steps:

1. Set the remote execution policy with this PowerShell command from the PowerShell interface:

```
Set-ExecutionPolicy RemoteSigned
```

When you run this command, you will see the warning message in Figure 3.4.

Figure 3.4: Execution policy warning message

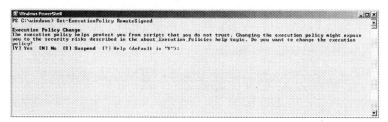

2. This message is again to inform you of the possible security risks by enabling this policy on your server. After you have reviewed the warning, press Y for yes.

3. To verify the command executed properly, you can view the remote execution policy of your server with this command:

   ```
   Get-ExecutionPolicy
   ```

   The command should return "RemoteSigned."

4. Close the Windows PowerShell interface, and open Windows PowerShell Modules to run the initial diagnostics. You should no longer see the error message.

Install Windows PowerShell on Windows Server 2008 R2 Server Core

You might be wondering if you read that correctly. Yes, you can install Windows PowerShell on Windows Server 2008 R2 Server Core. This is new and will provide even better support for you to administer your Server Core installations. This feature is possible because Server Core includes a customized copy of the Microsoft .NET Framework. The .NET Framework that is installed on Server Core provides enough support to run Windows PowerShell to function as a management tool on Server Core. What makes Windows PowerShell a great tool on Server Core is that it has the same functionality as it does on full server installations.

Windows Server 2008 R2 Server Core will provide you with cmdlets for Active Directory as well.

Install PowerShell on Server Core

Installing PowerShell on Windows Server 2008 R2 Server Core is straightforward; however, you will also be required to install the .NET Framework. You will use the dism tool as mentioned in Chapter 2 to install the features.

1. To verify what components have been installed on Server Core, run this command:

   ```
   dism /Online /get-features
   ```

2. If the .NET Framework is not listed in the results, you need to install the .NET Framework on Server Core. To do so, run this command, and hit Enter:

   ```
   dism /Online /Enable-Feature
   /Featurename:NetFx2-ServerCore
   ```

3. After you install the framework, then you can install Windows PowerShell by typing the following command. After the command is run, you will see Figure 3.5.

   ```
   dism /Online /Enable-Feature
   /Featurename:MicrosoftWindowsPowerShell
   ```

Figure 3.5: Server Core install

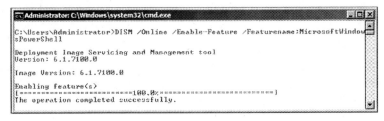

4. PowerShell is installed into the system32 directory. To run Windows PowerShell, you need to run the following command and then press Enter:

   ```
   C:\windows\system32\windowspowershell\v1.0\PowerShell.exe
   ```

After you run the command, you will see Figure 3.6; notice the PS before the command prompt.

Figure 3.6: Server Core running PowerShell

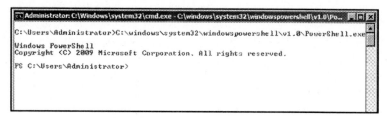

5. You will want to verify the installation of Windows PowerShell. You can run the following command, which will display basic system information about your Windows Server 2008 R2 Server Core:

```
Get-WMIObject Win32_ComputerSystem
```

Learn to Help Yourself to PowerShell

After you have installed PowerShell, you need to learn some simple and basic commands that will prove invaluable for working with PowerShell. The commands that you will see in this section will show you how to leverage the extremely powerful built-in help system.

Learn How to Help Yourself

You have probably heard the phrase "Give a man fish and he will eat for a day, but teach a man to fish and he will eat for a lifetime." To be successful with Windows PowerShell, you need to learn how to fish for yourself. Fortunately, PowerShell provides some very good tools to help you fish. There are two commands that you can use to find more information about commands and, more important, information how to use them.

The following two cmdlets will allow you to access PowerShell's built-in help system:

```
Get-Command
Get-Help
```

All Mixed up: PowerShell cmdlets and Case

When you begin to work with PowerShell cmdlets you will notice a variety of ways cmdlets are written. Some are upper case, some are lower, and some are all mixed up. For example, these three cmdlets provide you with the same results:

```
GET-COMMAND
get-command
Get-Command
```

The default standard for PowerShell is mixed case with each word being capitalized in the cmdlet; for example, Get-Command. Bottom line: Unless specifically noted for a particular cmdlet, PowerShell cmdlets *are not* case sensitive, and you can use the case that is most convenient for you.

As mentioned earlier, when you run the Get-Command cmdlet, you will see a list of the currently loaded cmdlets and functions on your Windows Server 2008 R2 server. However, you can also run Get-Command to learn about which particular commands will work against certain objects.

For example, you might want to use PowerShell to work with the services on Windows Server 2008 R2 but you are not sure what the available cmdlets are for doing this. To find out, you will use the following command:

```
Get-Command *-Service
```

You will see all the commands you can use on the services running on your Windows Server 2008 R2 server, as shown in Figure 3.7.

Figure 3.7: Get-Command *-Service

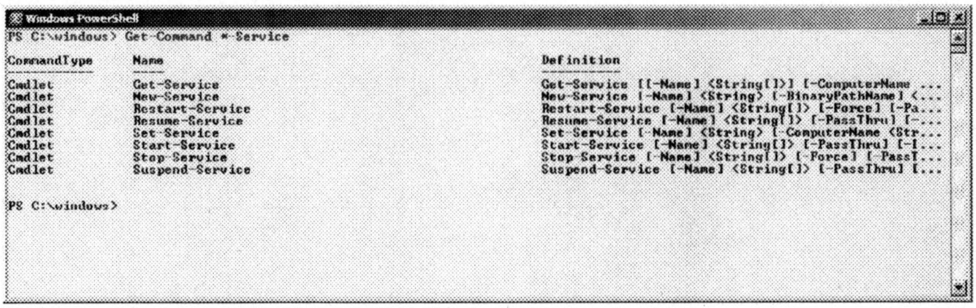

So, now that you know what commands you can use against the Service object, you might be wondering what the proper syntax is for those commands. This is where the Get-Help cmdlet comes to save the day. By itself, the Get-Help cmdlet by default will give you a generic help listing on how to use Get-Help—in other words, it's help on help.

However, the true benefit of the Get-Help cmdlet is when you run it in context. You can get the context you need when you run cmdlets, like the cmdlet from the earlier Service example. When you use the Get-Command and Get-Help cmdlets in conjunction, you can unlock virtually any information you need to learn PowerShell as well as get the proper syntax and usage needed to work with PowerShell cmdlets.

Let's return to the previous example for Windows Server 2008 R2 services. Let's say you want to learn how to properly stop a service. To find this out, you run the following cmdlet:

```
Get-Help Stop-Service
```

This cmdlet will give you the general information about what the cmdlet will do, how to use it, and any possible parameters that can be used with the cmdlet. You may need more information on the command or even examples of the cmdlet in action. There's no need to go search the Internet just yet. The PowerShell help system can provide you with even more information with the three following switches you can apply to your cmdlets.

If you learn by viewing examples, you would run the following cmdlet to see a list of examples of the cmdlet in action:

```
Get-Help Stop-Service -Examples
```

If you wanted to see even more detailed information about the cmdlet you are looking at using, you would run this cmdlet:

```
Get-Help Stop-Service -Detailed
```

If you wanted to see more technical information about the cmdlet you are running, you would run the following cmdlet. This cmdlet will also show you all the additional parameters and how they are used with the cmdlet. The -Full switch really provides an exhaustive explanation of the cmdlet:

```
Get-Help Stop-Service -Full
```

The -Example, -Detailed, and -Full switches can be used with virtually all of the cmdlets inside PowerShell. This provides a consistent
approach to how you can learn to use PowerShell. However, depending
on the command, sometimes the results for the detailed and example
switches will be identical.

PowerShell provides various other ways to get even more information
about how to run commands. For example, you could use the following
cmdlet to learn more about the Service keyword:

```
Get-Help Service
```

Although the results for this cmdlet may look the same as the
Get-Command *-Service cmdlet I showed you earlier, this cmdlet actually provides other areas that you can investigate with the help system.
Additionally, the help system will allow you to query based on the topic
you are interested in. Inside PowerShell there are several help files that
are built into the PowerShell interface. These are traditional-style help
files you can quickly access. To get a full listing of the available topics,
you can run this cmdlet:

```
Get-Help About
```

To explore one of the about topics you are interested in, it is a matter of just asking PowerShell. For example, what if you wanted to learn
more about parameters and how they are used in PowerShell? You would
run this cmdlet:

```
Get-Help About_Parameters
```

This last cmdlet offers a great example of working with the help
system inside PowerShell. Normally when you start looking at the information contained in the About help files, there will be several screens
of information generated when you access the file. This will require
you to scroll back up through the window to see all the information.
Fortunately, the help system has an alternative to viewing multiple pages.
If you want to have a break at each page so you read the information
before you move to the next page, you simply use the Help command
instead of the Get-Help cmd. When you use the Help command, you may
be required to press any key to move to the next page of information.
For example, notice the difference in behavior between the previous

cmdlet for looking at parameters vs. the following cmdlet one, which is shown in Figure 3.8:

```
Help About_Parameters
```

Figure 3.8: Scrolling pages with help

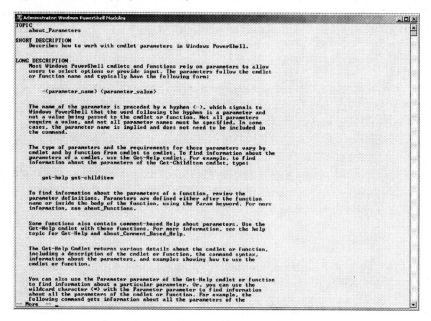

You can also get help with various levels of detail about the cmdlets and parameters you are interested in. For example, if you run the following cmdlet, you will learn more about the ComputerName parameter used in the Get-Service cmdlet, as shown in Figure 3.9.

```
Get-Help Get-Service -Parameter ComputerName
```

As you have seen, the help system is extremely useful and will provide you with the information you need to begin working with PowerShell. The examples you saw around services can be virtually duplicated for any of the commands that you may be interested in.

Figure 3.9: Parameter help example

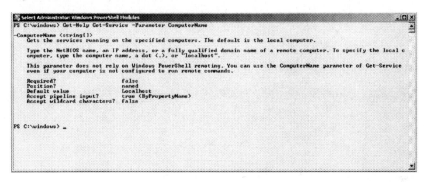

One last cmdlet you may use is the Get-Member cmdlet. This cmdlet will let you find out the properties and any operations for a particular object. These properties can provide additional information about the object you are interested in, such as the status of the object, how long the process has been running, and the required services that need to be running.

To fully utilize the Get-Member cmdlet, you need to have a quick briefing on *variables* for PowerShell. Using variables allows you to take a PowerShell cmdlet, abbreviate it for other functions, and store information for later use in your scripts. For example, instead of typing Get-Service -Name Bits, you could create a variable to assign to this command, a bit of shortcut. (BITS is the Background Intelligent Transfer Service.) To assign the variable $bits to the command string Get-Service -Name Bits, you would type this command in PowerShell:

```
$bits = Get-Service -Name Bits
```

Then you could simply type **$bits** to run the assigned cmdlet. Variables will also allow you to use the get-member cmdlet more effectively. To view all the currently loaded variables, you can run the get-variable cmdlet. For example, if you wanted to find all the properties and operations for a service using the previous variable, then all you would need to type would be this cmdlet:

```
Get-Member -i $bits
```

The -i represents the parameter input object used by the Get-Member cmdlet. Figure 3.10 shows an example of what Get-Member returns for results.

Figure 3.10: Get-Member

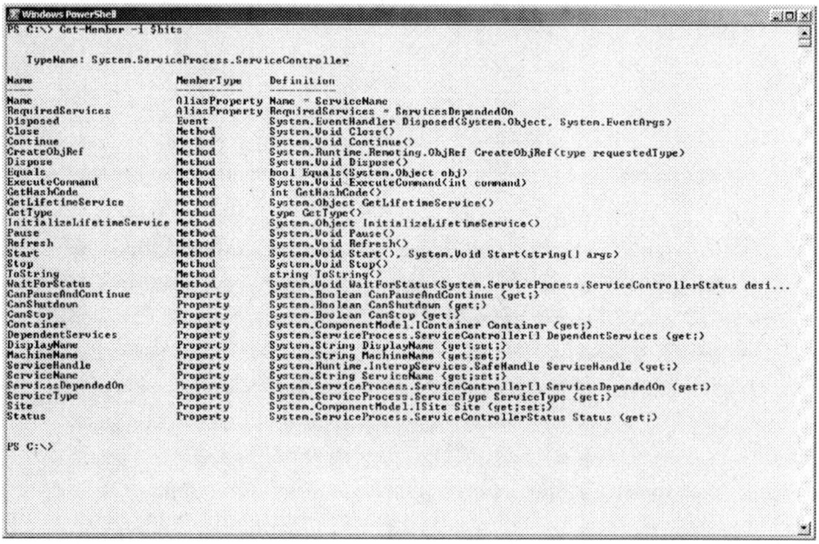

To see what the required services for the BITS service are it is a matter of using the following cmdlet:

```
$bits.RequiredServices
```

It is important to note these variables are temporary to your currently running PowerShell session, meaning when you close your PowerShell window, the variables will be cleared from memory.

You have seen how to generally work with services with PowerShell, which can prove to be very handy, especially when using remoting with PowerShell, discussed later in this chapter. Another useful way to use Get-Member is when you are looking for information about a particular process running on your Windows Server 2008 R2 server. You can determine fairly easily how long a process has been running on your system and whether you need to terminate the process.

For example, you will see the $process variable, which was created to follow the mspaint.exe process. To see what other processes are running on the system, you can run the Get-Process cmdlet.

After you have assigned a variable, you can see the start time of the process by running this command:

```
$process.StartTime
```

You then can use the environment variable to determine how long the process has been running using the Now system variable. The results of the following cmdlet will look similar to Figure 3.11:

```
[DateTime]::Now - $process.StartTime
```

Figure 3.11: Running time of a process

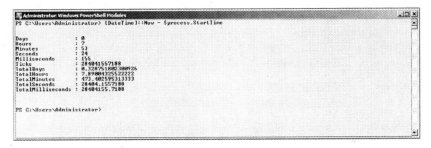

You then can stop the process using the variable again with the Kill() method used in this cmdlet:

```
$process.Kill()
```

Tab Completion: Discover the Power of the Tab

One of the last things you can utilize in PowerShell is tab completion. This feature of PowerShell will make sure you get the right names when you type in cmdlets. To use tab completion you simply need to hit the Tab key as you begin to type in your cmdlet.

For example, after you open PowerShell and you type in the Get verb and hit Tab, you will notice PowerShell will begin to cycle through all the different nouns you can use with the Get verb. If you hit the Tab key again you will see the next possible noun in alphabetical order. You can also type in partial spellings, or use wildcard characters for your commands: You could type ge or ge* and hit Tab and you would cycle through the commands as well. Tab completion will help save you time when your typing your cmdlets.

Take the Next Step

When you start working with PowerShell, you are going to also want to control the output from the various cmdlets and commands you will run to make sure you get the information you are most interested in. In a sense, you want to control the objects and their data. You can do this fairly easily with several built-in PowerShell commands that allow to you to work with multiple objects. Table 3.1 describes some of the common commands that will work with and manipulate multiple objects at the same time.

Table 3.1: Working with Objects

Command	Description
Compare	Compares two sets of objects. For example, you might want to compare what the previous state of a service is compared to the current state.
Group	Splits a set of objects into groups. For example, you might want to group the types of documents in a current file directory.
Measure	Measures some property on a set of objects. For example, you might want to count the number of files in a particular directory.
Select	Selects one or more properties from a set of objects. This allows you to control the type of data output. For example, you might want to see the name and ID of the currently running process.
Sort	Sorts a set of objects by one or more properties. There are several parameters you can use to control the sort, including the descending or ascending parameters.
Tee	Makes a copy of a set of objects. This command allows you to save the results of a command to a file or a variable.
Where	Filters a set of objects based on their properties and conditions. For example, you could use this command to find out the running services on your server.
ForEach	Provides a looping mechanism that allows you to act on every object meeting certain criteria. For example, you might want to stop a set of processes or services that meets a certain criterion.

You may also choose to export the information created from your cmdlets for documentation and reporting purposes. PowerShell provides several commands for outputting your information whether you are formatting the output on the screen or whether you want to create a file. PowerShell provides commands allowing you to convert objects into useful formats. Table 3.2 describes the common outputting commands.

Table 3.2: Output Formats

Command	Options	Description
Format	Custom List Table Wide	Converts objects into formatting records in a variety of choices. List formats the objects into a list for each property. Table formats the object in a table, with the selected properties taking a column in a table. Wide creates a table for an object with only one property displayed for each object. Custom allows you to use predefined views; you can find examples of predefined views in the *format.PS1XML files located in the Windows PowerShell directory.
Out	File Printer String GridView	Sends the output of your commands into different formats. File and Printer are straightforward. The host will output the commands into the command line. String will send the output to the host system as a series of strings. GridView will send the output into an interactive table created in a separate window. Note that GridView requires the .NET Framework 3.51 and the Windows PowerShell Integrated Scripting Environment (ISE) to be installed.
Export/Import	CliXML CSV	Converts objects into and out of common file formats. CSV is a comma-separated file, typically used for spreadsheet programs. CliXML will send the file into an XML file representation of the command.
ConvertTo	CSV HTML XML	Converts objects into other objects or formats; once again used to view data in a different manner.

To effectively use any of these commands, you will make a lot of use out of the built-in variable $_, which will always reference the current object being used in your cmdlet. You will also need to learn to use the | (pipe symbol). The | is used to combine one or more cmdlets into one line. The output of the first cmdlet is used as the input of the second cmdlet, and so forth.

Here are some useful examples of those commands to help you really work with PowerShell. You will see how many of the previous commands work very effectively when combined.

If you want to list all the services currently started on your server, you can use the Where-Object cmdlet to get the information, as shown in this example:

```
Get-Service | Where-Object { $_.Status -eq "Running" }
```

Alternatively, you could also see the stopped services by replacing the -eq parameter value with stopped. You could also use the and clause to see all the services as well as their dependent services.

```
Get-Service | Where { $_.Status -eq "Running"   -and
$_.DependentServices.Count -gt 0}
```

Notice that the previous command does not list the actual services that are dependent on each other. This is where you can use the sort and format commands to display the information you want to find. As you can see in the following, those two commands were added to produce the desired results, and this would look like Figure 3.12.

```
Get-Service |
where { $_.Status -eq "Running"
-and $_.DependentServices.Count -gt 0 } |
sort Name |
format-table Name,DisplayName,DependentServices -auto
```

Figure 3.12: Dependent services table

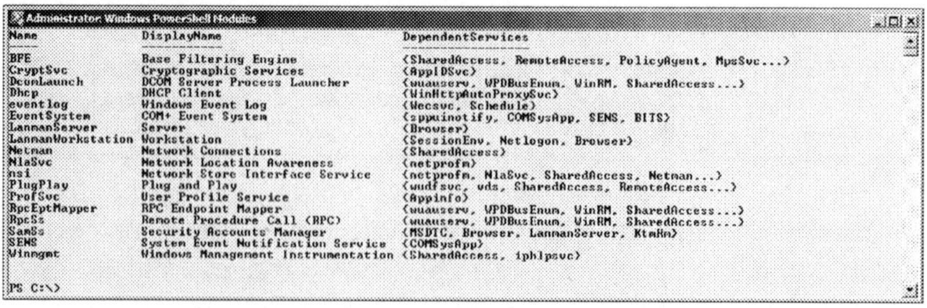

Another useful example using the sort and select properties can help determine why a particular server may not be performing well. You can quickly find the processes that are taking up the most CPU. The following command will list the top five processes taking up most of the CPU on the local machine:

```
Get-process | Sort-Object -Property CPU -Descending
| Select-Object -First 5
```

You can also execute commands on multiple objects at a time by using the ForEach-Object command, which will allow you to execute a script on every object. So, if you wanted to start all the services currently stopped that have dependent services, you would use ForEach to make this task easier to accomplish. You will notice for the previous commands there is a variable created called $services which will allow you to make effective use of the ForEach command.

The following command would create the variable:

```
$services = Get-Service |
Where { $_.Status -eq "Stopped" -and
$_.DependentServices.Count -gt 0 }
```

Then you can quickly start those listed services by running the following command. Now, this command will most likely fail on your Windows Server 2008 R2 servers because the proper roles and features may not be currently installed.

```
Get-Service |
ForEach { if ($_.Status -eq "Stopped" -and
$_.DependentServices.Count -gt 0)
{ $_.Start() } }
```

You can also list the individual objects in your command string that you want to perform actions on in the ForEach loop. For example, if you have the calculator and Notepad running on your server but want to stop them, you can use the following command:

```
Get-Process -Name calc,notepad | ForEach-Object { $_.Kill() }
```

Another powerful tool you can use with processes is Out-Gridview. This will create a nice interactive table to use with the output of the commands. You can click the column headers to quickly sort, and this command even has a built-in filtering mechanism to filter the data you want to see. For example, if you run the following command, you will create an interactive table, as shown in Figure 3.13:

```
Get-Process | Out-Gridview -Title "Processes Local Server"
```

You can also use the Compare-Object to see previous states of objects through PowerShell. For example, what if you wanted to see whether a certain service had been recently stopped? Here you will see two variables used to make the comparison command work effectively. Remember, variables are created at a point in time, so they can be used quite effectively in the Compare commands. If you create a variable like the following:

```
$services = Get-Service
```

and then stop a service either in PowerShell or the Services control panel and then create another variable like the following:

```
$updatedServices = Get-Service
```

then it is simply a matter of comparing the two variables and using some properties to generate some basic data with the following command:

```
Compare $updatedServices $services -Property Name,Status
```

Figure 3.14 shows a sample of the results.

These are just some of the basics; now you will see how to take some of the objects and leverage the Export/Import commands. The Export/Import commands will allow to you to work with objects in different file formats. How you are going to use the files will determine whether you choose to use XML or CSV files. What makes using these commands effective is that regardless of what file format you choose, the command will largely remain the same for either file format.

Figure 3.13: `Out-Gridview`

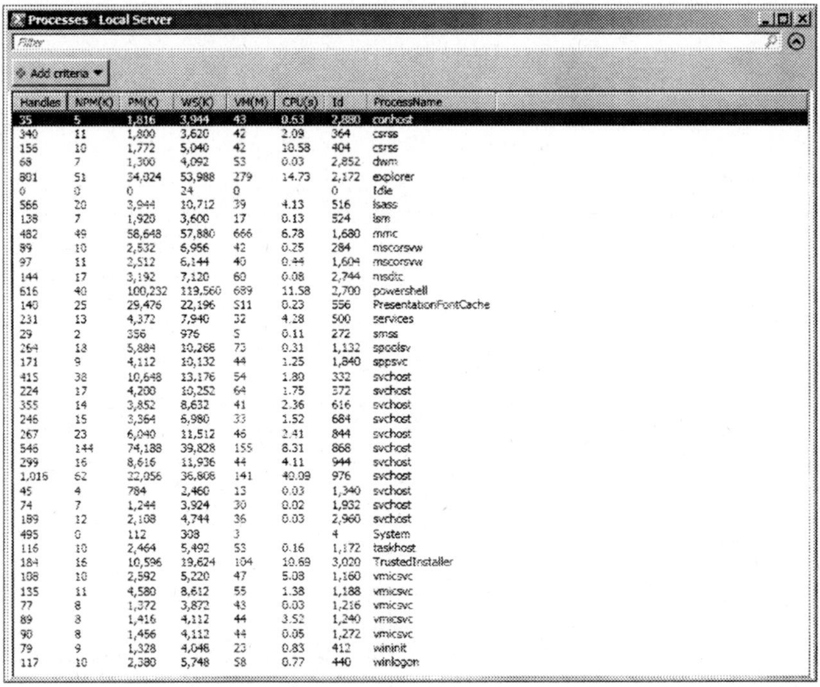

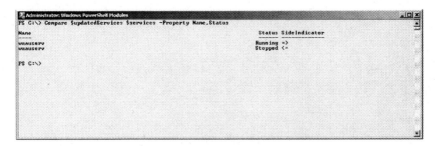

Figure 3.14: Compare in action

If you want to save a list of all the services currently on your server to a CSV file, you can use this command:

```
Get-Service | Export-Csv services.csv
```

Figure 3.15 shows you what the exported file will look like.

Alternatively, if you want to save the list to a CliXML file, you can change the `CSV` switch to `CliXML` and change the filename to reflect the different file format. You can also use the `ConvertTo` command to transform the output objects to HTML. The HTML format also has the added benefit of that you can format the HTML file inside your PowerShell commands. The following command will show some basic information about the local security authority subsystem service lsass process; lsass enforces the local security policy on your server:

```
Get-Process iexplore | ConvertTo-Html > processes.htm
```

Figure 3.16 shows what the file looks like.

This is not very nice looking, but if you apply a little formatting to your HTML reports with the following command, then you get the results you see in Figure 3.17.

```
gps iexplore |
Select Name, id, handles |
ConvertTo-Html -Title "Iexplore"
-Body "<H1>Info about Internet Explorer</H1>" > processes.htm
```

Figure 3.15: PowerShell CSV file

Figure 3.16: HTML outputted

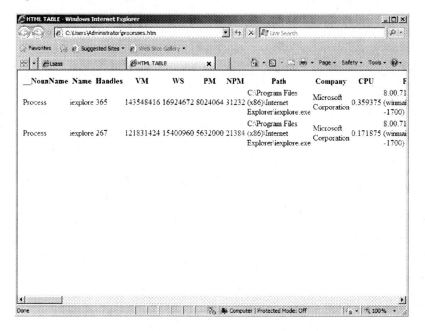

Figure 3.17: HTML formatted

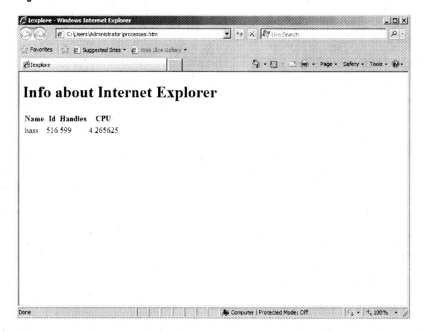

Use PowerShell Remoting

Previous versions of PowerShell were very powerful, but they lacked the ability to easily execute PowerShell scripts on remote servers. One of the new features in Windows Server 2008 R2 PowerShell v2 is called *remoting*. This new remoting infrastructure enables any PowerShell command or script to be run on remote servers.

For this to occur, the servers need to have Windows PowerShell v2 installed locally. Additionally, remoting has to be enabled on the servers. This allows you to run your PowerShell commands on remote servers, and you can even write configuration scripts or a script that starts services, all from your local computer.

What makes remoting a powerful addition to Windows Server 2008 R2 server is that you do not need really any major network infrastructure configuration. Once you know the script or command you want to run, it is then just a matter of executing the script on any number of computers without any knowledge of the underlying network and how it functions. In the end, PowerShell takes care of all the details of the network connection. Remoting allows you to run any number of PowerShell commands on any number of computers simultaneously.

The remoting functions are all built on WMI remoting, and this allows you to both execute commands on and work interactively with remote PowerShell sessions.

Enable PowerShell Remoting

Before you can use PowerShell v2 remoting, you have to enable it on the Windows Server 2008 R2 servers you want to run remote PowerShell sessions on. In this brief section, you will now see how to enable remoting on your Windows Server 2008 R2 server installations.

When you enable remoting on your server, it will do a few things for you:

- Start or restart the WinRM service, if it is currently running
- Set the WinRM service to start automatically
- Create a listener to accept requests on any IP address
- Enable the firewall exception for WS management traffic

To enable remoting, follow this procedure on either your Windows Server 2008 R2 full server or Server Core installation:

1. Open your PowerShell window in your administrator tools.

2. Run the following cmdlet:

   ```
   Enable-PSRemoting
   ```

3. Press Y and hit Enter to continue the process; you will see a screen similar to Figure 3.18.

Figure 3.18: Enabling remoting

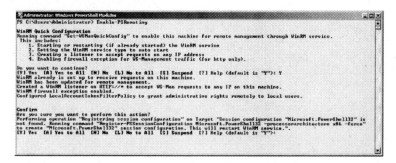

4. After you review the changes being made to your server, press Y and hit Enter to continue.

Run Remote Commands

In this section, you will see how to use remoting to run your PowerShell commands. To do this, you run the same commands that you would normally run locally. However, now you will use the invoke command (ICM) to begin the process, followed by your PowerShell cmdlet, and ending with the ComputerName parameter. The ComputerName parameter can except host names, fully qualified domain names (FQDNs), and IP addresses.

Trusted Hosts Error

If you see the following error message (also pictured in Figure 3.19), it could be for a few reasons:

Enter-PSSession: Connecting to remote server failed with the following error message : The WinRM client cannot process the request. If the authentication scheme is different from Kerberos, or if the client computer is not joined to a domain, then HTTPS transport must be used or the destination machine must be added to the TrustedHosts configuration setting. Use winrm.cmd to configure TrustedHosts. You can get more information about that by running the following command: winrm help config.

If you are using host names or FQDNs and you have an error with name resolution, you will see this error. One way you can verify whether you are having an issue with name resolution is to insert the IP address of the system you want to run the remote commands on. If the IP address works, this indicates you have a name resolution error.

Another reason you could be getting this error is if you can configure your WinRM trusted hosts. To see what trusted hosts are currently configured, you can run this command:

```
winrm Get winrm/config/client
```

To configure the trusted hosts, you can run the following command:

```
Set-Item WSMan:\localhost\Client\TrustedHosts
<computername> -force
```

Note that if you use the * wildcard, this will enable remote connection for all computers.

Figure 3.19: Remoting access error

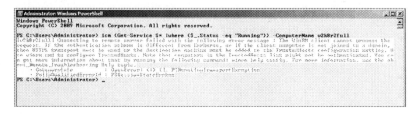

Running commands is a matter of using the parameters covered earlier. For example, if you wanted to see all the running services on the remote server, your PowerShell command would look like the following, and your results would look like Figure 3.20 for a server named WIN-NGKN55U121R. Notice that the PSComputerName column is now listed.

```
icm {Get-Service | Where {$_.Status -eq "Running"}}
-ComputerName <computername>
```

Figure 3.20: Remote service listing

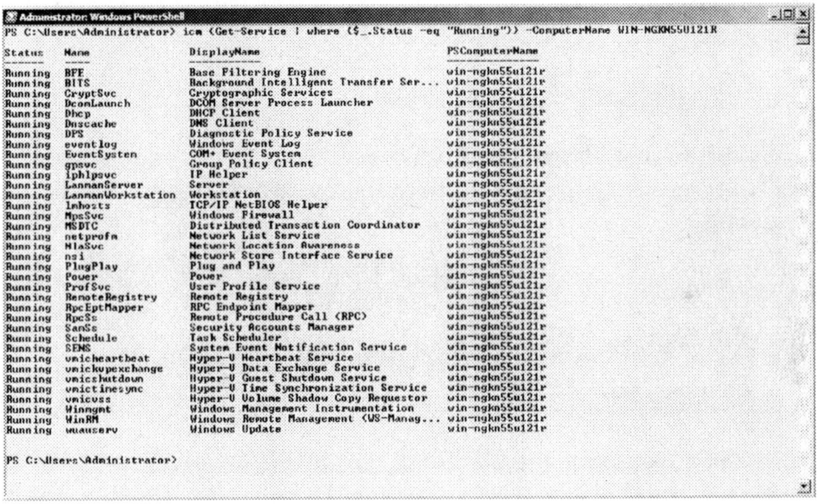

As you can see, this command is identical to the command you saw earlier in this chapter with three changes:

- The addition of the ICM at the beginning of the statement
- The command is wrapped in {}
- The command ends with the -computername parameter

Running your remote commands on servers with remoting enabled will more than most likely follow these guidelines. This allows you to quickly reuse your work and apply your knowledge of how to work with PowerShell locally.

For example, you can assign a variable to the previous command by using the following one. You see the output variable (OV) used to save the results into a variable called sv:

```
icm -Session $s {Get-Service | Where
{$_.Status -eq "Running"}} -OV sv
```

As you can see, you can work these objects as you would any other objects. You can even get more information with the get-member command using the following:

```
$sv | Get-Member
```

Or you can continue to manipulate the objects with the following command:

```
$sv | Select * | Out-GridView
```

As you read this book, you will see many more examples leveraging the basic knowledge covered in this section to help build your PowerShell knowledge.

Learn PowerShell Integrated Scripting Environment (ISE)

One of the powerful new tools for you to use in Windows Server 2008 R2 is the PowerShell Integrated Scripting Environment (ISE). The PowerShell ISE provides some great components. Specifically, it is the component required for the Out-Gridview output format. This component will also provide a GUI front end for PowerShell, which is a nice tool to use to create and validate your PowerShell scripts.

Work with the PowerShell ISE

The PowerShell ISE is Windows Server 2008 R2 feature, enabled by default on your server as well. Working with the PowerShell ISE is just a matter of loading it:

1. Go to the Start menu.
2. Click Search Programs And Files.

3. Type **PowerShell**.

4. Click PowerShell ISE or PowerShell ISE (86), and you will see a screen similar to Figure 3.21.

Figure 3.21: PowerShell ISE

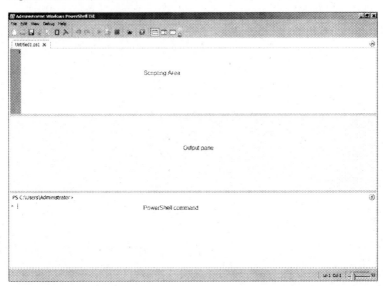

The PowerShell ISE is broken into three panes. The top pane is where you can create and edit your script. The bottom pane is your PowerShell scripting window and is where you can type in your commands just as you would in the command prompt window. The results of your command will appear in the middle output pane.

The true power of the PowerShell ISE tool is its ability to chain several of your PowerShell cmdlets together. All you need to do is type in your commands like you normally would and then tell it to execute by hitting your F5 key. The Windows PowerShell ISE also gives you some minimal debugging tools to set breakpoints in your PowerShell script.

PART II

Manage Active Directory and Local Users

IN THIS PART ▶

4

User and Group Maintenance

IN THIS CHAPTER, YOU WILL LEARN TO:

Manage Active Directory and Local Users

PART II

I n this chapter, you'll take a look at working with your users and groups and maintaining them. You will take a look at the local users and groups on a system, and a majority of the chapter will focus on the Active Directory (AD) users and groups.

AD users and groups really are the cornerstone of your infrastructure. Knowing how to properly maintain and leverage them is vital to a healthy network. Learning how to work with your users and groups not only offers agility to your network infrastructure but is also key to your enterprise-wide applications such as email.

Effectively managing your users and groups will help you perform your job easier and will ensure the integrity and security of your network infrastructure.

Understand Local Users and Groups

Even if you are leveraging Active Directory, you still need to understand how local users and groups work. Local users and groups provide a key role not only for maintenance but also for central administration.

In this section, you will see how to manage local users and groups on both Windows Server 2008 R2 full server installations and Server Core installations. You will also learn the default local users/groups and the default settings on these servers and how those settings impact your infrastructure.

Learn Default Local Users and Groups

Whether you are working with a Windows Server 2008 R2 full installation or with Server Core, managing local groups offers some great similarities. Starting with the default installations, both systems have the same default users and groups installed.

On your Windows Server 2008 R2 server, by default you have two user accounts that are created, Administrator and Guest.

- *Administrator* is the default built-in account for administering the local machine. The Administrator account is by default the only account that is enabled.

- *Guest* is the default built-in account for guest access to the system; however, the account is disabled by default.

Table 4.1 describes several other groups installed by default that you need to know.

Table 4.1: Default Local Groups

Group	Definition and Usage
Administrators	This group has unrestricted access to the local computer. This account is the main account to accomplish any task on a server. By default, the Administrator account is the only member of this group.
Backup Operators	This group, as the name suggests, is designed for the backup and restoration of files on the server.
Certificate Service DCOM Access	This group is allowed to connect to certificate authorities for enrollment in your preferred Public Key Infrastructure.
Cryptographic Operators	This group is allowed and authorized to perform cryptography operations on your server. These settings include the crypto settings in the IPsec policy of the Windows Firewall, among other settings.
Distributed COM Users	This group can activate and launch DCOM objects on the server. DCOM objects are used for the communications of the applications.
Event Log Readers	This group can work with and read the local event logs on the server.
Guests	Users of this group by default have the same access as the Users group, except for the Guest account, which is further restricted. By default, the only account in this group is the disabled Guest account.
IIS_IUSRS	This is the default group account for use with Internet Information Services.
Network Configuration Operators	Users in this group have some administrative privileges over managing the configuration of networking features on the server.
Performance Log Users	This group allows its users to schedule the logging of performance counters, enable trace providers, and collect event traces for the local server. The tasks can be performed locally or remotely.

Manage Active Directory and Local Users

PART II

Table 4.1: Default Local Groups *(continued)*

Group	Definition and Usage
Performance Monitor Users	This group can access the local performance counter data either locally or through remote administration.
Power Users	This group has limited administrative capabilities on the system and is primarily included for backward compatibility with previous operating systems.
Print Operators	These users can work with and administer printers on the local server system.
Remote Desktop Users	Users in this group are given the right to log on remotely to the server.
Replicator	This group is designed for file replication.
Users	Have limited administrative access to the system to prevent members from inadvertently making changes that can cause system-wide changes; however, users in this group can run and access most applications.

Placing user accounts in these local groups will grant those users access to the proper permissions and responsibilities for the groups. The basic concept behind using groups allows you to assign permissions just once to the group, thus granting permissions to all the members in the group. This offers an easy way for you to delegate administration for your server. For example, if you want to have a user perform a daily backup of your server, you would simply need to add them to the Backup Operators group, and they would be granted the necessary rights to perform backup and restore operations. Later in this chapter, you will see the impact of joining the domain to these local groups.

Administer Local Users and Groups

Managing local user groups on your server is just a matter of loading the correct snap-in for the Microsoft Management Console (MMC). You can manage either a Windows Server 2008 R2 full server installation or a Server Core installation. However, if you want to manage the local users and groups on your Server Core installation with the

MMC you will need to do that remotely. There are system commands allowing you to manage Server Core locally, and you will see those commands later in this section. To access the local user groups, you can go to the Control Panel to manage the accounts, or you may prefer a more thorough look at the users. You will see the local users and group management tools for both a full server and Server Core installation in the following steps.

1. Select Start ⇨ Run, type in **MMC**, and hit Enter. This loads a blank MMC, as shown in Figure 4.1.

Figure 4.1: Blank MMC

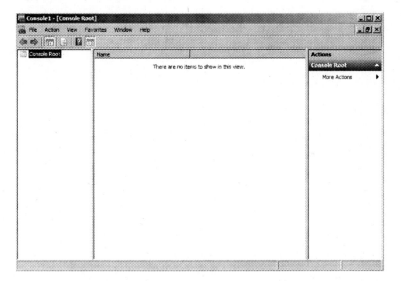

2. To perform work in any blank MMC, you need to load the appropriate snap-in. To load snap-ins, select File ⇨ Add/Remove Snap-In. This will load the Add Or Remove Snap-Ins dialog box, as pictured in Figure 4.2.

Figure 4.2: Adding snap-ins

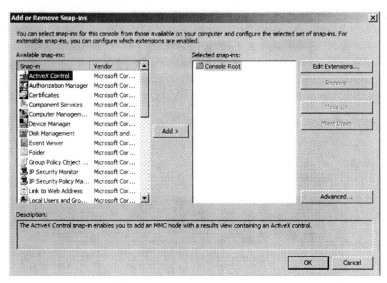

3. To manage your local users and groups, select the Local Users And Groups snap-in, and click the Add button. This will open the Choose Target Machine dialog box, as pictured in Figure 4.3.

Figure 4.3: Target machine

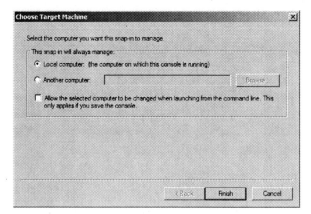

4. In the Choose Target Machine dialog box, you can either select the local computer to manage the users on the machine you're running the console from or select the Another Computer radio button and enter either the IP address or the name of the computer you want to manage. This option will allow you to manage the local users and groups on a remote server such as Server Core, if you have the appropriate permissions. After you make your selection, click Finish to return to the Add Or Remove Snap-Ins dialog box.

5. In the Add Or Remove Snap-Ins dialog box, click OK to load the snap-in into your MMC. Figure 4.4 shows a local users and group MMC.

Figure 4.4: Managing local users and groups

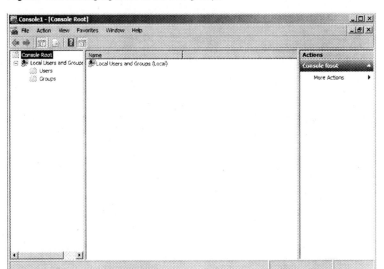

6. After you have loaded your snap-ins into the MMC, you can save your customized MMC for future use. To do so, select File ⇨ Save.

After you have loaded the MMC to manage local users and groups, you can easily work with your users and groups. Creating user IDs and groups, changing passwords, or other properties can all be easily done with the interface.

Manage Active Directory
and Local Users

PART II

Create a Local User Account

When you create a local user account, you are granting the account access to the local server, which is a straightforward process:

1. Inside the Local Users And Group MMC you created in the previous procedure, right-click the Users container.

2. Select New User, which will display the New User dialog box, as shown in Figure 4.5.

Figure 4.5: New User dialog box

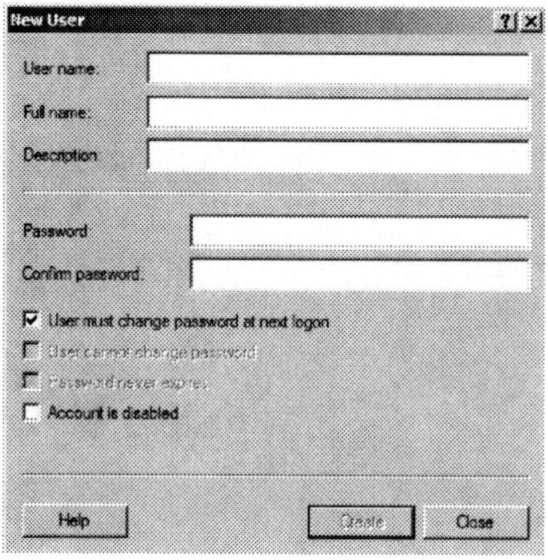

3. Type in the username, full name, and optional description, as well as the password. The password by default must follow the password complexity requirements listed in the "Default Password Requirements" sidebar. Additionally, you can mark the account disabled, if you know the account will not be in use for a period of time. You also have the following options regarding the setting of the initial password:

User Must Change Password At Next Log On   This is the default setting, and you should consider keeping this check box enabled when you create a new user account. The only time you should clear this check box is when the account you are creating will be a service account for an application. This setting allows the user to set their own personal password when they log on to the system the first time. All you need to do as the administrator is set an initial temporary password for the user. You may want to know the passwords for your users in case a user leaves the company or is on vacation. In reality, as long as you know the administrator password, you have the administrative right to reset a password temporarily and gain access into an account. Although it is good to have this ability, you should exercise it with caution and only when the situation warrants it.

User Cannot Change Password   By default this setting is grayed out and becomes available only when you clear the User Must Change Password At Next Log On setting, mentioned previously. This allows you to make sure the password for the account does not change. This is also good for service accounts for applications loaded on your server. This setting will also bypass any local machine password account policy. Default password policies will be covered later in this chapter.

Password Never Expires   By default this setting is also grayed out, and like the previous setting, it becomes available only when the User Must Change Password At Next Log On setting is cleared. The setting, as the name implies, locks down the password. This setting also will bypass any local machine password policy.

4. After you fill out the form, click Create to create the account. If your password does not meet the requirements for password complexity, you will see the screen in Figure 4.6.

Figure 4.6: Password complexity error

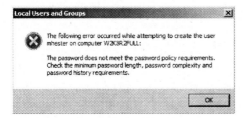

Manage Active Directory
and Local Users

PART II

Default Password Requirements

The default password requirements are the same for both the local user accounts and the Active Directory user accounts you will see later in this chapter. The default password requirements for a Windows Server 2008 R2 server are as follows:

- Cannot contain the user's account name or parts of the user's full name that exceed two consecutive characters

- Be at least six characters in length

- Contain characters from three of the following four categories:

  English uppercase characters (A–Z)

  English lowercase characters (a–z)

  Base 10 digits (0–9)

  Nonalphabetic characters (for example !, $, #, %)

5. If you have no more local users accounts to create, click Close. Otherwise, repeat steps 3 and 4 to continue creating local accounts on your server.

Create a Local Group

After you create your user accounts, you will most likely want to create groups to add your users to. Groups, as you may know, are used to grant permissions generally to files or printers located on the Windows Server 2008 R2 server. These local groups can be granted rights and permissions to resources only on the local server.

1. Inside the Local Users And Group MMC you created earlier, right-click the Groups container.

2. Select New Group, which will display the New Group dialog box, as shown in Figure 4.7.

Figure 4.7: New Group dialog box

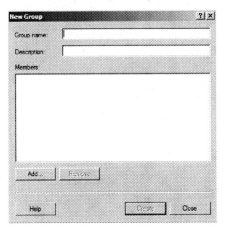

Manage Active Directory and Local Users

PART II

3. Type in the name of the new group and a description. To immediately add members to your group, click the Add button on the bottom of the screen. Clicking the Add button displays the Select Users dialog box, as shown in Figure 4.8.

Figure 4.8: Select Users dialog box

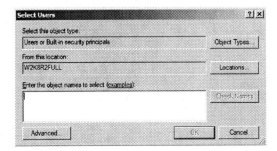

4. To add users, you can type them in the name text box. To verify the spelling of the user names you want to add, you can click Check Names, which will verify the usernames for you. You can also click the Advanced button, which will expand the dialog box to allow you to list all the user accounts on the system. This dialog box has a Find Now option to allow you to quickly list all the

users on the system. If you click Find Now, you will see a screen similar to Figure 4.9.

Figure 4.9: Advanced selecting users

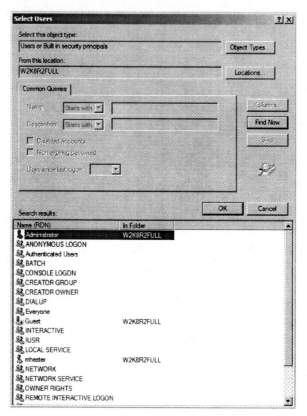

5. After you click Find Now, you will see a list of users on the system, as well as local system user and group accounts. Select the user or users you want to be in your group. To select multiple users, you can hold down the Ctrl key on your keyboard as you click. You could also select a list by using the Shift key. If you click the top item of your list, hold down the Shift key, and click the bottom item on your list, you will select all the items between and including your top and bottom selection.

Special Identity Groups

You may notice that when you were adding users to your group, you had several more accounts and groups that you did not create. These are special identity groups, and you cannot control the membership of these groups. Your users become members of these groups through the course of actions they perform on your servers or how they access servers, and the membership to these groups is temporary and normally changes given how the user will work with the system. System groups can be used to help set permissions based on how users access or interact with the server. Table 4.2 lists a few of the system groups you may encounter as you work with the server.

The groups that are not listed in the table are normally system groups that are reserved for the use of the operating system and the services running on your Windows Server 2008 R2 server. In particular, you need to pay particular attention to one special identity account, the SYSTEM account. The SYSTEM account represents the Windows Server 2008 R2 operating system. As you work with the files on your server and the user rights, you may encounter the SYSTEM account, and you should leave this account unmodified. If you make a change to the permissions or rights the SYSTEM account has on your server, you could disable your server, which may result in you reinstalling the operating system.

Table 4.2: Special Identity Groups

Group	Description
Anonymous Logon	This represents when users do not use credentials of any kind to access the system.
Authenticated Users	Users are automatically placed in this group when they log on locally to the system. Leveraging this group is a great way to make sure only valid, authenticated users can gain access to resources.
Creator Owner	When a user creates an object, such as a file or folder on the server, they are put into the Creator Owner group for that object. Generally speaking, the Creator Owner user has full control over the created object.
Dialup	When a user connects to the server via a dial-up connection, such as a remote VPN connection, they are added to this group.

Table 4.2: Special Identity Groups *(continued)*

Group	Description
Everyone	Everyone is a member of this group regardless of how they access the server.
Interactive	When a user logs on locally to the server (in other words, they have physical access to the server and log on physically to the server), users are placed in this group.
Network	When a user accesses the server remotely over a network connection, such as when they connect to a file share, they are placed in this group.
Remote Interactive Logon	When a user accesses the server remotely with a local user ID and actively logs on to the system to perform remote tasks, such as when an administrator logs on to the server from a remote workstation, they are placed in this group.
System	This is the account group ID used by the Windows Server 2008 R2 operating system.
Terminal Server User	When users access the server using Remote Desktop Services, they are automatically placed in this group.

Manage Your Local Users and Groups

After you are done creating your user groups, you will need to maintain and manage the local accounts. To begin managing local groups, just right-click the user or group you want to manage. They share some common tasks. When you right-click a user or group, you can delete, rename, open help, or view the unique properties for the object.

When you right-click the user, you can set a new password for the user. The only time you should set the password for an existing account is if the user has forgotten or lost their password. The user will lose access to information such as encrypted files, stored Internet passwords (although the user can re-create these with the new password), email that is encrypted with the user's public key, and any stored certificates (again, new certificates can be issued to still grant access). The potential risk here is losing data in files that have been encrypted by the encrypted file system (EFS). If you have backed up your recovery keys, you will be able to retrieve data; however, if there is no backup of the keys, you will not be able to access the data.

When you right-click a user account, you are presented with the choice to set the password. When you select the option, you will receive the warning shown in Figure 4.10.

Figure 4.10: Setting password warning

When you right-click a group and select Add to Group, this will start the same process to add members to your group as used in the previous procedure when you created the group. Additionally, when you select the Properties option after you right-click the group, it will take you to the properties where you can use the Add Members dialog box.

When you select the Properties option after you right-click will open a list of properties you can modify for the user account, as shown in Figure 4.11.

The properties listed here are part documentation and part account configuration. The tabs listed will allow you to configure basic username and description information and group membership. You can also set properties for Remote Desktop Services connections information, user profiles, home directory information, and dial-in access, as well as a variety of other properties you will see later in this chapter and throughout this book as the respective topics come up.

Figure 4.11: User properties

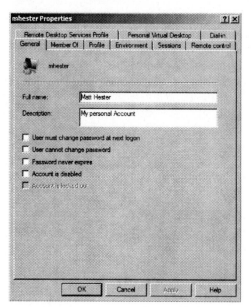

Manage Local Users and Groups on Server Core

You may not have access to a Microsoft Management Console, and you may need to make modifications to the local users and groups on a Windows Server 2008 R2 Server Core installation. You can add, delete, and modify all aspects of the local users and groups via the command prompt. Specifically, the net command is how you work with users and groups directly on Server Core. The net command will also work on a Windows Server 2008 R2 full server installation.

The net command has many functions, including starting and stopping services and configuring the IP address on the server. You will see in this section how to use the net command to work with your local users and groups.

All of the net commands begin with net; for users this will be followed by user, and for local groups this will be followed by localgroup. For example, to see the current list of your local users or local groups, type one of the following straightforward commands and hit Enter:

- Use net user to see a list of local users.

- Use net localgroup to see a list of local groups.

To add a user or local group to the system, the commands follow similar syntax. The commands will include the /add switch. For example, to add a user named Harold with a password of pass@word1 to your system, you would use the following command:

```
net user Harold pass@word1 /add
```

To add a local group called Writers to your server, you would use the following command:

```
net localgroup Writers /add
```

To add Harold to the Writers group, you would use the following command:

```
net localgroup Writers Harold /add
```

To see the current membership for the local group Writers, you would use the following command:

```
net localgroup Writers
```

The commands are straightforward and fairly intuitive to learn how to use. To learn more about commands to work with local users and groups, just use the built-in help system:

- Use net user /? to learn more about working with users.

- Use net localgroup /? to learn more about working with local groups.

Understand Local User Rights

You might be thinking that granting users permissions to your server is as easy as adding the user to the right group. Well, in part, you are correct; however, you need to understand what truly grants users the ability to do work on the Windows Server 2008 R2 server. Those abilities are called *rights* on a server, and in turn the local rights are assigned to the user or group. For example, when you add a user to the Backup Operators group, that group is granted a few built-in rights. A couple of those rights are Backup Files and Directories and Restore Files and Directories, for example.

View the Local User Rights

To see a list of the local rights on the server, you need to open the Local Security Policy MMC on the system. The local security policy will allow you to look at the local user rights and will show account policies, Windows Firewall, and other important security settings on your server. To view the local security policy, you need to be an administrator for the server.

1. Click the Start menu.

2. In Search Programs And Files, type **Local Security Policy**.

3. Click the Local Security Policy link, and you will see a screen similar to Figure 4.12.

Figure 4.12: Local Security Policy MMC

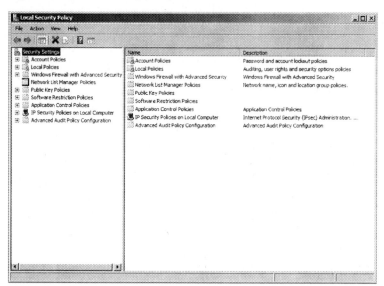

4. In the Local Security Policy MMC, click the + sign next to Local Policies to expand the console tree.

5. Click User Rights Assignment to view the currently assigned rights on the system, as shown in Figure 4.13.

Figure 4.13: Local user rights

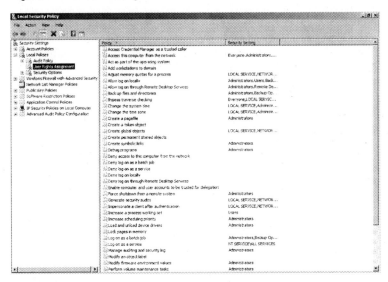

6. To see the currently assigned rights for any of the local users, simply double-click the appropriate object in the right pane. For example, if you double-click Backup Files And Directories, you will see that by default two local groups, Administrators and Backup Operators, have been granted the right.

WARNING   When you first look at the local security policy, you will see several of the user rights already assigned to various local built-in groups and special identities. If you're not sure what the user right is designed to accomplish, you should avoid making any changes to the default assignments on your server. In general, it is OK to make additions to the assigned local rights but not deletions to the default policies. Making the wrong deletion could prevent your server from functioning properly and could cause you to have to reinstall the server.

Even though you can make changes to the user rights, try to avoid this. If you need to grant users rights to perform actions on your server, check to see whether any of the built-in groups can accommodate your needs.

---

7. If you want to add any of the users or local groups you have created on the server to a user right, simply double-click the user right
   to view the properties of it.

8. Click Add to go through the familiar wizard for adding users to a
   group. The only difference is that during the wizard, you will see
   both users and groups.

Rights or Permissions

A common area that can cause confusion is the distinction between rights
and permissions. Even though they are similar, in a Windows Server 2008
R2 environment they are used for different purposes. Understanding the
difference will help you maintain your systems more efficiently. This concept of rights and permissions will follow you through all the work you
do regarding secure access to your Windows Server 2008 R2 servers, even
when you work with the Active Directory domain infrastructures.

Rights   One way you can think of rights, as you have seen from the
previous examples, is that they grant user abilities on the server. These
abilities are special and usually give your user extra access to a server.

Permissions   These grant the user the ability to access Windows
Server 2008 R2 resources, such as printers, files, and shares.
Permissions will determine your level of access to an object such as
a file or whether you can change the object or just read it, and they
will be determined by the permissions assigned to the object. You
will learn more about permissions in Chapter 7.

Work with Local Account Policies

You will need to manage the local account policies on your servers. The
local account policies on your server are designed to protect the integrity of your users and the passwords they use. Whether you are using a
stand-alone sever or an Active Directory domain for logon access, these
local policies have the same impact in both environments. They also help
lock out the accounts if there are too many invalid attempts to access a
given user account. Before you take a look at how to manage the account
policies of your server, you need to understand the importance of passwords and how the account policies are there to protect you.

A Word on Passwords

As you most likely know, there is nothing more important to the security of your environment than the passwords used by you and your users. Keeping these passwords protected is critical to any environment. You also want to always enforce password complexity and length to make sure your users passwords are hard to guess and can't be hacked.

You may have heard this phrase before:

> "Passwords are like bubble gum. They are strongest when fresh, should only be used by individuals and not a group, and if left laying around can create a sticky mess."

This is a fantastic way to think of passwords. What it means in a technical sense for you as an administrator is this: make sure you expire passwords on a regular basis to force users to regularly change passwords. This also goes hand in hand with password history and making sure that you keep track of users' former passwords so they cannot revert to old passwords. If you do not keep track of password history, what your users may do when their passwords expire is change their password to a new password and then change the password right back to their former password. Expiring passwords and keeping track of passwords will help keep your passwords fresh and secure.

If you have shared workstations in your network and have multiple users using a workstation, it is well worth your time to create individual accounts for each of the users. Not only will this protect the security of your environment, but it will also provide you with some flexibility when it comes to administering the users on the workstation.

Lastly, you may have seen or heard about users using sticky notes with the passwords written on them stuck to the monitor of their workstation. As you can imagine, this potentially opens your environment up to having users' passwords stolen. It is worth your time to occasionally patrol the hallways of your business to make sure this is not happening.

While on patrol, you may also notice unlocked desktops, which is another open avenue for you to be attacked. One way you can prevent this is with group policies and setting screensaver policies to lock the desktop after a predetermined amount of idle time. You will learn more about group policies in Chapter 6. Another, more nefarious way is that you can provide your users with a teachable moment when you find an unlocked desktop—send the user an email from themselves. Now, this method is more than likely prohibited by your employer, and I do not recommend this. It's just something to get you thinking about the potential danger of unlocked desktops in your organization. Now, you do not need to send the message to anyone other than the user who left their desktop unlocked. It would look something like this:

> From: Unlocked User
> To: Unlocked User
> Subject: Lock Your Desktop
> Message: Just think this message could have gone to your boss. So please, lock your desktop in the future.
> Sincerely,
> Your friendly neighborhood administrator

A Look at Account Policies

Your local account policies are also located in the local security policy for your server. The account polices are broken into two areas. One is for the password policy, as shown in Figure 4.14, and the other is your account lockout policy, as shown in Figure 4.15.

Figure 4.14: Password policy

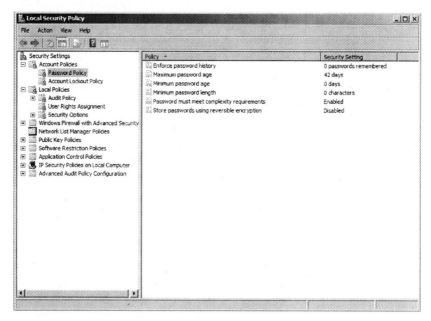

Figure 4.15: Account lockout policy

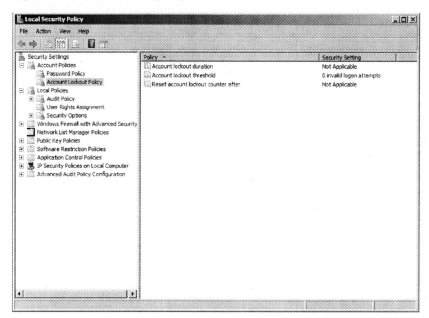

Working with your password policy allows you to control settings regarding password settings. Table 4.3 describes those settings and the default values. To change any of the settings on your server, you can use Group Policy or modify the settings by double-clicking them when you're viewing them in the Local Security Policy MMC.

Table 4.3: Password Policies

Policy	Description	Default Setting
Enforce Password History	This determines the amount of unique new passwords associated with the users on the system and can be set to 0–24. This allows your users to keep their passwords fresh.	0 for stand-alone servers 24 for domain controller

Table 4.3: Password Policies *(continued)*

Policy	Description	Default Setting
Maximum Password Age	Determines how many days a password can remain unchanged on a system and can be 1–999. If the setting is set to 0, then the passwords will never expire.	42 days until passwords expire
Minimum Password Age	Determines how many days a password has to be used before the user can change it and can be set to 0–998. You should change this value on your stand-alone servers. If the value is set to 0, your user can change the password immediately after a change.	0 days for stand-alone server 1 day for domain controllers
Minimum Password Length	Determines the minimum amount of characters a password has to be on the system.	0 for stand-alone servers 7 for domain controller
Password Must Meet Complexity Requirements	This determines whether the password has to meet the complexity requirements. If the minimum password length is set to 0, the complexity requirement of six characters will supersede the minimum password length setting; otherwise, the minimum password length setting will win.	Enabled
Store Passwords Using Reversible Encryption	This determines whether the passwords will be stored in a reversible encryption algorithm. This is akin to storing your passwords in plain text and should never be enabled unless you have an application or system requirement for this to be enabled.	Disabled

Working with account lockout policies allows basic control over failed logon attempts to your server. When an account is locked out, it effectively becomes disabled and cannot be used until the account is unlocked by an administrator or a preset amount of time has passed. All of those settings can be changed with Group Policy, or you can modify the settings by double-clicking them when you're viewing them in the Local Security Policy MMC. Table 4.4 describes the Account Lockout Policy settings and the default values.

Table 4.4: Account Lockout Policy

Policy	Description	Default Setting
Account Lockout Duration	Determines the amount of time the account will remain locked out until unlocking automatically. It can be from 0 to 99,999 minutes. If the policy is set to 0, then the account will remain locked out until an administrator explicitly unlocks the account. The setting has no pertinence until the Account Lockout Threshold policy is set.	None
Account Lockout Threshold	Determines the number of failed logon attempts before the account is locked out and can be set to 0–999 attempts. If it is set to 0, the account will never be locked out. Failed attempts include main logon at the Ctrl+Alt+Del, locked desktop logon, and password-protected screensavers.	0 invalid logon attempts
Reset Account Lockout Counter After	Each failed attempt to log on counts against the threshold counter. However, you can set a period of time when the counter is reset when a set amount of time passes. The setting can be a period of time from 0–99,999 minutes. The setting has no pertinence until the Account Lockout Threshold policy is set. If the threshold policy is set, this setting needs to be less than or equal to the Account Lockout Duration setting.	None

Manage Active Directory and Local Users

PART II

Understand Active Directory Users and Groups

Working with users and groups on Active Directory follows some of the same basic guidelines you have already seen in this chapter. However, Active Directory does add some layers of complexities because of the nature of how applications and other functions of the directory are handled. In this section, you will see some added complexity regarding groups and the amount of properties users have by default in a domain environment.

Learn Active Directory Users and Groups Terminology

When you create users in AD, they are very similar to local users, except for the extended properties and the ability to log on from any workstation in your infrastructure.

However, AD groups have some additional capabilities and complexity. Understanding how the groups work is key to working with permissions, rights, and even applications in your environment. Creating groups in your AD environment requires you to understand the basic terms and concepts. Before you begin working with groups, you want to make sure you understand the differences in the group types and group scopes listed in Table 4.5 and Table 4.6.

Table 4.5: AD Group Scopes

Group Type	Definition and Usage
Domain local	Domain local groups can be assigned permissions only to resources in the domain in which the group was created. Members in this group can be global groups, universal groups, other domain local groups from the same domain, and local user accounts. These groups are primarily used to control access to resources in their local domain.
Global	Global groups are used to control access to resources in the domain in which they are created, and they cannot travel outside the domain in which they exist. It is preferred to use global groups over other groups because they generate less replication traffic when you have groups with frequent changes. Members of this group can be other groups and user accounts located in the same domain in which the global group was created. This group is also the default group selection when creating a new group.

Table 4.5: AD Group Scopes *(continued)*

Group Type	Definition and Usage
Universal	Universal groups are groups that can travel across domain and forest boundaries and are used to assign members of the group access to resources outside of their forest. Members of this group can be any other accounts and groups from other domains or forests with the proper trusts. You want to avoid making frequent changes to the membership to this group, because each change will cause replication on the entire membership to all the global catalog servers in the forest. You can avoid replication traffic by nesting global groups in this group.

Table 4.6: AD Group Types

Group Type	Definition and Usage
Security	Security groups are used to assign permissions or user rights in order to quickly grant the members of the group access to resources or abilities in your network. These groups can also be used for email distribution, much like the distribution group mentioned next.
Distribution	Distribution groups are used only for your email applications, like Exchange Server or Lotus Notes. These groups are not security enabled and cannot be assigned access to resources.

Organize Your Users and Groups

As you begin to create your users, groups, and computer accounts in AD, you are going to want to organize your AD environment into logical containers. In AD, these logical containers are called *organizational units* (OUs). OUs are the way you can easily organize the various users, groups, computer accounts, and so on, in your AD infrastructure. You create OUs to provide a logical structure, and you can design them in a variety of ways. You can create an OU structure following the business functions of your business. For example, you could create OUs for marketing, sales, finance, and so on. This is probably the most common OU design structure. Another popular method is geographic; for example, you create OUs where businesses reside, such as North America, Asia, Europe, and so on. Additionally, you can nest OUs inside of each other to logically represent your business. This logical design helps you organize your AD environment, delegate administration, and provide a key part to working with your Group Policy design. You will learn more in Chapter 6.

Computer Accounts

Before you begin to learn how to work effectively with AD groups and users, you need to understand computer accounts. Computer accounts are the objects that represent the client computers and servers in your domain. If a server or client desktop does not have a computer account, the system will not be able to be managed by the domain, and users will not be able to log on to the domain from the system. Having computer accounts in your domain allows additional auditing capability and network authentication services. You manage, delete, reset, add, and do other administrative tasks for computers similar to users. As you work with users and groups, you will see computer accounts in your Active Directory structure.

Join an Active Directory Domain as a Member

Before your users can log on and work in your AD domain, you need to join them to your domain. Each server or client system in your domain requires a computer account in your domain. To join a domain, all you need to do is configure the system:

1. Click the Start menu.
2. Right-click Computer, and select Properties.
3. Under Computer Name, Domain, And Workgroup Settings, click Change Settings.
4. In System Properties on the General tab, click Change.
5. Select the radio button for Domain, type in your domain name, and click OK.
6. Type in your administrative account ID and password.
7. In the Welcome To Domain box, click OK.
8. Click OK to acknowledge the reboot is required.
9. Click OK to exit System Properties, and click OK to reboot the system.

When the system reboots, you will then be able to log on with your domain credentials.

Work with Active Directory and Local Groups

You may be confused about which groups to use and about the best way to work with groups and manage them. More important, you may be wondering about the best way to quickly grant access to user rights or permissions to the many objects in your infrastructure. You will want to know the interrelationship between your AD groups and the local groups on your servers that have resources.

The preferred process for this can be summed up in a one-word acronym, UGLY:

U is for **users**.

G is for **global groups**.

L is for **local groups** (where the resource resides).

Y is for **your permissions** on the local resources.

You may be thinking that this sums up the confusion, but learning this process will provide you with an efficient and effective way to quickly manage and control access to resources in your domain. When you access a resource in the same domain, this is how UGLY can be applied:

1. Place your users in the global group for the domain on which they both reside.

2. Place the global group in the local group on the system with the resource.

3. Grant the local group your desired permissions, and grant members access to the resource.

If the resource is another domain, you will have one more step, and the acronym changes a little. UGLY becomes UGULY, but the basic premise is still the same:

1. Place your users in the global group for the domain in which they both reside.

2. Place the global group in the universal group in the same domain.

3. Place the universal group in the local group on the system with the resources.

4. Grant the local group your desired permissions, and grant members access to the resource. The reason you nest the global groups into the universal groups is to avoid replication traffic that can occur when universal groups change. This way, you can modify the global groups, and only those groups are changed, which will allow the nested members to gain access to resources.

For example, in a single domain, if you wanted a user in your domain to back up a client desktop or member server in your domain, after you created the user, you would create a global group, called something like Global Backup. You would place the user in Global Backup and place Global Backup into the local group Backup Operators. In this case, you are using the built-in Backup Operators group, which has already been assigned the necessary rights and permissions to perform the backup on the system.

Manage Users and Groups in Active Directory

To manage user and groups, you can use a number of tools built in to Windows Server 2008 R2. Three tools allow you to work with Active Directory users and groups:

- Server Manager

- Active Directory Users And Computers

- Active Directory Administrator Center, a new tool in Windows Server 2008 R2

Using Server Manager or Active Directory Users And Computers will take you to the same set of tools. Server Manager is a new tool introduced in Windows Server 2008 and is a consolidated management tool with several management tools, including Active Directory Users And Computers. The Active Directory Users And Computers tool found in Administrative Tools is a dedicated tool just for managing users and groups.

You can find both tools in the Administrative Tools group on the Start menu, as shown in Figure 4.16.

Figure 4.16: Administrative Tools group

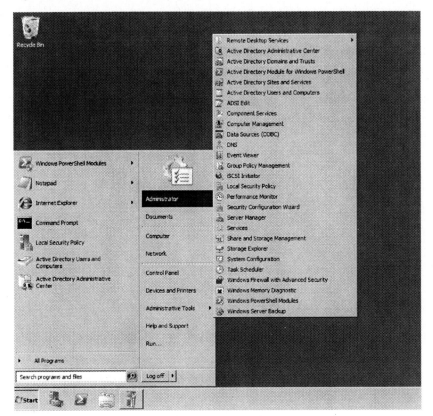

When you want to work with the AD Users and Groups, load either tool, and you will be able to see the AD Users and Groups. If you open AD Users and Computers, you are taken directly to working with your AD objects. However, there is one difference. If you load Server Manager, you will have to navigate to the AD Users and Groups.

1. Load Server Manager.

2. Click the + next to Roles.

3. Click the + next to Active Directory Domain Services.

4. Click the + next to Active Directory Users And Computers.

5. Click the + next to your domain name.

6. Click Users to begin managing your AD users and groups, and your screen should look like Figure 4.17.

Figure 4.17: AD user management

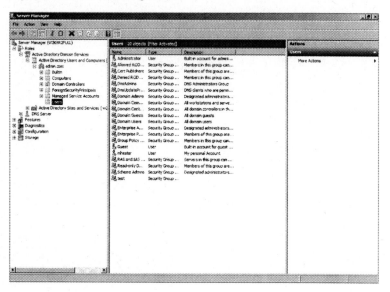

Once you have opened your chosen administrative console, then it is matter of creating the groups and other objects you need.

Create Organizational Units

Once you have loaded the console, you can start creating AD objects. OUs are one of the first objects you may create. To create an OU, follow these steps:

1. Right-click the level of domain where you want to create the OU.

2. Select New.

3. Select Organizational Unit.

4. Type a name for your OU. You will also notice a default check mark for Protect Container From Accidental Deletion. This will prevent administrators from accidentally deleting the object.

Create Users

Creating users is similar to creating local users in a nondomain environment. To create a user, follow these steps:

1. Right-click the container of domain where you want to create the user.

2. Select New.

3. Select User, and you will see a screen similar to Figure 4.18.

Figure 4.18: New AD user

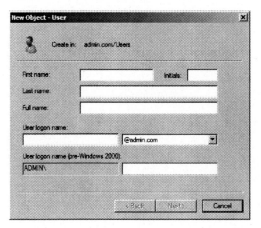

4. Fill the form, assign a logon name to the new user, and click Next.

5. Set the default password information for the user, and click Next.

6. Review the summary, and click Finish to create the user.

Just like users on a local machine, after you create the user, you can right-click and view all the properties for the user. You will notice there are several more properties for the AD users. After you create the user, you can later move the user by simply dragging and dropping the user into the appropriate OU.

Create Groups

To create groups, follow these steps:

1. Right-click the container of the domain where you want to create the group.

2. Select New.

3. Select Group, and you will see a screen similar to Figure 4.19

Figure 4.19: New AD group

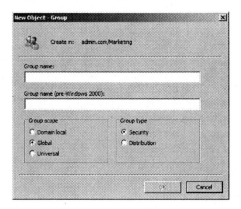

4. Fill out the form, and make the appropriate selections for the group type and scope.

5. Click OK to finish creating the group.

Viewing Advanced Features

When you first view the default containers and properties of objects inside AD, you are not seeing the whole picture. There are several other AD objects and additionally a Security tab becomes visible in the properties for the various AD objects. To see these additional objects and tabs, you just need to view the advanced features. To view the advanced features, when you're managing your AD users and groups, go to the View menu and select Advanced Features. If you do not want to see the advanced features anymore, simply go back to the View menu and deselect the Advanced Features options.

After you create the group, you can add members to the group by right-clicking the group, selecting Properties, and clicking the Members tab. You can then simply click Add, and the Find Users dialog box will function similarly to the one for local users. Also while in the Properties window, you can change the group's existing group type and scope.

Active Directory Administrator Center

One of the new tools in Windows Server 2008 R2 to make your life easier when working with objects inside AD is the Active Directory Administrator Center (ADAC). This tool makes it easy to search and reset passwords and perform other administrative tasks. You can also create users and groups with this tool. To load the tool, select Start ⇨ Administrative Tools ⇨ Active Directory Administrator Center, as shown in Figure 4.20.

Figure 4.20: ADAC

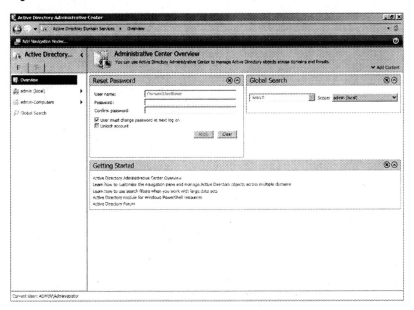

The tool is intuitive; it's tasked based, and it can be quite easy to run. The ADAC consists of customizable panels that represent the most common tasks you can perform. You can add and remove panels and customize the overview page to enable you to quickly get to the tasks you perform most often.

A good use for the ADAC is searching your AD for various objects. Similar to saved queries in the AD Users And Computers, it is a quick way to find objects you're interested in. In the overview pane on the right side, you'll see Global Search. Type in your search parameter, and click the magnify glass icon. Your results would look similar to Figure 4.21.

Figure 4.21: ADAC search

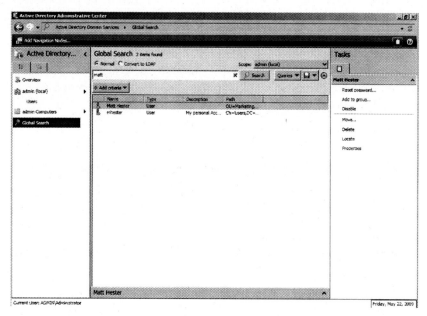

Fundamentally, creating new users and groups follows the same guidance mentioned in the previous sections. However, the ADAC provides a much more detailed interface to allow you to create users and groups easier. To create a user, you navigate to the container or OU as you may have done in the past, right-click the container, and select New User. You will see that the new user is a form that allows you to populate all the needed properties for a user and much more. The interface will highlight required fields with a red asterisk (*). Figure 4.22 shows the new user screen.

Creating groups follows the same form-based interface as the users. Figure 4.23 shows the new group interface.

Figure 4.22: New user in ADAC

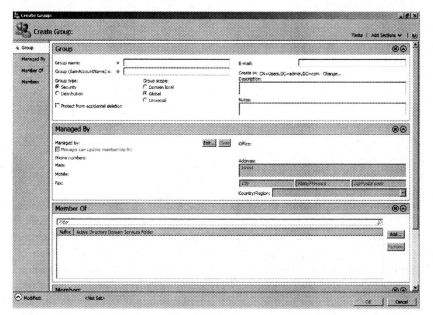

Figure 4.23: New group in ADAC

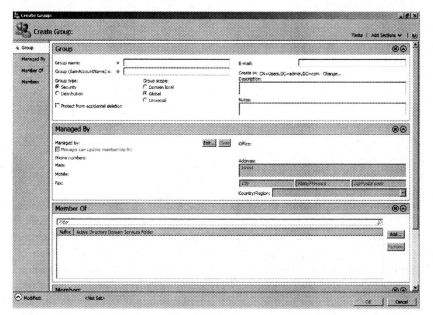

The viewing of properties also takes on the new enhanced interface of the tool. When you view the properties of a user in ADAC, you will see a screen similar to Figure 4.24.

Figure 4.24: ADAC user properties

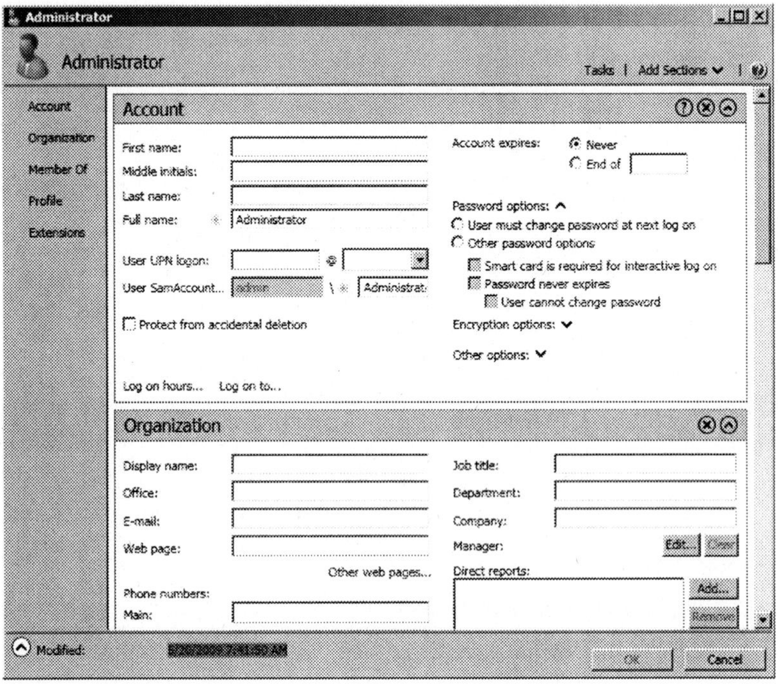

It is up to you if you want to use the standard tools or the new ADAC. They both will take you to the same management place. With Windows Server 2008 R2, you should get to know the ADAC, because it may provide you with a more intuitive interface to working with AD.

Automate User and Group Management

With PowerShell, you have a great tool to help you automate users and groups in your AD environment. In the prior versions to Windows Server 2008, you could use PowerShell to manage objects, but it was cumbersome and not an easy task to accomplish. However, in Windows Server 2008 R2, there are several improvements and additions for easy management with Windows PowerShell. Specifically, there are newly created PowerShell cmdlets and the AD Recycle Bin, which provides easier access to working with AD at a PowerShell level. You will see both of those in this section.

Load AD PowerShell Modules

Before you can begin using the new cmdlets, you need to load the AD PowerShell modules. The AD PowerShell modules are installed by default on a server when Windows PowerShell and the Microsoft .NET Framework 3.5.1 are installed. You can load the AD cmdlets in one of two ways:

1. Select Administrative Tools ⇨ Active Directory Module For Windows PowerShell.

or

1. Load a normal Windows PowerShell session, and run this cmdlet:

```
Import-Module ActiveDirectory
```

2. Verify the module was loaded by running this:

```
Get-Module
```

If you want to see a list of all the commands available from managing AD objects and resources, you can run this command:

```
Get-Command *ad*
```

Work with Users and Groups in PowerShell

You can also use the AD PowerShell cmdlets to manage your users, groups, and OUs just like you can with the tools previously mentioned in this chapter. The reasons for using PowerShell are the same generally with any scripting tool. You may have a preference for using command-line and scripting tools. Potentially, you may also find yourself repeating the same tasks over and over again, and using PowerShell will provide you with a consistent and repeatable approach to these tasks.

When working in the AD PowerShell, you can also use directory-style commands to move around the AD structure. For example, you can run this command to get to the top of your AD structure:

```
cd AD:
```

When you run the command, you will see command prompt change to the following:

```
PS AD:\>
```

The command prompt will continue to change to reflect your current location in the directory hierarchy. From there you can run dir to see the objects at the root. To navigate to the actual domain, you will need to run a command similar to this:

```
cd "dc=yourdomainname,dc=com (or your FQDN ending)"
```

To change to an OU or container, after you have navigated to your domain structure, you can run this command:

```
cd cn=containername
```

If you want to switch to OU, the command is slightly different:

```
cd ou=Organizational Unit
```

Figure 4.25 shows an example of the previous commands and a dir command, which will show all the objects in the container.

Figure 4.25: Browsing the AD structure

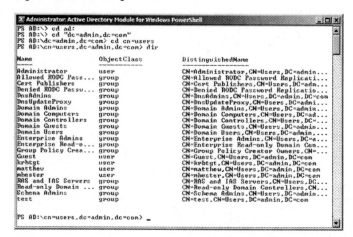

Table 4.7 lists some of the common tasks for working with PowerShell with your users and groups. When you run the commands listed in the table, they run from the directory you are currently located in. If you need more information, do not forgot about the built-in help system. You can use get-help with any of the following commands to learn more.

Table 4.7: Common PowerShell AD Commands

cmdlet	Description	Example
Get-ADobject	Lists multiple AD objects. Like with users and groups, works similar to other **get** cmdlets. This command uses filter, ldapfilter, and searchbase to query the information. You can also combine this with the format and output switches of PowerShell to work with the command's output.	This command will list all the objects in AD: Get-ADObject -Filter {name -like "*"}
Get-ADuser	Lists the AD users in the domain. This command uses filter, ldapfilter, and searchbase to query the information. You can also combine this with format and out switches to work with the command's output.	This command will list all the users at your current level of the AD hierarchy: Get-ADUser -Filter {name -like "*"}
New-ADuser	Creates a new user in your AD environment. You can also control most of the properties for this cmdlet. You will need to set a password and enable the account for use.	This command will create a user called John Smith in the Marketing OU in the admin.com domain, with display name and given name filled out: New-ADuser john-smith -GivenName "Smith" -Surname "John" -Displayname "John Smith" -Path 'OU=Marketing,DC=admin,DC=com'

Table 4.7: Common PowerShell AD Commands *(continued)*

cmdlet	Description	Example
Set-ADaccountpassword	Sets the password for an AD account. Depending on the nature of how you use this command, you may be presented with a series of prompts to set the password. When you run this command, you do not need to specify the OU or domain name if you are located in the OU that contains the user.	This command will reset the password of John Smith with a new password of p@ssw0rd: `Set-adaccountpassword -identity johnsmith -reset -newpassword (ConvertTo-SecureString -AsPlainText "p@ssw0rd" -force)`
Remove-ADuser	Removes a user from AD. When you run this command, you do not need to specify the OU or domain name if you are located in the OU that contains the user.	This command deletes John Smith: `Remove-aduser johnsmith`
New-ADgroup	Creates a new group. You can also modify the group type, scope, and other properties of the group.	This command will create a new global security group called Accounting: `New-adgroup Accounting -groupscope global`
Add-ADGroupMember	Allows you to modify the membership of an AD group.	This command adds John Smith to the Marketing group in the **admin.com** domain. `Add-ADGroupMember -Member John Smith`
New-ADorganizationalunit	Creates a new AD organizational unit.	This command creates a new OU called Finance in the **admin.com** domain: `New-ADOrganizationalUnit -Name "Finance" -Path "DC=admin,DC=com"`

Use the AD Recycle Bin

You may have at one time deleted a user by accident. In previous versions of Windows, when an accidental deletion occurred, you had to implement AD disaster/recovery scenarios to recover the deleted object. This method, as you may know, was complex. Accidental deletions also became the number-one reason you may have implemented your AD disaster recovery scenarios. With Windows Server 2008 R2 you can now use the new functionality called the Recycle Bin as apart of your overall backup and recovery strategy; even though the Recycle Bin provides you with the ability to recover AD objects, you will still need to perform your regular backups in your environment.

One of the new additions to Windows Server 2008 R2 is the AD Recycle Bin. This is an optional tool you can enable on your Windows Server 2008 R2 domain controller. The Recycle Bin provides a tool for you to recover deleted users, groups, OUs, and so on. All attributes of the object are automatically restored, including the description, password, group membership, and managed by properties, as well as many of the other properties of the user objects, including the formerly problematic "linked attributes."

Enabling the Recycle Bin can increase the size of the Active Directory database file by about 5 to 10 percent when you install on a new DC. The amount of growth of the database really depends on the size and frequency of object deletions in your domain.

When you delete the object, the object will have a lifetime of 180 days by default before it is put into the normal tombstone and collection process in AD. You can modify the value manually by modifying the msDS-deletedObjectLifetime attribute. This applies only to newly deleted objects. Any objected deleted before you enable the Recycle Bin will follow normal deletion properties.

WARNING   The Recycle Bin requires Windows Server 2008 R2 forest functional level in Windows Server 2008 R2. This is required in order to ensure that all DCs preserve the attributes necessary to complete a successful object recovery.

When you raise the functional level, by itself it really has no effect other than allowing optional features to be enabled, like the Recycle Bin. This allows you to raise the functional level with confidence and avoid any unnecessary side effects.

Manage Active Directory and Local Users

PART II

Enable the AD Recycle Bin

To work with the Recycle Bin, you need to enable the optional feature in your AD PowerShell:

1. Load AD PowerShell.

2. Type the following command, and hit Enter to enable the Recycle Bin:

   ```
   Enable-ADOptionalFeature "Recycle Bin Feature"
    -Scope ForestorConfigurationSet -Target 'your domain name'
   ```

3. Press Y to enable the feature.

4. Verify the Recycle Bin has been enabled by running the following command and hitting Enter. Your screen will look similar to Figure 4.26:

   ```
   Get-ADOptionalFeature -Filter {Name -Like "*"}
   ```

Figure 4.26: Enabled Recycle Bin

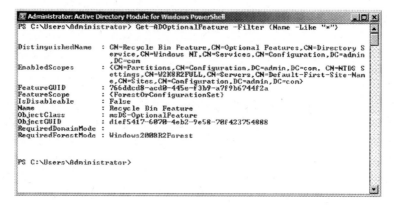

Using the AD Recycle Bin

If you have deleted a user and need to recover the user from the Recycle Bin, you will need to do this in PowerShell:

1. Load AD PowerShell.

2. Type the following command to view the objects in the Recycle Bin:

```
Get-ADObject -SearchBase
 "CN=Deleted Objects,DC=your domain name,DC=Com"
-ldapFilter "(objectClass=*)"
-includeDeletedObjects | format-list
```

You could also use the out-gridview object to see a GUI of the deleted objects. Your results may look like Figure 4.27.

Figure 4.27: Recycle Bin

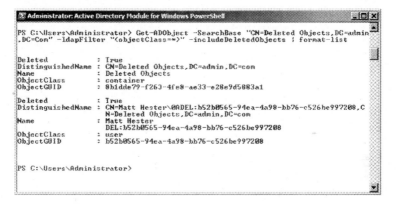

3. Write down or copy the ObjectGUID for the object you want to recover. This is the identity of the object you have deleted:

    ▪ To copy text from a command prompt, right-click and then select Mark. Highlight the text to copy and then press Enter.

    ▪ To paste, right-click and then click Paste.

4. Recover the object with the following command:

```
Restore-ADObject -Identity ObjectGUID from step 3
```

5

Managing and Replicating Active Directory

IN THIS CHAPTER, YOU WILL LEARN TO:

Manage Active Directory and Local Users

PART II

A n Active Directory database brings some tremendous benefits to a network of users and computers. Authentication, organization, permission controls, policy applications, resource management, and sharing are all key benefits. When you implement Active Directory, it is imperative to understand that it will indeed be "active." In other words, it will be exposed to changes on a regular basis. In addition, it is important that you understand the processes by which changes are made and shared with other domain controllers that have a role in maintaining the directory database. It is also essential that you take a proactive approach to managing and maintaining the directory database in order to prevent possible difficulties in database functionality or replication. This chapter will talk about key operations related to managing the directory database and replicating the database.

Manage the Active Directory Database

For all of its fanfare and cool functions, when you take off all the pretty interfaces and controls, Active Directory (AD) is at its core a database named NTDS.DIT. It has a defining schema, a set of partitions, and tables much like any other database. It shares the data contained within the database among a series of authoritative and nonauthoritative servers called *domain controllers* (DCs) and *read-only DCs*, respectively. The directory database relies on the physical hardware on which it resides to maintain consistent performance. If the hardware has significant limitations of speed, capacity, or other performance aspects, those limitations will be inherited by the directory database. In a like manner, if the physical hardware suffers failures, those failures will be perpetuated through the directory database. This section covers how to manage the directory database by managing the hardware on which the database resides.

So, how exactly should you do this? Here's how many successful clients have done it:

1. Install the operating system on a mirrored partition.

2. Install the NTDS.DIT database on a RAID 5 volume.

3. Install the log files associated with AD on a separate mirrored partition.

This straightforward implementation provides performance and fault tolerance to the operating system, directory database, and log files by distributing the processor and disk workload across multiple physical platforms. It does take a fair number of disks to implement, but the resulting benefits in performance and fault tolerance are well worth it.

What about other options for installation? Couldn't you install the OS, directory database, and log files on a single local drive? In short, yes, you could install them all on the same physical drive. Please don't do this, though. It just places too much of a workload on a single point of failure. When that drive fails (and it will), you will lose everything. Bite the bullet up front, and set up your directory for performance and fault tolerance. Once your directory database is happily running on its physical hardware, which you will be constantly monitoring to maintain its health and performance, then it's time to start considering some important topics.

Maintain FSMO Roles

Active Directory is stored in writable form on multiple DCs. Usually having all these writable copies of the directory database is just fine. On rare occasions, it can be problematic having all of these DCs have write access, such as when you are creating new domain objects, when you are changing the schema of the directory, or when you are changing a user's password.

These are the FSMO (pronounced "fizz-mo") roles:

Schema master   The schema master domain controller controls all updates and modifications to the schema. To update the schema of a forest, you must have access to the schema master. This role would be used in conjunction with the adprep or domainprep command. There can be only one schema master in the whole forest.

Domain naming master   The domain naming master domain controller controls the addition or removal of domains in the forest. There can be only one domain naming master in the whole forest.

Infrastructure master   The infrastructure master is responsible for updating references from objects in its domain to objects in other domains. It is also used in conjunction with adprep or domainprep and to update SID attributes and distinguished name attributes for objects that are referenced across domains. At any one time, there can be only one domain controller acting as the infrastructure master in each domain.

Relative ID (RID) master The RID master is responsible for processing RID pool requests from all domain controllers in a particular domain. These RID pools are used to create new user accounts, computer accounts, or groups. At any one time, there can be only one domain controller acting as the RID master in the domain.

PDC emulator The PDC emulator is a domain controller that advertises itself as the primary domain controller (PDC) to workstations, member servers, and domain controllers that are running earlier versions of Windows. It is also the domain master browser, and it handles password discrepancies and updates to user and computer account passwords. At any one time, there can be only one domain controller acting as the PDC emulator master in each domain.

TIP Please see http://support.microsoft.com/kb/324801 and http://support.microsoft.com/kb/255504 for additional details on the FSMO roles.

The real questions begin when you start to consider that the initial DC that is built in each forest (referred to as the *forest root server*) will by default hold all five FSMO roles. Should they stay there when you add DCs? If not, how do you move them? What if, heaven forbid, the server that holds your FSMO roles crashes and burns? What do you do then?

On the day it is installed, the forest root server does in fact hold all five FSMO roles, and while you are setting up your other DCs, that forest root server will likely do just fine holding all five roles. Remember that the roles come in two types: forest-wide roles, one per forest, and domain-wide roles, one per domain. Each forest will have a single schema master and domain naming master regardless of the number of domains you create. These roles are just fine to stay on your forest root server. Each domain will have its own PDC emulator, RID master, and infrastructure master. As you create new domains in your directory database and add new domain controllers to manage those domain directory resources, the first DC created in each domain will take on the domain-based roles for that individual domain. This all proceeds quite nicely in an organized fashion as you build the infrastructure of your directory. Assuming that you are allocating sufficient server resources for each DC, you will not have any problems with FSMO roles.

It is possible to relocate the FSMO roles to another domain controller for reasons of personal preference or in the event of a failure by a current role holder. The circumstances surrounding the transfer of roles will determine the process of the role change. If all the DCs are still online and you are making a role change in a nice controlled environment, that's a *role transfer*. If the server that holds the role is offline for any reason, such as it has failed, you will take the role from it in a process called *seizing* the role.

Although the absence of an FSMO role holder can have serious consequences, it is much more likely that the failure of a FSMO role holder can be tolerated in most situations for at least a limited amount of time, allowing you to "fix" whatever caused the DC to fail.

Transfer FSMO Roles

Ideally, you will be doing a nice planned transfer of roles from one operating DC to another. In this case, you have a couple of options:

- Use the graphical user interface tools to view role ownership and initiate transfers. The graphical tools can be used only if the server that is the original role holder is still online. If the original role holder is not currently online, then the transfer of roles (seizure) can be performed using the command-line utilities only.

- Use the command-line utility called NTDSUTIL to script the transfer or seizure of roles.

The GUI tools for viewing and transferring FSMO roles include Active Directory Users And Computers for working with the RID master, PDC emulator, and infrastructure master.

1. Open the Active Directory Users And Computers tool.

2. Right-click Active Directory Users And Computers.

3. Choose All Tasks.

4. Choose Operations Masters.

You can click Change here to change the role to another server, as illustrated in Figure 5.1.

Manage Active Directory and Local Users

PART II

Figure 5.1: The Active Directory Users And Computers tool shows the three domain-based FSMO roles.

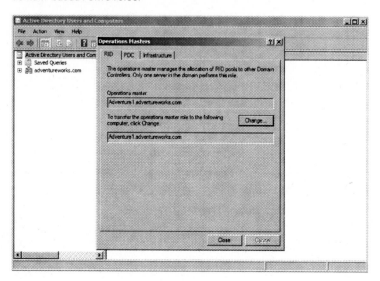

You must be connected to the server that you want to change to. The GUI tool for viewing the forest-wide tools is Active Directory Domains And Trusts for changing the domain naming master.

1. Open the Active Directory Domains And Trusts tool.

2. Right-click Active Directory Domains And Trusts.

3. Choose Operations Master.

Figure 5.2 illustrates how you can view the role holder and change it to another computer.

The GUI tool for viewing the schema master role is a little trickier. By default there is no built-in or enabled GUI tool that you can use to work with the schema master role. You need to both enable and add the Active Directory Schema snap-in to the Microsoft Management Console (MMC) in order to have GUI access to the schema master role. This tool is not enabled by default. To enable the Active Directory Schema snap-in, follow these steps:

1. Select Start ➪ Run.

2. Type **regsvr32 schmmgmt.dll,** and hit Enter.

3. A message will appear confirming that DLLRegisterServer in schmmgmt.dll succeeded. Click OK.

Figure 5.2: The Active Directory Domains And Trust tool shows the domain naming master FSMO role holder.

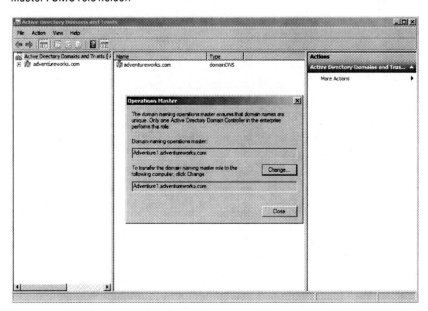

You are not done yet. Now that you have enabled the tool, you will need to add it to the MMC in order to actually use it.

To add the Active Directory Schema snap-in to the Microsoft Management Console, follow these steps:

1. Select Start ⇨ Run.

2. Type **MMC**.

3. Select File ⇨ Add/Remove Snap-In.

4. Select Active Directory Schema.

5. Click Add.

6. Right-click Active Directory Schema, and select Choose Operations Master.

Figure 5.3 shows how to view the schema master and change the server that hosts this role.

Figure 5.3: The Active Directory Schema snap-in shows the schema master FSMO role holder.

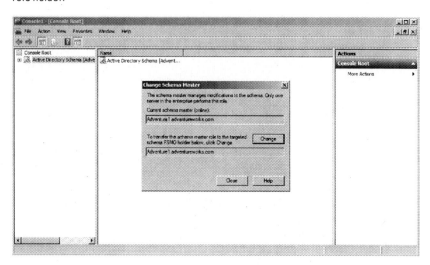

It is not always possible to use the GUI tools to work with FSMO role changes. What if the server you want to transfer a role from is offline? Connecting to an offline server is not possible. You will have to take more drastic action. As is often the case when working with Windows Server 2008 R2, you can get significantly more options by using the command-line tool NTDSUTIL. This utility will allow you to transfer FSMO roles and can also be used to seize these roles without the express permission of the original role holder.

NOTE Once you have seized a role from the original role holder, you will need to make certain that the original role holder is not brought back online in that network.

Seize FSMO Roles with NTDSUTIL

To seize roles using NTDSUTIL, you can follow these steps:

1. Select Start ➪ Run.

2. Type **ntdsutil** in the Open text box, and then click OK.

3. Type **roles**, and then press Enter.

4. Type **connections**, and then press Enter.

5. Type **connect to server** *servername*, where *servername* is the name of the domain controller that you want to assign the FSMO role to, and then press Enter.

6. At the server connections prompt, type **q**, and then press Enter.

7. Type **seize** *role*, where *role* is the role that you want to seize. For a list of roles that you can seize, type **?** at the fsmo maintenance prompt, and then press Enter. For example, to seize the RID master role, type **seize rid master**. The one exception is for the PDC emulator role, whose syntax is seize pdc, not seize pdc emulator.

8. At the fsmo maintenance prompt, type **q**, and then press Enter to gain access to the ntdsutil prompt.

9. Type **q**, and then press Enter to quit the NTDSUTIL utility.

TIP   For more information on NTDSUTIL and FSMO roles, please review the article at http://support.microsoft.com/kb/255504.

Defragment the Directory Database

A directory database gets fragmented as you add, change, and delete objects to your database. Like any file system–based storage, as the directory database is changed and updated, fragments of disk space will build up so it needs to be defragmented on a routine basis to maintain optimal operation. By default, Active Directory performs an online defragmentation of the directory database every 12 hours with the garbage collection process, an automated directory database cleanup, and IT pros should be familiar with it. However, online defragmentation does not decrease the size of the NTDS.DIT database file. Instead, it shuffles the data around for easier access. Depending on how much fragmentation you actually have in the database, running an offline defragmentation—which does decrease the size of the database—could have a significant effect on the overall size of your NTDS.DIT database file.

Manage Active Directory and Local Users

PART II

There is a little problem associated with defragmenting databases. They have to be taken offline in order to have the fragments removed and the database resized. In Windows Server 2008 R2, there is a great feature that allows you to take the database offline without shutting down the server. It's called Restartable Active Directory, and it could not be much easier to stop and start your directory database than this. Figure 5.4 shows the Services tool and how you can use it to stop the Active Directory service.

1. Start the Services tool from the Control Panel.

2. Right-click Active Directory Domain Services, and select Stop.

Figure 5.4: You can use the Services tool to stop and restart Active Directory.

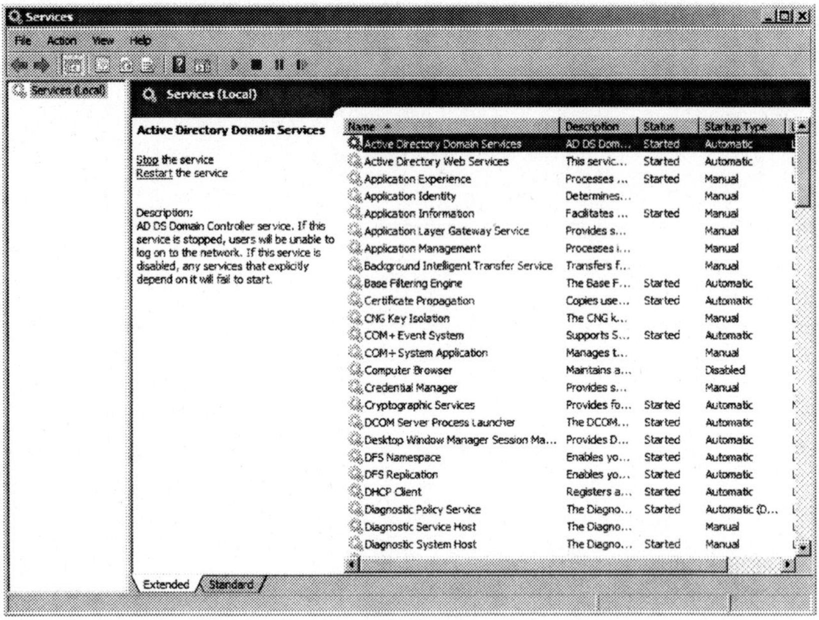

That's it! Now when you stop Active Directory Domain Services, any other dependent services will also be stopped. Keep in mind that while the services are stopped, they cannot fulfill their assigned role in your network. The really cool thing about Restartable AD is that while the directory services and its dependent services are stopped, other services on the local machine are not. So, perhaps you have a shared printer running on your DC. Print services still run, and print operations do not stop. Nice!

Offline Directory Defragmentation

Now that you have stopped Active Directory services, it is time to get down to the business of offline defragmentation of the directory database:

1. Back up the database. This will be covered in more detail in Chapter 8.

2. Open a command prompt, and type **NTDSUTIL**.

3. Type **ACTIVATE INSTANCE NTDS**.

4. Type **FILES**, and press Enter.

5. Type **INFO**, and press Enter. This will tell you the current location of the directory database, its size, and the size of the associated log files. Write all this down.

6. Make a folder location that has enough drive space for the directory to be stored.

7. Type **COMPACT TO DRIVE:\DIRECTORY**, and press Enter. The drive and directory are the locations you set up in step 5. If the drive path contains spaces, put the whole path in quotation marks, as in `"C:\ database defrag"`.

   A new defragmented and compacted NTDS.DIT is created in the folder you specified.

8. Type **QUIT**, and press Enter.

9. Type **QUIT** again, and press Enter to return to the command prompt.

10. If defragmentation succeeds without errors, follow the NTDSUTIL prompts.

11. Delete all log files by typing **DEL x:\pathtologfiles*.log** where x is the drive letter of your drive.

12. Overwrite the old NTDS.DIT file with the new one. Remember, you wrote down its location in step 4.

13. Close the command prompt.

14. Open the Services tool, and start Active Directory Domain Services.

Defragmenting your directory database using the offline NTDSUTIL process can significantly reduce the size of your database depending

Manage Active Directory and Local Users

PART II

on how long it has been since your last offline defrag. The hard thing about offline defrag is that every network is different, so making recommendations about how often to use the offline defrag process is somewhat spurious. I recommend you get to know your directory database. Monitor its size and growth. When you think it is appropriate to defragment offline, then do it. A pattern will emerge for you, and you will find yourself using offline defragmentation on a frequency that works well for your network and your directory database. One of the cool things about offline defragmentation is that if you should happen to have an error occur during the defragmentation process, you still have your original NTDS.DIT database in place and can continue using it with no problems until you can isolate and fix any issues.

Audit Active Directory Service

Windows Server 2008 R2 not only allows you to audit changes to Active Directory but also allows you to see the actual values entered into the directory before the change was made and after the change is made. It was possible in Windows 2000 Server and Windows Server 2003 to audit directory service access to see whether a change had been made, but this auditing allowed you to see the results of the change only, not the "before and after" settings.

In Windows Server 2008 R2, the Audit Directory Service Access setting policy is divided into four subcategories:

- Directory Service Access

- Directory Service Changes

- Directory Service Replication

- Detailed Directory Service Replication

When you want to see changes, you will implement the Directory Service Changes Policy. This policy will allow you to see the changes made by any security principal including create, delete, modify, move, or undelete operations. This policy will record not only the new values but also the original values in the event of a modify or undelete operation. In the event of a move operation, the original location of the object will also be logged.

You can enable auditing in Windows Server 2008 R2 through the use of three mechanisms. First, you can choose to enable a global audit policy for all the directory service subcategories mentioned previously.

This setting is in the default domain controller policy on the Domain Controllers OU and is *not* enabled by default on Windows Server 2008 R2 DC. Therefore, if you want to audit directory service changes, you will need to implement this setting. One item of note is that the ID number for directory service changes has been updated to 4,662 instead of Windows 2000 Server and Windows Server 2003's 566 ID designation.

Second, you can also enable auditing through the use of system access control lists (SACLs). The SACL of an object determines whether access to an object will or will not be audited. It determines which operations are to be audited and for whom. SACLs are controlled by those security administrators who have rights to the local system. The Administrators group would hold this right by default. So, it is technically possible to edit the access control entry (ACE) of an object and remove the auditing requirement of the object even though Directory Services Changes has been enabled.

Finally, there is also a set of schema controls that you can use to create exceptions using search flag properties for what is being audited. For more on schema auditing exceptions, see http://technet.microsoft.com/en-us/library/cc731607.

Enable Group Policy Auditing in Group Policy Management Console

To enable directory services auditing, you need to use Group Policy. Use the Group Policy Management Console to make the suggested changes.

1. Select Start ⇨ Administrative Tools ⇨ Group Policy Management.

2. In the console tree, double-click the name of the forest, expand Domains, expand the name of your domain, select Domain Controllers, right-click Default Domain Controllers Policy, and then click Edit.

3. Under Computer Configuration, expand Policies, expand Windows Settings, expand Security Settings, expand Local Policies, and then click Audit Policy (see Figure 5-5).

4. In the details pane, right-click Audit Directory Service Access, and then click Properties.

5. Select the Define These Policy Settings check box.

6. Under Audit These Attempts, select the Success check box, and then click OK.

Figure 5.5: Auditing enabled in Group Policy Management Console

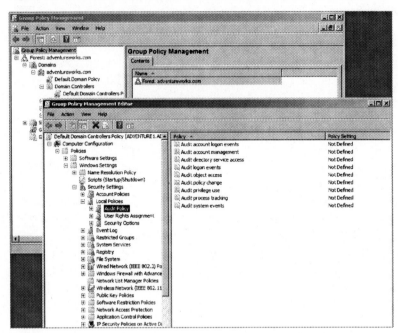

Enable Auditing Using the Command Line

Although you will most likely enable auditing using the Group Policy Management Console, sometimes you may prefer to use the command line. Here are the steps:

1. Click Start, type **cmd** in the search box to locate the command prompt, and then right-click and choose Run As Administrator.

2. Type the following command, and then press Enter:

```
auditpol /set /subcategory:"directory service changes"
/success:enable
```

Configure Auditing in the Object SACLs

SACLs hold the real power in auditing. They define the permissions and functions for auditing on any given object or file location. It is possible to configure auditing of Active Directory on the SACL:

1. Select Start ➪ Administrative Tools ➪ Active Directory Users And Computers.

2. Right-click the organizational unit, or any object, for which you want to enable auditing, and then click Properties.

3. Click the Security tab, click Advanced, and then click the Auditing tab. (If you do not see the Security tab, you may need to enable Advanced Features from the View menu.)

4. Click Add, and under Enter The Object Name To Select, type **Authenticated Users** (or any other security principal). Then click OK.

5. In Apply Onto, click Descendant User Objects (or any other objects).

6. Under Access, select the Successful check box for Write All properties.

7. Click OK.

Directory Service Changes auditing can add a powerful tool to your toolbox of management features in Window Server 2008 R2.

Use Fine-Grained Password Policy

Password policies provide you with a way to set strict enforcement of the length, age, and complexity of the passwords used in your network. In the Windows 2000 Server and Windows Server 2003 versions of Active Directory, there was a single password policy that could be set, and it was created by default as part of the Default Domain Policy. If you had an environment where you wanted to implement another password policy, for whatever reason, you were stuck creating a new domain to get a new Default Domain Policy object wherein you could create your new password policy. It seems a little silly to create a new domain simply to get an additional password policy object, but that is how it was done. Windows Server 2008 R2 will let you create more than one password settings object (PSO) per Active Directory domain. This means it is now possible to create multiple password policies and their corresponding lockout restrictions in a single-domain environment. This ability to create multiple password policies that have differing levels of impact on different users and groups has been termed *fine-grained password policies.*

To use these policies, Windows Server 2008 R2 relies on two object classes in the Active Directory schema called Password Settings Container and Password Settings. The Password Settings Container object class is created by default in the System container in the domain. It is responsible for storing the PSOs for the domain.

When you build a fine-grained password policy for your domain, there are some things to consider. First, although your domain is probably organized into organizational units, PSOs will need to be applied to security groups. This will mean that moving a user from one OU to another will require updating group memberships to meet password policy requirements. Why not just apply the PSO to the OU? There are several reasons:

- Groups are a lot more flexible for managing users than OUs are.

- You have already used a systematic set of groups in your Active Directory deployment in Domain Admins, Enterprise Admins, Schema Admins, Backup Operators, Account Operators and so on. It works!

- Using groups makes deploying fine-grained password policy so much easier because you don't have to restructure OUs to match your password policy structure, which can really be a pain, not to mention have negative side effects on the Group Policy inheritance you have worked so hard to get right.

Before you create your first PSO, there are some important rules to know:

- By default, only members of the Domain Admins group can create PSOs. They are the only ones who have write permissions to the PSO once it is created and therefore are the only ones who can tie the PSO to an object.

- PSOs apply only to user objects and global security groups. They *cannot* be applied to computer objects.

- You can delegate Read permissions to the default security descriptor of the PSO to any other group in the domain or forest. (For example, you might want to delegate Read permissions to your help-desk group.)

Create PSOs

So, you are ready to go to work building your own PSO. There are actually two tools that can be used to build a PSO. You can build PSOs with the Active Directory Service Interfaces Editor (ADSI Edit) or LDAP Data Interchange Format Directory Exchange (LDIFDE.)

Realistically, ADSI Edit is sufficient for the majority of cases in which you will create PSOs. For the purposes of this example, you'll use ADSI Edit:

1. Select Start ⇨ Run, type **adsiedit.msc**, and then click OK.

2. If this is the first time you have run ADSI Edit on this machine, then in the ADSI Edit snap-in, right-click ADSI Edit, and then click Connect To.

3. In Name, type the fully qualified domain name (FQDN) of the domain in which you want to create the PSO, and then click OK.

4. Double-click the domain.

5. Double-click DC=<domain_name>.

6. Double-click CN=System.

7. Click CN=Password Settings Container, as shown in Figure 5.6.

8. Right-click CN=Password Settings Container, click New, and then click Object.

9. In the Create Object dialog box, under Select A Class, click msDS-PasswordSettings, and then click Next.

10. In Value, type the name of the new PSO, and then click Next.

Figure 5.6: Using ADSI Edit to create a password settings object

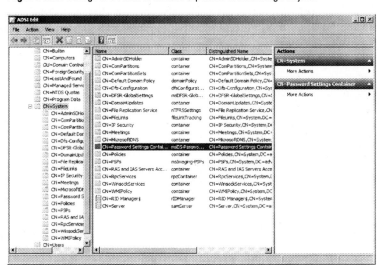

Manage Active Directory and Local Users

PART II

11. Continue with the wizard, and enter appropriate values for all must-have attributes, as shown in Table 5.1.

12. On the last screen of the wizard, click More Attributes.

13. In the Select Which Property To View menu, click Optional or Both.

14. In the Select A Property To View drop-down list, select msDS-PSOAppliesTo.

15. In Edit Attribute, add the distinguished names of users or global security groups that the PSO is to be applied to, and then click Add.

16. Repeat step 15 to apply the PSO to more users or global security groups.

17. Click Finish.

Table 5.1: PSO Attribute Values and Settings

Attribute	Description	Values	Sample Value
msDS PasswordSettingsPrecedence	Password Settings Precedence	Values greater than 0	7
msDS PasswordReversible EncryptionEnabled	Reversible Encryption settings for User accounts	True/false	False (recommended)
msDS PasswordHistoryLength	Password History Length	0 through 1024	30
msDS PasswordComplexityEnabled	Password Complexity Requirement	True/false	True (recommended)
msDS MinimumPasswordLength	Minimum Password Length	0 through 255	8

Table 5.1: PSO Attribute Values and Settings *(continued)*

Attribute	Description	Values	Sample Value
msDS MimimumPasswordAge	Minimum Password Age	None or 00:00:00:00 through the msDS MaximumPasswordAge value	02:00:00:00 (2 days)
Ms DS MaximumPasswordAge	Maximum Password Age	msDS MinimumPasswordAge through (Never)	30:00:00:00 (30 days)
msDS LockoutThreshold	Lockout Threshold	0 through 65535	15
msDS LockputObservationWindow	Lockout Observation Window	(none) or 00:00:00:01 through the msDS LockoutDuration value	00:00:15:00 (15 minutes)
msDS LockoutDuration	Lockout duration	None , Never, or any value between the msDS LockoutObservation Windows through (Never)	00:00:30:00 (30 minutes)
msDS PSOAppliesto	Links PSO to objects	Distingushed names of users or global security groups	"CN=user1, CN=users, DC=Server1, DC=xyz, DC=com"

Please note that as you create the values in the PSO, they must exactly match the syntax and formatting shown in Table 5.1, or you will not be successful in creating the object.

Once you have created your PSO and associated it to your user or group accounts, you are ready to go. Now what happens if you decide that there is another group that you want this PSO to apply to? Do you have to go back to ADSI Edit and reassociate the PSO to the group? You could do that, but an easier way is to simply use Active Directory Users And Computers to associate the PSO to the group.

Manage Active Directory and Local Users

PART II

Associate a PSO to an Additional User or Group

To associate a PSO to an additional user or group, follow these steps:

1. Select Start ⇨ Administrative Tools ⇨ Active Directory Users And Computers.

2. On the View menu, ensure that Advanced Features is selected.

3. In the console tree, navigate to Active Directory Users And Computers*domain node*\System\Password Settings Container.

4. In the details pane, right-click the PSO, and then click Properties.

5. Click the Attribute Editor tab.

6. Select the msDS-PsoAppliesTo attribute, and then click Edit.

7. In the Multi-valued String Editor dialog box, enter the distinguished name of the user or the global security group that you want to apply this PSO to, click Add, and then click OK.

   To get the distinguished name of a global Security group, you can right-click the group and choose Properties. On the Attribute Editor tab, view the value of the Distinguished Name attribute.

PSOs can be managed in much the same way they were created using ADSI Edit. Let's say you wanted to delete a PSO for whatever reason. To do so, you simply go back to ADSI Edit, locate the PSO, right-click, and choose Delete. If you wanted to make changes to the settings of a PSO, you would use Active Directory Users And Computers to navigate to the Password Settings objects container. Right-click the object, and edit its attributes.

PSOs make it possible for you to have a flexible password policy, which in turn will help you enrich the security of your directory database.

Understand Active Directory Replication

Active Directory is a database. The really cool thing about Active Directory is that it has multiple points of authoritative input. Objects can be added, deleted, changed, and so on, from any domain controller (with the obvious exception of the read-only DC, which we will discuss later). This distributed database capability adds tremendous flexibility to Active Directory. It makes administration and management much easier and much more efficient. So, you might be wondering how a distributed database with write permissions at each DC can share those changes across a network to get true synchronization. The process is called *directory replication*.

Understand the Components of Replication

Remember that a directory database is really just a file called NTDS.DIT. It would seem like you could just pass around the most current copy of the NTDS.DIT file and make sure each DC had the most current copy and this whole process would be academic. That would be just fine if your directory database remained at its default size of around 15MB. The problem is that as you add more and more objects to your directory, it grows and grows and grows. Passing 15MB between DCs is not such a big deal. If the file is 10, 20, or 50 times that size, then you have some real bandwidth issues to deal with. You cannot feasibly pass full-size copies of the directory database around between DCs. You have to break the database down into smaller component parts and pass those parts around as updates to each domain controller.

Each directory database is broken down into three separate subsections called *partitions*, or naming contexts. The partitions are the schema partition, configuration partition, and domain partition.

The *schema partition* is replicated to all DCs in the directory forest. It contains the information about the directory schema, which provides definitions to all the objects in the directory.

The *configuration partition* is replicated to all DCs in the directory forest. It contains information about the physical structure of the actual directory.

The *domain partition* is replicated only to DCs within a single domain. Each domain in a directory forest will have its own unique domain partition information. This is where you would find the actual users, groups, computers, and other objects associated with the domain.

Each of these partitions is replicated independently of the others. This allows partitions that have lots of changes, such as the domain partition, to have a limited effect on partitions that don't change very often, like the schema partition.

Manage Active Directory and Local Users

PART II

Types of Updates

Each domain controller has the ability to write changes to the directory database. This means that when you think about replication, there are really two types of updates that can be made to a directory database. The update could be what is termed an *originating update*, meaning an object was created on this DC in the local copy of the database. It does not exist elsewhere on other DCs in the forest. Once the originating update has occurred, it needs to be sent to the other DCs in the domain. When the other DCs receive the update, they are not creating the original object. Instead, they are making what is termed a *replicated update*. They are replicating data from another DC.

Metadata

The question of how a DC knows whether it is making an originating update or a replicated update is significant. Each DC uses metadata to manage the replication of objects. This means that in addition to the objects themselves, the directory service also sends key bits of information about the DC where the object originated, when the change was made, and what update was made (where in the sequence of updates this one fits). All this metadata is used by the receiving DC to determine whether this update should be written and whether it should be sent to other partner DCs called *replication partners*.

Metadata items include the following:

- *Update sequence numbers (USN)*: These sequence numbers are specific to the DC. When a change is made to an object, the DC increments the USN by 1. Each DC maintains its own USN independent of the other DCs in the directory. The USN of a DC is shared with its replication partners.

- *High watermark vector (HWMV)*: This piece of metadata is used to help the DC limit the changes that are being sent across the wire at each replication.

- *Globally unique identifier (GUID)*: This piece of metadata identifies the remote DC and prevents possible confusion if the DC were to be renamed.

- *Up-to-dateness vector (UTDV)*: This piece of metadata is used to prevent the same replication changes from being sent out over and over again. This data is kept by each DC for each of the other DCs associated with each of the three directory partitions.

Through the use of these metadata controls, it is possible to get consistent and rapid replication updates throughout a directory forest without having to send the entire copy of the directory database at each replication attempt.

TIP For more information on metadata used in replication, see http://technet.microsoft.com/en-us/magazine/ 2007.10.replication.aspx.

Understand the Physical Constructs of Replication

As you learned earlier in this book, Active Directory has two types of constructs. There are *logical* constructs, such as forests, trees, domains, and organizational units, and there are *physical* constructs, such as sites and domain controllers. When replication is discussed, it is the physical constructs of Active Directory that we are concerned with. Replication is all about passing information about changes to objects in the directory database to each domain controller within and between the physical sites in the network topology.

By definition, a site is composed of one or more IP subnets connected by high-speed links. We like to define a high-speed link as one that has at least 512KB of "available bandwidth." This means that the bandwidth can be entirely dedicated to the directory service traffic of the site. If the IP subnets in your network are not connected by high-speed links, then generally you would create additional sites. One of the reasons you build sites is to provide a framework on which replication can be built. We hope you are smiling right now with the realization that replication comes in two flavors: replication within the same site, which is referred to as *intrasite* replication, and replication that occurs between sites, which is referred to as *intersite* replication.

Active Directory uses a set of standards in replication to make it as effective and efficient as possible. These standards are referred to as the *replication model* for Active Directory. In short, these standards mean that all replication in Active Directory will follow a multimaster replication model. Every domain controller can receive updates to data for which it is authoritative, and all replication is "pull-based," meaning DCs request changes rather than push or send them. This way, only desired changes arrive at the DC. Each domain controller communicates with a subset of all the DCs in the forest and "stores and forwards" changes, instead of having a single DC responsible for sending all updates. Finally, each DC tracks the state of replication updates through partner DCs using metadata to ensure synchronization while minimizing network bandwidth usage.

Latency in directory replication is always a concern. *Latency* refers to some delay in time between an originating update and its replication throughout the directory to the appropriate DCs. When all changes have been updated throughout the directory, the directory is said to have achieved *convergence*. The goal of replication is to build a topology where latency is minimized and you achieve convergence.

Now that we have laid the groundwork, it is time to see how all of these components work together to build effective replication (and all of this is done without any help from us humans, thankfully!).

Knowledge Consistency Checker

The replication topology of your directory is generated by a built-in component of the directory service called the Knowledge Consistency Checker (KCC). The KCC runs locally on each domain controller; it reads configuration data and writes connection objects for DCs in the site. The KCC also writes local nonreplicated values that define the replication partners from which to request replication updates. This little application is the engine that defines and consequently drives the topology of directory replication. There is one designated KCC in each site that is responsible for writing the connections to other DCs in other sites. This KCC is given the title of Intersite Topology Generator (ISTG). Through defined connections within and between sites, metadata and actual updates are then passed to the DCs that make up a directory service replication topology.

The KCC uses a host of information about topology to build replication partnerships. In the case of the ISTG, much of that information is user-defined as you configure the information about the site objects and how those sites are to be connected and when (and using what method) replication should occur between sites.

Viewing Replication Data

When working with Active Directory replication, it is sometimes desirable to see the replication topology of your network. You can use the built-in command-line tool called REPADMIN.exe to view and manage replication data in your directory.

Start REPADMIN by opening a command prompt (run as administrator) and typing **REPADMIN.exe**.

You will be presented with the supported commands that can be executed with REPADMIN. This tool is exceptional at reporting replication data. You might be thinking, "Wasn't there another Microsoft Tool called REPLMON that was included with Windows Server 2003?" There was, but it was graphical-based, not command-line-based. It is not included with Windows Server 2008 R2, but if you were to go to the support tools folder on a Windows Server 2003 DVD, you could install the REPLMON tool on a Windows Server 2008 R2 machine, and it would work. Please keep in mind that it is *not* supported as a replication monitoring tool in Windows Server 2008 R2. Use REPADMIN to be on the safe side.

TIP   For detailed information about the operation of REPADMIN, visit http://technet.microsoft.com/en-us/library/ cc770963(ws.10).aspx.

Manage Active Directory and Local Users

PART II

6

Maintaining and Controlling the Centralized Desktop

Manage Active Directory and Local Users

PART II

A s you begin to manage the systems for your network, servers, or workstations, you will want to strive for consistency. In Windows Server 2008 R2 Active Directory, as in previous versions of Windows Server, you have a tremendously powerful tool at your disposal called Group Policy.

Group Policy provides a great asset for controlling and maintaining your users' desktops. Group Policy can help configure either the computers or the users in your Active Directory. By targeting a computer with Group Policy, you can maintain the desktop but also ensure any user who uses the desktop has a default configuration that you mandate for your systems. In addition, when you target users with Group Policy, the policy will travel with the users. In other words, regardless of which system in your AD environment the user logs on to, the policies applied to the account will apply.

Group Policy allows you to define your corporate desktop, and there are thousands of settings you can configure. For example, you can set what applications are installed, what the background is for the desktop, whether the user can use Control Panel applets, what the logon scripts are, and more. Group Policy also provides mechanisms to configure many security settings. This provides you with a tool for not only maintaining and configuring your infrastructure but for also protecting it.

Learning how to use Group Policy is a key benefit you can provide to your infrastructure. Being effective with Group Policy can save you time and energy when working with the desktops and users in your environment by providing you with a method to maintain and control your environment. In this chapter, you'll learn some of the ins and outs of Group Policy and how to get started using it.

Understand Group Policy

Using Group Policy, you can easily deliver one-to-many management of users and computers. Group Policy allows you to enforce your IT policies, implement any necessary security settings, and implement a standard computing environment. Having a standard environment provides a consistent base and helps to alleviate support-desk calls. Group Policy will also help simplify your day-to-day administrative tasks and leverage your existing Active Directory environment.

Before you begin working with Group Policy, you need to be aware of some basic terms. Refer to Table 6.1 to get up to speed with some of the terminology behind this powerful tool. Then you'll learn about the scope of policy management as well how client systems process group policies.

Table 6.1: Group Policy Terminology

Term	Description
Group Policy Management Console (GPMC)	This is the main tool where you create your Group Policy objects. GPMC creates the links defining what objects the GPO will target and the three main scopes managed in GPMC: sites, domains, and OUs.
Group Policy object (GPO)	GPOs are the objects that contain all the settings you want to apply to your users or computers. GPOs are also what you link to your organizational units (OUs), sites, or domains.
Group Policy Object link	The GPO link is what links the GPO to the portion of your Active Directory environment where you want the GPO to be applied. This is referred to as the *scope*, and there are three main levels you apply GPOs to: site, domain, and OU.
Group Policy Management Editor	This is the tool you use to modify the settings in the GPOs. The available settings are based on the administrative templates currently loaded.
Administrative template files (ADMX files)	These files have two purposes. One is to define the settings and configuration location (on the local system) for those settings. The second is to create the interface you use to modify the setting in the Group Policy Management Editor.
Group Policy preferences	Preferences provide an alternative to working with company-wide images to manage settings previously not easily configured in Group Policy. The settings initially set by the administrator reflect a default state of the operating system, and these settings are not necessarily enforced.
Resultant Set of Policy (RSOP)	RSOP is the set of policy settings applied after all the Group Policy processing is complete. This could be a combination of many levels of group policies.

Know the Difference Between Policy and Preferences

As you begin to work with Group Policy settings, you will notice that there are two ways to configure systems: policies and preferences. Both policies and preferences can modify user and computer objects;

however, the reasons to use them are very different. The main difference is enforcement; policies are enforced, while preferences are not strictly enforced. In this section, you will see the difference between the two.

Policies

When you are working with policies, the settings and interface are based on administrative templates. Policies make changes to the registry as directed by the administrative template. There are special sections in the registry hives that are controlled by Group Policy. The Group Policy settings stored in these locations are known as *true policies*.

Specifically, Group Policy works with these two locations for computer settings:

- HKEY_LOCAL_MACHINE\SOFTWARE\policies (preferred location)
- HKEY_LOCAL_MACHINE\SOFTWARE\Microsoft\Windows\ CurrentVersion\policies

For the user settings, Group Policy works with the following two locations:

- HKEY_CURRENT_USER\SOFTWARE\policies (preferred location)
- HKEY_ CURRENT_USER\SOFTWARE\Microsoft\Windows\ CurrentVersion\policies

Every time a system processes a policy and gets the RSOP, these registry hives (all the keys and values) are erased and rewritten with the new RSOP. This occurs only as long as a valid group policy is still being applied to the computer or user.

Lastly, you can also make your own policy settings by modifying one of the administrator templates or creating your own. This allows you to work with the entire registry (except for the keys mentioned earlier). However, it is important to note these settings will "tattoo" the registry. In other words, the settings are permanently set until you specifically reverse them in Group Policy. This means if you just delete your GPO, these types of settings do not go away; you must reverse them by hand.

Preferences

Introduced in Windows Server 2008, preferences provide an alternative to using scripts to perform common tasks. These tasks were traditionally not done easily if at all in Group Policy. Preferences allow you to modify local registry settings, local users and groups, files and folders, printers, local services, mapped drives, and many other local settings. Since preferences are not enforced on local systems, users have the ability to make changes. Additionally, preferences are useful for non-Group-Policy-aware applications and system settings. However, even if a user decides to make changes, they most likely will not have the permission to make the change because a majority of the preferences require some kind of administrative credentials.

You can also target individual preference items through Group Policy filtering, which you will learn about later in this chapter. This is very different from true policies, in that you do not target individual settings inside Group Policy settings.

In Windows Server 2008 R2, the targeting of preferences has been dramatically improved. You now can leverage the Targeting Editor, as shown in Figure 6.1.

Figure 6.1: Targeting Editor

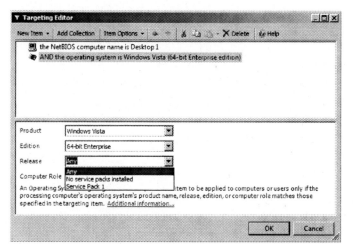

The Targeting Editor is a straightforward rules-based tool that allows you to create how you want to target the preference. You can target based on computer name, operating system (including version, service pack, 64-bit), RAM, CPU, and so on. This makes item-level targeting very flexible. To access the targeting editor, choose the Common tab while modifying your preference setting and select Item-Level Targeting, as shown in Figure 6.2.

Manage Active Directory and Local Users

PART II

Figure 6.2: Selecting Item-Level Targeting

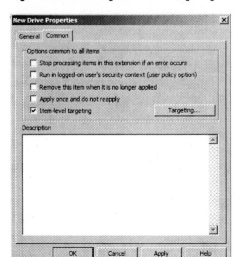

Understand the Scope of Group Policy Management

As you begin working with Group Policy, you'll start to see how an effective AD design provides the basis for managing Group Policy. You can apply group policies to the site, domain, and organizational unit levels. Table 6.2 describes the impact and recommendations for using the different levels to apply group policies.

Table 6.2: Scopes of Group Policy Management

Scope	Objects Impacted	Recommendation
Site	All the domains and the objects in the AD site are impacted; this is the largest scope of impact.	It is not recommended you use the site scope for a typical Group Policy setup. However, sites are useful when you are setting network security settings, such as a proxy server or IPsec policies. You also need to be an Enterprise Administrator to link GPOs at this level.

Table 6.2: Scopes of Group Policy Management *(continued)*

Scope	Objects Impacted	Recommendation
Domain	All the objects in the chosen domain are impacted.	This is also not a recommended scope for applying group policies. The domain scope is used for your password policies (length, complexity, expiration, and so on) and other security settings where you want to apply them consistently.
Organizational unit	All the objects in the chosen OU as well as any nested OUs and their objects are impacted.	This is the recommended scope for applying group policies. OUs provide the easiest-to-manage location for all of your Group Policy needs.

As mentioned in Table 6.2, organizational units are the recommended way you should apply Group Policy. One of the benefits of having a good OU design is that it can assist you in applying group policies by allowing you to target the unique needs for the users and computers in each OU.

Understand and Control the Order of Precedence

When you create group policies, you are not limited to just one GPO or one scope of management. By default, the RSOP is the culmination of all the scopes and all of the GPOs, and policies are cumulative. In other words, the RSOP could be the combination of multiple GPOs from multiple scopes. You could have an RSOP containing settings from the site, domain, and OU scopes. Typically, there is very little conflict when working with policies, and all the settings will apply as you go through the levels.

However, it is important you understand the default order of precedence. This becomes important when you have two or more group policies that have conflicting settings. The following is the general rule of thumb when working with multiple GPOs:

The GPO closest to the object (user or computer) wins.

The following is the default order of precedence:

1. Local policies

   Local policies live on the local system and are applied first, including multiple local policies on Windows Vista systems or later.

2. Site

3. Domain

4. Parent OU

5. Child OU

If you have nested OUs, these are called *child* OUs, and they can have separate settings as well.

For example, if you have a setting to remove the run command at the domain scope and a setting to enable the run command at the object's OU, the setting at the OU level will "win," and the run command will be enabled.

With Group Policy you also have the ability to link multiple GPOs per site, domain, or OU. When this happens, you need to understand link order. In Figure 6.3, you can see an OU with two GPOs linked to the OU. Link order determines the order in which policies are applied. The link with the highest order (with 1 being the highest order) is applied last and therefore has the highest precedence for a given site, domain, or organizational unit. So, in Figure 6.3, the run command would be disabled since it has a link order of 1 and is processed last. By changing the link order, you determine the order of processing. You can move a link up or down in the list to the appropriate location.

Figure 6.3: Link order

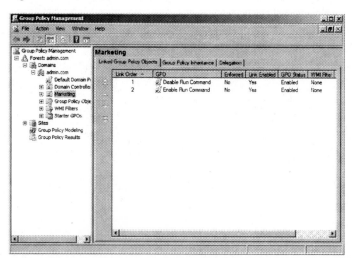

There are two other ways you can control how Group Policy is processed: block inheritance and enforce (known as *no override* in previous operating systems).

Block inheritance prevents GPOs from higher scopes from being inherited and thus from being applied by the child scopes further down the chain. The only exception is if the GPO has been marked as enforced. Block inheritance is selected at either the domain level or the OU level. For example, if you did not want domain-wide policies applying to the children OUs, you could block inheritance at the OU level, and the domain policies would not be inherited.

Enforce is applied to the Group Policy link and marks the GPO to be processed last regardless of where the policy falls in the scope of management. In other words, an enforced policy will always win unless another enforced policy is further down the scope of management. This also means that when you use an enforced policy, it will also override the block inheritance setting.

Learn Group Policy Processing

Understanding Group Policy processing is key to understanding how to apply settings and can really assist you in troubleshooting. Policy processing will also impact when you see the Group Policy settings take effect on your targeted systems and users.

You also need to understand that Group Policy is processed differently for computer settings and user settings. There is also a difference on the client operating system; specifically, the client operating system can affect how group policy is applied. We'll discuss this in the "Learn How Group Policies Process on the Client Side" section later in this chapter.

Computer settings are applied at two times: during startup of the operating system and during shutdown. User settings are applied when the user logs on to and logs off from the system. With the user settings being applied second, by default they take precedence over computer settings unless you have configured loopback processing mode.

When you make changes to Group Policy via the GPMC, they may not immediately take effect but may also not require any action by the user or computer. There is a background process controlling the refresh of policies. Policies are updated in the background at various intervals; the intervals are also configurable via Group Policy settings. If the system is a domain controller, the policy is refreshed by default every 5 minutes. On all other systems, the refresh interval is by default 90 minutes plus a random interval of 30 minutes, so a policy could take up to 2 hours before the changes you made to the GPO are reflected on the targeting system.

Loopback Processing Mode

When you apply both computer and user settings via Group Policy, they are processed at separate times. With the user settings applied after computer settings, there is a potential that your computer settings will be overridden by the user settings. Even though there are only a few settings that can conflict in this way, ultimately this behavior may not be what you desire. You can control the order of processing of computer and user settings by configuring loopback processing mode. Loopback processing mode will enable the computer settings of the GPO to take precedence over the user settings in the GPO.

Loopback processing mode is configured via Group Policy and is located under Computer Configuration\Policies\Administrative Templates\System\Group Policy. The setting is User Group Policy Loopback Processing Mode, as shown here.

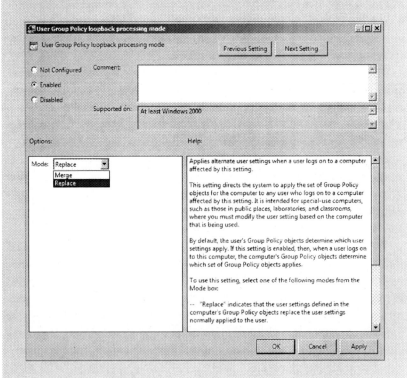

The settings has two modes:

Merge: This allows the settings in both the computer and user areas of Group Policy to be combined. If there is a conflict between the two settings, the settings in the computer configuration will take precedence.

Replace: This allows the settings in the computer area to replace the settings in the user portion of Group Policy.

Not all policies are processed in the background; by default policies are not reapplied if the policy has not changed. Additionally, software installation, scripts, and folder redirection are not reapplied during background processing. Those policies are applied when either a computer restarts or a user logs off or logs back on. However, there is one exception to the order of processing for GPOs. If a GPO is in the startup or shutdown settings for computer objects or in the logon or logoff settings for user objects, those policies will process the next time the sequence will occur. In other words, if a policy is updated in the background and is in the startup settings, then those policy changes will not take place until the next time the system is restarted.

Security settings are also treated separately from other Group Policy settings. Security settings are those settings listed under both the User Configuration and Computer Configuration under Windows Settings\ Security Settings. They include such things as Account Policies, Local Security Policies such as Auditing and User Rights, Event Log size and retention settings, Restricted Groups, System Services, Registry and File System access, Public Key Policies, Software Restrictions, and IP Security, to name the general categories. These settings are reapplied every 16 hours even if the GPO has not changed. You can modify this duration through the registry.

Lastly, some policies are not applied if a slow link is detected. Specifically, application deployment, scripts, folder redirection, and disk quotas are not applied by default when a slow link is detected. A slow link is determined by the responsiveness of the domain controller delivering the policies to the targeted systems. By default, when processing a GPO client, operating systems prior to Windows Vista will try four times to ping a domain controller. If the average of the four ping attempts is greater than the default or that set by the GPO, then only registry settings, security policies, EFS recovery policy, and IP security policies will be applied. With Windows Vista, this has changed. Instead of pings, Vista uses the Network Location Awareness handler, which verifies whether a domain controller is available.

Manually Update Group Policy Settings

You may not be willing to wait for background policy processing. You can manually update Group Policy settings on targeted systems by running the command gpupdate.exe from the target system. When testing Group Policy, you should usually run gpupdate /force before logging off or rebooting the computer. This will allow you to make sure that Group Policy settings are flowing down to the system. This simple command can save you time, especially when you are troubleshooting. You can run gpupdate.exe from a command prompt. The command has a few parameters, making the tool very useful, as listed in Table 6.3.

Table 6.3: gpupdate.exe

Command	Function
gpupdate	Reapplies just the policies that have changed since the last update for both computer and user settings
gpupdate /force	Reapplies all the policy settings for both computer and user settings regardless if they have changed
gpupdate /targetComputer or gpupdate /target:User	Reapplies only the computer or user settings as reflected by the choice you set in the command

Learn How Group Policies Process on the Client Side

One last consideration you need to be aware of regarding Group Policy processing is how they are applied to the system. There are two types of Group Policy processing modes: synchronous and asynchronous. *Synchronous* processing is when you have a series of processes where the series is processed one step at a time; in other words, one process must finish running before the next one begins. *Asynchronous* processing, on the other hand, can run on different threads simultaneously because their outcome is independent of other processes.

Client-side systems (Windows XP, Windows Vista, Windows 7) process group policies asynchronously. The main reason for asynchronous processing on the client-side systems is fast logon optimization. Fast logon optimization is designed to enable the systems to quickly present the desktop to the users. This could result in some policies not being applied initially to the targeted systems.

Server-side systems (Windows Server 2003, Windows Server 2008, Windows Server 2008 R2) process group policies synchronously, which ensures the Group Policy settings are processed. With synchronous processing, all the Group Policy settings will be applied. You will notice this may delay logon; however, when you see the logon screen, you will know the computer settings have been applied, and likewise when the desktop is displayed, you will know that all the user settings have been applied. Group policies are processed synchronously on Windows 2000 systems at startup and asynchronously during Group Policy refreshes.

As you can see, this is important to understand when it comes to maintaining and troubleshooting Group Policy. You can also control this setting on the client-side systems by modifying the Always Wait for the Network at Computer Startup and Logon setting; this will allow you have the client-side systems process group policies synchronously. You can find this setting in Group Policy under Computer Configuration\Policies\Administrative Templates\System\Logon, as shown in Figure 6.4. By enabling the setting, you control the processing behavior on the client-side systems.

Figure 6.4: Setting for synchronous processing

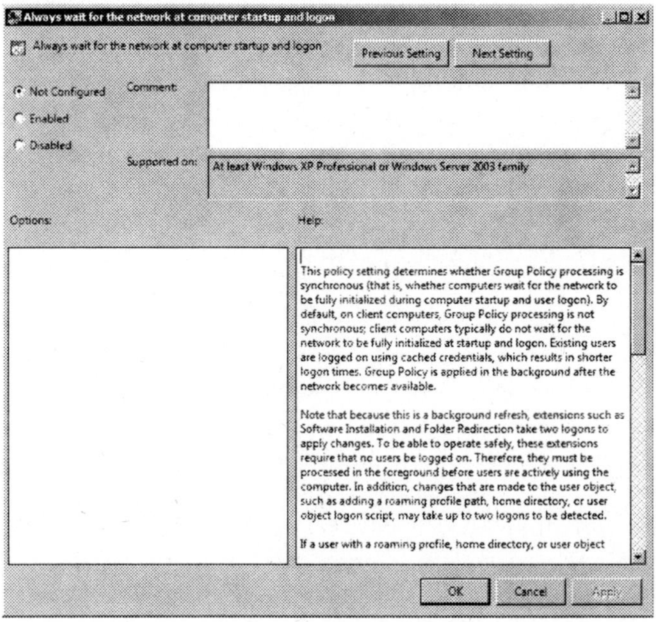

Service Running Group Policy Processing

On operating systems prior to Windows Vista, group policies were processed by the netlogon service. As a result, the netlogon service sometimes was the culprit for issues with Group Policy.

In later versions of Windows (2008, 2008 R2, Vista, and 7), there is a dedicated service for Group Policy, aptly called the Group Policy service. The service is responsible for applying settings configured through Group Policy.

This change is important because it offers better reliability for Group Policy and enables better efficiency and reduction of resources for background processing of Group Policy. The dedicated service provides the ability to read to new files and allows the Group Policy service to take on the workload provided by multiple services in other versions of Windows.

Administer Group Policy

Now that you have seen how group policies are processed, it is time to take a look at how to work with Group Policy. Managing Group Policy is straightforward after you have deployed your AD environment. To work with Group Policy, you will use primarily two tools: the Group Policy Management Console (GPMC) and the Group Policy Management Editor (GPME). In this section, you will get to take a look at both tools and see how to use them.

Use the Group Policy Management Console

The Group Policy Management Console is the main tool where you manage the deployment of Group Policy. This includes creating and linking your GPOs to the appropriate site, domain, or organizational unit. You also can manage security filtering, WMI filtering, administration delegation of Group Policy, and various other tasks with the GPMC. In addition, you can also use it to gain access to the GPME to edit the settings for your GPOs (you will learn about the GPME in the next section). You can also view the settings for your various Group Policy objects. You can find the GPMC in the administrative tools on your Windows Server 2008 R2 server. Select Start ⇨ Administrative Tools ⇨ Group Policy Management to load the GPMC; your screen will resemble Figure 6.5.

Figure 6.5: Group Policy Management Console

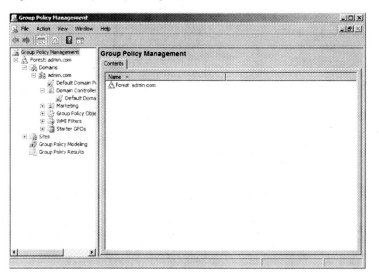

When you first open the GPMC, expand the management tree; you will see two GPOs that are configured by default: the Default Domain Policy and the Default Domain Controllers Policy. These two policies contain the default security policies for the domains. To view the settings of the default policies, follow these steps:

1. Open GPMC.

2. Click the + sign to expand the Forest container.

3. Click the + sign to expand the Domains container.

4. Click the + sign to expand the appropriate domain to view the Default Domain Policy. If you want to view the Default Domain Controllers Policy, continue in the domain you expanded, and expand the Domain Controllers container by clicking the + sign.

5. Click either Default Domain Policy or Default Domain Controllers Policy, depending on which you want to view.

6. In the details pane to the right, click the Settings tab, and you will see a screen similar to Figure 6.6, which shows the Default Domain Policy.

Figure 6.6: Default Domain Policy

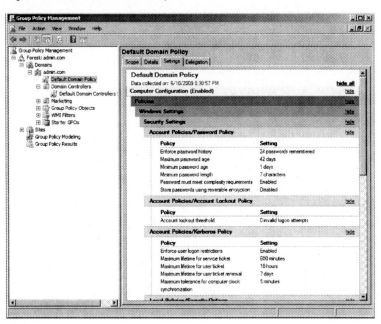

WARNING   The Default Domain Policy sets the basis for security in your domain. Specifically, the Default Domain Policy sets the default domain password policy, Kerberos, and public key policies. These provide protection for your users' passwords, and the Kerberos and public key policies help provide secure authentication mechanisms for your domain.

The Default Domain Controllers Policy sets the local security rights for the domain controllers. The rights govern the administrative access to the domain controllers in your domain. These rights help harden the server and keep it secure for the right people in your organization.

You should seriously consider any changes to the Default Domain Policy before you make them. Whether the change is an addition or a deletion, you should consider making separate policies for your preferences. The default policies are designed to provide you with a solid, secure network, and you should never really change them.

Work with Group Policies

Creating, linking, and setting security for group policies starts with knowing what scope you want to apply the policy to. Additionally, you want to know what users in the scope you want to apply the policies to.

1. Select the scope where you want to create your GPO.

2. Right-click the scope, and you will see a screen similar to Figure 6.7.

3. Select Create A GPO In This Domain And Link It Here.

4. Enter the name of the GPO, and select a starter GPO, if any exists. Click OK to finish creating your GPO.

Figure 6.7: Creating a GPO

You can also create a GPO without having the policy linked directly to a scope initially, and you can create a policy via the GPO container. After you create the GPO, you can easily link the GPO to a scope by simply dragging and dropping the GPO on the scope you want the policy to apply to.

1. Click the Group Policy Objects container.

2. Right-click the container, and select New.

3. Enter the name of the GPO, and select a starter GPO, if any exists. Click OK to finish creating your GPO.

Work with Starter GPOs

Starter GPOs allow you to create a template for quickly creating new GPOs, with a predefined list of settings. They can save you a lot of time because part of the challenge of working with GPOs is the number of settings you can modify. There are literally thousands of settings you can manipulate with Group Policy. Learning which settings work best in your environment is key to using Group Policy effectively. By using starter GPOs, you can reuse a list of frequent settings when you create new GPOs, which will save you time. It is important to note that starter GPOs contain settings only from the Administrative Templates section of Group Policy. You edit the settings in the GPOs just like any other GPO.

To create a starter GPO, click Starter GPOs in the GPMC tree. If this is the first time you have clicked Starter GPOs, you will see a screen similar to Figure 6.8.

Figure 6.8: Creating a starter GPO

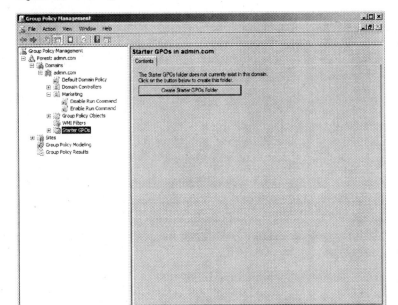

You need to create a folder to store the starter GPOs, so click the Create Starter GPOs Folder button to create the folder. Once you create the folder, you will see a few starter GPOs provided by Microsoft by default. There are two acronyms you'll see with all the built-in starter GPOs, and these provide the key to what type of settings are in the policies. EC stands for "enterprise client" and provides basic security and power settings, among others, for your infrastructure. SSLF stands for "specialized security limited functionality," which provides robust security-enabled clients. Note this starter may cause compatibility issues with applications. To view the settings for any of these starter GPOs, select one, and click the Settings tab.

Work with Group Policy Object Links

After you create the GPO, you will see the link of the object associated with your container. You should take note that is this the link for the GPO, not the GPO itself. This is an important distinction to make, because there are different administrative tasks that you can perform for either the GPO link or the GPO itself. To see a list of all the GPOs in your domain, click the Group Policy Objects container located in your management tree.

Working with GPO links provides you with the ability to set the enforced setting, as mentioned earlier. You can also enable or disable the link on the scope. You also control all the filtering of the GPO by working with the link. To access and see the tasks you can perform on links, you can either right-click the link and select the appropriate option (link enabled or enforced). You can also select the link and click the Action menu and you will see same options (link enabled or enforced) to control the link.

Working with the GPOs provides you with the ability to back up and recover them. You can also import settings from previously backed up items. To access these tasks, as with GPO links, you can simply right-click the object and you will see the various actions you can perform (backup, import and so on), or you can highlight the object and then click the Action menu. Remember, you can link GPOs to more than one scope of management. While viewing the objects, you can also link the GPO to other sites, domains, or OUs. To link a GPO to a scope, you can either drag and drop the object on the scope you want to target or right-click the scope and select Link An Existing GPO. When you edit the GPO, you are modifying the object, and all the changes you make will apply to all the scopes linked to the GPO.

Manage Active Directory and Local Users

PART II

There are a few common tasks that you can perform on both the links and the GPOs. You can access the Group Policy Management Editor by selecting Edit, and you can save all the settings into an HTML file by selecting the Save Report Action item, as shown in Figure 6.9.

Figure 6.9: Settings report

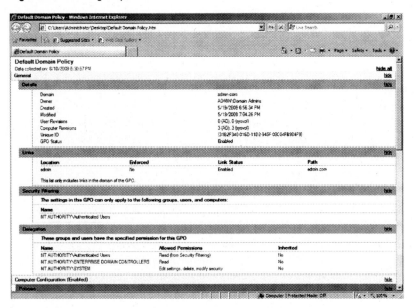

GPO Status

One of the special tasks you can perform on the GPOs is to control which sections of the GPO are applied. When you right-click the GPO (or select the GPO and click the Action menu), one of the items you can select is GPO Status, as shown here.

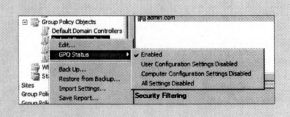

The GPO has four status options:

- *Enabled:* Both user and computer settings are enabled.
- *User Configuration Settings Disabled:* User settings are disabled, and computer settings are enabled.
- *Computer Configuration Settings Disabled:* User settings are enabled, and computer settings are disabled.
- *All Settings Disabled:* Both user and computer settings are disabled.

The purpose of these settings is for GPO processing efficiency. When you create a GPO, you can have both user and computer settings in the GPO. However, you may create a GPO without one of the two settings; if you do this, it is recommended that you disable the portion that has no settings. This will improve how the targeted systems process group policies.

Manage Active Directory and Local Users

PART II

Filter Group Policies with GPMC

When working with Group Policy links, you have additional control over the objects targeted by your GPO. Typically, when you link a GPO to an OU, for example, you want all the objects in the OU impacted by the GPO. However, there may be some scenarios where you want only some of the objects to have the group policy applied to them. In Group Policy, you have two main mechanisms for filtering GPOs. Two of the filters you can work with are Windows Management Instrumentation (WMI) filters and security filters.

WMI filtering provides a very powerful filtering tool that allows you to leverage WMI scripting to filter which objects are targeted by your GPOs. WMI scripting leverages an industry standard for how to work with systems across network infrastructures. In a nutshell, WMI scripting will allow you find out various inventory types of information about computers—from what OS they are running to what applications are installed to what type of hardware, and so on. What this provides for GPOs is the ability to target systems meeting very specific criteria. For example, you could use Group Policy to install a software application and then use WMI filtering to make sure only systems having the required amount of free hard drive space to support the application have the application installed on them. To see what WMI filters are currently installed on the system, look in the WMI Filters container in the GPMC. To see some examples of WMI, take a look at http://technet .microsoft.com/en-us/library/cc758471.aspx.

Security filtering is another great way to filter objects. To access the security filter for a GPO link, click the link you want to view, and make sure you are on the Scope tab for the GPO link. You can see the list of users and groups in the Security Filtering section. By default, the group Authenticated Users is added to the security for all GPOs. When you work with security permissions, there are two permissions required for your users to process a Group Policy object targeted on the OU:

- Read
- Apply Group Policy

You can use security filtering to prevent applying a GPO to security groups or users. For example, say you have an OU containing a group of people including Harold, the manager, of the group, and you want the policy to apply to everyone in the OU except Harold. You could simply add Deny access to either Read or Apply Group Policy for Harold. You can see an example of this in Figure 6.10.

Figure 6.10: Denying a user a group policy

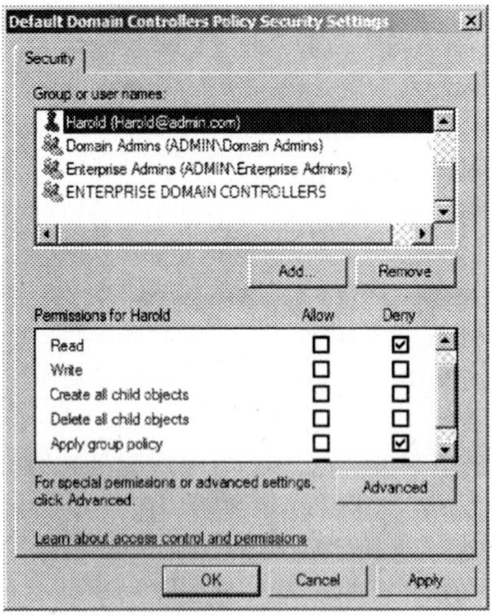

You can view the security filtering for a GPO by clicking the GPO link for the targeted scope. On the Scope tab, you will see the current security filtering for the GPO in the Security Filtering section of the details pane inside the GPMC. To modify the security filtering for a GPO, follow these steps:

1. Click the GPO you want to apply filtering to.

2. Click the Delegation tab.

3. Click the Add button to open the user/group selection dialog box.

4. Find or enter the group or user you want to work with, and click OK, which will bring up the Add Group Or User dialog box, as shown in Figure 6.11. This dialog box allows you to choose the base security level for the user or group you have selected.

Figure 6.11: GPO base security filter

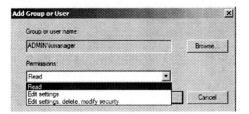

5. Choose the appropriate level from the three choices, and click OK. Read will give the ability to read and apply the GPO, "Edit settings" grants the ability for modifying the GPO settings themselves, and the last choice of "Edit settings, delete, modify security" allows basic administration over the GPO link.

6. To further modify the security, click Advanced on the Delegation tab, which will bring up an advanced view of the security settings, as shown in Figure 6.12.

7. Click the user you want to modify, and choose the appropriate security settings for the user. It is important to note that Deny permissions supersede any Allow permissions. In other words, if you have selected the user to have Allow for Read and Deny for Read, the user would have Deny permissions for that setting. In the example you saw earlier, if you did not want Keith to be able to have the GPO applied, simply select Deny for Read, and deselect Allow for Read, as shown in Figure 6.13. When you are finished modifying permissions, click OK.

Figure 6.12: GPO advanced security filtering

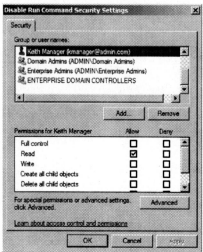

Figure 6.13: Denying Read for a GPO

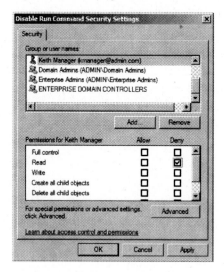

Advanced Group Policy Management Tool

Another tool you may be able to take advantage of is the Advanced Group Policy Management (AGPM) tool. You can find this tool in the Microsoft Desktop Optimization Pack (MDOP); it's available only to volume license customers with Software Assurance as part of the licensing agreement. You can also download the evaluation version if you are an MSDN or TechNet subscriber. The tool does provide some nice benefits to working with Group Policy, including change management, auditing, reporting, and offline editing of GPOs. To learn more and to see whether you can leverage this tool, refer to http://technet.microsoft.com/en-us/library/cc749396.aspx.

Use the Group Policy Management Editor

To access the Group Policy Management Editor, all you need to do is select the GPO link or GPO to edit, and select Action ⇨ Edit (or right-click the GPO and select Edit). Whether you choose to edit from the link or from the GPO, they both will modify the GPO, meaning any other scopes linked to the GPO will be affected. When you edit the GPO, there are two main containers to work with the settings: Computer Congifugration and User Configuration. To work with a Group Policy setting, open the appropriate container, and click the setting you want to edit.

If you have worked with GPO in previous versions, the interface for the GPE was different. The new interface in Windows Server 2008 R2 is easier to use, and it displays all the settings for a particular setting in one page, which means...*no more tabs*! This is a nice addition to the Group Policy Management Editor. One of the great features in Group Policy is the built-in documentation. With every setting in the editor, you will see an explanation of what it does, and you can see the explanation as you are expanding the tree or double-clicking a setting to configure it. Figure 6.14 shows an example of a setting and the explanation. You will notice that the setting will include the minimum required OS for the setting to be applied to the targeted system. This is important when you are working with a variety of OSs connecting to your domain.

Figure 6.14: GPO setting

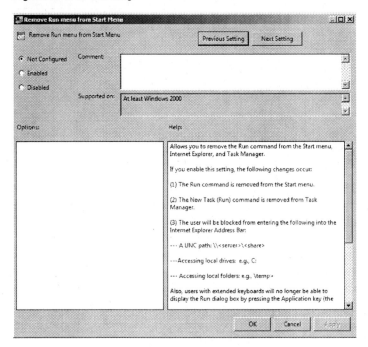

As mentioned previously, you can configure more than 1,000 settings. In this section, you will see the main areas explained and what types of settings you can expect to find. When working with the editor, the settings are broken down into two main containers, one for computers and one for users. Inside both Users Configuration and Computers Configurations, you will see policies and preferences. Table 6.4 describes the computer and user policies you'll find in specific policy areas.

Table 6.4: Overview of Computer and User Policies

Policy Area	Description
Software Settings	In this section of Group Policy, you can configure installations of software packages to the targeted computers or users. Typically the packages are in the Windows Installer (MSI) format. You can deploy applications by assigning or publishing them to the target. If you assign an application in the computer configuration, the application will be installed on the targeted system the next time the system reboots. If you assign the application to a user, the application will appear on the Start menu, and the first time a user clicks the icon or opens a file associated with the application, the application will be installed.

Publishing an application is available only if the target is a user. Publishing an application will allow the application to appear in the Add or Remove Programs applet. The user will need to go into the Control Panel to install the application. |
| Computer Windows Settings | This contains several important Windows settings specific to the computer. This is where you would configure your startup and shutdown scripts, networking Quality of Service (QoS) settings, and security settings. In the security settings, you can configure IPsec, wireless or wired network configuration and security settings, the firewall, and a variety of other security settings. You will also find a new policy in Windows Server 2008 R2 called Name Resolution, which is used for configuring DirectAccess, which only really applies to Windows 7 computers and DNS security settings. |
| User Windows Settings | This contains several important Windows settings that are specific to the user. This is where you configure your logon and logoff scripts, additional networking QoS settings, and security settings. The security settings for the users have two sections: Public Key Policies and Software Restriction Policies. Public key policies, commonly referred as PKI, are used for configuring the client-side certificate security settings. Software restriction policies allow you to configure which applications are restricted on your client systems. You can also configure folder redirection for users' common directories, which is particularly useful when your users have roaming profiles. |

Manage Active Directory and Local Users

PART II

Table 6.4: Overview of Computer and User Policies *(continued)*

Policy Area	Description
Administrative Templates	This is where you find a majority of all the settings available for Group Policy and is where you can configure most of the aspects of the interface for users and computers. Administrative templates are also unique in that you can add templates you have created or get from other software applications. For example, Internet Explorer 8 has its own administrative template with more than 1,300 settings just for the browser.
	There is also a new category in Windows Server 2008 R2 inside Administrative Templates called All Settings, which is very useful when you are using filtering for searching for a particular setting.

You can also work with preferences in the Group Policy Management Editor. Table 6.5 gives you a quick reference for the type of settings you will find in the tool.

Table 6.5: Overview of Computer and User Preferences

Preference Area	Description
Window Settings	You can configure system-wide environment variables and modify registry settings and INI files for any application. You can also work with the local file system by configuring files, folders, and network shares.
Control Panel Settings	You can configure local system devices, local users, and groups. Also, you can set power options here to help optimize the power consumption of your desktop operating systems. This is also where you can configure printers on the network and local-based devices. You also have the ability to work with services and the Task Scheduler.

These two tables are meant to give you just a brief glimpse into the setting areas. The best way to learn how to use the settings is to look through them and their categories; it is worth your time to be familiar with the setting locations.

Filter Group Policy with the Editor

Prior to Windows Server 2008, there was no built-in way to search through Group Policy settings. You had to work with the Group

Policy settings reference file, which is a free downloadable spread-sheet. You can find the current Group Policy settings reference file at www.microsoft.com/downloads/details.aspx?familyid=2043B94E-66CD-4B91-9E0F-68363245C495&displaylang=en.

In Windows Server 2008 and Windows Server 2008 R2, you can filter the administrative template settings inside the Group Policy Management Editor. To work with the built-in filter, follow these steps:

1. Right-click Administrative Templates, and select Filter Options. You will see a screen similar to Figure 6.15.

Figure 6.15: Filter options

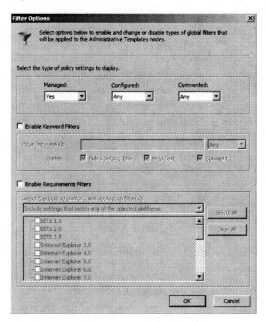

2. You can filter based on several criteria including keyword filters and software requirements. You will also notice the two options to filter: Managed and Configured. Managed policies are true policies and are managed directly by Group Policy; unmanaged policies are persistent settings, sometimes referred to as *tattooing* the registry. Configured is a useful option to allow you quickly find only the settings you have configured. By default all policies are marked as not configured, so by setting the Configured option to Yes, you will only find the settings that have been configured.

Manage Active Directory and Local Users

PART II

3. After you're done setting the options, click OK, which will enable the filter. To turn the filter off, click the Filter icon.

Automate Group Policy Administrator Tasks

When you work with Group Policy, it is recommended that you perform common administrative tasks such as backup and recovery on a regular basis. These tasks can be performed through the GPMC, as well as PowerShell. In Table 6.6, you can see a few general PowerShell commands to help you with working with Group Policy.

Table 6.6: Group Policy PowerShell Commands

PowerShell Command	Description
Get-Help *-gp*	Lists all the possible commands involved in working with GPOs. As you learned in Chapter 3, you can access help for individual commands listed by this command.
Get-GPO -all	Lists all the GPOs in your current domain.
Backup-GPO -all -path 'c:\gpobackup\'	Backs up all the group policies in the domain to the c:\gpobackup directory.
Import-GPO	Is a useful command for importing GPOs from a backup server to a new server.
Restore-GPO -all -path 'c:\gpobackup\'	Restores all the group policies in the domain from the c:\gpobackup directory. Typically, you would use this command with the GUID for the GPO you are restoring to find the GUID. In GPMC, click the GPO located in the Group Policy Objects container, and click the Details tab or use get-gpo cmdlet.
Get-GPResultantSetofPolicy -ReportType html -Path 'c:\rsop\rsop2.html'	Generates an HTML report showing you the RSOP for the policy applied to a particular system. This is a particularly useful tool for troubleshooting.

Troubleshoot Group Policy

When working with Group Policy, which has several moving parts, learning some tools to troubleshoot the application of group policies will help save you administrative time and hassle. Understanding the processing covered in this chapter can offer a clue or two on why a group policy is not being applied. In this section, you will see some of the built-in tools designed to help you with troubleshooting Group Policy.

The built-in tools focus on predicting how your policy settings will be applied and how to find out the results on how the policy was applied. The tools are the Group Policy Modeling Wizard (GPMW) and three tools for generating the RSOP: the Group Policy Results Wizard (GPRW), GPResult.exe, and the RSOP snap-in. Ultimately, these tools will allow you to see the Group Policy order of precedence in action. You can see which policies were applied to the system and which polices "win."

In addition, since Group Policy relies on the network, all the tools you use to test the network—from ping to name resolution—still apply when troubleshooting Group Policy. For example, you can run the RSOP tool, which will inform you if a policy was not applied. If you check your GPO and it is all correct, this will generally indicate it's a network or replication issue.

Use the Group Policy Modeling Wizard

The GPMW allows you to preview your group policies. The tool models the results of group policies before they are deployed. This tool compiles reports based on what is configured at the site, domain, and OU levels for both computer and user objects. Based on the rules for applying group policies, the tool will give you a snapshot at what policies will be applied. GPMW can also show you how any security or WMI filtering will affect the application of group policies.

The GPMW is located in the GPMC, and you can find it in the Sites container. It is important to note that the GPMW evaluates only the theoretical RSOP based on all GPOs and filtering set via AD. It does not take into account any physical issues on the network that may affect GPO application.

Manage Active Directory and Local Users

PART II

To create a model, perform the following:

1. In the GPMC right-click Group Policy Modeling, and select Group Policy Modeling Wizard.

2. On the welcome page, click Next.

3. Select the domain controller you will use to process the requests for modeling, and click Next.

4. Determine what you want to model. You can choose an individual user, individual computer, or a whole scope (domain or OU) for either a user or a computer. You can also model a combination of any of these. For example, you could model just one user for user settings and an entire domain for computer objects. After you have selected your target, click Next.

5. You also have the ability to simulate a slow network or a loopback address in the Advanced Simulation dialog box, make your selection, and click Next.

6. In the Alternate Active Directory Paths dialog box, you have the ability to choose other locations for the simulation. (You may not see this dialog box option, based on what choices you made in step 3.) Make your selection, and click Next.

7. You can also simulate changes to a user's security group. After you make your selection, click Next.

8. Like with users, you can also simulate changes to a computer's security groups. After you make your selection, click Next.

9. The WMI Filters For Users setting allows you to control which filters are used. After you make your selection, click Next.

10. The WMI Filters For Computers setting allows you to control which filters are used for your computer accounts. After you make your selection, click Next.

11. On the summary screen, review your selections, and click Next to create the model.

12. When the model is done being created, click Finish to see the report. The report is saved under the Group Policy Modeling node. You can rerun the model at any time by right-clicking the model and selecting Re-run. Figure 6.16 shows an example of the report.

Figure 6.16: Group Policy modeling report

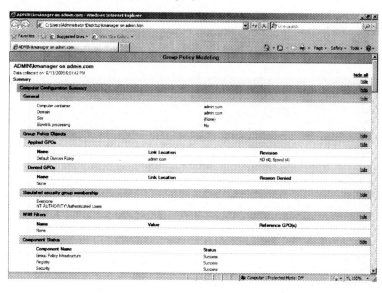

Use Tools to See the RSOP

Several tools will allow you to see the RSOP. One of the tools is built into the GPMC. The Group Policy Results Wizard is similar to the GPMW, and it is also located in the GPMC. To run the GPRW, go the Sites container, and perform the following steps:

1. Right-click Group Policy Results, and select Group Policy Results Wizard.

2. On the welcome page, click Next.

3. You can select the local computer or a remote computer. Make your selection, and click Next.

4. Select the user account you want to see the RSOP for, and click Next. It is important to note that you will see only users who have already logged onto the system.

5. Review the summary screen, and click Next.

6. After the wizard runs successfully, click Finish to return to the GPMC and view the report.

7. The report is saved under the Group Policy Modeling node. You can rerun the model at any time by right-clicking the report and selecting Re-run Query. Figure 6.17 shows an example of the report.

Figure 6.17: Group Policy results report

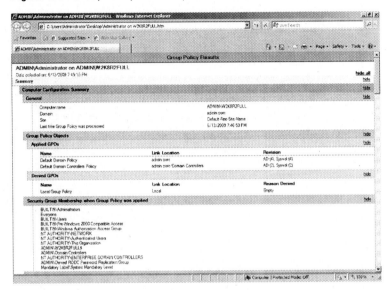

The second tool is a command-line tool called GPResult.exe. This tool will allow you to see the results of Group Policy either for the local system and current user or for remote systems and other users. Like many other commands, several switches/parameters are available providing additional information. You can pipe the results to a text file and utilize the command in batch files or scripts.

Lastly, the Resultant Set of Policy snap-in is available by loading the Microsoft Management Console (MMC) and adding it. You can also find the tool in the Active Directory Users And Computers tool, as shown in Figure 6.18.

This tool is similar to the GPRW, but it is able to display the results of multiple GPOs. This is a great tool to troubleshoot your GPOs if the GPMC is not currently available. The tool also has two modes: planning mode and logging mode.

Figure 6.18: RSOP in ADUC

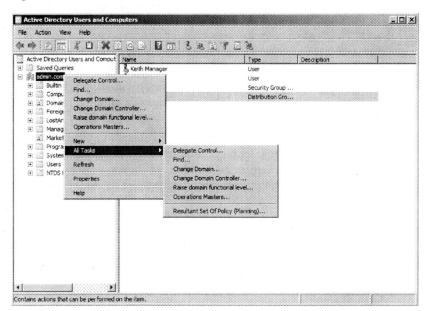

The main difference between the modes is how you are provided the RSOP. Planning mode, which is similar to the GPMW, simulates the processing of Group Policy. Logging mode queries a specific computer's WMI database, which is collected when Group Policy is applied. You can view user information with this tool only if the user has logged onto the system. Additionally, you will see only those policies that have been processed by the system.

Both modes have benefits. The main benefit of planning mode is that it generates a report based on what settings will be processed before they are processed. Planning mode allows you to simulate behaviors and troubleshoot your group policies before you apply them into production. The main benefit of logging mode is accuracy since the report is based on what has actually been processed.

Manage Active Directory and Local Users

PART II

NOTE   When you are working with Group Policy, one of the popular debates is how many settings to make per GPO. Do you create one GPO with all of your desired settings, or do you create more GPOs with a few settings? Well, the answer to the question is one of the favorites in all of IT administration: it depends.

Seriously, you do not want to create one GPO for every individual setting or create one massive GPO with all the settings. The answer lies in balance, performance, how often you make changes, and how you delegate administration.

Generally speaking, if your group policies do not change, you can consolidate your policies into fewer GPOs, which will increase client processing time. However, this method sometimes can be hard to track changes and troubleshoot. Another method is to create GPOs based on the settings they are processing and segment if they are computer-based or user-based settings. For example, create a GPO for just the security settings of a computer, and create another for the security settings for the users. Although this method will cause more client-side processing, it does help mitigate frequent changes to your group policies.

PART III

Data Access and Management

IN THIS PART ▶

Data Access and Management

PART III

7

Configuring Folder Security, Access, and Replication

IN THIS CHAPTER, YOU WILL LEARN TO:

Data Access and Management

PART III

A network of servers has one central purpose, and that purpose is to provide controlled access to resources that have been shared in that network. The resources could be files, folders, web pages, databases, printers, or a whole host of other things. The point of the servers is to provide access to all this "stuff." If there is no "stuff," then there is nothing to secure and protect and therefore no need for Windows Server. The need for Windows Server 2008 R2 is greater now than ever before. The sheer amount of data that you are storing in your networks is constantly growing, while the demand for methods to secure and access that data are keeping pace right along with amount of data.

Implement Permissions

A *file system* is by definition a hierarchical structure of folders that house files and secure those files through a series of access control lists (ACLs) and access control entries (ACEs) that define the type of permissions that are granted or denied to those same folders and files. This means that in the Windows Server 2008 R2 world, the primary methodology for securing folders and their files is the use of permissions.

Permissions come in two varieties: share-level permissions and NTFS permissions. If you think about it, this makes perfect sense. When you create a folder in the file system, there is a default set of permissions that are assigned to the folder. The system itself, the user who created the folder, and the local Administrators group on the server where the folder was created all need some level of access to the folder, as shown in Figure 7.1.

NTFS permissions are assigned when the folder is created but can be edited at any time by a user or group member who has the permission to change permissions on the folder.

NTFS folder permissions come in two types called *standard permissions* and *special permissions*. Standard permissions come in the form of Full Control, Modify, Read & Execute, List Folder Contents, Read, and Write. Each of these permissions can be either allowed or denied. Because you have the option to allow or deny permissions on a folder in an NTFS file system, you have incredible flexibility over the level of access on a given folder.

Figure 7.1: Default NTFS permissions

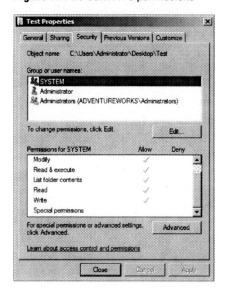

In addition to the standard permissions, there are also special permissions that can be set on each folder or file. Special permissions do more than simply provide access to the folder on which they are applied. They provide the basis for folder ownership as well as the ability to change permissions for a folder and the hierarchy that could exist beneath the folder in the file system.

Set Standard NTFS Permissions

Setting or changing standard NTFS permissions is a straightforward process. Follow these steps to get started:

1. Open Windows Explorer.

2. Locate the desired folder.

3. Right-click the folder.

4. Choose Properties.

5. Select the Security tab.

6. Click Edit.

Data Access and Management

PART III

At this point, you can select an existing user or group from the list of users and groups that have existing permissions, or you can click the Add button to add new users or groups to which permissions may be assigned.

You can add users and groups from the local accounts available on the physical machine or from the Active Directory database if the folder resides on a server that is part of an Active Directory forest. In the event that you are interested in removing permissions, you can simply select the user or group account from the list of users and groups and then click the Remove button, as illustrated in Figure 7.2.

Figure 7.2: Setting and removing standard NTFS permissions

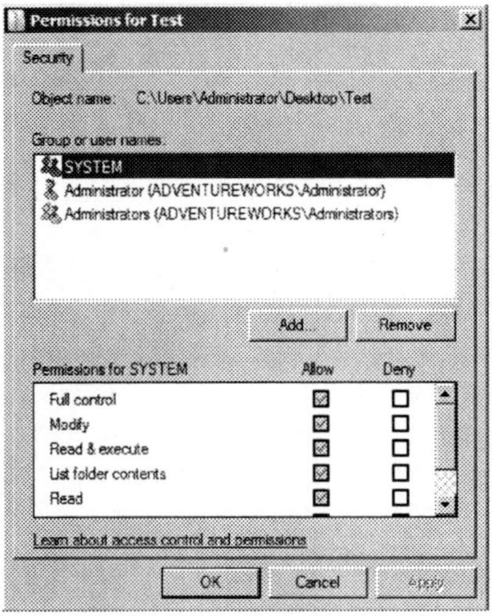

Please keep in mind that not just anyone can add, change, or remove NTFS permissions on a folder. You need to have permissions to a folder in order to change its permissions. The permissions to change permissions or take ownership of a folder are special permissions.

Set Special NTFS Permissions

Like with standard permissions, adding or changing special permissions is a fairly straightforward process. Follow these steps to get started:

1. Open Windows Explorer.
2. Locate the desired folder.

3. Right-click the folder.

4. Choose Properties.

5. Select the Security tab.

6. Click the Advanced button.

At this point, the Advanced Security Settings dialog box for this folder is displayed, as shown in Figure 7.3.

Figure 7.3: Advanced Security Settings dialog box

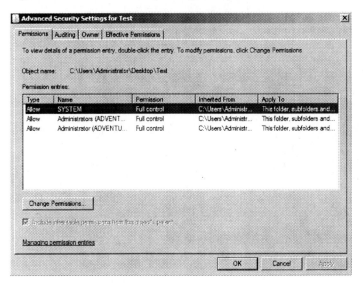

On the Permissions tab, you can click Change Permissions and add, edit, or remove the special permissions. Note the check boxes at the bottom of the window to include inheritable permissions from this object's parent and to replace all child object permissions with inheritable permissions from this object. NTFS file systems have a system of inheritance that is built in to the file system. This means that permissions added higher up in the file system hierarchy can flow down to the folders that are beneath them in the hierarchy. This is valuable when you want to assign permissions to users or groups to a section of the NTFS file system. It can also present some interesting challenges when you are trying to figure out exactly what permissions a given user or group has been granted on a given folder. To help with this issue, you can use the Effective Permissions tab in the Advanced Security Settings dialog box as shown in Figure 7.4.

Figure 7.4: Advanced Security Settings dialog box

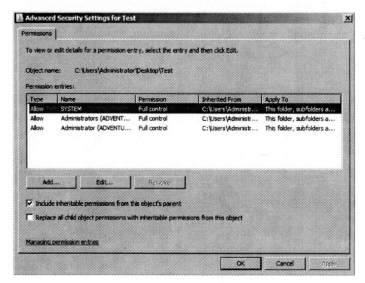

View Effective NTFS Permissions

To view the effective NTFS permissions, follow these steps:

1. Open Windows Explorer.
2. Locate the desired folder.
3. Right-click the folder.
4. Choose Properties.
5. Select the Security tab.
6. Click the Advanced button.
7. Select the Effective Permissions tab.
8. Click Select.
9. Select the user or group whose effective permissions you want to view.
10. Click OK to view them, as shown in Figure 7.5.

Figure 7.5: Effective Permissions tab

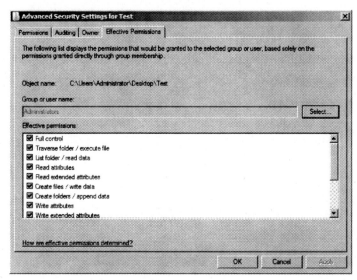

Notice in Figure 7.5 that on the Effective Permissions tab you can view both standard and special permissions for the user or group that you select. This can be a very valuable tool to aid you in determining the permissions on an NTFS folder.

Take Ownership of an NTFS Folder

By now you may have noticed that a set of default permissions is given to each folder created in an NTFS file system. There is a special set of permissions given to the creator of an NTFS folder. These permissions can be defined as "ownership" of the folder. The owner of the folder has full control of the folder and both its standard and special permissions. The Administrators group is also given special permissions, including the permission to take ownership of the folder. This means that at any given point in time anyone in the Administrators group might choose to take ownership of an NTFS folder and thus take control of its associated permissions. In order to take ownership of a folder, though, you need to have that special permission assigned to your user or group. If you do not have permissions to take ownership of a folder, you cannot simply "force" your way to ownership. By the same token, if you are the owner, you can deny the ability to take ownership to all parties with the exception of yourself. Now that's control!

Data Access and Management

PART III

If you have the permission to take ownership, the process works like this:

1. Open Windows Explorer.
2. Locate the desired folder.
3. Right-click the folder.
4. Choose Properties.
5. Select the Security tab.
6. Click the Advanced button.
7. Select the Owner tab.
8. Click Edit. You'll see Figure 7.6.

Figure 7.6: Taking ownership

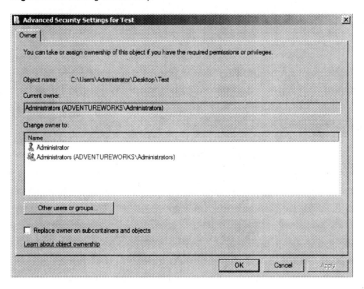

Notice that when you click Edit, the current owner is displayed, and the users or groups that can take ownership are displayed in the Change Owner To box. It is also important to consider the Replace Owner On Subcontainers And Objects check box. If you take ownership of a folder, you also have the option to take ownership of the folders beneath it in the hierarchy. This may be desirable if your intent is to take control of a section of the file system.

NTFS folder and file permissions are a great way to control permissions to a local resource. The problem you will have is that in a network environment the users are almost never sitting at the server where the resources are located. How do you provide access and permission controls for folders that are not on the same physical system that the user is on? You share them!

Share Folders

Sharing a folder makes it visible and accessible to the users and groups that have been granted share-level permissions across the network. Share-level permissions are different from NTFS permissions. NTFS permissions are rooted in the file system, while share permissions provide for network accessibility to a folder. When you implement folder sharing, you will also set permissions for each of the shares that are created in your network.

Create a Shared Folder

When you are ready to start making folders available across your network, you will need to do the following:

1. Open Windows Explorer.
2. Locate the desired folder.
3. Right-click the folder.
4. Choose Properties.
5. Select the Sharing tab.
6. Click Share. The File Sharing dialog box will open (see Figure 7.7).
7. Type in the name of the user or group with whom the folder will be shared, and click Add.

   By default the user permissions will be assigned as Read unless you change them to Read/Write.

8. Set the desired permission level.
9. Click the Share button.

   Notice that the network path to the share is displayed.

10. Click Done.

Data Access and Management

PART III

Figure 7.7: File Sharing dialog box

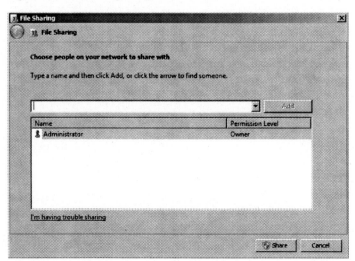

Once a folder is shared, it becomes accessible from other network locations. The permissions on the share provide some degree of control on the level of access to the folder.

Share permissions are implemented with either an Allow or Deny option. The levels of permission are Full Control, Change, and Read.

Implement Advanced Sharing

To implement advanced sharing, follow these steps:

1. Open Windows Explorer.

2. Locate the desired folder.

3. Right-click the folder.

4. Choose Properties.

5. Select the Sharing tab.

6. Click the Advanced Sharing button. The Advanced Sharing dialog box will open (see Figure 7.8).

   At this point, you have the option to select the box to share the folder. One of the great features of using advanced sharing is the ability to limit the number of simultaneous users on a shared folder. You will notice that by default "only" 16,777,216 users can connect to this share. That seems a little high to us. Change that to a number that is appropriate for your share.

7. Click the Permissions button.

8. Click Add to include users or groups for permissions to this share.

9. Click OK to close the Permissions dialog box.

10. Click OK to close the Advanced Sharing dialog box.

Figure 7.8: Advanced Sharing dialog box

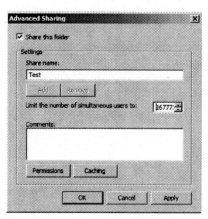

We know you saw that extra button labeled Caching and wondered why it was there. In short, caching can make the share available to users when they are not actually connected to the network. There will be more detail on offline file caching later in the chapter.

Resolve Permission Conflicts

When you implement shared folders from an NTFS file system, there are two different permissions that are going to be applied to each user or group that attempts access to the folder. If these two types of permissions are *complementary*, meaning that they are both set to allow the same level of access, then there are no real issues to address. However, if there is a difference in the level of permissions assigned, then the level of access will be limited.

When resolving disparate permissions in shared NTFS folders, a couple of simple rules make this process easy to understand:

- *Rule 1*: Deny permissions always override Allow permissions.

- *Rule 2*: When the share and NTFS permissions are different from one another, the most restrictive permission will be applied.

Data Access and Management

PART III

Let's say you had a shared folder that had a test user who was assigned Read permissions to the share. The same test user is also assigned Write permissions to the NTFS folder. The two permissions are not complementary, so the most restrictive takes precedent. The user would have an effective permission of Read.

Let's say that test user 2 has Full Control permission on the same share and has been denied Read access on the NTFS folder. These permissions are definitely not complementary, and the Deny permission would override Allow Full Control. The effective permission would be Deny Read.

These two simple rules will suffice to handle the vast majority of cases in which permissions are not complementary between NTFS and shared folders. The recommendation is that you plan as you assign permissions to folders in NTFS and folder shares.

Configure Offline File Caching

In today's business world, you need access to information from many different locations. You aren't always connected to the network that hosts your folders and file shares. If you take your laptop with you when you leave your network, why not take the essential files that you need with you too? With offline file caching, you can do just that.

Working with offline file caching is really pretty simple. You choose the files and folders that you want to make available offline. Windows Server will automatically create a copy of each file or folder as you connect to it and store it on your computer. These files are called *offline files*. The files can be opened, modified, and saved the same way as if you were connected to your network. This means that the caching is completely transparent to the user accessing the files. If the user accessed the files by going to \\fileserver\share when connected to the network, they could also type the same path when off the network and the files would still be accessible. When you are offline, any changes that are made to these files will be stored on your local computer and then will be synchronized the next time you connect to your network.

Before you can use offline files on your server, you will need to enable Desktop Experience under Features in Server Manager. Without this feature enabled, offline files will not be an available option for you to enable. Offline files must be enabled before they can be used. To enable offline files, follow these steps:

1. Click Start.

2. Type **manage offline files** in the search box.

3. Press Enter.

4. Click Enable Offline Files, as shown in Figure 7.9.

5. Restart the computer.

Figure 7.9: Offline Files dialog box

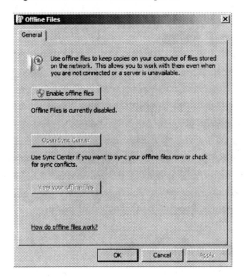

Once offline files have been enabled, you can right-click any file or folder and select the option to make the files always available. These files will be copied to your local machine for use offline. In the case of a shared folder, you can click the Caching button to enable offline files for the share. It is also possible to make offline files available through the use of Group Policy objects (GPOs). If you had implemented folder redirection using GPOs, for example, those redirected folders would be made available using offline files.

When you use offline files, there is a potential for multiple versions of the same file. If you have a file and are working with it offline and another user in your network makes changes to the file in its online version, there is going to be a conflict. You can resolve these conflicts using a tool called the Sync Center. You can find the Sync Center in the Control Panel. The Sync Center is responsible for more than managing conflicts. It is responsible for keeping offline files synchronized with their online counterparts each time you connect to the network.

You can also access the Sync Center through the Manage Offline Files tool. The Manage Offline Files tool has a component that will allow you to view all your offline files. This allows you to see folders, mapped network drives, and shares that you are caching for offline access.

Secure Folders and Files

Files and folders contain data. That data may be innocuous data that you use regularly and that requires little or no protection, or it might be critically sensitive data requiring extensive protection. In each case, you will need to implement a strategy to protect your sensitive data. A strategy for protecting data will include but not be limited to a structured design for permissions, storage, encryption, and auditing. So far, this chapter has addressed permissions. Storage will be addressed in Chapters 8 and 9, which cover backups and disk management, respectively. That leaves encryption and auditing. You will need to understand both.

Configure the Encrypting File System

The Encrypting File System (EFS) is a feature of Windows that you can use to encrypt files and folders on your hard drive to provide a secure format of storage. EFS is a core file encryption technology used only on NTFS volumes. An encrypted file cannot be used unless the user has access to the keys required to decrypt the file. The files do not have to be manually encrypted or decrypted each time you use them. They will open and close just like any other file. Once EFS is enabled, the encryption is transparent to the user.

Using EFS is similar to using permissions on NTFS files or folders. However, a user who gets physical access to encrypted files would still be unable to read them because they are stored in an encrypted form.

You can encrypt or decrypt files or folders by setting the encryption property attribute for the file or folder. The encryption property is an attribute that is applied much like the attributes of read-only, compressed, or hidden files or folders, as shown in Figure 7.10.

To encrypt a file or folder, follow these steps:

1. Select the file or folder you want to encrypt.

2. Right-click the file or folder.

3. Choose Properties.

4. Click the Advanced button.

5. Select the Encrypt Contents To Secure Data box.

Figure 7.10: Advanced Attributes dialog box

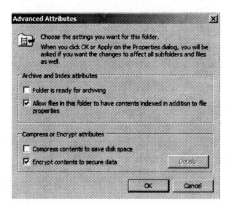

It is important to note that the attributes of compression and encryption are mutually exclusive of one another. You cannot do both. If you have a file that is compressed and you decide you want to encrypt it, you must remove the compression bit before the file can be encrypted, and vice versa.

The following are some additional considerations when using EFS:

- Only files and folders on NTFS volumes can be encrypted. You can use Web Distributed Authoring and Versioning (WebDAV), which also works in NTFS volumes to transfer encrypted files and folders in their encrypted form.

- Encrypted files and folders are decrypted if you move them to a volume that is not NTFS.

Data Access and Management

PART III

- Moving unencrypted files or folders into a folder that has been encrypted will result in the encryption of the moved files or folders; however, the reverse is not true. Files or folders that are moved from an encrypted NTFS folder to an unencrypted folder will *not* automatically be decrypted. Files must be explicitly decrypted.

- Files marked with the system files attribute and files residing in the system root directory structure cannot be encrypted with EFS.

- Marking the encryption attribute of a file or folder does not prevent a user with the appropriate NTFS permissions from deleting or listing files or directories if their NTFS permissions allow those functions. Use EFS in conjunction with NTFS permissions.

- You can encrypt or decrypt files and folders on a remote computer that has been enabled for remote encryption. When you do, the data is transmitted over the network in its decrypted form. Other protocols such as Secure Sockets Layer (SSL) or Internet Protocol Security (IPsec) must be used to encrypt the traffic.

As you would expect, you can also implement EFS through the use of Group Policy. These settings are located in Computer Configuration\ Windows Settings\Security Settings\Public Key Policies\Encrypting File System.

Through these settings, you can choose whether you want to allow or deny the use of EFS for your entire network. You can also choose to allow or deny the use of Elliptic Curve Cryptography (ECC) encryption. ECC allows your network to be complaint with Suite B encryption standards. Suite B standards meet the Advanced Encryption Standard (AES) with key sizes of 128 and 256 bits for symmetric encryption, Elliptical Curve Digital Signature Algorithm (ECDSA) for digital signatures, Elliptic Curve Diffie-Hellman (ECDH) for key agreement, and Secure Hash Algorithm (SHA-256 and SHA-384) for message digest.

EFS is a great tool to help you secure files and folders. As you implement an EFS program in your network environment, you can provide access to files and folders while maintaining very good security for those same files and folders.

But what about those system files?

Configure BitLocker Drive Encryption

In the previous section, you learned that EFS will not provide encryption to any files marked with the system attribute or files located in the system root directory. So, what do you do with them? How do you secure the system files? The answer is a tool called BitLocker. BitLocker was designed to encrypt the partition on which the operating system files reside. Unlike EFS, which allows the user to pick and choose files and folders for encryption, BitLocker encrypts entire partitions or drives. BitLocker can be used to encrypt the locally attached drives, while a tool called BitLocker To Go can be used to encrypt devices such as USB sticks that may be temporarily attached to the system. If a hacker were to attempt to get at your system files, the files would be encrypted. If your drive were stolen and put into another machine, the data would be inaccessible. BitLocker makes use of a hardware module on the motherboard called a Trusted Platform Module (TPM) chip. BitLocker uses it to seal the keys that are used to unlock the encrypted operating system drive. When you start your operating system, BitLocker requests the key from the TPM chip and then uses it to unlock the drive.

When using a BitLocker-encrypted drive, if you add new files to the drive, they are automatically encrypted. Drives (fixed or removable) can be unlocked with a password or a smart card, or you can set the drive to automatically unlock when you log onto the computer.

BitLocker can be used in conjunction with EFS. We recommend a strategy that maximizes the security needs of your data, while minimizing the impact on the users who will need access to that data.

Turn On BitLocker

BitLocker sounds like a good idea, but how exactly do you turn it on?

First you will need to turn on the TPM chip in your system BIOS. This is required for use of BitLocker in Windows Server 2008 R2. Next you will need to add the BitLocker feature through Server Manager and install it:

1. Open Server Manager.

2. Right-click Features.

Data Access and Management

PART III

3. Click Add Features.

4. Select BitLocker Drive Encryption, as shown in Figure 7.11.

5. Restart your computer.

6. Close the Server Manager window.

7. Click Start.

8. Type **BitLocker** in the search box.

9. Hit Enter to open the BitLocker Drive Encryption tool, as shown in Figure 7.12.

   Figure 7.12 shows the BitLocker Drive Encryption tool. It is not a bad idea to click What Should I Know About BitLocker Drive Encryption Before I Turn It On? to read more about it. There is some very good information there. Once you are comfortable with the fact that you will be encrypting your drive, you can continue.

10. Click Turn On BitLocker.

    Just after adding the BitLocker feature, although you may have multiple drives and partitions on your system, only the system partition is available for BitLocker. After you turn on BitLocker and encrypt the system partition, the other drives and partitions will then show up in the list as available for BitLocker encryption.

11. Click Yes to start the BitLocker setup.

12. If you haven't turned on TPM in the BIOS, you will be prompted to do so now, and the process will actually be automated for you. Click Yes. (This is kind of cool.)

13. Log back on to your computer.

14. BitLocker will prompt you to encrypt the drive.

15. Click Next.

    At this point, BitLocker asks how you want to store your recovery key (Figure 7.13). This is important! If your BitLocker drive becomes inaccessible, you are going to need this key.

16. Pick the option that works best for you, and click Next.

17. Select the box to run the BitLocker system check.

18. Click Start Encrypting.

Figure 7.11: Installing BitLocker Drive Encryption

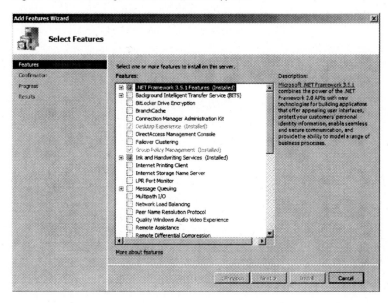

Figure 7.12: Turning on BitLocker Drive Encryption tool

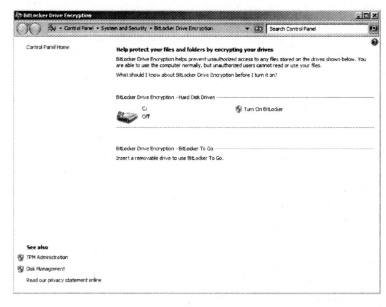

Figure 7.13: Recovery key storage options

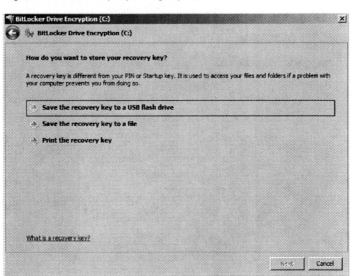

At this point, the drive will begin its encryption process. Some words to the wise: do not do the initial BitLocker drive encryption on your key servers during peak operating hours. The initial encryption takes some time and will slow down your performance. Find a time when the servers are less busy and initialize BitLocker on them then.

BitLocker can now be configured for other drives and partitions on your system using the same BitLocker Drive Encryption tool.

Recover BitLocker

We don't need to tell you that sometimes things can go wrong with servers. What do you do if things go wrong with a server that is running BitLocker?

What if the TPM module that contains the keys necessary to start the operating system is unavailable? What if your user forgets their PIN? What if the hardware crashes on the box and you are trying to salvage the hard disk?

Luckily, there is a system for recovering BitLocker. The process relies on one very important component, the recovery key. When you turned on BitLocker, you were prompted for a location in which to store the BitLocker recovery key. If you have access to this key, you are well on your way to recovering the BitLocker drive. The process is simple and straightforward:

1. Boot the computer.

2. The computer will present a message indicating that it cannot locate the keys necessary to start decrypting the operating system. One of your options will be to recover BitLocker.

3. Type in the 48-digit (yes, 48 digits) recovery key.

4. The system will decrypt and start the operating system as normal.

At this point, you will need to make some decisions. If you still have the original key, you can reestablish connectivity to that key. If you do not have the original key, you will need to generate a new one by turning off BitLocker, which will decrypt the drive, and then turn BitLocker back on to create a new set of keys for the system.

Use the BitLocker To Go Tool

BitLocker To Go introduces the benefits of an encrypted partition to a removable drive. Instead of using a file encryption tool, you can use BitLocker to encrypt the contents of a removable drive. This drive could be a USB device, a memory stick, an SD card, or some other type of removable storage. The benefit of using BitLocker To Go is that you can enjoy the ease and portability of a USB storage device without worrying about the data on that device falling into the wrong hands. If someone were to steal the device, the data would be encrypted and therefore inaccessible.

Once you have added and enabled the BitLocker feature on your Windows Server 2008 R2 machine, you will notice that there is an option in the BitLocker Drive Encryption tool called BitLocker To Go. If you insert a removable storage device, that device will be added to the tool as an additional drive under the BitLocker To Go section, shown in Figure 7.14.

Data Access and Management

PART III

Figure 7.14: BitLocker To Go tool

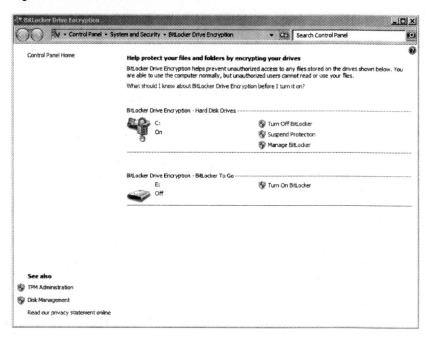

At this point, you can simply click the link to turn on BitLocker for the removable drive. The setup tool will prompt you to start BitLocker setup for this drive.

BitLocker To Go is a little bit different from the traditional BitLocker tool in that there is no TPM chip to hold keys for BitLocker To Go. You will need to make a choice about how you want to unlock the drive. It can be unlocked through the use of a password that you supply during setup or through the use of a smart card and PIN.

Just like traditional BitLocker, there is also a recovery key associated with BitLocker To Go. Save this file carefully to a location where you will not lose it, or better yet, print it and add it to your network log book. Remember, if the drive becomes inaccessible for whatever reason, the recovery key is your only ticket back to that data.

The drive will be encrypted in much the same way as your system drive was encrypted, albeit probably a little quicker since the size of the removable device is likely much smaller than your system drive.

Once the drive is encrypted, when the user plugs the drive into a physical machine, they will be prompted for the password or smartcard

PIN in order to unlock the drive. Any files that are copied or moved to the drive will be encrypted.

BitLocker To Go provides excellent security to files and folders stored on a removable drive.

One of the cool things about BitLocker To Go is that you can use Group Policy to require BitLocker To Go in order to use thumb drives and require that the keys are stored in Active Directory.

Implement the Distributed File System

If you are trying to make data accessible, you have lots of options such as creating shared folders and using offline files. If you want to extend the availability of your files and folders, you might consider building more than one server to house the same data and then copying or replicating that data between the various servers so that it stays consistent. Replicating data to multiple servers increases data availability and gives users in remote sites fast, reliable access to files. Replication is configured via Distributed File System (DFS) namespaces. DFS namespaces allow you to group shared folders located on different servers by transparently connecting them to one or more namespaces. A *namespace* is a virtual view of shared folders in an organization. When you create a namespace, you select which shared folders to add to the namespace, design the hierarchy in which those folders appear, and determine the names that the shared folders show in the namespace. When a user views the namespace, the folders appear to reside on a single, high-capacity hard disk. Users can navigate the namespace without needing to know the server names or shared folders hosting the data.

The path to a namespace is similar to a universal naming convention (UNC) path of a shared folder, such as \\server1\shares\test. If you are familiar with UNC paths, you know that, in this example, the shared folder, Shares, and its subfolder, Test, are all hosted on the server called server1. Now, assume you want to give users a single place to locate data, but you want to host data on different servers for availability and performance purposes. To do this, you can deploy a namespace.

To build a namespace, you will need a namespace server. A namespace server hosts a namespace. The namespace server can be a member server or a domain controller.

Data Access and Management

PART III

To install DFS, you will need to add the DFS role located under File Services in Server Manager:

1. Open Server Manager.

2. Right-click Roles.

3. Choose Add Roles.

4. Select File Services.

5. Click Next.

6. Check the box to add the Distributed File System.

   This will add both the DFS Namespaces and DFS Replication role services.

7. Click Next.

8. Click Create A Namespace Later Using The DFS Management snap-in in Server Manager.

9. Click Next.

10. Click Install.

11. Click Close.

Configure a DFS Namespace

After you have installed the DFS role service, you can begin the process of creating the DFS namespace and configuring the DFS root:

1. Open Server Manager.

2. Expand Roles.

3. Expand File Services.

4. Select the DFS Management snap-in.

5. Click New Namespace.

6. Type the name of the server, or click Browse to select it from a list (see Figure 7.15).

7. Click Next.

8. Type a name for the namespace. This is what the users will see after the server name in the UNC path. If you want to edit the settings of this share, you can click the Edit Settings button to change those settings.

9. Click Next.

Figure 7.15: Creating a new namespace

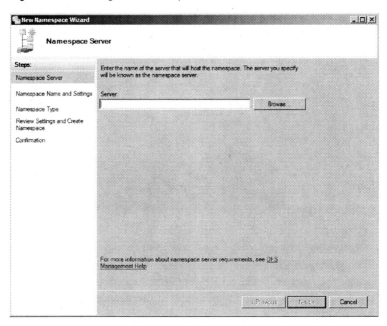

At this point, you are prompted to choose the type of namespace. You can choose either a domain-based namespace or a stand-alone namespace. The domain-based namespace begins with a domain name, and its metadata is stored in Active Directory. A domain-based namespace can be hosted on multiple namespace servers. A stand-alone namespace is stored only on the namespace server, but it can be hosted on a server cluster. The path begins with the namespace server name. A dedicated namespace server should be used to host a namespace that contains more than 5,000 replicated folders. Figure 7.16 summarizes the settings and creates the namespace.

Figure 7.16: Reviewing the DFS settings and creating the namespace

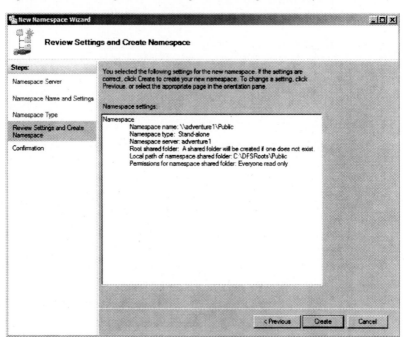

You have just successfully created your first DFS namespace. This namespace is called the *DFS root*. When you expand the DFS Management tool in the Server Manager and then expand Namespaces, you will see the existing namespaces. The namespace is really just the location that will be used to hold targets that will point to the location of resources located elsewhere on the network. A folder may have one or more folder targets that may be added using the Add Folder Tool displayed in Figure 7.17.

This is where you start to see the real potential of DFS. If you have more than one target location that hosts shared data, you can configure multiple targets for the same folder in your DFS namespace. The namespace will route requests from users to the appropriate folder target based on the site information for that user. This way, you can maintain multiple shared folders containing the same data and maximize referrals to users using DFS namespaces. We know what you are thinking here. What happens if a user changes the contents of one of the shares? How will the other targets be updated? Not to worry, there is a built-in replication system in DFS called Distributed File System Replication (DFSR).

Figure 7.17: Adding a new folder to DFS

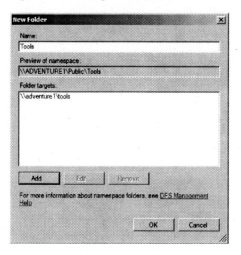

DFSR uses something called Remote Differential Compression (RDC), which replicates only the changes in files. In Windows Server 2008 R2, DFSR can even replicate SYSVOL using RDC, resulting in a dramatic reduction in bandwidth consumption while maintaining the integrity of your folder targets.

Configure Replication Groups

Replication groups define the relationships that DFS will use to replicate data between partners in a DFS replication topology. You will choose the partnerships and the types of replication that occur between those partners.

1. Open the DFS Management tool, select Replication.

2. In the Actions pane, select New Replication Group.

3. Select the type of replication group.

4. Click Next.

5. Type a name and a description, and select the domain for the replication group.

6. Click Next.

7. Click Add to select two or more servers to become members of the replication group.

Data Access and Management

PART III

8. Click Next.

9. Select a topology for replication.

10. Select a replication schedule. This is one of the coolest things about DFSR. You can pick the amount of bandwidth that will be used by DFSR and the schedule for when the replication will occur.

11. Click Next.

12. Use the drop-down menu to select a primary member.

    When you first set up replication, you must choose a primary member. Choose the member that has the most up-to-date files that you want replicated to all other members of the replication group, because the primary member's content is considered "authoritative." This means that during initial replication, the primary member's files will always win the conflict resolution that occurs when the receiving members have files that are older or newer than the same files on the primary server. After the initialization of the replicated folder, the "primary member" designation is removed. The member that was previously the primary member is then treated like any other member, and its files are no longer considered authoritative over those of other members who have completed initial replication.

13. Select the path to the folders that you want to replicate.

14. Click Next.

15. Define the local path on the other servers for the folder you want to replicate on the other members of the replication group.

16. Click Next.

17. Review the summary settings for the replication group, as shown in Figure 7.18.

18. Click Create.

19. Review the results of the wizard, and click Close.

Please keep in mind at this point that the replication will not start immediately. Based on the settings and schedule that you provided during setup, the initial replication will proceed when DFSR is ready and only after the new configuration settings have been picked up by all the members of the replication group. This can take some time depending on how your Active Directory replication is occurring.

Figure 7.18: Summary settings to create replication group

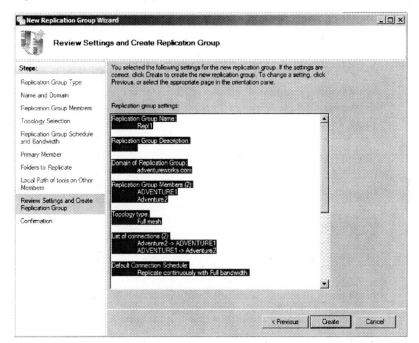

Enable Previous Versions of Files

So, let's say you have been working for the past few hours modifying a file. Your boss calls and says he would like a copy of the same file you are working on only without all the current changes. If you were really lucky, you used Save As and started your editing with a new file. (We know that's not very likely.) But if you had enabled previous versions, you could simply smile and say, "Sure, Boss! The file is on its way."

You can use the previous versions feature to allow your users to access previous versions of their files and folders that they have stored on the network. The service that is working behind the scenes to make this all possible is called the Volume Shadow Copy Service. To use previous version of files and folders, you will need to enable shadow copies of shared folders on the file server.

1. Click Start.

2. Navigate to Administrative Tools, and then click Computer Management.

3. In the console tree, right-click Shared Folders.

4. Go to All Tasks, and click Configure Shadow Copies.

5. Select the drive on which you want to enable shadow copies.

6. Click Enable.

   You are going to get a notice warning you of the potential problems of enabling shadow copies on servers that have high I/O loads. Heed the warning, as shown in Figure 7.19.

7. Click Yes to enable shadow copies.

Figure 7.19: Shadow copies warning

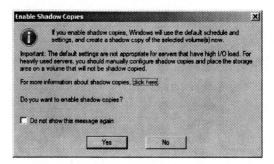

Now your enabled shares will maintain previous versions of files.

Restore a Previous Version

Restoring previous versions of files and folders is a pretty straightforward process:

1. Locate the file or folder you want to restore.

2. Right-click, and choose Properties.

3. Click the Previous Versions tab.

4. Select the version of the file that you want to restore.

   A warning message will appear about restoring a previous version of a file or folder.

5. Click Restore.

It is really important to understand this point! Restoring a previous version will delete the current version. When you restore the shadow copy, you will replace the current version with the file or folder at a previous point in time, and your changes since that point in time will be lost. To avoid losing your changes, you can choose to copy the previous version to a different location, thus preserving your changes and allowing you to use the previous version as well.

These are a few other things to consider when working with previous versions:

- If the Previous Versions tab does not appear in the Properties dialog box, then shadow copies might not be enabled on that server. Remember that shadow copies are enabled on a server-by-server basis.

- If there are no previous versions listed on the Previous Versions tab, then that file has not changed since the oldest copy was created. The Previous Versions tab shows only unique versions of the file.

- When you restore a file to its existing folder, the file permissions will not change. When you copy a previous version to a new folder location, the files will inherit the permissions of the target folder.

- If you choose to restore a large folder, it will put a heavy workload on the file server and can result in previous versions being deleted. Best practice is to restore individual files instead of folders or directories.

- Previous files should not be used as a substitute for a good backup solution!

The previous versions feature is an excellent resource for your network. It enables users to manage basic recovery operations of shared files and folders.

Data Access and Management

PART III

8

Backing Up and Recovering Your Server

Accidents happen. There are many scenarios in which data can get lost, deleted, infected, or corrupted—from a user accidently deleting a file to a hard drive failing to an operating system failing to a full disaster scenario during which Mother Nature decides to go after your data. It is time for you to shine as the hero for your data and bring it back!

One of the most important tasks you need to perform as an administrator is backing up your server. Performing regular backups on your server is a necessity to help protect you from any number of potential problems. Backups can save you time and money, and, more important, they allow you to sleep well at night. If you have performed proper backups and are proficient in the proper procedures to restore your data, you can quickly identify the proper backup media to begin recovering the data. No one wants to spend thousands of dollars to pay a recovery company to bring back data that you could retrieve yourself with the proper safety measures in place.

Backing up your data is just one part of the process. Learning recovery techniques is just as important. Understanding recovery techniques goes hand in hand with understanding backup solutions. Also, in certain situations you may be able to enable your users to help recover their own lost data. If you know your backup procedures backward and forward, this will allow you to get your recovery operation underway quickly and properly.

Knowing the terminology and when and where to perform backups will allow you to perform the task of backing up and recovering your date efficiently and effectively. This will also allow you to establish proper policies and procedures to gain consistency in protecting your organization. In this chapter, you will learn the tools and terminology behind performing backups and recovery.

Understand Backup and Recovery

In this section, you will learn the terminology behind backup and recovery, as well as the many tools at your disposal to perform the tasks necessary to protect your data. The tools you will see in this chapter are all built in to your Windows Server 2008 R2 server, so they will incur you no additional costs. In fact, not having your data protected using these simple tools can definitely have some cost consequences.

In Windows Server 2008 R2, Microsoft has made several improvements to the backup tool. You now have the ability to back up specific files and folders. In Windows Server 2008 RTM, you had to back up an entire volume. In Windows Server 2008 R2, you can include or exclude folders or individual files. You can also exclude files based on the file types, and you can perform incremental backups of system state. Previously, you could only perform a full backup of the system state by using the wbadmin.exe utility. Now you can perform incremental backups of the system state by using the Windows Server Backup utility, the wbadmin.exe utility, or a PowerShell cmdlet. You can also perform scheduled backups to volumes or network shares. Lastly, Windows Server 2008 R2 has built-in PowerShell cmdlets for managing backups and restores.

Understand Backup and Recovery Terminology

When working with backup and recovery technologies in Windows Server 2008 R2 or any Windows environment, it is necessary to learn the lingo used by the operating system. Table 8.1 defines some of the key terms you will see used throughout this chapter.

Table 8.1: Backup Terms

Term	Definition
Normal or full backup	Normal backups, sometimes known as full backups, are the slowest for the backup process to complete. The time your backup will take is determined by how much data you are backing up. However, if you can perform a normal backup every night and have it completed during off-hours, this is the preferred way to protect your system. This is also the default setting for Windows Server Backup.
Incremental backup	Incremental backups are the fastest backup process because this type of backup tracks only the changes to your data since the last backup of any kind. Incremental backups will also control how your restore process will work. When you want to restore data with incremental backups, you first need to restore the latest normal backup followed by all the incremental backup sets in order. This method may also impact your servers' performance.

Table 8.1: Backup Terms *(continued)*

Term	Definition
System state	System state contains most of the system's configuration information. It does not contain all the needed configuration for your system; you should always consider using this in conjunction with a full backup. Also, the roles you currently have installed on the server will determine what components make up the system state. See the "Perform a System State Backup" section to see what is backed up.
Bare-metal recovery	A bare-metal recovery allows you to recover a full server environment based on a backed-up image you had created previously (without first installing an OS). This allows you to recover a server that may otherwise have been inoperable because of any number of errors that a regular backup and recovery could not fix. Bare-metal recovery is one of your last lines of recovery to bring back a failed system.
Shadow copies	Shadow copies are point-in-time copies of data typically located on file shares. A shadow copy provides your users with a self-service method of recovering files they have deleted or overwritten accidentally.
Volume Shadow Copy Service (VSS)	VSS is the master service inside Windows Server 2008 R2 governing the majority of the backup infrastructure. It is also the service providing you with the ability to create shadow copies.

Use Backup and Recovery Tools

Three tools allow you to access the backup and recovery tool set in Windows Server 2008 R2. You have a fully functioning GUI management tool called Windows Server Backup, you have a command-line tool called wbadmin.exe, and lastly you have PowerShell cmdlets at your disposal to perform these commands. On a Windows Server 2008 R2 Server Core installation, you only have wpadmin.exe and PowerShell cmdlets to back up a Server Core installation.

In addition to these tools, another valuable tool you can leverage to help protect data located in the file shares is Volume Shadow Copy Service. This tool creates point-in-time backup copies of your file on shared resources. This powerful utility gives your users the ability to protect themselves from accidentally deleting or overwriting files and even allows them to compare versions of a file.

Install Windows Server Backup Tools on a Full Server

Before you can use any of these tools, you need to first install the tools on their respective server environments. Even though you will see the Windows Server Backup utility in the administrative tools on your Windows Server 2008 R2 server, the feature is not installed by default, and you will see a message similar to Figure 8.1 when you first try to run it.

Figure 8.1: Windows Server Backup message

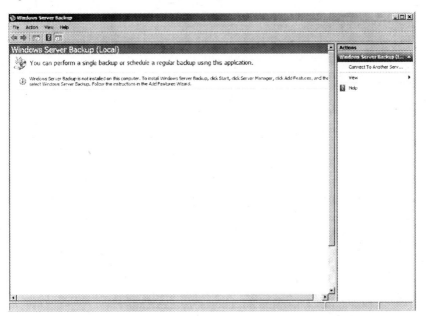

To install the tools, you just need to install the built-in Windows Server 2008 R2 feature:

1. Open Server Manager.

2. Click Features in the tree menu on the left.

3. Click Add Features in the details pane on the right to begin the installation.

4. Scroll down the feature list to find Windows Server Backup Features. Click the + sign next to the feature name. You will see you have two options to install, as shown in Figure 8.2.

Figure 8.2: Installing Windows Server Backup

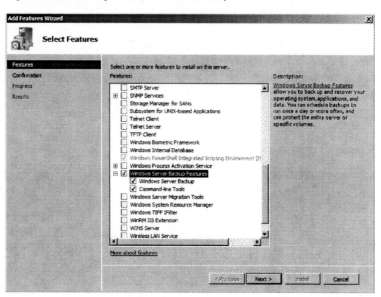

The Windows Server Backup choice installs the GUI management tool for your backup administration, and the Command-Line Tools option installs the wbadmin.exe command-line tool and the PowerShell cmdlets.

5. Select the management tools you want to install, and click Next.

6. Review the Confirm Installation Selections screen, and when ready, click Install to install the backup tools.

7. After the installation completes, click Close to use the tools.

Install Windows Server Backup Tools on Core Server

Windows Server Core has the same built-in backup tools and functionality as a full Windows Server 2008 R2 server installation. Because of the nature of the Server Core installation, there is no GUI tool; however, you can install either the wbadmin.exe command-line tool or the PowerShell backup cmdlets. Just like the Windows Server 2008 R2 full installation, the backup tools are not installed by default.

1. Log on your Server Core server.

2. Type the following command and hit Enter to see the current state of the backup tools (as well as other features installed on Server Core):

   ```
   dism /online /get-features
   ```

   You are looking for the two features called WindowsServerBackup and WindowsServerBackupCommandlet, and by default the current state for both will be Disabled.

3. Type in one or both of the following commands to install the backup tools on the Server Core server.

   To install the wbadmin.exe tool, type the following command, and hit Enter:

   ```
   dism /online /enable-feature
   /featurename:WindowsServerBackup
   ```

   Make sure you have enabled PowerShell on your Windows Server 2008 R2 server before you install the backup cmdlets. To install the PowerShell commands for backup, type the following command, and hit Enter:

   ```
   dism /online /enable-feature
   /featurename:WindowsServerBackupCommandlet
   ```

4. To verify the tools installed properly, you can run the following command and hit Enter. You will see the current state of your backup tools as Enabled, and you will see a screen similar to Figure 8.3.

   ```
   dism /online /get-features
   ```

Figure 8.3: Server Core backup tools enabled

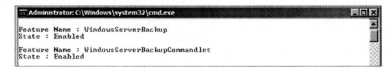

Data Access and Management

PART III

Enable Shadow Copies

Shadow copies help protect data located in the file shares and drives of your Windows Server 2008 R2 server. Shadow copies are point-in-time backup copies of your files on shared resources. They're enabled at the volume level. This means that when you enable this on a volume you protect all the resources and shares residing on the volume. While you cannot select individual shares to turn this on or off for, you will still be able to recover information individually if needed because the volume is protected.

When a shadow copy is created for a file, only the incremental changes are stored for the file. This means the amount of storage needed for your network could be minimal, based on how many files and changes are made to the files. The copies you create can be stored on the same volume the data is stored. You can move the shadow copies to another volume, which will help the performance of the shadow copies and the volumes themselves. Before you enable shadow copies, you should also be aware you can have only 64 copies on the volume at one time. This will impact the schedule you choose as well, which is Monday through Friday from 7 a.m. to 12 p.m. (noon) by default. Shadow copies are run by the Volume Shadow Copy Service (VSS). When you enable shadow copies, there is a 100MB backup file automatically created. Additionally, by default the maximum size used for the backups is set to 10 percent of the volume's total space. What this means is that if you run out of space, VSS will start deleting older versions of your shadow copies.

Allowing your users to work quickly with these volumes will save you from having to use your recovery media to help restore lost data. However, shadow copies are not a replacement for your current backup and recovery implementation. Rather, they provide a nice complement for your backup and recovery tool belt.

For more information on Shadow Copy, take a look at the following:

```
http://technet.microsoft.com/en-us/library/cc771305.aspx
```

Enabling shadow copies is just a matter of enabling the volume, and you can do this for both Windows Server 2008 R2 full and Server Core installations.

1. Open Computer Management by selecting Start ➪ Administrative Tools ➪ Computer Management.

2. In the Computer Management tree on the left, right-click Shared Folders, and select All Tasks ⇨ Configure Shadow Copies. You will see a screen similar to Figure 8.4.

Figure 8.4: Enabling shadow copies

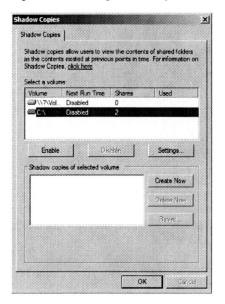

3. Select the volume where the shares are located that you want to enable this feature on.

4. To modify the settings for shadow copies, click Settings; you will see a screen similar to Figure 8.5. The Settings screen will allow you to control the location and schedule for the shadow copies. You can change the storage location for the shadow copies only when they are disabled on the volume. So, you want to make sure you change the location of the shadow copy storage before you enable shadow copies.

Data Access and Management

PART III

Figure 8.5: Shadow copy settings

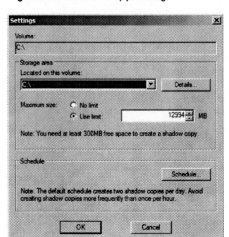

5. After you have modified the settings, click Enable to enable shadow copies on your selected volume; you will see the warning shown in Figure 8.6.

Figure 8.6: Shadow copy warning

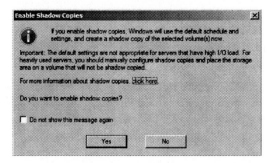

6. Click Yes to enable shadow copies. You can also select the Do Not Show This Message Again check box to not see the warning again.

Manage Backup and Recovery

Now that you have seen some of the tools for backups and recovery, it is time to put them to use. When you perform backups traditionally, you want to have the backups on a schedule so you are sure they are happening at regular intervals. This will make finding the right media for recovery easy. Even though backup and recovery are performed separately, they are joined together in form and function. The type of backup you perform will always dictate the recovery options available to you. In reality, the backup strategy is determined by your recovery requirements and what your service-level agreement is with your users and business. Is it OK if a user has to wait 24 hours to recover a file? What if the user is the CEO? Is it OK to turn off a server during work hours? What if the server is mission critical to your organization? These are all key questions, among many others, that you need to address when defining your policies and procedures and determining the best way to handle the needs of your organization.

Whether you choose to perform backup and recovery tasks with the GUI, command-line tool, or the PowerShell cmdlets, you are essentially performing the same task. In this section, you will learn how to use the backup and recovery tools to perform your daily tasks. Not that to perform either backup or recovery, you do need to be a member of the Backup Operators or Administrators groups.

Back Up Your Server

After you have determined your backup strategy, it is time to back up the server. When you back up your server, you want to make sure you schedule your backup times to not impact your network or your users. Try to schedule the backups after-hours, when the system is being used the least. You also want to make sure your backups complete in a timely manner; this is where knowing the difference between full and incremental backups can offer value to you and your organization.

Configure Backup Settings

Before you perform your backup, you may need to define your backup settings. You have only a few selections to make to configure your backup. Specifically, you need to determine whether you want to perform a full/normal backup, an incremental backup, or a custom combination of both of these methods. To configure your server, perform the following steps:

1. Start Windows Server Backup by selecting Start ⇨ Administrative Tools ⇨ Windows Server Backup.

2. In the right Actions task pane, click Configure Performance Settings; you will see a screen similar to Figure 8.7.

Figure 8.7: Backup performance settings

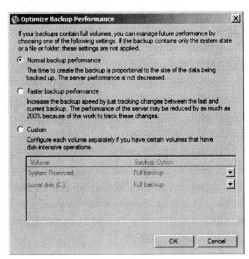

The three options listed determine how the backup will be performed. It is important for you to know the choices you make here will not be applied if you are backing up only system state.

-   Normal Backup Performance is the default method for Windows Server Backup, and this method will perform a normal backup.

-   Faster Backup Performance will perform an incremental backup for your system.

-   Custom will allow you to choose a combination of the previous two options for your drives. For example, you could perform a full backup on your data volume but only an incremental backup on your system drive.

3. Select the setting for your system, and click OK.

Back Up Your Server

After you have installed the backup tools, it is now just a matter of setting up the tasks to begin protecting your system. When you are ready to perform the backup and you know what files and folders you want to protect, you are ready to set up the backup test and schedule.

The first time you load the tool, you will see a message telling you no backup has been configured and you need to either set up a backup schedule or set up a backup once to begin protecting your system. Whether you choose to create a backup schedule or perform a backup once, the choices in the wizard are the same, with the exception of configuring the schedule:

1. Start Windows Server Backup by selecting Start ⇨ Administrative Tools ⇨ Windows Server Backup.

2. To launch the backup wizard, in the Actions pane on the right, select Backup Schedule to create a regular backup task, or select Backup Once if you just want to perform an immediate backup. For this set of tasks, you will see the Backup Schedule choice.

3. Review the Getting Started screen, and click Next to see a screen similar to Figure 8.8.

Figure 8.8: Configuring the backup

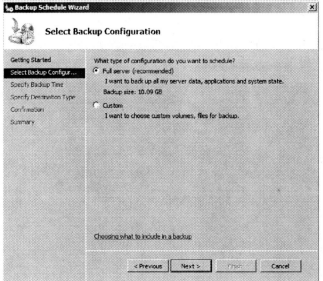

Data Access and Management

PART III

4. Select Full Server (Recommended), and click Next.

5. Set your schedule; the default is once a day at 9 p.m. You can also configure multiple times a day to perform the backup. After you set your schedule, click Next.

6. On the Specify Destination Type screen, as shown in Figure 8.9, you'll see two new choices in Windows Server 2008 R2; these allow you to store your backup to another volume and to a network share. These methods provide flexibility for your backup process that did not exist in prior versions of Windows servers. However, make sure you make note of the performance costs to your additional volume or network. You will have to decide what the right balance is for you and your organization. After you make your selection, click Next.

NOTE The first time you run the backup wizard, you may be asked to format the destination drive. When you select the default choice of Backup To Hard Disk That Is Dedicated For Backups, it will reformat the selected disk before the backup process begins. Make sure you have saved any necessary data off the drive. The format of the drive has to be NTFS; also, make sure you have at least 1½ times the free drive space compared to what you are backing up.

Figure 8.9: Backup destinations

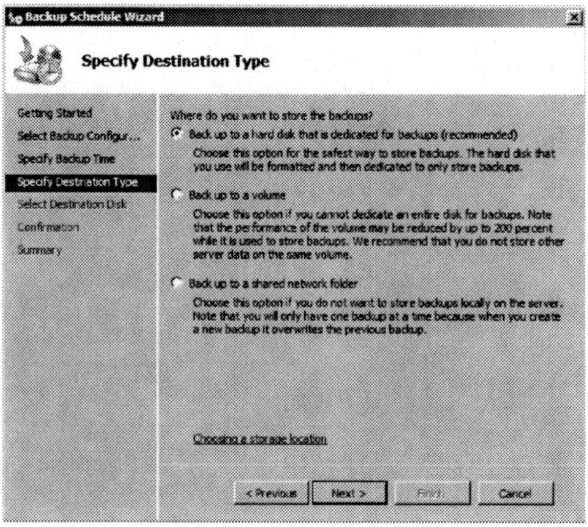

7. On the Select Destination Disk page, select where you want to store your backups. For a scheduled backup, this can be another hard drive or a network share. It cannot be an optical drive or removable media. However, you can use optical drives or removable media for backup-once backups, and these media choices provide a great choice for bare-metal backups. After you make your selection, click Next.

8. If you are presented with a warning to format the disk and you are positive you want to use the selected disk, click Yes. Otherwise, click No, and select another drive to store your backup.

9. Review the Confirmation screen, and click Finish to create the scheduled task for backup and format the volume (if this is your first time using Windows Server Backup). If you chose Backup Once, you will click Backup to immediately perform the backup.

10. Review your Summary screen, and click Close.

NOTE After you have run the backup wizard the first time, the next time you run it you will see a screen similar to Figure 8.10. This allows you to modify the existing backup or stop the backup process. You can still configure the backup once if you need to create new backups for different files or needs, like bare-metal recovery.

Figure 8.10: Modifying the existing backup schedule

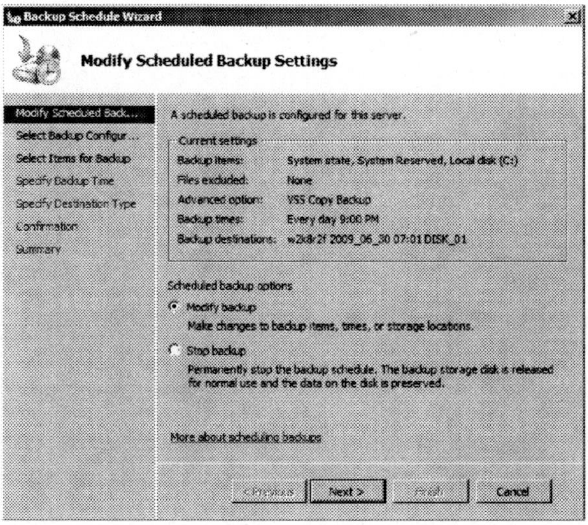

Back Up Specific Files

In Windows Server Backup in Windows Server 2008, you had to back up the entire volume. In Windows Server 2008 R2, you now can include or exclude folders or individual files. You can also exclude files based on the file types with filters. For this purpose, you will see how to modify an existing backup schedule.

1. Start Windows Server Backup by selecting Start ⇨ Administrative Tools ⇨ Windows Server Backup.

2. To launch the backup wizard, in the Actions pane on the right, select Backup Schedule.

3. On the Modify Backup Schedules screen, verify that Modify Backup is selected, and click Next.

4. Select Custom, and click Next.

5. On the Select Items For Backup screen, you will see what you are currently backing up. If want to add or remove from the backup, click Add Items, and you will see a screen similar to Figure 8.11.

Figure 8.11: Backup item selection

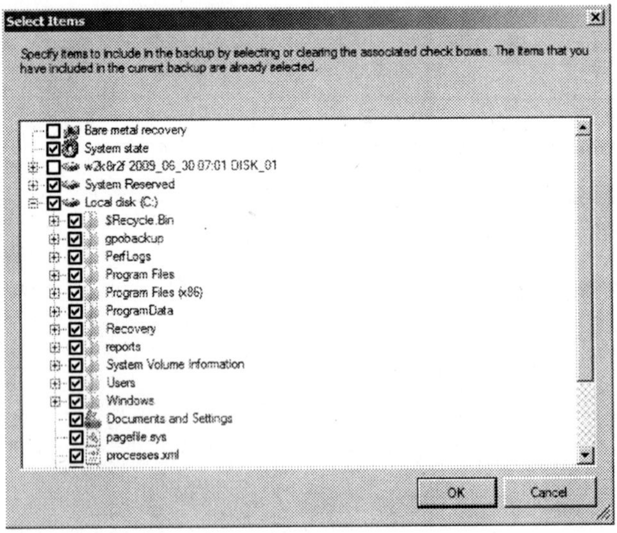

6. Select the items you want to add to or remove from the backup by selecting or deselecting the check boxes next to the items. If

you want to select specific folders, click the + sign next to your listed hard drives to expand the directory tree and then make your folder selections. When you are done selecting items to back up, click OK.

7. If you want to exclude certain files from your backup, such as temporary files (*.tmp) or music files (.wmv, .mp3, and so on), click the Advanced Settings button.

8. Click Add Exclusion to select the drive or folders you want to apply your exclusions.

9. Select the drive you want to use. Typically you will want your full volumes to have the exclusion applied. However, you can select individual folders or files to exclude directly. When you're done selecting your locations, click OK.

10. To exclude certain files, click in the File Type column, and type in your exclusion. You can also specify whether you want apply the filter to the subfolders. For example, if you wanted to exclude .tmp files from your backup, type *.**tmp**. Your screen would look similar to Figure 8.12.

Figure 8.12: Backup exclusions

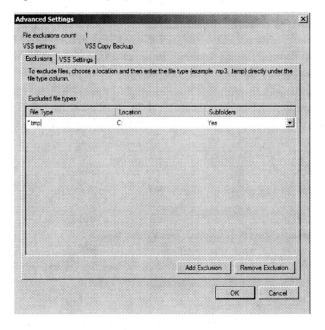

Data Access and Management

PART III

If you want to add more exclusions, click Add Exclusion, and repeat the process. Likewise, if you want to remove the exclusion, you can select it and click Remove Exclusion.

11. When you are finished creating exclusions, click OK to proceed through the rest of the wizard.

12. Set or modify your schedule, and click Next.

13. Select your destination type, and click Next.

14. Select the destination disk, and click Next.

15. If you are presented with a warning to format the disk and you are positive you want to use the selected disk, click Yes. Otherwise, click No, and select another drive to store your backup.

16. Review the Confirmation screen, and click Finish to create the scheduled task for backup and format the volume (if this is your first time using Windows Server Backup). If you chose Backup Once, you will click Backup to immediately perform the backup.

17. Review your Summary screen, and click Close.

Perform a System State Backup

When you back up the system state, you are backing up a majority of the system configuration information. In Windows Server 2008 R2, you can perform the system state backup inside the Windows Server Backup Tool, and you do not have to solely use wbadmin.exe. Also, if you have installed additional roles on the Windows Server 2008 R2 server, your system state will contain more data. By default, on a server with no additional roles, the system state backup always contains the following components:

- Registry
- COM+ class registration database
- Boot files, including system files
- System files under Windows File Protection

If the system is a domain controller in addition to the default system state data, system state will contain the following:

- Active Directory service
- SYSVOL directory

If you have installed clustering on the server, the system state data will contain the clustering services information.

If you have installed a certificate services server, the system state data will contain the certificate services database.

If you have installed IIS, the system state data will contain the IIS metadirectory.

1. Start Windows Server Backup by selecting Start ⇨ Administrative Tools ⇨ Windows Server Backup.

2. To launch the backup wizard, in the Actions pane on the right, select Backup Schedule to create a regular backup task, or select Backup Once if you just want to perform an immediate backup. For this set of tasks, you will see the Backup Schedule choice.

3. Review the Getting Started screen, and click Next.

4. Select Custom, and click Next.

5. On the Select Items For Backup screen, click Add Items.

6. Click System State, click OK, and then click Next.

7. If presented with a scheduling window, set or modify your schedule, and click Next.

8. Select your destination type, and click Next.

9. Select the destination disk, and click Next.

10. If you are presented with a warning to format the disk and you are positive you want to use the selected disk, click Yes. Otherwise, click No, and select another drive to store your backup.

11. Review the Confirmation screen, and click Finish to create the scheduled task for backup and format the volume (if this is your first time using Windows Server Backup). If you chose Backup Once, you will click Backup to immediately perform the backup.

12. Review your Summary screen, and click Close.

Perform a Bare-Metal Backup

Another backup option that will provide you with a great option in case of a catastrophic failure is a bare-metal backup. The bare-metal backup will back up your system state, your system volume, and the system reserved data. This backup set is also unique in that you will need the Windows Server 2008 R2 installation media available during recovery.

This is a good time to use a USB drive or another portable media to store this backup. The main reason is because to perform the restore, you need to boot the system into the Windows Recovery Environment using a Windows Server 2008 R2 installation DVD.

1. Start Windows Server Backup by selecting Start ⇨ Administrative Tools ⇨ Windows Server Backup.

2. To launch the backup wizard, in the Actions pane on the right, select Backup Schedule to create a regular backup task, or select Backup Once if you just want to perform an immediate backup. For this set of tasks, you will see the Backup Schedule choice.

3. Review the Getting Started screen, and click Next.

4. Select Custom, and click Next.

5. On the Select Items For Backup step, click Add Items.

6. Click Bare Metal Recovery, and click OK; then click Next.

7. If presented with a scheduling window, set or modify your schedule, and click Next.

8. Select your destination type, and click Next.

9. Select the destination disk, and click Next.

10. If you are presented with a warning to format the disk and you are positive you want to use the selected disk, click Yes. Otherwise, click No, and select another drive to store your backup.

11. Review the Confirmation screen, and click Finish to create the scheduled task for backup and format the volume (if this is your first time using Windows Server Backup). If you chose Backup Once, you will click Backup to immediately perform the backup.

12. Review your Summary screen, and click Close.

Look at the Scheduled Tasks

Whenever you create a backup schedule, you may be wondering where the task is stored. The task is stored in the Task Scheduler tool, and you can view your backup tasks there. You can also run the task directly from the Task Scheduler. The tasks in the Task Scheduler have several properties you can modify, as shown in Table 8.2.

Table 8.2: Task Property Tabs

Property Tab	Definition
General	Contains the description, author, and what account will be used to run the command.
Triggers	Determines when the task will be performed. In the case of a backup, the trigger is date and time.
Actions	Determines what programs or commands will be run.
Conditions	Specifies additional options, combined with the triggers, that determine whether the task should run.
Settings	Controls additional behaviors of the task. An important setting here is Allow Task To Be Run On Demand. If you want to be able to run your tasks directly from the Task Scheduler, you have to select this setting to turn it on.
History	Shows the past history of the task when it was run.

1. Click Start ⇨ Administrative Tools ⇨ Task Scheduler.

2. Expand the tree to view the backup tasks. Click the + to expand Task Scheduler Library ⇨ Microsoft ⇨ Windows, and then click Backup.

3. Double-click the task to view the properties of the backup task, and you will see a screen similar to Figure 8.13.

Figure 8.13: Backup task

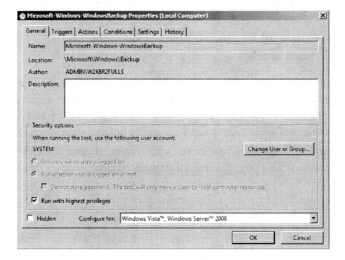

PART III

Data Access and Management

You can also view the status of your backups and get more details on the main console page of the Windows Server Backup window, as shown in Figure 8.14.

Figure 8.14: Windows Server Backup

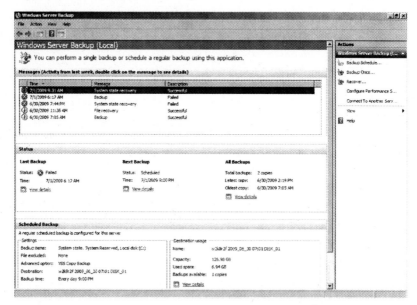

From the main console window, you can view the details, status, and next schedule for your backups and recovery processes. The Windows Server Backup Tool will show all the events with your backups and restores in this main console window.

Recover Your Data

I hope recovering your data is not a daily task. However, you should know how to recover data just in case. Fortunately, the recovery tool is straightforward to use presuming you have performed a proper backup. The method used to back up your data will always determine what recovery method you will need to perform. Your desired outcome will impact what and how you need to perform your recovery.

Restore Specific Files or a Full Volume

If the time comes that you need to recover the files, it is just a matter of knowing what files and what time frame you need to restore.

1. Start Windows Server Backup by selecting Start ⇨ Administrative Tools ⇨ Windows Server Backup.

2. To launch the recovery wizard, in the Actions pane on the right, select Recover.

3. Select where you have stored the backup, and click Next. If the backup is stored locally on an internal hard drive, verify This Server is selected, click Next, and proceed to step 7. If the backup is stored elsewhere, select A Backup Stored On Another Location, and click Next.

4. Depending on the location of the backup, click Local Drives or Remote Shared Folder, and click Next. If you specified Remote Shared Folder, you will need to type in the UNC name for the backup in the form of \\servername\sharename.

5. On the Select Backup Location screen, verify your backup set, and click Next.

6. Select the server data you want to recover, and click Next.

7. On the Select Backup Date screen, select the date and possible time for the backup set you want to recover from, and click Next.

8. On the Select Recovery Type page, select what you want to recover.

   - Select Specific Files Or Folders if you trying to recover a specific file or folder. When you select this option and click Next, you will see a screen similar to Figure 8.15, allowing you to expand the tree to recover the file from.

   - Select Volumes if you need to recover the entire volume from a backup set. When you select this option and click Next, you will be provided with a list of volumes to select from.

   - Select System State if you want to recover system state.

Data Access and Management

PART III

Figure 8.15: Recovering a specific file

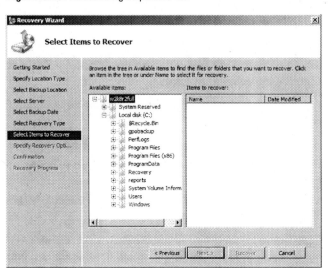

NOTE   You may also notice a choice called Applications. Depending what applications you have installed on your server, some may have registered with Windows Server Backup. If they have, you have the ability to recover those applications as well.

---

   9. After you make your selection for the recovery of files, click Next.

 10. The Specify Recovery Options screen will look like Figure 8.16. This screen gives you a few options on how you want to recover the file. You can recover to the original location or an alternative location. You can also control whether you create a copy of the file to make sure you have both versions, overwrite any existing version of the file, or do not recover the file if one already exists. You can also bring back any security permissions on the file. After you make your selection, click Next.

 11. Review the Confirmation screen, and click Recover.

 12. After the recovery process is complete, review the results, and click Close.

Figure 8.16: Recovery options

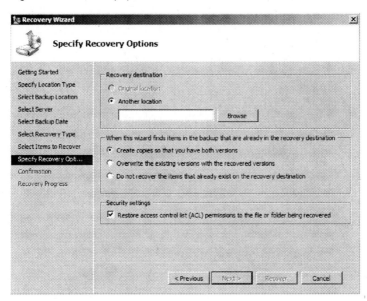

Perform a System State Restore

When you want to recover system state data, you need to take an extra bit of precaution and planning when recovering this data. Because of the nature of the data being recovered, you have the potential to render your system unbootable. Specifically, when this restore process is started, it cannot be stopped or interrupted. If it is, this process could render your server unbootable. In other words, use caution when recovering the system state. Of course, if you are using this process, chances are you are not too far from having to rebuild your server anyway.

1. Start Windows Server Backup by selecting Start ⇨ Administrative Tools ⇨ Windows Server Backup.

2. To launch the recovery wizard, in the Actions pane on the right, select Recover.

3. Select where you have stored the backup, and click Next. If the backup is stored locally on an internal hard drive, verify that This Server is selected, click Next, and proceed to step 7. If the backup is stored elsewhere, select A Backup Stored On Another Location, and click Next.

4. Depending on the location of the backup, click Local Drives or Remote Shared Folder, and click Next. If you specified Remote Shared Folder, you will need to type in the UNC name for the backup in the form of \\servername\sharename.

5. On the backup location screen, verify your backup set, and click Next.

6. Select the server data you want to recover, and click Next.

7. On the Select Backup Date screen, select the date and possible time for the backup set you want to recover from, and click Next.

8. On the Select Recovery Type screen, select System State to recover the system state information, and click Next.

9. Select the area you would like to recover your system state data to, either the original location or an alternate location. If you are trying to recover, make your selection, and click Next.

10. On the Summary screen, review your selections, and then click Recover.

11. After the recovery process is complete, review the results, and click Close.

Recover System State Data Containing Active Directory Data

If your system state backup contains Active Directory information, you will not be able to recover the data via the recovery wizard unless you specify an alternate location to recover to. If you try to recover the data in the Windows Server Backup tool, you will see an error message similar to the one shown in Figure 8.17.

Figure 8.17: System state with Active Directory data error

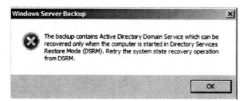

To perform a system state recovery of your Windows Server 2008 R2 server containing Active Directory information, you need to boot the operating system into Directory Services Restore Mode (DSRM). Specifically, you will be performing an authoritative restore.

Before you can boot into DSRM, you need to configure your boot process:

1. Click Start, type **msconfig**, and click the Msconfig program under Programs.

2. Click the Boot tab.

3. In the Boot Options section, select the Safe Boot check box, and select the Active Directory Repair option. Click OK. Your screen should look like Figure 8.18.

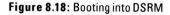

Figure 8.18: Booting into DSRM

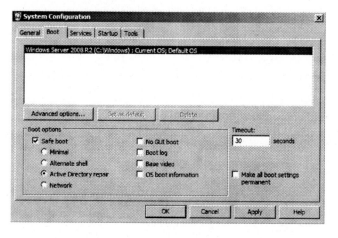

4. Restart the server.

5. Log on to the server with the local administrator ID and the DSRM password you created while installing the server.

6. Start Windows Server Backup by selecting Start ➪ Administrative Tools ➪ Windows Server Backup.

7. To launch the recovery wizard, in the Actions pane on the right, select Recover.

8. Select where you have stored the backup, and click Next. If the backup is stored locally on an internal hard drive, verify that This Server is selected, click Next, and proceed to step 12. If the backup is stored elsewhere, select A Backup Stored On Another Location, and click Next.

9. Depending on the location of the backup, click Local Drives or Remote Shared Folder, and click Next. If you specified Remote Shared Folder, you will need to type in the UNC name for the backup in the form of \\servername\sharename.

10. On the Specify Backup Location screen, verify your backup set, and click Next.

11. Select the server's data you want to recover, and click Next.

12. On the Select Backup Date screen, select the date and possible time for the backup set you want to recover from, and click Next.

13. On the Select Recovery Type screen, select System State to recover the system state information, and click Next.

14. Select Original Location, and select Perform An Authoritative Restore Of Active Directory files, as shown in Figure 8.19.

Figure 8.19: Authoritative restore

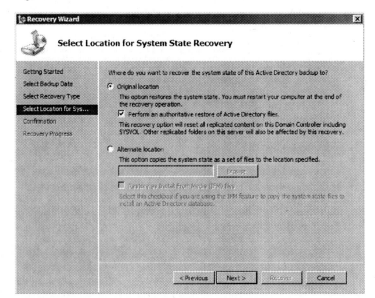

15. You will receive a warning noting that all replicated content on the server will be resynchronized and that this can cause potential latency on your server and network. Acknowledge the message by clicking OK.

16. On the Summary screen, review your selections, and then click Recover.

17. You will receive another warning message stating that system state recovery cannot be paused or canceled once it has started. Click Yes to proceed with the recovery, or click No to complete the recovery at a later time.

18. After the recovery process is complete, review the results, and click Close.

19. Before you restart the server, you need to turn off DSRM.

20. Click Start, type `msconfig`, and click the Msconfig program under Programs.

21. Click the Boot tab.

22. In the Boot Options section, deselect the Safe Boot check box. Click OK.

23. Restart the server, and log on with your normal domain credentials.

24. If you see a command prompt window notifying you the status of your recovery, review the message, and press the Enter key.

Perform a Bare-Metal Restore

Sometimes you run into problems that a simple file restore or a system state recovery cannot fix. If you have created a bare-metal recovery image, then you can recover your full server using the recovery process. This recovery process is different from recovering just files or the system state. The bare-metal recovery process is part of the Windows Recovery Environment, and to get to it, you need a Windows Server 2008 R2 DVD to boot the operating system to, and you need access to the drive containing the bare-metal backup. Typical USB drives can work really well in this scenario presuming your BIOS supports USB at boot.

Additionally, this recovery process is destructive, meaning when you run a bare-metal recovery all the data on your drives will be replaced with data from the system image. You also have the potential during

Data Access and Management

PART III

the recovery process to partition and format the drives, in other words, restoring the server completely to a previous working state.

1. Make sure your backup media is attached to the server, and insert and boot to your Windows Server 2008 R2 DVD.

2. Select your language preferences, and click Next.

3. In the Install Now window, click the Repair Your Computer option located in the lower left of the installation window.

4. To recover from your bare-metal backup, select the Restore System Using A System Image You Created Earlier radio option, and click Next. You can also get to the image via the Recovery Tools option.

5. The system image will scan your system's drives for an image for you to restore from; you will see a screen similar to Figure 8.20. You can select the image provided to, usually the most current, or you can select a different image by selecting Select A System Image. When you have the proper image selected, click Next.

Figure 8.20: Bare-metal image selection

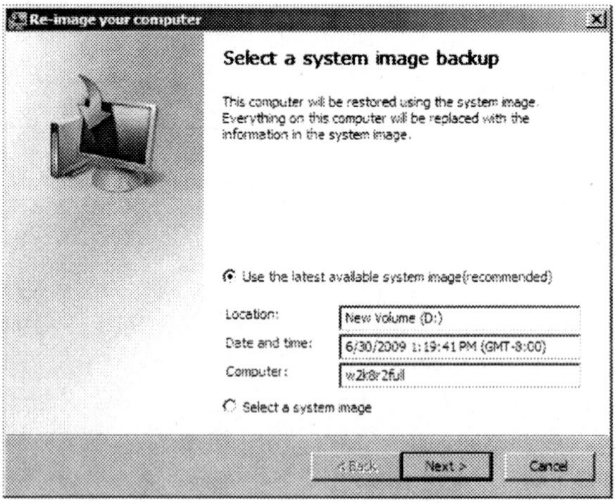

6. On the Choose Additional Restore Options screen, you have the ability to control how your drives and partitions are handled, as shown in Figure 8.21. You can repartition and format the drives. You can also exclude drives from the partition, which is particu-larly useful when you want to keep other drives intact. By clicking

Advanced, you will see a window similar to Figure 8.22. This window allows you to control whether you want restart upon completion. It will also allow you to perform a hard disk scan to check and possibly repair errors. After you're done, select your options, and click Next.

7. Review your selections, and click Finish to begin the bare-metal restoration.

Figure 8.21: Bare-metal recovery options

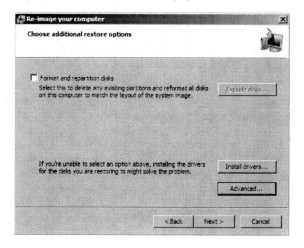

Figure 8.22: Advanced options

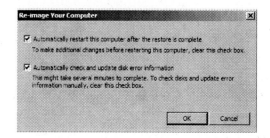

8. You will be presented with a warning reminding you that the process will replace existing data from the bare-metal backup image. If this is what you want to do, click Yes to finalize the restoration

process. This process could take a long time to complete based on how much data you need to recover.

9. When the recovery is complete, you will prompted to restart, or the system will restart automatically (the default option).

Windows System Recovery Tools

During the bare-metal restore process, you saw an option to load the Windows system recovery tools. The Windows system recovery tools provide you with three options to further troubleshoot your environment:

▶ **System Image Recovery** will take you to the bare-metal recovery wizard to allow you to fully recover your system.

▶ **Windows Memory Diagnostics** will perform diagnostic checks on the memory of your system to see whether faulty memory is to blame for any system errors. When you select this option, you will asked to either restart the system immediately to check for problems or schedule the memory check for the next time you restart the system. Pressing F1 will allow to control the types and number of memory tests you can perform. When the test is running, you will see a screen similar to this one.

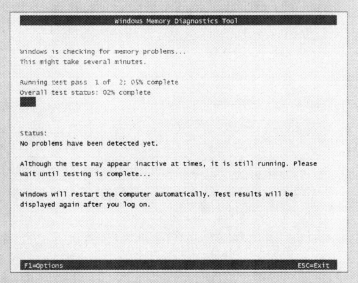

▶ **Command Prompt** will load a command prompt to allow you to perform a variety of command prompt actions.

Recover via Shadow Copy

Recovering files via a shadow copied shared volume is something you can teach your users to do. It is very straightforward to work with when it is enabled and as easy to access as right-clicking the file or folder you want to perform the recover. To access the shadow copies on your Windows Server 2008 R2 server, the users must be running an operating system that supports the Shadow Copy Client. Windows Vista, Windows 7, Windows Server 2003, Windows Server 2008, and Windows Server 2008 R2 all have built-in support for the Shadow Copy Client. For Windows XP or Windows Server 2000 SP3 or later, you need to download the client located from this location:

http://support.microsoft.com/kb/832217

Using the Shadow Copy Client to recover a file is just a matter of knowing where the file is located and knowing how you want to recover the file. Shadow copies are great if a user has accidentally deleted a file or folder or inadvertently overwritten a file, such as by choosing Save instead of Save As. You can work with the shadow copy files or folders just like you would any regular file or folder.

When restoring with shadow copies, you have three options, as listed in Table 8.3.

Table 8.3: Shadow Copy Options

Option	Usage
Open	Allows you to open a shadow copy of the file or folder to view any changes. You can copy and paste between the shadow copy and the original file or folder. This method is very useful when you want only to recover a file from a folder instead of the whole folder.
Copy	This will make a copy of the shadow copy and store it in a different location. This is also useful when you want to compare files or folders side by side.
Restore	This will restore the file in the original location. Be careful if you restore a folder with this method because it will restore all the contents of the folder.

You can access the shadow copies either locally if the shadow copy has been enabled on your local volume or via a network share after you have opened the folder or share where you want to recover data from.

Data Access and Management

PART III

1. Right-click the file or folder you want to restore with the shadow copy. You can also right-click the whitespace of an opened folder.

2. Select Properties.

3. Click the Previous Versions tab; your screen will look similar to Figure 8.23.

Figure 8.23: Shadow copy restore

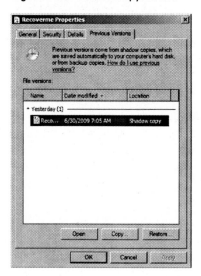

4. Select the shadow copy you want to use; they are stored by date and time.

5. Select Open, Copy, or Restore.

6. When you are finished, click OK.

NOTE If you do not see any shadow copies listed, the most likely cause is that the file has not changed. Remember, shadow copies store only the changes for the files, and if there are no copies listed, the file is the original.

It is important you also know that shadow copy is not retroactive. The feature will not protect you until the feature is enabled. In other words, if a user makes changes to files or deletes a file prior to enabling shadow copy, the act of enabling shadow copy will not allow you to retroactively make copies of files and folders.

Perform Backup and Recovery with Command Tools

You may choose to back up and recover your systems with command-line tools. Specifically, in the case of a Windows Server 2008 R2 Server Core installation, two options are available to you; they are the command-line tool wbadmin.exe (the command-line equivalent of the Windows Server Backup GUI) and PowerShell cmdlets.

Regardless of which tool you use, the techniques, terminology, and processes in this chapter still apply. These tools provide the same capabilities as the GUI for Windows Server Backup. Therefore, you do not need to relearn all the previously mentioned information—the command-line versions are just an alternative way to access the tools.

In this section, you will see how to back up and recover your systems with the command-line tools.

Use wbadmin.exe

Using the command-line tool wbadmin.exe provides you with a method to create scripts for backup as well as a method to back up servers like Server Core installations where there is no GUI present. Table 8.4 describes some of the common switches for the wbadmin.exe backup. For more information on how to use wbadmin.exe, in a command prompt, type the following command and hit Enter:

```
wbadmin /?
```

Table 8.4: wbadmin.exe Common Switches

Switch	Explanation
enable backup	Allows you to modify or create a backup schedule
start backup	Performs a one-time backup
get disks	Lists the current disks available and online
start systemstatebackup	Allows you create a system state backup
start recovery	Begins the recovery process from an existing backup

wbadmin.exe Examples

Here are some examples on how you can use `wbadmin.exe` to perform the various tasks of backup and recovery.

Before you back up the systems, you will need to see what drives are available on the system. When you create a backup, you can use the drive letter if one exists, or you will need the disk identifier. To see what drives are available, run the following command:

```
wbadmin get disks
```

Your output will look similar to Figure 8.24.

Figure 8.24: Available online disks

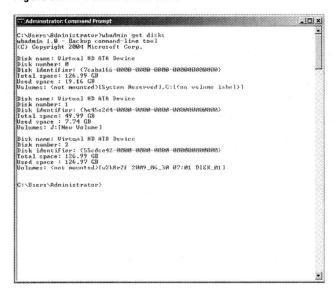

The following command will create a backup of the C and D drives and would occur daily at 4 a.m. and 10 p.m. The backup would be stored on the disk {7caba166-0000-0000-0000-000000000000}.

```
wbadmin enable backup
-addtarget:{7caba166-0000-0000-0000-000000000000}
-schedule:04:00,22:00 -include:c:,d:
```

If you wanted the backup to occur just once, the command would look like this:

```
wbadmin start backup
-backuptarget:{7caba166-0000-0000-0000-000000000000}
-include:c:,d:
```

The following command would back up the system state to the disk {7caba166-0000-0000-0000-000000000000}:

```
wbadmin start systemstatebackup
-backuptarget:{7caba166-0000-0000-0000-000000000000}
```

To be able to restore items with wbadmin.exe, you need to know two things: the backup version identifier and what items are stored in the backup. You use wbadmin get versions to find out what backups you currently have available. Specifically, you are looking for the version identifier, which is formatted as a date and timestamp. You would run the following command to see the items backed up on June 30, 2009, at 2:05 p.m.

```
wbadmin get items -version:06/30/2009-14:05
```

The results would look similar to Figure 8.25.

Figure 8.25: wbadmin.exe get items

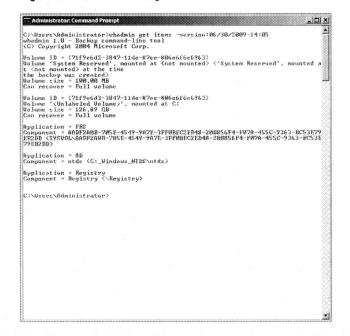

The following command would restore the C volume from the backup taken on June 30, 2009, at 2:05 p.m.:

```
wbadmin start recovery -version:06/30/2009-14:05
-itemType:Volume -items:c:
```

Use PowerShell

Using the backup and recover cmdlets for Windows Server 2008 R2 follow the same syntax and language from Chapter 3. These cmdlets provide another tool to perform your server recovery. If you choose to install the command-line tools for Windows Server Backup, you will have access to the PowerShell backup and restore cmdlets as well. Before you can run these tools, you have to verify the PowerShell snap-in for backing up has been loaded.

To verify the tools have been loaded, run the following command from a PowerShell window. Then verify you see Windows.ServerBackup as the loaded snap-in.

```
Get-PSSnapin
```

If you do not see Windows Server Backup in your loaded snap-ins, you will need to run this command:

```
Add-PSSnapin windows.serverbackup
```

Working with the PowerShell is quite a bit more complex than working with wbadmin.exe to perform backup tasks. You need to create a PowerShell script to accomplish your tasks. Although PowerShell can be more complex, it does offer some nice flexibility to performing backups. All the capabilities of PowerShell are determined by what backup policy you set. The backup policy for PowerShell is stored in an object called WBPolicy. The WBPolicy object contains all the settings for the backup, including the schedule, backup types, backup targets, and so on.

Working with PowerShell and backup, you need to understand how to set the values for the WBPolicy object. Table 8.5 describes some of the common PowerShell commands used for backup and recovery and how to set the parameters for WBPolicy. For a full listing of the PowerShell cmdlets for backing up the system, run the following cmdlet:

```
Get-Command *wb* -CommandType cmdlet
```

Table 8.5: PowerShell Backup Cmdlets

cmdlets	Explanation
Get-WBPolicy	Displays the current settings for the WBPolicy object on the server
Set-WBPolicy	Allows you to set the parameters for the WBPolicy
Add-WBVolume	Adds a volume to the WBPolicy object to be backed up
Add-WBSystemState	Adds the system state to the WBPolicy object to be backed up
Set-WBSchedule	Sets the time for your daily backup schedule
Start-WBBackup	Starts a one-time backup
Get-WBJob	Shows the current status of a running backup job

PowerShell Examples

As you can see in Table 8.5, only a few of the commands are available to work with PowerShell in Group Policy. This section gives a couple of examples to allow you to get used to using PowerShell.

The following two lines will back up your system with your current backup policy settings. You can create a PowerShell script to run these commands, or you can run each line separately by hitting Enter after each line:

```
$policy = Get-WBPolicy
Start-WBBackup -Policy $policy
```

This first line sets the $policy variable to the current settings in WBPolicy. The second line starts the backup process with settings currently in the WPObject object's $policy variable.

The following script will back up the C, D, and system state on your system to your Z drive. Notice you will be using a variety of the Add cmdlets to modify the value of the variable $policy, as well as variables for target and paths:

```
$policy = New-WBPolicy
$volume = Get-WBVolume -VolumePath c:
Add-WBVolume -Policy $policy -volume $volume
$volume1 = Get-WBVolume -VolumePath d:
```

```
Add-WBVolume -Policy $policy -volume $volume1
Add-WBSystemState -Policy $policy
$target = New-WBBackupTarget -VolumePath Z:
Add-WBBackuptarget -Policy $policy -target $target
Start-WBBackup -Policy $policy
```

9

Managing Disks and Disk Storage

IN THIS CHAPTER, YOU WILL LEARN TO:

Data Access and Management

PART III

I n this chapter, you will learn some of the fundamentals of working with the hard drives on your system. You will get to see the basics of hard drive management and learn how to create, format, and delete your partitions. You will look at the tools needed to make sure your disks are running properly and are properly formatted.

You will also take a brief look at leveraging software RAID levels to provide your Windows Server 2008 R2 server with some software-level redundancy, and you will learn what levels are supported by Windows Server 2008 R2.

This chapter will also introduce you to the built-in tools used to manage large hard drive arrays and volumes. You will learn that some built-in tools allow you to control how much space your users can use on your server, preventing them from taking over the hard drive space on your servers.

Understand the Basics

As you begin to work with managing the disks and storage for your Windows Server 2008 R2 server, you need to have a firm handle on the basics of the terminology used. We'll define some key terms and then go into how to work with storage, how to work with partitions, and how to use DiskPart.

Learn Disk Management and Storage Terminology

Before you start creating and working with the drives on your server, it is important to have a solid understanding of the basic terminology associated with using the disk storage on your server. Table 9.1 defines some of the basic terms.

Table 9.1: Basic Disk Management Terminology

Term	Definition
Basic disk	These are the default disk types in a Windows environment and have been around since MS-DOS.
Dynamic disk	Dynamic disks are used to create volumes that will span multiple hard drives. These drives can also be used for simple volumes.

Table 9.1: Basic Disk Management Terminology *(continued)*

Term	Definition
Foreign disk	You will see a Foreign Disk option when you take a dynamic disk from one server and place it in another server.
Partitions	These define how you break up your physical drives. Partitions can be primary partitions, extended partitions, or logical drives.
Simple volume	This is the most basic type of volume and can be created and used only on one physical disk.
Spanned volume	Spanned volumes combine two or more physical disks and allow you to create a volume larger than a single physical disk on your system. The disks in a spanned volume need to be dynamic disks.
Striped volume	Striped volumes combine two or more physical disks. The data stored on these volumes is striped, which means when data is written to the drives, it is written alternatively in equal amounts across both physical drives. Striped volumes are faster than spanned or mirrored volumes; however, they do not provide any redundancy. The disks in a striped volume need to be dynamic disks. This is also known as RAID 0.
Mirrored volume	Mirrored volumes combine two disks that are duplicates of each other. This provides you with an identical copy of data stored on two different disks and therefore some protection against data loss. This is also known as RAID 1.
RAID	RAID stands for Redundant Array of Independent (or Inexpensive) Disks. RAID drives are broken into different levels, and with the exception of RAID 0, all levels of RAID offer data protection and redundancy from a failed drive or volume.
Master boot record (MBR)	The MBR is part of the hard drive system used by the BIOS. The MBR is used to store all the initial boot-processing information for performing the initial boot sequence of the operating system. The MBR has been around for a long time and is primarily used for smaller hard drives and is not recommended if your drive is larger than 2TB.
GUID partition table (GPT)	The GPT, like the MBR, is another system used by the BIOS to load the initial boot sequence of the hard drive. The GPT is a newer form of the MBR but utilizes the extensible firmware interface for working with the drives. GPT drives can have more than four partitions and are designed to work with large and small drives, particularly drives larger than 2TB. However, GPT drives are not recognized by all previous versions of Windows.

Work with Your Storage

You'll now learn how to work with your disks and create partitions. Although these may not be day-to-day activities, this will create the foundation for storing data on your server. To begin working with your storage on your Windows Server 2008 R2 server, you'll need to open the Disk Management utility for your server. This utility will work with your locally connected hard drives; however, USB- and FireWire-connected drives are not supported by the Disk Management utility.

1. Open Server Manager by selecting Start ⇨ Administrative Tools ⇨ Server Manager.

2. In the Server Manager tree, click Storage.

3. In Storage, click Disk Management, and you will see a screen similar to Figure 9.1.

Figure 9.1: Disk Management utility

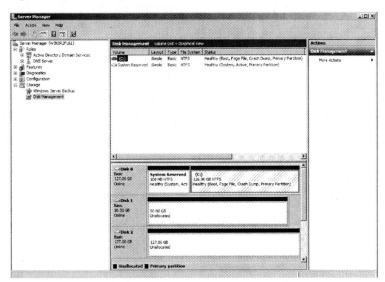

Convert a Basic Disk to a Dynamic Disk

In the Disk Management tool, you will see your volumes and disks listed on your server. When you first put your physical disks on the system, they will most likely be basic disks. You can choose to leave them as basic or convert them to dynamic. You will want to convert these disks to dynamic disks when you need to create spanned and striped volumes. It is recommended that you convert these disks prior to creating partitions or placing any data on the volumes.

To convert a disk to dynamic, follow these steps:

1. Open Server Manager by selecting Start ➪ Administrative Tools ➪ Server Manager.

2. In the Server Manager tree, click Storage.

3. In Storage, click Disk Management.

4. Right-click the disk you want to convert.

5. Select Convert To Dynamic Disk.

6. Select the disk or disks in the bottom window of the middle pane you want to convert, and click OK.

Import a Foreign Disk

When you move a dynamic disk from one server to another server, the drive will be labeled as Foreign. You can see an example of a foreign disk in Figure 9.2.

Figure 9.2: Foreign disk

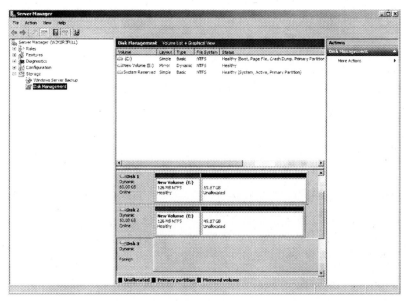

Before you can use the drive, you need to import it:

1. Open Server Manager by selecting Start ⇨ Administrative Tools ⇨ Server Manager.

2. In the Server Manager tree, click Storage.

3. In Storage, click Disk Management.

4. Right-click the disk in the bottom window of the middle pane you want to import.

5. Select Import Foreign Disks.

6. On the Import Disk screen, select the disks you want to import, and click OK.

7. In the Foreign Disk Volumes dialog box, you will see what volumes currently exist on the drive, as shown in Figure 9.3. Review the volumes, and click OK.

Figure 9.3: Foreign volumes

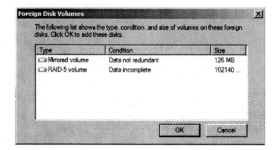

WARNING   You may see a warning about some of your volumes losing data, as shown here. This typically will occur when you import disks and volumes that may have been part of a RAID volume. If you are ready to import and have reviewed the message about your volumes and lose data, click Yes.

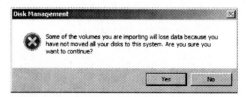

Create Simple Volumes

Before you can use your disks for storage, you will generally need to create volumes on the drives for use within your server. Creating simple volumes is fairly straightforward:

1. Open Server Manager by selecting Start ⇨ Administrative Tools ⇨ Server Manager.

2. In the Server Manager tree, click Storage.

3. In Storage, click Disk Management.

4. Right-click the unallocated space in the bottom window of the middle pane you want to create the volume on.

5. Click New Simple Volume.

6. On the Welcome screen, review the message, and click Next.

7. Select the size you want to make the volume, and click Next.

8. Select how you want to mount the volume. You can choose to mount to a drive letter, mount to a folder on an existing drive, or not assign any mount point. After you make your selection, click Next.

9. Next, you can select how to format the drive. After you make your selection, click Next. You will see a screen similar to Figure 9.4.

10. Review the summary screen, and click Finish.

Figure 9.4: Format partition options

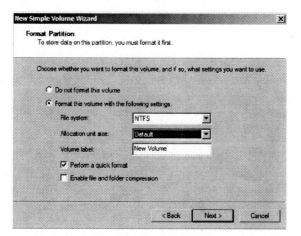

Data Access and Management

PART III

Create Spanned and Striped Volumes

Creating spanned and striped volumes is similar to creating simple volumes. These types of drives require your disks to be dynamic disks, and they require two or more drives to create. The ability to create these types of volumes is determined by the number of drives and amount of unallocated space you have available on your Windows Server 2008 R2 server. When you right-click the unallocated space and you see the options grayed out, as shown in Figure 9.5, this will tell you do *not* have the needed disks or unallocated space to create the volumes.

Figure 9.5: Grayed-out options

Creating a spanned volume is similar to creating a simple volume:

1. Open Server Manager by selecting Start ➪ Administrative Tools ➪ Server Manager.

2. In the Server Manager tree, click Storage.

3. In Storage, click Disk Management.

4. Right-click the unallocated space in the bottom window of the middle pane you want to create the volume on.

5. Click New Spanned Volume.

6. On the Welcome screen, review the message, and click Next.

7. On the Select Disks screen, as shown in Figure 9.6, select the disks you want to use for the volume, and click Add to place them in the Selected section.

Figure 9.6: Selecting disks

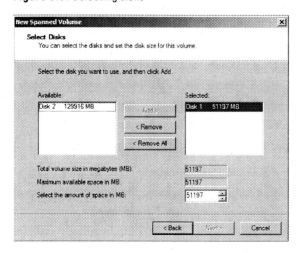

8. Select the size you want to make the volume, and click Next.

9. Select how you want mount the volume. You can choose to mount to a drive letter, mount to a folder on an existing drive, or not assign any mount point. After you make your selection, click Next.

10. Next, you can select how to format the drive. After you make your selection, click Next.

11. Review the summary screen, and click Finish.

12. You will see a warning dialog box, as shown in Figure 9.7, if the drives need to be converted to dynamic drives for spanned volumes. After you review the warning, click Yes.

Data Access and Management

PART III

Figure 9.7: Dynamic disk conversion warning

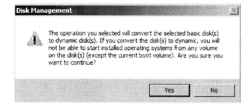

Creating a striped volume is similar to creating spanned volumes. It is important for you to understand that striping helps improve the performance of your hard drive. However, it does have one risk. If you lose one hard drive from the striped volume, you will lose all the data across the entire volume. Take a look at the "Work with RAID Volumes" section in this chapter to learn more about RAID and how it functions.

1. Open Server Manager by selecting Start ⇨ Administrative Tools ⇨ Server Manager.

2. In the Server Manager tree, click Storage.

3. In Storage, click Disk Management.

4. Right-click the unallocated space in the bottom window of the middle pane you want to create the volume on.

5. Click New Striped Volume.

6. On the Welcome screen, review the message, and click Next.

7. On the Select Disks screen, select the disks you want to use for the striped volume, and click Add to place them in the selected option.

8. Select the size you want to make the volume, and click Next.

9. Select how you want mount the volume. You can choose to mount to a drive letter, mount a folder on an existing drive, or not assign any mount point. After you make your selection, click Next.

10. Next, you can select how to format the drive. After you make your selection, click Next.

11. Review the summary screen, and click Finish.

12. You will see a warning dialog box, as shown in Figure 9.7, if the drives need to be converted to dynamic drives for striped volumes. After you review the warning, click Yes.

NOTE   When you create a striped volume, it will make the partitions on all disks the same size. (You can see an example of a striped volume later in the chapter in Figure 9.8.)

Figure 9.8: Striped volume

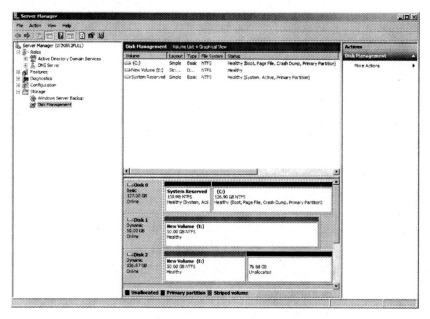

Work with Partitions

After you create your partitions, you can perform a variety of tasks on the drives, including reformatting, deleting, and extending. All of these tasks are done in the Disk Management utility. In addition, you can perform almost all of these tasks by merely right-clicking the volumes.

Format a Partition

You need to format a partition to prepare the drive for use. When you format the volume, you will lose all your existing data, so make sure you have a backup of the volume if you want to save any of the data on it.

1. Open Server Manager by selecting Start ➪ Administrative Tools ➪ Server Manager.

2. In the Server Manager tree, click Storage.

Data Access and Management

PART III

3. In Storage, click Disk Management.

4. Right-click the volume you want to format.

5. Select Format.

6. Next, you can select how to format the drive. After you make your selection, click Next.

7. Review the warning about erasing the data on the volume, and click OK.

Delete a Partition

If you need to repurpose the drive or get rid of an existing partition, you can delete your partitions. Remember, when you delete a volume, you will lose all your existing data, so make sure you have a backup of the volume if you want to save any of the data from it.

1. Open Server Manager by selecting Start ⇨ Administrative Tools ⇨ Server Manager.

2. In the Server Manager tree, click Storage.

3. In Storage, click Disk Management.

4. Right-click the volume you want to delete.

5. Select Delete.

6. Review the warning about erasing the data on the volume, and click Yes.

Extend a Partition

You may find you have an existing volume that is not large enough to meet your current needs for data storage on your server. In that case, you can extend the volume with disks that have unallocated space on them. When you extend an existing volume, you create a new spanned volume.

1. Open Server Manager by selecting Start ⇨ Administrative Tools ⇨ Server Manager.

2. In the Server Manager tree, click Storage.

3. In Storage, click Disk Management.

4. Right-click the volume in the bottom window of the middle pane you want to extend.

5. Select Extend Volume.

6. On the Welcome screen, click Next.

7. On the Select Disks screen, select the disks you want to use to extend the volume, and click Add to place them in the selected option.

8. Select the size you want to make the volume. You can select a size for each disk individually. Click Next.

9. Review the summary screen, and click Finish.

10. You may see a warning dialog box about the drives needing to be converted to dynamic drives. After you review the warning, click Yes.

Shrink an Existing Volume

If you have an existing volume you want to shrink, you can reduce the size through the Disk Management utility. After you shrink the volume, any space you removed from the volume will become unallocated space.

1. Open Server Manager by selecting Start ⇨ Administrative Tools ⇨ Server Manager.

2. In the Server Manager tree, click Storage.

3. In Storage, click Disk Management.

4. Right-click the volume in the bottom window of the middle pane you want to shrink

5. Select Shrink Volume.

6. You can select the size you want to shrink the volume by; you will see a screen similar to Figure 9.9. This allows you to choose the amount you want to reduce from the volume. You cannot shrink the volume to smaller than the existing data on the volume. After you make your selection, click Shrink.

Figure 9.9: Shrinking a volume

Shrink F:	×
Total size before shrink in MB:	242549
Size of available shrink space in MB:	242457
Enter the amount of space to shrink in MB:	242457
Total size after shrink in MB:	92

ⓘ You cannot shrink a volume beyond the point where any unmovable files are located. See the "defrag" event in the Application log for detailed information about the operation when it has completed.

See Shrink a Basic Volume in Disk Management help for more information.

[Shrink]   [Cancel]

Use DiskPart

You may want to use the command prompt to work with your drive partitions, and in the case of Server Core installation, you will *need* to use the command prompt to work with your partitions. Windows Server 2008 R2 provides a command-line utility called DiskPart that you can use to work with disks and partitions. To access DiskPart, follow these steps:

1. To open a command prompt, select Start ⇨ All Programs ⇨ Accessories ⇨ Command Prompt.

2. At the command prompt, type **diskpart,** and hit Enter. You will see a screen similar to Figure 9.10, with the DiskPart utility loaded and waiting for you to enter commands.

Figure 9.10: DiskPart

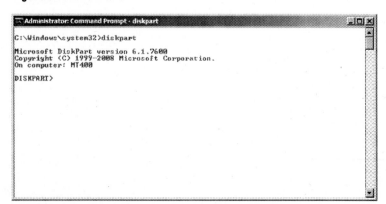

```
Administrator: Command Prompt - diskpart                          _ □ ×

C:\Windows\system32>diskpart

Microsoft DiskPart version 6.1.7600
Copyright (C) 1999-2008 Microsoft Corporation.
On computer: MT400

DISKPART>
```

After you load DiskPart, you need to use commands to perform tasks such as creating volumes, formatting partitions, extending volumes, and so on. You can also take the commands, combine them in a script, and then use DiskPart to process the commands in the file. For example, typing **diskpart /s c:\diskscript.txt** will run DiskPart with the commands listed in diskscript.txt.

Table 9.2 describes some of the common commands used in DiskPart.

Table 9.2: DiskPart Switches

Switch	Description
select	This allows you to select the disk, partition, or volume. Using the select command allows you to access the information about the select object with the detail or list command. Before you can use the detail or list commands, you need to use the select command to set the object you want to work with.
detail	This displays detailed information about the object you have currently selected.
list	This displays existing information about your server's storage; you can list the disk, volume, or partitions.
create	This allows you to create volumes, partitions, or volumes.
format	This allows you to format the partitions. This command's true power comes from using it in a script.
extend	This allows you to use the command prompt to extend an existing volume.

NOTE When you are working with disks and using the select command to target disks on your system, it is important to note how the drives are numbered. Drives are numbered beginning with 0. That means the first drive in your system is drive 0. So, if you wanted to use the select command to select the first disk, the command would look as follows:

```
select disk 0
```

Data Access and Management

PART III

DiskPart Script Examples

Here are some examples of basic scripts you can run with DiskPart to help you see how you can utilize this powerful command. You can create simple script files using Notepad. If you have created the script file, you can type **diskpart /s <path and name of the script file>**.

The following script will select and list the partitions of disk 1 and output detailed information about partition 1:

```
select disk 1
list partition
select partition 1
detail partition
```

The following script will convert disk 2 to dynamic, format the disk with NTFS, create a new volume that's 1GB, assign a drive letter of G, and add a label of "New DiskPart Drive":

```
select disk 2
convert dynamic
create volume simple size=1000 disk=2
assign letter g
select volume g
format FS=NTFS label="New DiskPart Drive" quick
```

The following script will convert disk 2 and disk 3 to dynamic, create a mirrored volume of 2GB, assign a drive letter of M, format the new mirrored volume with NTFS, and add a label of "New Mirrored Drive":

```
select disk 2
convert dynamic
select disk 3
convert dynamic
create volume mirror size=2000 disk=2,3
assign letter m
select volume m
format FS=NTFS label="New Mirrored Drive" quick
```

As you can see, DiskPart is extremely powerful, and it provides a great tool for scripting your disk management tasks.

Work with RAID Volumes

A Redundant Array of Independent Disks (RAID) is a special type of volume providing you with redundancy on your drives or volumes. RAID is designed to provide you with protection from failures of the drives on your sever. RAID does not replace the need to perform regular backups of your systems; it offers an additional level of protection to your system and is designed to work in conjunction with regular backups. In most cases, RAID will tolerate a loss of one hard drive, meaning you will not lose any data; however, the performance of the RAID volume is reduced until you replace the failed drive. RAID is designed to not only help protect your data but also to help improve the performance of the overall drive system. RAID can be implemented either via hardware or software. You will now see how Windows Server 2008 R2 implements RAID at the software level.

Understand RAID Levels

Essentially, RAID volumes (commonly called *arrays*) create duplicates of the data and spread the data over the drives in the volume. In the case of a RAID mirror, the data is completely duplicated in a one-to-one fashion across two drives. However, in other versions of RAID, a concept called a *parity bit* is introduced. One of the keys to understanding how RAID works is knowing how the parity bit works. The parity bit is the copy of the data; however, the parity is spread evenly across the drives.

When you begin to work with RAID, it is important to know what the implications are for the chosen level of RAID for your server. Windows Server 2008 R2 supports only RAID 0, RAID 1, and RAID 5 at the software level. Several of the more common RAID levels are listed in Table 9.3.

Table 9.3: RAID Levels

RAID Level	Description
RAID 0	RAID 0 is commonly known as *striping*. This is the only level of RAID that does not provide you any protection from a failed volume. That means if you lose one drive, you will lose all of the data across your volumes. Striping is designed to provide improved drive performance.
RAID 1	RAID 1 is commonly known as *mirroring*. RAID 1 uses only two drives, and as you write to one drive, a duplicate copy is written to the second drive at the same time. If you lose one drive in the mirror, the second drive contains the backup, and you will not lose any data unless you lose the second drive. This is also the slowest version of RAID.
RAID 5	RAID 5, commonly known as *striping with parity*, is a combination of performance and redundancy. RAID 5 requires three (or more) drives or volumes and provides protection if one of the drives fails. RAID 5 spreads the data and the parity (copy of the data) evenly across all three drives. If a RAID 5 volume loses a drive, the overall performance of the drive will be reduced until you replace the drive. Additionally, RAID 5 may cause a performance impact for your memory and I/O. This will occur with all writes, since the parity bit must be calculated and then written.
RAID 6	RAID 6 is commonly known as *striping with dual parity*. It is nearly identical to RAID 5, but it creates an additional copy of the parity information. This provides you with the additional ability to lose up to two drives without losing your data.
RAID 10	RAID 10, sometimes referred to as RAID 1+0, is a combination of striping and mirroring. RAID 10 is essentially a striped mirror, which offers a nice hardware-level version of RAID with performance and mirroring.

Say, for example, you create a RAID 5 volume with three hard drives of 100GB each. Your total available hard drive space for the volume would be 200GB. The reduced space is because of the parity bit, which is the copy of the data. When your data is written to this volume, it will be spread evenly across the drives, and during the write, a parity bit will be written to help maintain the copy of the data in case a drive is lost.

Figure 9.11 shows an example of a RAID 5 volume. Additionally, if you look at Figure 9.12, you will see the drive and how it appears in My Computer. It is important to note the drive is only about 100GB even though three 50GB drives were used to create the volume.

Figure 9.11: RAID 5 volume

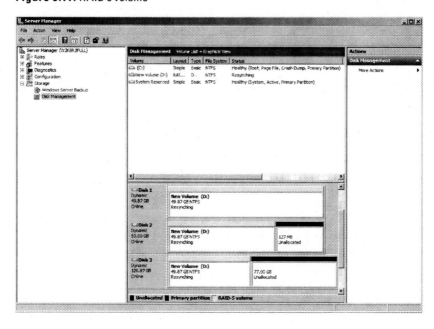

Figure 9.12: RAID 5 drive size

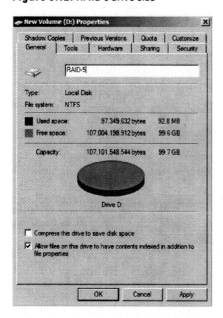

Implement RAID

The number of drives or volumes you have available to you will determine what level of RAID you can implement. In this section, you will see how to create a RAID 5 volume with three drives in the Windows Server 2008 R2 software. If you want to use a hardware solution to create RAID 5, please consult the manufacturer of your system.

Create a RAID 1 or Mirrored Volume

Creating a mirrored volume is similar to creating spanned and striped volumes. Additionally, like with striped volumes, the partitions on the mirrored disks will be the same size. Figure 9.13 shows an example of a mirrored volume.

1. Open Server Manager by selecting Start ⇨ Administrative Tools ⇨ Server Manager.

2. In the Server Manager tree, click Storage.

3. In Storage, click Disk Management.

Figure 9.13: Mirrored volume

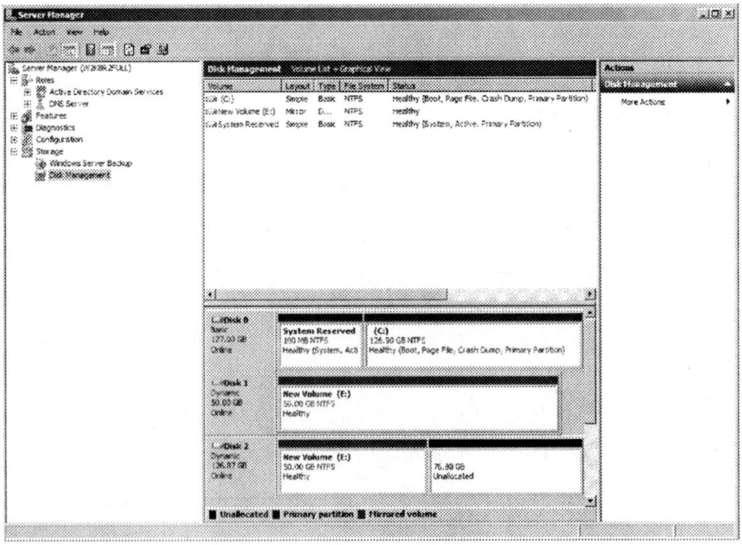

4. Right-click the unallocated space in the bottom window of the middle pane you want to create the volume on.

5. Click New Mirrored Volume.

6. On the Welcome screen, review the message, and click Next.

7. On the Select Disks screen, select the disks you want to use for the mirrored volume, and click Add to place them in the selected option.

8. Select the size you want to make the volume, and click Next.

9. Select how you want mount the volume. You can choose to mount to a drive letter, to mount a folder on an existing drive, or to not assign any mount point. After you make your selection, click Next.

10. Next, you can select how to format the drive. After you make your selection, click Next.

11. Review the summary screen, and click Finish.

12. You will see a warning dialog box if the drives need to be converted to dynamic drives for mirrored volumes. After you review the warning, click Yes.

Repair a Mirrored Volume

If you lose a hard drive in a mirror, the mirror has failed redundancy. You will need to replace the failed drive, remove the existing mirror, and then re-create the mirror.

1. Open Server Manager by selecting Start ⇨ Administrative Tools ⇨ Server Manager.

2. In the Server Manager tree, click Storage.

3. In Storage, click Disk Management.

4. Right-click the half of the mirror in the bottom window of the middle pane that is still working.

5. Select Remove Mirror; you will a screen similar to Figure 9.14.

Figure 9.14: Removing a mirror

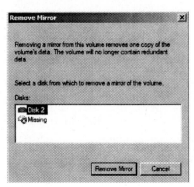

6. Select the drive that has failed on your server to remove the mirror from. When you remove the mirror for the drive, this will remove the mirror. Then you are ready to re-create the mirror.

7. To re-create the mirror, right-click and select Add Mirror.

8. In the Add Mirror dialog box, select the new volume you want to create the mirror on.

9. You will see a warning dialog box if the drives need to be converted to dynamic drives for mirrored volumes. After you review the warning, click Yes.

10. You will see the drive status of synching, and when the drive has completed the sync, you will see a status of Healthy.

Break a Mirror

You may choose to stop using an existing mirror. Maybe you want to choose a different RAID level or need to repurpose one of your disks for additional storage. You can at any time break your mirror. You do not need to worry about seven years' bad luck. Also, unlike when a real mirror breaks, you will not lose any data. In fact, you will have two copies of the data on two separate volumes.

1. Open Server Manager by selecting Start ⇨ Administrative Tools ⇨ Server Manager.

2. In the Server Manager tree, click Storage.

3. In Storage, click Disk Management.

4. Right-click one of the volumes in the bottom window of the middle pane in the mirror.

5. Select Break Mirrored Volume.

6. Review the warning about removing the fault tolerance from the drive. Remember, you will not lose data, just the redundancy of the mirror. Click Yes to break the mirror.

Create a RAID 5 or Striped Volume with Parity

After you have determined which volumes you are going to use for your RAID 5 volume, you will use Disk Management to create the RAID 5 volume:

1. Open Server Manager by selecting Start ➪ Administrative Tools ➪ Server Manager.

2. In the Server Manager tree, click Storage.

3. In Storage, click Disk Management.

4. Right-click the unallocated space in the bottom window of the middle pane you want to create the volume on.

5. Click New RAID-5 Volume.

6. On the Welcome screen, review the message, and click Next.

7. On the Select Disks screen, select the disks you want to use for the RAID 5 volume, and click Add to place them in the selected option. Remember, you need at least three drives.

8. Select the amount of space to allocate on each disk selected, and click Next.

9. Select how you want mount the volume. You can choose to mount to a drive letter, to mount a folder on an existing drive, or to not assign any mount point. After you make your selection, click Next.

10. Next, you can select how to format the drive. After you make your selection, click Next.

11. Review the summary screen, and click Finish.

12. You will see a warning dialog box if the drives need to be converted to dynamic drives for striped volumes. After you review the warning, click Yes.

Data Access and Management

PART III

Repair a RAID 5 Volume

If you lose a hard drive in a RAID 5 volume, you will need to repair the volume. When you are working with Disk Management and see a screen similar to Figure 9.15, with the words *failed redundancy*, one of your hard drives may have failed. To fix the RAID 5 volume, you need to replace the failed drive and then use Disk Management to repair the volume and reestablish redundancy.

1. Open Server Manager by selecting Start ⇨ Administrative Tools ⇨ Server Manager.

2. In the Server Manager tree, click Storage.

3. In Storage, click Disk Management.

4. Right-click one of the volumes, in the bottom window of the middle pane, in the existing RAID 5 set.

5. Click Repair Volume.

6. You will see a screen similar to Figure 9.16, asking you which volume you want to use to repair the RAID 5 volume. Select the new hard drive, and click OK.

Figure 9.15: RAID 5 failure

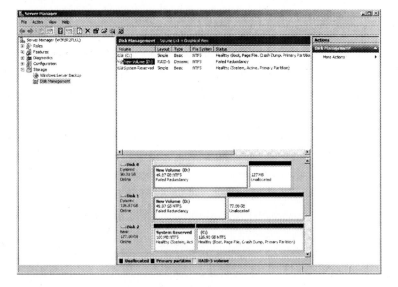

Figure 9.16: Repairing RAID 5

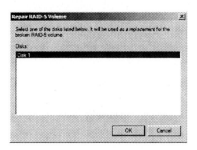

7. You will see a warning dialog box if the drives need to be converted to dynamic drives for striped volumes. After you review the warning, click Yes.

8. Your drives will begin the process of resynching. This process could take several minutes. During the resync process, you will see a screen similar to Figure 9.17.

Figure 9.17: Resynching RAID 5

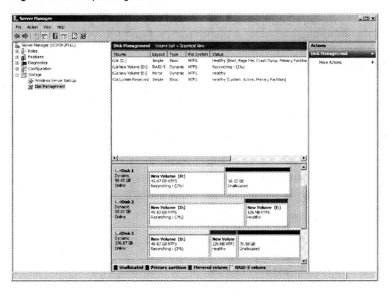

Data Access and Management

PART III

Manage Disk Storage

One of the keys to working with your drive storage is being able to manage how your storage is being used and how the data is being stored on the drives. With Windows Server 2008 R2, you have the ability to create storage *quotas* for your drives. The quotas allow you to limit how much space your users can use. In Chapter 5, you saw a little bit about the File Resource Manager. In this section, you will learn how to enable and manage storage quotas that are natively part of the Windows Server 2008 R2 disks.

Manage Disk Storage Quotas

Managing storage quotas is simply a matter of enabling quota management on the volumes you want to have managed. Then, after enabling the management of the volumes, you can set a quota for everyone using the volume, or you can set individual entries for users or groups through the quota management utility. Normally, you will want to enable quotas on the drive before you enable access to your users. Before you can work with disk quotas, you need to enable them on the drives. You can enable them by accessing the properties for the drive or volume you want to manage. You can access the properties for the drive either through Windows Explorer or through Disk Management. For the steps you see here, you'll use Disk Management:

1. Open Server Manager by selecting Start ⇨ Administrative Tools ⇨ Server Manager.

2. In the Server Manager tree, click Storage.

3. In Storage, click Disk Management.

4. Right-click the volume you want to enable quotas on, and click Properties. You will see a screen similar to Figure 9.18.

5. Click the Quota tab.

6. Click Enable Quota Management to turn on quotas.

7. Click OK to close the properties window; you will see a screen similar to Figure 9.19, which tells you the drive will be scanned to verify and update current storage statistics.

Figure 9.18: Volume properties

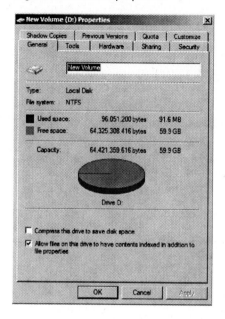

Figure 9.19: Quota initial scan

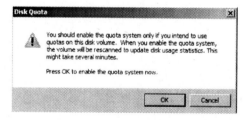

If you want to turn off quotas, simply reverse the process you used to turn on the quota system.

After you enable quotas, you can choose the amount of space all the users are limited to on your server. You can also choose when they receive a warning—when they are about to have the quotas be enforced or just when they near their quota limit. You can also enable individual quota entries for your users or groups. This provides you with a tool to allow exceptions for certain users or groups. You can create exceptions that are less than your set default or exceptions exceeding your default. By default, the Administrators group does not have quotas applied to it.

1. After you have enabled quotas on the volumes, you then need to set defaults for all your users. You set the defaults by modifying the select default disk space and warning levels for your users. Figure 9.20 shows a quota limit of 100MB with a warning given to the user at 90KB of usage space. You will always set the warning to be less than the limit. By default this quota applies to all of your users.

Figure 9.20: Disk quota limit

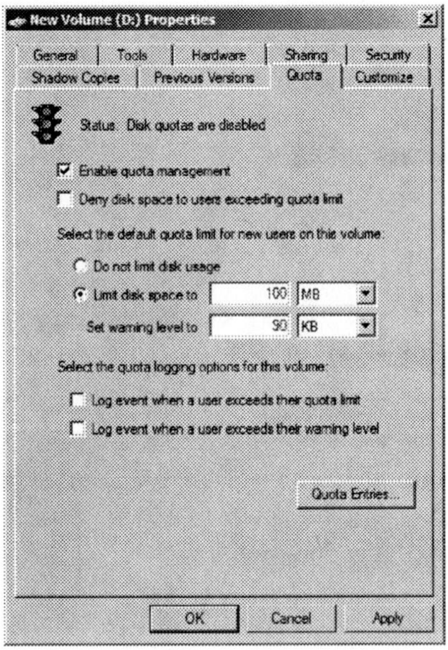

2. If you want to enable individual entries on the Quota tab, click the Quota Entries button.

3. Click the New Quota Entry button, which looks like a blank piece of paper.

4. Type in your users or groups, or click the Advanced button to search. This process is similar to working with users and groups.

When you're done adding users, click OK; you will see a screen similar to Figure 9.21.

Figure 9.21: Quota entry

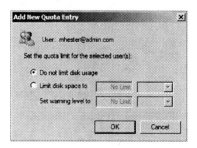

5. Modify the limits for the user or group, and when you are finished, click OK.

6. When you are done adding entries, close the window to return to the quota management screen.

7. Click OK to close the volume's properties when you are finished.

After you have enabled quota management and added your quota entries, you now have a choice to make. By default the quotas are *soft*, or unenforced, quotas, which means your users can exceed the limits you have set. If you want to keep the soft quota, you should also enable logging by selecting the logging options on the Quota tab, as shown in Figure 9.22. This will allow you to track events in Event Viewer when your users get warnings or exceed the limits.

Figure 9.22: Quota logging

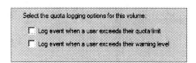

However, if you want to enforce your quotas, select the Deny Disk Space To Users Exceeding Quota Limit box on the Quota tab. This will ensure your users will not exceed the amount of space you have granted them. Also, when you enforce the quota, your users will then see the

Data Access and
Management

PART III

visual notifications for warnings and when they exceed the limit. In Figure 9.23, you can see an example of a user who has exceeded the limit.

Figure 9.23: Enforced quota

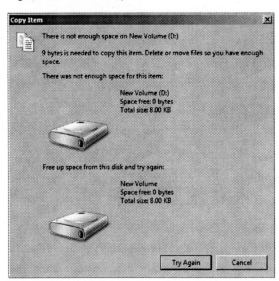

PART IV

Network Configuration and Communication

IN THIS PART ⊙

10

Maintaining Your Web Server

In this chapter, you will learn how to work with Internet Information Services (IIS). The IIS server role provides your environment with the ability to have web services for both internal- and external-facing websites. IIS also provides several other key components that you will see in this chapter. IIS in Windows Server 2008 R2 is a new version, labeled IIS 7.5.

In addition, IIS has several key improvements to assist administrators; it now includes PowerShell modules and supports the ability to install IIS on Windows Server 2008 R2 Server Core. You will learn some of the key features for application support for IIS, including support for PHP applications. You will also take a look at installing IIS on a server and will take a brief tour of where your web files are and the tools to manage your websites.

Install Internet Information Services

In this section, you will learn how to install Internet Information Services. You will see how to install IIS on a full Windows Server 2008 R2 installation and on a Windows Server 2008 R2 Server Core installation. You will also see how Windows Server 2008 R2 Web edition can be installed for the purpose of supporting an IIS server. Being able to install IIS on Windows Server 2008 R2 Server Core provides a new workload capability to Server Core. The ability to install IIS on Windows Server 2008 R2 Server Core is available because of the .NET application framework provided by Server Core. You will also get a brief overview of the various components IIS can provide to your environment.

Understand Internet Information Services Role Services

When you are installing IIS on your server, you will see a screen of role services you can choose to install, as shown in Figure 10.1. Understanding which components you will need to install will help you support your web server requirements in addition to any needed web applications. Prior to installing IIS, you need to talk with your web developers to make sure you are providing the proper level of support for their applications.

Figure 10.1: IIS role services

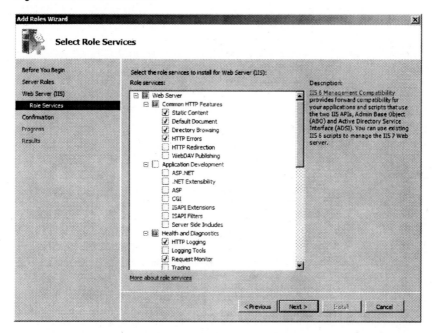

The role services are broken into three main categories:

- Web Server: This category contains all the components for your websites from basic HTML websites to complex web applications. This is the main role of an IIS server and has several components and capabilities to provide you with the web infrastructure your environment will need.

- Management Tools: This category provides you with the tools necessary to manage and administer your web servers. You will also be able to select management tools for previous versions of IIS, mainly IIS 6.0.

- FTP Server: This category allows you to install and set up a basic FTP server for your infrastructure.

The Web Server role service is broken into five major sections. The first component is Common HTTP Features, which provides the web server with basic functionality. Primarily basic and static HTML pages are provided by these features, as described in Table 10.1.

Table 10.1: Common HTTP Features

HTTP Feature	Description
Static Content	This provides the support needed for HTML pages and graphics and provides the basic level of functionality for your IIS server. This feature is installed by default.
Default Document	This provides the web server with the ability to offer users of your website a default document when they reference your site without a specific file request. Essentially, the default document is the home page for your web server. This feature is installed by default.
Directory Browsing	This allows your users, if they have the proper permissions, to browse the directory for the contents on your web server. This feature is installed by default.
HTTP Errors	This provides the customizable error messages that users of your website will see. For example, when you see an error message like "Error 403: Access Denied/Forbidden," this is the service that provides the error message. This feature is installed by default.
HTTP Redirection	This provides you with the ability to redirect users of your websites to a different location. This is great to use when you want to send users to a different URL than what they typed in. This is useful when you want or need to rename or change your domain for your website.
WebDAV Publishing	Web Distributed Authoring and Versioning (WebDAV) provides the needed capability to allow files to be published via HTTP to your web server. This is commonly used by web applications. Outlook Web Access is an example of an application requiring WebDAV.

The second category is Application Development. This unlocks the true power of a web server by providing the web server with the necessary infrastructure to support web applications and in general extend the functionality of IIS. This component allows you to support the many different programming languages your developers can use to write web applications. It is vital that you understand how these components are installed and configured. However, you may be wondering which of the components, listed in Table 10.2, you need to install. This is an important question, and generally speaking, this is for your web developers to help you make the proper decision to support the applications they are programming. It is good to take some time and chat with the developers so you can install the proper components. By default, none of the Application Development components are installed.

Table 10.2: Application Development Components

Component	Description
ASP.NET	ASP.NET is an object-oriented programming environment. Installing this component will allow your web server to support sites built using managed code via the ASP.NET framework. If you install this component, you will also need to install ISAPI Filters, ISAPI Extensions, and .NET Extensibility to properly support this environment.
.NET Extensibility	This allows your developers to change, add, and extend your web servers. This component provides the necessary framework to support ASP.NET.
ASP	Active Server Pages (ASP) is a scripting environment commonly used to build websites. ASP provides support for VBScript and JScript. This is primarily used for older application support, and your developers may be using ASP.NET for any new projects. Installing ASP will require that you install ISAPI Extensions.
CGI	Common Gateway Interface (CGI) is another scripting-based language commonly used to create websites. Depending on the applications you need to support, you may need to install the support for CGI. PHP applications typically will require CGI to be installed on the IIS server. This component provides a key framework for interoperability for non-Microsoft-based applications.
ISAPI Extensions	Internet Server Application Programming Interface (ISAPI) provides support for dynamic content that is written using ISAPI.
ISAPI Filters	The ISAPI filters help determine how requests are processed by your web applications. The filters are files allowing you to change the functionality of IIS to support your web applications.
Server Side Includes (SSI)	SSI is another scripting-based language allowing you to dynamically include common web clients on other web pages in your environment. For example, if you wanted to have a common menu appear on all the web pages on your site, your programmers could use SSI to provide the menu.

Health and Diagnostics provides the basic functionality to monitor and tune your IIS server. Table 10.3 describes the features.

Table 10.3: Health and Diagnostics

Component	Description
HTTP Logging	As the name implies, with this you can track website activity on your IIS server. The type of events logged are typically when an HTTP transaction occurs (such as a web page request). This feature is installed by default.
Logging Tools	This allows you to manage your logs, as well as provide the functionality to automate common logging procedures.
Request Monitor	This provides the ability for you to monitor the health of your web applications. This allows you to see when you have a process running slowly or not responding. This allows you to identify the process to help identify any issue. This feature is installed by default.
Tracing	This is another tool allowing you to monitor your web applications, typically used for hard-to-find problems in your website, such as when your website times out or performs slowly because of poor performance.
Custom Logging	This provides you with the ability to customize and create your own logging format. You can create or use your own logging components by installing this component.
ODBC Logging	This provides logging for the Open Database Connectivity (ODBC) activity generated by your web server when it is connecting to an ODBC-compliant database. Most modern-day databases are ODBC compliant, which provides a framework for you to log web activity to those databases.

The next section, "Security," is vital in not only protecting your IIS servers but also protecting your applications and data. The "Security" section provides you with the ability to determine your level of secure authentication support in IIS. By protecting the authentication mechanisms, you can control how users will access your web server environment. You will also need to speak to your web developers to determine which authentication mechanisms are supported by the applications they are currently writing. You will need to find the right blend of secure authentication, performance, and application compatibility. IIS has the capability to have multiple authentications supported on the server. In Table 10.4, you can find a list of the different authentication mechanisms and descriptions.

Table 10.4: Security Components

Component	Description
Basic Authentication	This method is the weakest of the authentication methods; this method stores passwords in an easily decrypted format during transmission. If you need to use basic authentication, make sure you also use SSL. Basic authentication is used generally when you need to offer compatibility to a variety of web browsers.
Windows Authentication	This is a secure authentication mechanism, allowing you to leverage your existing Windows Active Directory domain environment for authenticating your users. You should use this solution for internal websites only, not for users who access your website from behind proxy servers or firewalls.
Digest Authentication	This provides a more secure authentication methodology over basic authentication. This method will also leverage your Windows Active Directory domain environment, by sending a secure password hash to the domain controllers. This method should be considered if you need your users to have access to your website if they are behind proxy servers or firewalls.
Client Certificate Mapping Authentication	This allows you to use client certificates to authenticate your Active Directory users, in a one-to-one mapping across multiple web servers.
IIS Client Certificate Mapping Authentication	This is a faster performance model than client certificate mapping but also uses client certificates to identify your users. This method can use either one-to-one or many-to-one mappings and is typically used in heterogeneous directory environments.
URL Authorization	This provides you with a security mechanism to prevent access to websites in your web servers. URL authorization gives you a tool to explicitly allow or deny access to a directory on your web server either by username or by role. You can use rules based on users, groups, or the header verbs of your HTTP pages.
Request Filtering	This method provides a layer of security at the web server to help prevent many common hacking attacks to your server. This helps filter attacks that may make odd requests or that may use long URLs to target your server. This method screens all inbound requests of your server. This provides you with a mechanism to help mitigate attacks on your server. This feature is installed by default.
IP and Domain Restrictions	This allows you to allow or deny access to your web content, based on the IP address or domain name of the requestor. This provides an additional layer of security to your groups, your roles, or even your NTFS permissions.

The last section is Performance. There are two choices in this section: Static Content Compression and Dynamic Content Compression. Static Content Compression is installed by default and provides your server with the ability to improve bandwidth utilization. As the name implies, this is useful only for static content on your web server, and it has the additional benefit of not affecting the CPU performance on your server.

Dynamic Content Compression also allows you to improve the bandwidth utilization of dynamic content for your web server. However, this method will also potentially have a negative impact on your server's CPU performance. If your Windows Server 2008 R2 server is already heavily taxed for usage with your CPU, you should not install this component.

Install IIS on Windows Server 2008 R2 Full Server Installation

After you have determined which components you want to install for your version of IIS, you now have to install the IIS role with the required components. Like all the roles on Windows Server 2008 R2, you begin the process in Server Manager:

1. To open Server Manager, select Start ⇨ Administrative Tools ⇨ Server Manager.

2. In Server Manager, click Roles.

3. Click Add Roles.

4. Review the welcome screen, and click Next.

5. On the Select Server Roles screen, select Web Server (IIS), as shown in Figure 10.2, and click Next.

6. On the Server Role services screen, review the notes, and click Next.

7. Select the necessary role services to support your web application platform, and click Next.

8. Review the confirmation screen and your selections, and when you are ready, click Install.

9. Review the summary screen, correct any error messages, and click Close.

Figure 10.2: Installing IIS

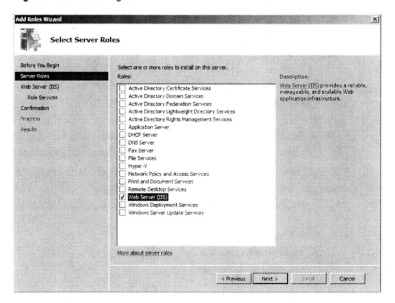

NOTE   If you accept just the default selections, you will have a basic web server. The web server will have basic static content and functionality. More than likely, you will want to add some development components to provide your developers with a platform to build applications to support your company's business internally and externally.

Install IIS on Windows Server 2008 R2 Core Server

The inclusion of the .NET Framework on Windows Server 2008 R2 Server Core provides you with another platform to install web server roles. Like many other roles, you will use the Deployment Image Servicing and Management (dism) command-line tool on the server to install the IIS role. Because of the complexity and the numerous additional roles required, you will want to add the components separately as you build your IIS server, even though you can run this all in one command.

1. After you log on to Server Core, type the following command to install the .NET Framework:

```
DISM /Online /Enable-Feature
 /Featurename:NetFx2-ServerCore
```

2. After the .NET Framework is installed successfully, you then can proceed to install the IIS role on Server Core. To begin the process, type the following command. Please note the name of the role, in this case WebServerRole, is case sensitive. This command will install IIS with all the default components on Server Core:

```
DISM /online /enable-feature
 /featurename:IIS-WebServerRole
 /featurename:IIS-WebServer
```

3. To verify the installation and the necessary components, you can run the get-features switch for the dism command, as in dism /online /get-features. You will see a screen similar to Figure 10.3.

After you run the command, you will see all the IIS features (enabled or disabled) listed in the feature list. These are all the role services for IIS, and they all begin with IIS.

Before you install any additional features on your IIS server, it's important to install the prerequisite features. For example, if you want to install ASP.NET on Windows Server 2008 R2 Server Core, you need to install the following features: ISAPI Filters, ISAPI Extensions, and .NET Extensibility. When you are installing these components on a Windows Server 2008 R2 full server edition, the GUI wizard will handle the prerequisite installation for you. Figure 10.4 shows an example of what you will see on a Windows Server 2008 R2 full edition server.

This is not the case for Server Core; you will need to install the required features prior to installing the main feature. For example, if you ran the command to enable ASP.NET, prior to installing the required features, you would see an error message similar to Figure 10.5.

Figure 10.3: IIS Server Core role services

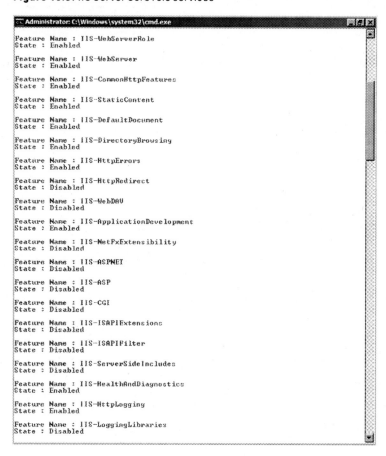

Figure 10.4: ASP.NET requirements

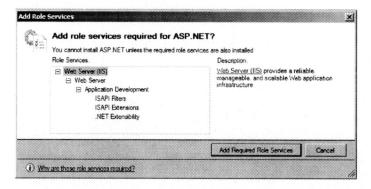

Figure 10.5: ASP.NET error

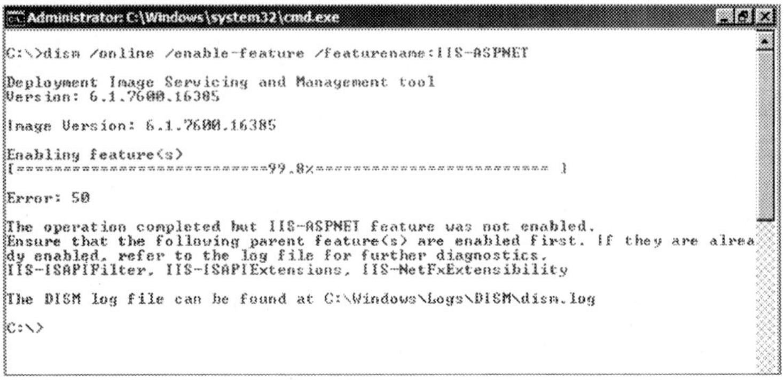

The error message will inform you of the required features you need to install. In the example of installing ASP.NET on Server Core, you would need to run the following command prior to installing the ASP.NET feature:

```
dism /online /enable-feature
    /featurename:IIS-ApplicationDevelopment
    /featurename:IIS-ISAPIFilter
    /featurename:IIS-ISAPIExtensions
    /featurename:IIS-NetFxExtensibility
```

After the command runs successfully, you can then enable the ASP.NET feature by running the following command:

```
dism /online /enable-feature /featurename:IIS-ASPNET
```

Install IIS on Windows Server 2008 R2 Web Edition

If you purchased Windows Server 2008 R2 Web edition, you probably purchased this server edition with the sole purpose of it being a web server for your organization. To install the Web edition server, you simply need to select the Web edition on the operating system selection screen, as shown in Figure 10.6.

The Web edition can be installed on either a full edition or Server Core. After you install the Web edition server, then all you need to do is install the IIS role. What makes the Windows Server 2008 R2 Web edition unique is that the server contains only two server roles, DNS and Web Server (IIS). When you go to add the roles on the Web edition, you will see a screen similar to Figure 10.7.

Figure 10.6: Web edition

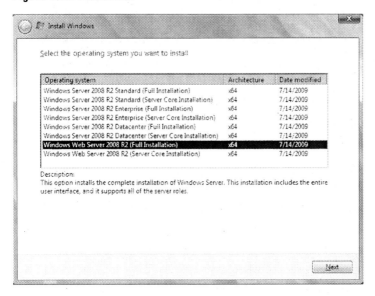

Figure 10.7: Web edition add roles

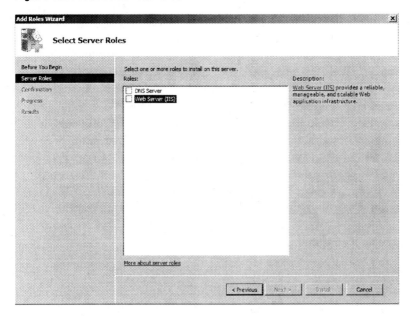

Even though you can install only two roles on the Web edition, IIS will install like IIS on a Windows Server 2008 R2 full edition server.

1. To open Server Manager, select Start ➪ Administrative Tools ➪ Server Manager.

2. In Server Manager, click Roles.

3. Click Add Roles.

4. Review the welcome screen, and click Next.

5. On the Select Server Roles screen, select Web Server (IIS),

6. On the Server Role services screen, review the notes, and click Next.

7. Select the necessary role services to support your web application platform, and click Next.

8. Review the confirmation screen and your selections, and when you are ready, click Install.

9. Review the summary screen, correct any error messages, and click Close.

Manage Internet Information Services

After you have installed IIS, you will have access to the default tool to manage the web server. This tool is the IIS Management Console. However, you may need to install additional components depending on the management needs for your Windows Server 2008 R2 web server or web server farm. The IIS Management Console will also provide you with the ability to manage IIS 7.0 from Windows Server 2008.

IIS also provides the ability for you to manage and support your previous IIS 6 installations. If you need to have these capabilities, simply select them during the IIS server installation. This section will focus on managing IIS 7.5, which is built into Windows Server 2008 R2.

Work with the IIS Management Console

You can access the IIS Management Console in one of two ways. You can access the tool via Server Manager under Roles, or you can access the console via the administrative tools. Depending on the screen resolution of the workstation you are managing the server on, you may consider using the selection in the Administrative Tools group. The IIS Management Console can take up a lot of screen real estate. To load the IIS Management Console from the Administrative Tools group, simply select Internet Information Services (IIS) Manager. To access the console, click Start ⇨ Administrative Tools ⇨ Internet Information Services (IIS) Manager. When you load the console, you will see a screen similar to Figure 10.8.

The start page gives you some basic tasks, allowing you to connect to other websites and applications. You will also be able to access online websites and help files. One resource specific for IIS you will want to make note of is www.iis.net, which is great website with tons of references and examples for you to use when maintaining your web server.

Figure 10.8: IIS Management Console

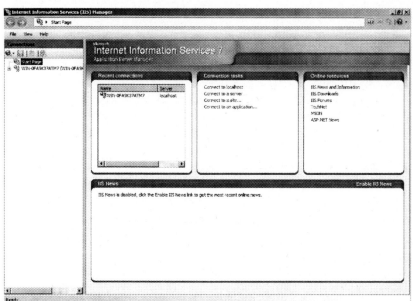

IIS Configuration Files

In prior versions of IIS, configuration was stored in a location called the *metabase*. You may have used this very unwieldy file. Now in IIS, the configuration is XML-based and is centralized on the server. Three main files make up the IIS manager configuration. The files, by default, are located in your Windows directory in the System32\Inetsrv\Config folder:

- administration.config: This configuration file contains all the management settings for your IIS server and your management console.

- applicationhost.config: This stores all the settings for the websites located on your web server.

- redirection.config: This file allows you to have centralized settings. You can use this file to redirect the IIS server's configuration to a centralized server location.

These files create the main default settings for your web server. A good reference for you to learn more about the configuration files is at http://learn.iis.net/page.aspx/122/getting-started-with-iis-7-configuration/.

The true power in the IIS Management Console is when you first click a server in your management console; you will see a screen similar to Figure 10.9.

As you can see, this screen is broken up into three panes, typical of most Microsoft Management Consoles, with tree navigation on the left pane, details of the selected object in the middle pane, and actions in the far-right pane. As you navigate the tree or components regarding your website, your details and actions will change.

When you first click your server in the IIS Management Console, your IIS Management Console will show only the components you have currently installed for IIS. With a default installation of IIS only, you will notice your management screen will be broken into three areas: ASP.NET, IIS, and Management. This allows you to navigate quickly around the areas on your IIS server you want to manage. You can also change the view to Category or just list the different areas for you to manage on your server. To change how the IIS management tasks are organized, you can click the Group By option on the toolbar in the console and select your desired view. In Figure 10.10, you can see an example of an IIS server with ungrouped tasks.

Figure 10.9: IIS server tasks

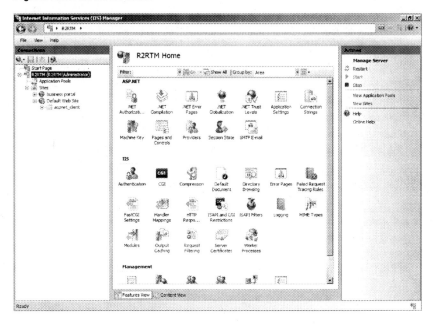

Figure 10.10: IIS tasks ungroup

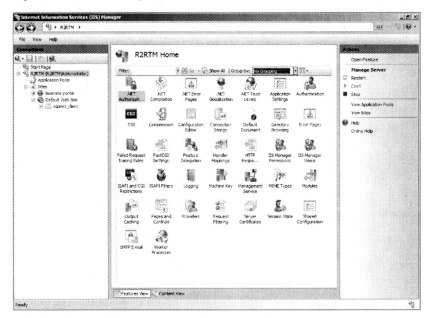

When you click a site, you will see several of the same administrative tasks you can perform. When you are working with sites, it's important you select the proper level you want to administer. When you first select the server level, all the changes you make will impact the websites on the server. However, you can override the settings by making changes at the website level. The website level allows you to have customized settings of that website.

One of the things you will notice is the tasks all work the same way, and once you learn how to manage tasks at the server level, it is quite easy to apply the same knowledge to the website level. Table 10.5 describes some of the common tasks you can perform when managing IIS.

Table 10.5: Common IIS Tasks

Task Name	Description
Authentication	This allows you to control which authentication mechanisms are currently enabled. As you may recall, when you install IIS, you can have multiple authentication methods installed. With the Authentication task, you can control which sites use which authentication mechanism.
Default Document	Default Document is an important setting for you to use when users connect to a website or server but do not specify a specific page. The default document is what is displayed. You can list many default documents to be used, and they are processed in order.
Error Pages	When a user encounters an error on your web server or site, you can customize the error messages that users will see. This provides you with a tool to assist the user but also to assist your troubleshooting efforts.
Handler Mappings	Handler mappings work similarly to file extensions for documents. For example, when you double-click an `.xlsx` file, Excel opens. In the web server handler, mappings work with requests for applications. For example, if you open a web page, IIS will know to open the page and, if necessary, open the proper application as in the case of `.php` websites, for example.
Logging	If you have installed the logging role service, you will be able to control the default location, how log files are generated, and when logging will occur.

Table 10.5: Common IIS Tasks *(continued)*

Task Name	Description
Management Service	If you have installed the remote management service, you will be able to configure the service with this task.
Request Filtering	Request filtering allows you to work with and filter content based on protocol or even IP settings. This essentially allows you to set what content will be served to users of your websites.

Work with Failed Request Tracing Rules

One of the tasks you can use to help troubleshoot errors on your web server is failed request tracing. To be able to take advantage of failed request tracing, you need to install the Tracing role service of IIS.

1. To open Server Manager, click Start ➪ Administrative Tools ➪ Server Manager.

2. In Server Manager, click + next to Roles.

3. Right-click Web Server (IIS), and select Add Role Services.

4. Select Tracing, and click Next.

5. Review the summary screen, and click Install.

6. Review the installation summary, and click Close.

Once you have successfully installed the Tracing role service, you will be able to trace requests to your websites that have failed. This allows you to set certain rules and conditions that, when met, allow you to see what happened and why the error occurred. You can then, ideally, track down the source of the error.

You can create failed request tracing rules at the server level or the site level. However, by default failed request tracing is not enabled at the site level. To enable failed request tracing, you need to modify the site settings:

1. To open the IIS Management Console, click Start ➪ Administrative Tools ➪ Internet Information Services (IIS) Manager.

2. In the navigation tree, click Sites.

3. Click the site on which you want to enable failed request tracing.

4. In the Actions pane on the right, click Failed Request Tracing; you will see a screen similar to Figure 10.11.

Figure 10.11: Enabling site failed request tracing

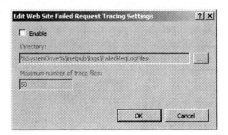

5. Click Enable, and set your directory for the log and how many trace files you want to maintain.

6. Click OK; you will then be able to create tracing rules.

Creating tracing rules at the web server or site level follows the same procedures; the only difference is the scope of the rule. Creating failed request tracing rules follows a similar procedure to creating an email rule:

1. To open the IIS Management Console, click Start ➪ Administrative Tools ➪ Internet Information Services (IIS) Manager.

2. In the navigation tree, click the server or sites you want to manage.

3. Double-click Failed Request Tracing Rules in the center pane.

4. In the Failed Request Tracing Rules screen, click Add in the right Actions pane.

5. Select the content you want to look for, and click Next.

6. On the Conditions screen, set the conditions you are looking to trace; you can trace status codes, timeouts, and even the severity level. Before you can continue, you must select either Status Code or Time Taken. Even though these are check boxes that do not seem to be dependent on each other, one of the first two must be selected even if you just want the event severity. When you are done selecting your conditions, click Next.

7. In the Trace Providers step, you can select which providers you want to trace and to what level of detail you want to see in your log. The more verbose your logs, the bigger the files, but the better chance for you to trace the error. When you are done, click Finish.

Remotely Manage IIS Servers

While you're using the IIS console to manage your local web server, you can also manage other IIS servers by using the IIS Management Console to connect to them. However, before you can remotely manage IIS on other servers, you have to configure remote management of the services. Specifically, you need to add the IIS management service and configure and start the service to be able to remotely manage your web servers.

First you need to install the remote management component of IIS either via Server Manager or via the command prompt. To add the component in Server Manager, follow these steps:

1. Open Server Manager by selecting Start ⇨ Administrative Tools ⇨ Server Manager.

2. Right-click the Web Server (IIS) role; you will see a menu similar to Figure 10.12. Select Add Role Services.

Figure 10.12: Adding role services

3. Select the Management Service box to add the remote management service; you may also want to select the IIS Management Scripts And Tools box to provide management capabilities via the command prompt. You can see an example of these services being installed in Figure 10.13.

Figure 10.13: IIS remote management and scripting services

4. Review the confirmation screen and your selections, and when you are ready, click Install.

5. Review the summary screen, correct any error messages, and click Close.

To add the IIS management service via the command prompt, as in the case of a Windows Server 2008 R2 Server Core installation, type in the following command:

```
dism /online /enable-feature
    /featurename:IIS-ManagementService
```

After you have installed the service, you then need to configure the registry to enable the remote management service:

1. Click Start ⇨ Run.

2. In the Run dialog box, type **regedit.exe**, and press Enter.

3. In the registry, open the following location: HKEY_LOCAL_MACHINE\ Software\Microsoft\WebManagement\Server.

4. Set the EnableRemoteManagement key to the value of 1; you can see an example of this service enabled in Figure 10.14.

5. Close the registry editor.

Figure 10.14: Enabling web management in the registry

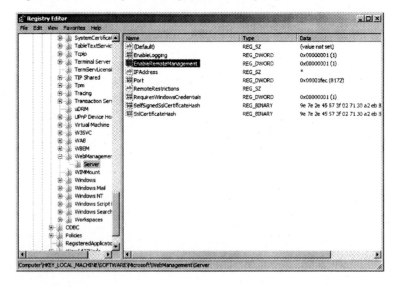

After you have enabled the service in the registry, you need to configure the service to start and run. You can configure the service in the Services control panel, or you can use the command prompt to start the service. To use the Services control panel, follow these steps:

1. Open Services by selecting Start ➪ Administrative Tools ➪ Services.

2. Select Web Management Service, and click Start. If you want the service to start automatically, you can right-click the service and click Properties. You will see a screen similar to Figure 10.15.

3. Set the service to start automatically, and click OK.

Figure 10.15: Web management service

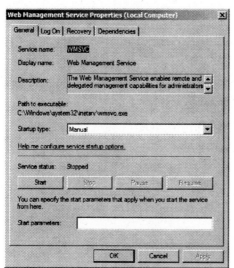

If you want to start the service temporarily or start the service from the command prompt, you can just run the following command. This will not change the startup properties of the service, and the service is only temporary until the service is stopped or the server is rebooted.

```
net start wmsvc
```

If you want to have the service started automatically, for example, you are configuring Windows Server 2008 R2 Server Core, you can type in the following command:

```
sc config wmsvc start= auto
```

After you have followed those steps, you can remotely manage IIS web services from the IIS Management Console on a centralized workstation or server system. To connect to the remote servers, follow this procedure:

1. Open the IIS Management Console by selecting Start ⇨ Administrative Tools ⇨ Internet Information Services (IIS) Manager.

2. On the tree root on the left side of the console, right-click Start Page, and click Connect To Server.

3. Type in the FQDN name or IP address of the server you want to remotely manage, and click Next.

4. If you are prompted for credentials, type in the necessary administrative credentials, and click Next.

5. Give your connection a new name if you desire, and then click Finish.

You then will be able to manage the new web server from your centralized console. This will make working with your web servers, particularly your Server Core installations, easier and more efficient. The new servers will appear in the tree on the left side of the console. You can see an example of the IIS Management Console connected to three web servers (the local server, Web edition, and a Server Core) in Figure 10.16.

Figure 10.16: IIS managing multiple servers

Manage IIS with PowerShell

One of the new additions to Windows Server 2008 R2 server is for the support of PowerShell cmdlets and IIS. Managing IIS with PowerShell gives you another avenue to manage and maintain your web servers. Also, with the added PowerShell support to Windows Server 2008 R2 Server Core, PowerShell provides you with an alternative to work with and configure your IIS servers on Server Core installations.

Before you can use the PowerShell utilities in IIS, you need to install the IIS Management Scripts and Tools role service for IIS:

1. Open Server Manager by selecting Start ➪ Administrative Tools ➪ Server Manager.

2. In Server Manager, click + next to Roles.

3. Right-click Web Server (IIS), and select Add Role Services.

4. Select IIS Management Scripts And Tools, and click Next.

5. Review the summary screen, and click Install.

6. Review the installation summary, and click Close.

Network Configuration and Communication

PART IV

After you have installed the scripts and tools, you have to make sure your PowerShell cmdlets, specifically your Web Administration module on your IIS servers, has been loaded.

1. Load PowerShell by selecting Start ➪ Administrative Tools And Windows PowerShell Modules.

2. Run the following command:

```
Get-Module -all | Where {$_.moduletype -eq "Binary"}
 |Format-List moduletype, name
```

Verify Microsoft.IIS.Powershell.Provider is listed in your output list; you can see an example of this command in Figure 10.17.

Figure 10.17: IIS PowerShell module

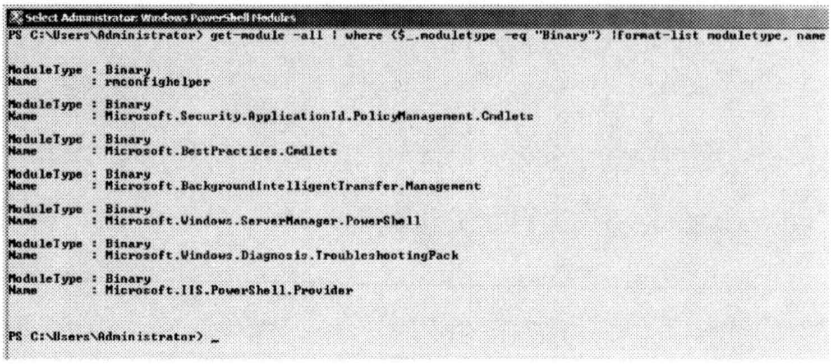

3. If you do not see the IIS PowerShell provider loaded, run the following command to load the IIS PowerShell module:

```
import-module WebAdministration
```

4. After you have loaded or verified the IIS PowerShell module is loaded, you can then work with IIS Web Administration module.

After you have loaded the module, you can manage several aspects of the IIS environment from in PowerShell; if you want to see all the commands, you can type the following command in PowerShell:

```
get-command –pssnapin WebAdministration
```

You will see a list of all the PowerShell commands, as shown in Figure 10.18.

Figure 10.18: IIS PowerShell cmdlets

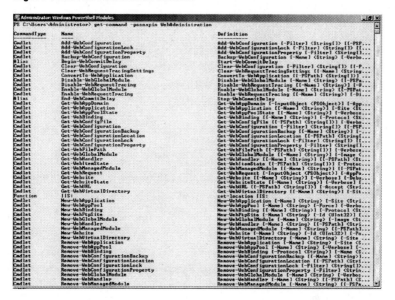

Table 10.6 describes some of the common cmdlets in IIS.

Table 10.6: IIS cmdlets

cmdlets	Description
get-website	This shows the basic configuration of the website, including the directory location for the web files, port bindings, and locations.
backup-webconfiguration	This backs up your existing web configuration information.
restore-webconfiguration	This allows you to restore the backup in case of an IIS failure.
stop-website	This stops the website, . You can start, remove, or even stop websites from the PowerShell command prompt.
new-website	This allows you to create a new website with any settings you want to use.

If you wanted to create a new website called business portal on port 8080 with the website stored on the c:\bp drive, you would run the following PowerShell command:

```
new-website "business portal" -port 8080
-physicalpath "c:\bp"
```

You will notice there is one function listed, which is the IIS: function. This function allows you to navigate directly into the IIS configuration. When you type in the following command, you will be able to navigate the IIS configuration using common commands:

```
cd IIS:\
```

You can then navigate three different areas of IIS configuration: application pools, sites, and SSL Bindings. You can view or modify any of those areas by using directory navigation commands, such as cd and dir to view the information. For example, if you wanted to view some basic information about all the websites currently on the IIS server, you can perform the following steps:

1. Open PowerShell, and verify the IIS administration module has been loaded.

2. Enter **cd iis:**, and hit Enter.

3. At the command prompt, type the following to navigate to the site information: **cd sites**. Then hit Enter.

4. Your command prompt should read PS IIS:\sites>. Type in **dir**, and you will see basic information about your websites. Figure 10.19 shows an example.

Figure 10.19: Sites in IIS PowerShell

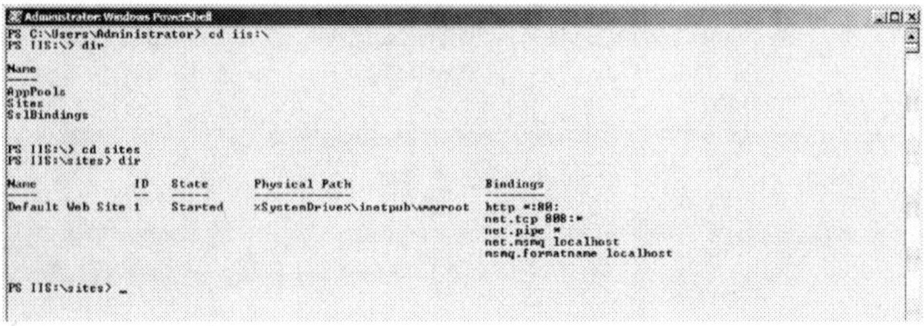

Work with Websites

After you have learned to work with the many tools in IIS to manage the environment, you will need to learn how a website is stored and how to work with the applications your website may need to support. In this section, you will see a basic understanding on how IIS can provide support for your websites.

Understand the Basics of IIS Websites

Before you can work with applications, you need to understand the basics of how websites are used in IIS. Even though your websites may have a combination of simple static web pages and complex applications, all websites have one thing in common. The files supporting the website are stored on the server. Being able to quickly navigate and work with these files provides you with a quick path to fix, replace, or even troubleshoot your applications.

Typically, before you start to work directly with your websites by looking into the directories, you will normally have a testing process in place. The testing process is essential so that when you modify the website currently in production, you do not crash the website or cause your users or even customers any issues.

By default your websites files are stored on your system drive under the inetpub\wwwroot directory. When your website programmers want to change the files, they can quickly navigate directly to the directory and work with the files on your websites. You can also view the website contents directly in the IIS Management Console. This is especially useful if the website is on a Windows Server 2008 R2 Server Core installation. To view the content in the IIS Management Console, you need to be in the content view.

1. Open IIS Management Console by selecting Start ➪ Administrative Tools ➪ Internet Information Services (IIS) Manager.

2. In the navigation tree, click the server where the website you want to manage is located.

3. In the middle pane toward the bottom of the IIS Management Console window, click Content view.

Network Configuration and Communication

PART IV

4. Double-click the site you want to manage, and you will see a screen similar to Figure 10.20.

Figure 10.20: Content view in IIS

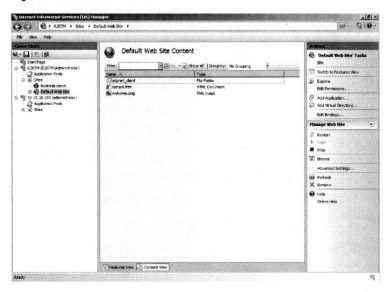

5. From the content view window, you can right-click any whitespace in the console and select Explore. This will take you directly to the Windows Explorer view of the directory where you can modify and work with your files.

One of the nice things about being able to work with your websites directly like this is that it does not require a lot of administrative burden when you need to move the application's files and settings. Even if the application is connected to a server, at the end of the day you are just moving files and not changing the configuration of the applications. You still want to test and verify your applications prior to moving the files.

Moving the location of your websites from one physical location to another involves two steps. First you configure the website's physical directory, and second you copy/cut and paste the files into the new directory. Moving the physical path for your websites is the same procedure regardless of the application you are moving. You could be moving a .NET application or a PHP application. Keep in mind you are just changing the location of the files, not the configuration. Changing the physical directory is just a matter of modifying a setting inside the IIS Management Console:

1. Open IIS Management Console by selecting Start ⇨ Administrative Tools ⇨ Internet Information Services (IIS) Manager.

2. In the navigation tree, click the server where the website you want to manage is located.

3. Double-click Sites in the middle details pane, and click the site you want to change.

4. In the right Actions pane, click Advanced Settings; you will see a screen similar to Figure 10.21.

Figure 10.21: Website advanced settings

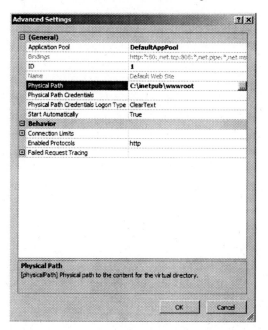

5. Click the physical path parameter, and either type in the new path location or click the ellipsis button to browse to the new location.

6. After you have configured your new directory, click Finish.

7. After you have changed the configuration in IIS, go to the original file location for the website, and copy and paste the contents to the new location.

Network Configuration and Communication

PART IV

Work with Applications

Most of your websites will contain some type of dynamic content, most likely generated from an application on your web server. One of the areas you need to understand is how IIS works with applications. Specifically, you need to understand the nature of application pools and how they provide your server stability.

Application pools allow you to separate running applications on your web server. Therefore, if one application crashes on your server, it will not impact any other applications currently running on your web server. Working with application pools allows you to configure how applications are run on your server. However, working with application pools means you need to understand how the applications need to run on your server. Often times, you will need to speak to a website developer to make sure you provide the proper support for the application.

When you create an application pool, you will need to know a couple of aspects about the application you are going to support. First, you need to know whether the application is running using managed code; this typically means the application requires the .NET Framework to run properly. Second, you will want to know how the application pipe will be managed so you know if you should choose either Integrated or Classic. Classic is provided for backward compatibility for application support and simply means IIS will not use the IIS integrated pipeline for managed code. Again, take the time for a quick conversation to help provide adequate support to your web developers.

Recycle Applications

One last task you may need to perform from time to time is recycling your application pool. This will help free up resources on your web server in case an application encounters an error. Recycling your application pools periodically will allow you to maintain your applications and keep them running smoothly. You can set recycling to occur on regular intervals, or you can recycle an application pool immediately. When you recycle an application pool, you essentially clear up system resources and system state information. This could negatively impact users of your website, so you need to try to recycle the applications in off-hours. When you recycle an application pool on your server, all existing session state data will be lost on your server. If the application you are recycling depends on the session state data, any users with active connections may encounter problems when you recycle the application pool. This is why you should try to make sure you recycle the applications during downtime, if possible, to minimize the impact on your users.

1. Open IIS Management Console by selecting Start ⇨ Administrative Tools ⇨ Internet Information Services (IIS) Manager.

2. In the navigation tree, click the + sign next to your server to expand the container.

3. Click Application Pools.

4. Click the application pool you want to recycle.

5. If you want to recycle the application pool immediately, click Recycle in the Actions pane on the right. The recycle request will process immediately. If you want to set regular recycle intervals, click Recycling in the Actions pane on the right.

6. If you clicked Recycling, you will see a screen similar to Figure 10.22.

Figure 10.22: Recycling application pools

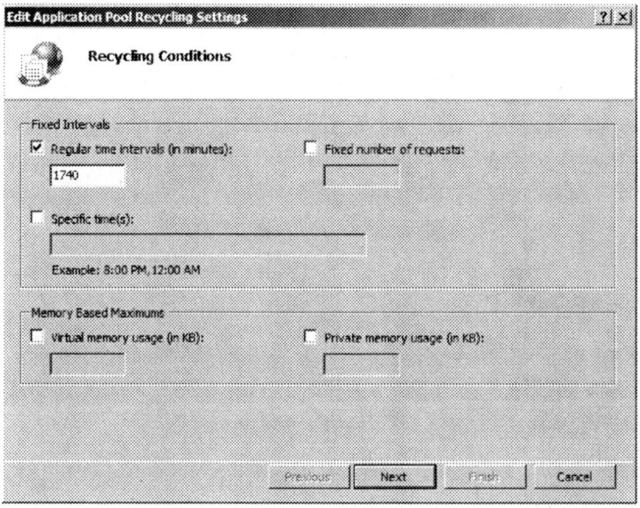

7. The recycling conditions will allow you to set a variety of conditions when you recycle. You can set the time, number of requests, specific time, or even the memory usage of an application. When you are done selecting your conditions, click Next.

8. You can also create event log entries when a recycling process has occurred on your server. The choices you will see here will be based on the selections you made on the recycling conditions. When you are done selecting your logging options, click Finish.

Integrate PHP Applications in IIS

One of the tasks you may be asked to perform as a web administrator is to provide support of PHP applications on your IIS web server. At first you might be inclined to think that PHP applications are not supported on a Microsoft platform like IIS. Fortunately, IIS provides full support for working with PHP applications on the IIS platform. All you need to do from an IT perspective is to know how the components in IIS provide support for these applications and how you can maintain them. One of the great things about this support is that to IIS, whether the application is PHP or not, it is treated like any other applications. It will have application pools, and you will be able to support multiple versions of PHP on the same server.

Before you can begin working with your PHP applications in IIS, you need to make sure you have installed the proper IIS component to provide the PHP applications with the back-end support they will need. In the case of IIS, you will need to install the CGI component located under the Application Development section of IIS. This component installs the underlying framework called FastCGI that provides the necessary support for PHP applications to run properly on IIS.

Install CGI on IIS

You can install CGI during the normal install of IIS or after you have already installed IIS. To install CGI if you already have installed IIS, you will need to install the additional role service.

1. Open Server Manager by selecting Start ➪ Administrative Tools ➪ Server Manager.

2. Click the + next to Roles to expand the tree.

3. Right-click Web Server (IIS), and select Add Role Services.

4. Select CGI in the Application Development section, and click Next.

5. Review the confirmation screen and your selections, and when you are ready, click Install.

6. Review the summary screen, correct any error messages, and click Close.

After you have installed CGI onto your IIS server, you will then need to download the version of PHP required for your web server. When you go to download the PHP package, you will see two versions for Windows; one titled thread-safe, and another is non-thread-safe. You want to download the non-thread-safe version of PHP for your IIS server on Windows Server 2008 R2. The built-in FastCGI component will handle the necessary thread process checks for process integrity normally handled by the thread-safe version of PHP. This means better performance for the PHP applications loaded on your server.

Thread-Safe vs. Non-Thread-Safe in IIS FastCGI

Using thread-safe PHP will typically ensure your applications' threads run properly, in order, and safely. Typically this is a very good thing. Even though this may impact performance, making sure the applications run properly and smoothly is vital.

Non-thread-safe applications are going to try to execute the threads process as quickly as the threads can be called and executed. This sometimes means the threads bump into other threads or run improperly. The advantage of non-thread-safe applications is typically performance.

So, this is the age-old question of performance vs. reliability and is why IIS is so special. The FastCGI component built in to IIS on Windows Server 2008 R2 will make sure the threads are executed safely. In a sense, it takes the place of the thread-safe version of PHP in regard to thread safety. You can expect the non-thread-safe PHP package to run faster with reliability on your IIS server.

Network Configuration and Communication

PART IV

You also need to make several changes to your PHP.ini file for the applications to run properly. You have to locate and uncomment the following sections in your PHP.ini file:

- Set fastcgi.impersonate=1.

- Set cgi.fix_pathinfo=1.

- Set cgi.force_redirect=0.

- Set open_basedir to point to a folder or network path where the content of the website is located. By default, on a IIS server, this is c:\inetpub\wwwroot.

- Set extension_dir to the location where the PHP extensions reside. If you have installed PHP with the default settings, you would most likely set this parameter to extension_dir = "./ext".

Lastly, you need to set the application association for PHP applications when they are accessed by your web server. In IIS this is called the *handler mappings* and is similar to mapping a file extension to a program such as .doc for Microsoft Word. The PHP applications will have the .php extension. IIS will need to know how to process the files when the requests come in. With the newer PHP for Windows packages, this handler mapping is created; however, if it does not exist, you will have to configure the IIS handler mapping. This will make sure that when it processes a .php file, it passes the component to the FastCGI component.

1. Open IIS Management Console by selecting Start ⇨ Administrative Tools ⇨ Internet Information Services (IIS) Manager.

2. Click your server or website in the console tree on the left.

3. Double-click Handler Mappings in the center pane of the IIS console.

4. Look for an option in the Path column with a value of *.php. If one exists, double-click the mapping, and your settings should be similar to Figure 10.23.

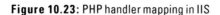

Figure 10.23: PHP handler mapping in IIS

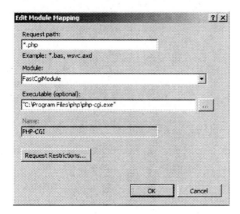

5. If you do not see a *.php handler mapping, click Add Module
    Mapping on the right action list. Configure the mapping with the
    following settings, which assumes you used the default installa-
    tion settings for PHP:

    - Request Path: *.php

    - Module: FastCGI

    - Executable: Location of PHP installation (for example,
      c:\program files\php\php-cgi.exe)

    - Name: Can be any value you want

For more information on providing support for PHP applications,
take a look at this website:

        http://learn.iis.net/page.aspx/246/using-fastcgi-to-host-
        php-applications-on-iis-70

11

Administering DNS

Network Configuration and Communication

PART IV

N ame resolution services are critically important in every network! They provide name resolution for Active Directory, applications, and the Internet, and they provide the mechanism for network connectivity. DNS is the service responsible for name resolution in Windows Server 2008 R2, and a clear understanding of DNS and how to administrate it effectively will ensure both internal and external connectivity for the users, computers, and applications in your network.

Add and Remove DNS Servers

Domain Name System (DNS) servers are used to provide name resolution services to your TCP/IP network. DNS is built on a client-server model where the server stores a database of records that maps TCP/IP addresses to the corresponding name type. Clients send queries to the DNS server in order to resolve names to their corresponding TCP/IP address. If your clients cannot resolve names to IP addresses, then communication will be limited at best and nonexistent at worst. If you can ensure that your clients have access to a DNS server, your ability to facilitate network connectivity increases.

DNS is very flexible; it can be run on a Windows Server machine in a stand-alone environment or as part of a domain-joined Active Directory (AD) network. If Active Directory is running in your network, you will want to add the DNS Server role to your domain controllers. The really cool thing about this is that you can maintain the directory services database and the DNS database simultaneously. One option for DNS is to install what is called a *caching-only* DNS server. These servers simply perform name resolution and maintain a list of the results of the queries they receive. They do not have authority for any DNS zone. This option can be very desirable in situations where you have multiple sites connected by wide area network (WAN) links that have limited bandwidth.

There is no right or wrong way to deploy DNS; the key is that you understand the name resolution needs of your network and then deploy the DNS servers to meet your network's needs.

Add a DNS Server

As you install your first DNS server, begin with a simple configuration change. Whether you are planning on running DNS with Active Directory or running it on a stand-alone server, you will want to configure the local network adapter card with a static IP address. Please don't use a dynamically assigned IP address with a DNS server. The headaches are just not worth it.

The interesting thing about DNS is that it is required for Active Directory installation. If you were building a new AD forest, you would actually need to configure DNS first. What if you didn't know you had to configure DNS before you ran DCPromo (dcpromo.exe) and installed AD? Not to worry. The AD installation wizard will actually install and configure a local DNS server for you. Although this process is certainly easy and it works just fine, we recommend you take the time up front to install your own DNS.

So, how exactly do you install DNS? First you will need membership in the Administrators (or better) group in order to add DNS. Then follow these steps:

1. Open Server Manager.

2. Right-click Roles, and choose Add Roles.

3. Click Next on the Before You Begin page.

4. Select the DNS Server box, as shown in Figure 11.1.

5. Read the DNS info page. There is a lot of good information here.

Figure 11.1: Installing the DNS role

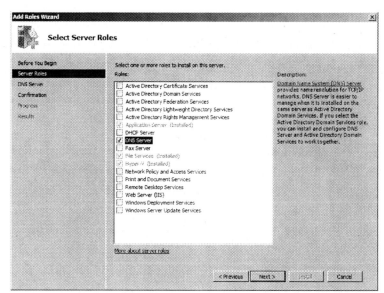

6. Click Next.

7. Click Install.

8. Click Close.

Now that DNS is configured as a role service on the server, you need to configure the DNS server. You can do this with two different tools: DNS Manager, which is a GUI tool, or dnscmd, which is a command-line tool. Although it is technically possible to use a standard text editor to work with DNS entries, it is *not* recommended.

Configure a New DNS Server

When you install DNS on a server that is not an Active Directory domain controller, you will need to do three main things:

- Create a forward lookup zone to facilitate name resolution to IP address, and create a reverse lookup zone to facilitate IP address to name resolution, as shown in Figure 11.2.

- Configure each zone for updates and determine how those updates will occur (secure or nonsecure).

- Define what happens when your server gets a query that it cannot solve. Usually you will want to forward unsolved query requests to another DNS server.

Figure 11.2: Configured forward and reverse lookup zones

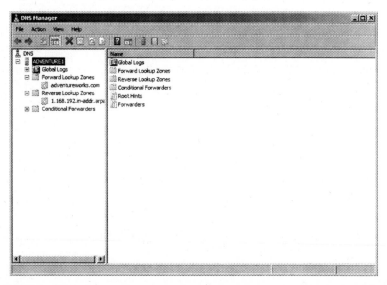

To configure a new DNS server, follow these steps:

1. Start DNS Manager.

2. Right-click the name of the DNS server, and choose Configure A DNS Server.

3. Click Next on the Welcome page of the Configure A DNS Server Wizard.

4. Select the radio button to create the zones you desire. You will likely choose to create both forward and reverse lookup zones on your initial server. Click Next.

5. Select the Yes radio button to create a forward lookup zone, and click Next.

6. Select the type of zone you want to create, and click Next.

7. Type in the zone name, and click Next.

8. Choose Create A New File With This File Name.

9. Choose the type of updates you will allow this zone to accept. (If you are installing DNS on a DC, the option to allow only secure dynamic updates will be enabled.) Click Next.

10. Choose to create a reverse lookup zone, and click Next.

11. Select the type of zone you want to create, and click Next.

12. Choose to create a reverse lookup for IPV4. You can come back and create a reverse lookup zone for IPV6 at a later time. Click Next.

13. Enter the network ID, and click Next.

14. Accept the new filename for the reverse lookup zone, and click Next.

15. Choose the type of updates you will allow for the reverse lookup zone, and click Next.

16. Choose whether you will forward unresolved queries, add the address of the server that queries will be forwarded to, and click Next.

17. Click Finish.

Network Configuration and Communication

PART IV

Of course, you could do all this configuration from the command line using the dnscmd tool. To view the options and syntax, open a command prompt, and type **dnscmd /config /help**.

Now that you have configured your initial forward and reverse lookup zones, have specified how updates will occur, and have chosen forwarders for unresolved DNS queries, your DNS server is ready to service host name resolution requests from your clients. Of course, you will need to tell your clients that you have a DNS server for them to use. You can do this by directly configuring the DNS server entry on each network adapter card configuration, or you can build an option for DNS into your Dynamic Host Configuration Protocol (DHCP) server.

Once the clients know to look to the DNS server for name resolution, your DNS infrastructure is ready to go.

Add Query Forwarding

Once the DNS Server is installed and configured, you will want to consider how to get name resolution for names that your DNS servers are not authoritative for. If you think about the way DNS servers resolve names, you'll realize they use a process of recursive queries to find an authoritative server that will resolve a name to an IP address. Your DNS servers simply do not know all the possible host names and IP addresses in the world's networks. To resolve host names for domains outside of the ones your servers are authoritative for, you will need to configure *query forwarding*.

Your network will likely have several DNS servers. If you configure one of those servers to pass queries from inside your network to the Internet, you have really just designated that server as a forwarder. You would change your network firewall settings to allow that DNS traffic from the forwarder through the firewall and out to the Internet. Queries will be returned from the Internet to the forwarder, and then the forwarder will pass those responses to the appropriate internal server. Do not host a local DNS zone on your forwarder! It is exposed to the Internet, and any zone stored on the forwarder will also be exposed to the Internet. You really don't want your internal DNS zone data becoming available online.

Maybe you don't want to simply forward all your unresolved queries through a single forwarder. Maybe you want to forward requests for certain domains through a specific forwarder. This concept of setting conditions under which queries are forwarded and through which server they are forwarded is called *conditional forwarding*. It offers a little more flexibility than traditional forwarding, and it can be far more effective than traditional forwarding if you are in a private network that hosts multiple domains, each with their own DNS zones. To add forwarders to your DNS architecture, you will use DNS Manager:

1. Open DNS Manager.

2. Right-click the server name.

3. Choose Properties.

4. Select the Forwarders tab.

5. Click Edit. The Edit Forwarders dialog box opens, as shown in Figure 11.3.

6. At this point you can add the desired server to your forwarders list.

Figure 11.3: Adding DNS forwarders

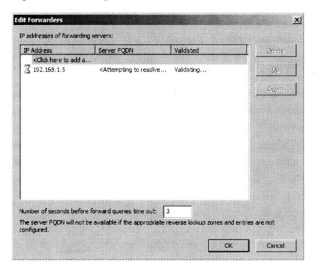

Configure a Caching-Only DNS Server

All DNS servers resolve queries and then cache the results of queries for a limited time. They also perform other functions such as updating records and doing zone database maintenance. You might want a server that simply resolves queries and caches the results. A *caching-only*

Network Configuration and Communication

PART IV

server is especially useful when DNS resolution is needed but when you don't want to create a separate zone for that location.

With a caching-only server, query information is gathered over time from other DNS servers as the caching-only server resolves client queries. That information is then stored by the caching-only server for future use. This process usually results in a decreasing amount of network traffic over time between the location containing the caching-only server and those other locations that contain full-version DNS zones. The benefit comes in the reduced use of the WAN link for DNS resolution while increasing name resolution performance for the local clients. The caching-only server does not perform zone transfers like other DNS servers, and so the WAN is not impacted by this traffic.

1. On the server where you want to configure the DNS caching-only server, open DNS Manager.

2. Right-click the name of the server, and select Configure A DNS Server.

3. Choose to configure the root hints only. Do not configure a forward or reverse lookup zone.

4. Click Finish.

This process really could not be much easier. You now have a caching-only DNS server that will take client requests and perform recursive DNS name queries. When the server resolves a query, it will store the answer locally. There are no zones to maintain or update. No zone transfers are necessary, and the clients get the benefit of a local DNS server.

Manage Root Hints

We know some of you out there are scratching your heads and thinking, "What in the world is a root hint?" By definition, a *root hint* is a piece of DNS data stored in the DNS database that identifies the authoritative servers for the root of a given DNS namespace. If you want to resolve a query for a namespace, you have to find the server responsible for resolving requests for that space. DNS names are hierarchical in structure, and each level of the hierarchy is separated by a period (or a *dot*). So, for example, if you had a client who was trying to resolve the hierarchical name www.microsoft.com, you would begin the process at the root, which in this case is com. Where is the com server? Wouldn't it be nice if you already had a list of commonly used roots (like com, mil, gov, edu, net, org, and so on) and their corresponding IP addresses? These are the root hints.

By default DNS contains a standard list of commonly used root hints. The root hints contain the name server (NS) records and the host (A) resource records for the internet root servers. All of this works very well if you are on the Internet. What if you are on a private network and want to configure your own root servers? You can configure your own root zone and add the associated NS and A records to root hints as follows:

1. Open DNS Manager.

2. Right-click your DNS server, and choose Properties.

3. Select the Root Hints tab, as shown in Figure 11.4.

Figure 11.4: Managing root hints

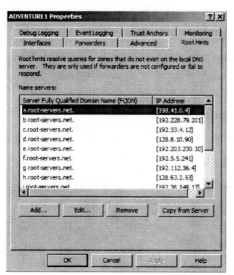

At this point you can add, edit, or remove root hints, or you can choose to copy the root hints from another server.

Network Configuration and Communication

PART IV

Remove a DNS Server

There may come a time when you want to remove a DNS server from your network. When you remove a DNS server, it is important to remember that your DNS server is likely part of a larger DNS infrastructure, and it likely performs key functions and contains records referencing those functions to the other DNS servers and clients in your organization. You would not want to simply delete the server from DNS and remove the DNS Server role from Server Manager without first making sure that there will not be an interruption of the name resolution service. Make sure that as you remove a DNS server that its functions are being taken over by another server and that the records and references to those services have been updated in your DNS database.

This process consists of four steps:

1. Delete the host (A) record for the server.

2. Modify the NS records for the zone so that the server being removed is no longer included on the list of authoritative servers.

3. Modify the Start of Authority (SOA) record for the zone to point to the new server responsible for the zone. (If you are using an Active Directory integrated zone, this is not necessary.)

4. Use the NSLookup tool to verify zone delegation to be certain that the resource records used for delegation are functioning with the appropriate changes and that they no longer look to the removed server.

   a. Open a command prompt.

   b. Type `nslookup (rootserveripaddress)`, and press Enter.

   c. Type `nslookup`, and press Enter.

   d. Type `set norecurse` (this tells the root server not to perform a recursive query), and press Enter.

   e. Type `set q=ns` (this sends the query for name server records to the root server).

   f. Type the fully qualified domain name of the domain you are testing followed by a period. A list of name servers will be displayed.

   g. Verify the NS and A records for the existing name server in the domain.

Manage a DNS Server

After you have installed a DNS server, you might perform several different tasks to maintain or enhance the operation of DNS in your network. For example, you might need to make changes to the IP address of the server, change the way that DNS works with Active Directory, or maybe change the default settings of DNS to improve the security of your environment. Each of these tasks will change the function of DNS slightly, allowing you some flexibility in how you implement DNS in your network and, more important, how DNS operates within your network infrastructure.

Change the Address of a DNS Server

If circumstances arise that demand you to change the IP address of your DNS server, you will need to make a simple change to the A record. If the name of the server has not changed, then neither the NS record nor the SOA record will need to be changed. Make sure that you make the change in the zone records as well as check the records of the parent zone. Remember that your DNS server is updating records to zone database files. Therefore, a change in a single location does not guarantee updates to parents or other zones. Verify that these changes are made; otherwise, your zone updates may fail because of inconsistent records.

1. Open DNS Manager.
2. Expand the server.
3. Right-click the forward lookup zone, and choose Properties.
4. Select the Name Servers tab.
5. Edit the IP address of the chosen name server, as shown in Figure 11.5.
6. Click OK to accept your changes.

Network Configuration and Communication

PART IV

Figure 11.5: Changing the DNS server IP address

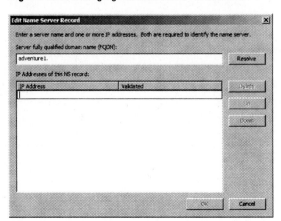

Configure a DNS Server to Listen Only on a Selected Address

Let's say you have a server that has more than one network adapter connected to your network. If the server is running DNS, you may want to configure the server so that DNS listens for queries on only a single network adapter. This can actually increase the security of your server by allowing DNS to listen to queries only on the network IP address that you have configured on the clients.

The process is fairly easy to complete:

1. Open DNS Manager.

2. Right-click the DNS server, and choose Properties.

3. Select the Interfaces tab.

4. On the Interfaces tab, select Only The Following IP Addresses.

5. Select the boxes of the addresses you want to use, as shown in Figure 11.6.

6. Click OK.

By restricting the IP address that the DNS server listens to, you can effectively limit access to the single routed segment that your clients will be using to query DNS and eliminate potential threats or unwanted queries from other unrelated subnets.

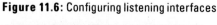

Figure 11.6: Configuring listening interfaces

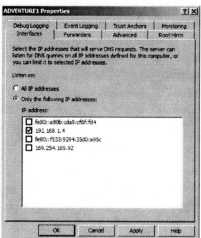

Scavenge Properties for DNS

The DNS server performs queries and then stores the results of those queries as part of the zone database files. Over time the size of a DNS database can really grow. Because of the nature of host name records, they will change over time. IP addresses are changed, names are changed, or both. It doesn't make sense to simply keep resolved queries in the zone database file indefinitely. Instead, it is desirable that you age records in the database and then *scavenge* them out of the database when they are no longer valid. This is where things get a little tricky. How long should a record stay in DNS? How old is too old? What is the usable life of a cached DNS record? Windows Server 2008 R2 uses two values associated with aging and scavenging called the *refresh interval* and the *no-refresh interval*.

- The refresh interval is the time between the earliest moment when a record timestamp can be refreshed and the earliest moment when the record can be scavenged. By default this value is set to seven days. The question is, "Is seven days the right value?" The answer is, "Probably!" We know that is not really an answer, but in most cases seven days will work just fine. If you have a reason to change the value, you are more than welcome to do so. Please do not feel like you have to keep the default value if something else will work better for your network.

- The no-refresh interval is the time between the most recent refresh of a record timestamp and the moment when the record can be refreshed again. This value is also set by default to seven days. Like the refresh interval, the no-refresh interval can be changed to suit the needs of your organization. In layman's terms, the no-refresh interval is really just a definition of how long DNS should wait until it refreshes a record. You want to make sure that your DNS server is not constantly refreshing records. Once a record is refreshed, the no-refresh interval defines how long to wait until the record is refreshed.

You can change both of these values using DNS Manager:

1. Open DNS Manager.

2. Right-click the DNS Server, and choose Set Aging/Scavenging for all zones.

3. Select Scavenge Stale Resource Records. (This is not enabled by default.)

4. Change the no-refresh interval to your desired value.

5. Change the refresh interval to your desired value, as shown in Figure 11.7, and click OK.

Figure 11.7: Changing DNS aging and scavenging properties

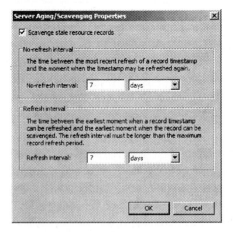

Manage DNS Integration with Active Directory

One of the great things you can do with DNS is integrate it with Active
Directory. As you might recall from earlier in the chapter, DNS is
a requirement for installing AD. Active Directory has the ability to
integrate DNS zone database information into the NTDS.DIT Active
Directory database. This can have significant benefits for the security
and replication of DNS data. In a typical Active Directory forest, there
is more than one DC. When the AD database is replicated, the DNS
database is replicated right along with it. This adds a degree of fault tolerance to the DNS data. Even if a server fails, you still have other DCs
running DNS that can pick up the workload.

When you install AD using the dcpromo.exe tool, you are prompted
to install DNS on the DC. This is the most common way of building
DNS integration within AD. It is also possible to build something called
Active Directory integrated zones that are not actually part of your AD
namespace.

Integrate DNS with AD Domain Services

When you install Active Directory from Server Manager by adding
the Active Directory role service, you will need to run dcpromo.exe to
complete the installation of Active Directory. You will be given the
option to install and configure a DNS server, as shown in Figure 11.8.
If you choose to do this, the resulting server will be integrated with AD
Domain Services. The nice thing about having your DNS integrated
with AD is that when it comes to replication, the DNS zone information
is going to be replicated along with the AD database. If you add DNS
to the several DCs in your network, you get a built-in secure replication
topology for DNS and a built-in fault tolerance strategy.

Build a DNS Application Directory Partition

The Active Directory database consists of partitions. Data from DNS
zones can be stored in the domain partition or a partition called the
application directory partition. If you store DNS zone data in the
domain partition, it will inherit the replication parameters of the partition, which in short means you don't really control how the DNS data is
replicated. Whatever the replication rules are for the domain partition

**Network Configuration
and Communication**

PART IV

become the rules for the DNS zone. That is not necessarily a bad thing. What if you wanted to control the replication parameters independent of the domain partition? You would build an application directory partition for DNS. By building an application directory partition, you have differentiated the DNS zone data from the AD domain data. In short, this gives you the opportunity to control the replication of the application directory partition without influencing or affecting the domain partition.

Figure 11.8: Installing AD with DNS

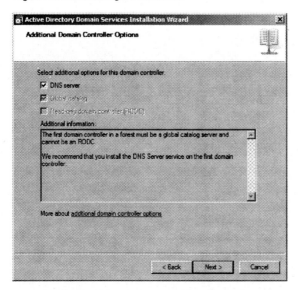

To create your own application directory partition for DNS, you will need two things. First, you will need membership in the Enterprise Admins security group, and second, you will need to know enough about dnscmd to enter a one-line command:

```
dnscmd (yourservername) /CreateDirectoryPartition (FQDN)
```

Your server name can be specified by name or by IP address. If you are working from the local DNS server, you could simply use a period to indicate the local server. When you use this command, it is important to know that the FQDN will specify the name of the new application directory partition. You must use an FQDN, such as dnspartition.xyz.com.

With a DNS application directory partition, you have a great tool for managing replication and fault tolerance. When you create the partition, there is only a single DNS server that is part of the partition. If you want to have additional servers participate as part of the partition, you need to add them to the partition. The technical term for this process is called *enlisting* a DNS server in an application directory partition. Much like creating the partition, enlisting servers requires that you use the dnscmd tool with the following syntax:

```
dnscmd (servername) /EnlistDirectoryPartition (FQDN)
```

The parameter requirements are similar to those you used in creating the application directory partition, where (servername) is the server name you are enlisting and (FQDN) is the fully qualified domain name of the application directory partition you created earlier, dnspartition. xyz.com.

There is one last concept associated with application directory partitions that you need to be aware of before moving to another topic. It is essential that once you create your application directory partition and enlist your DNS servers in the partition that you verify the application directory partition and its enlisted members. Again, you will use the command line:

```
dnscmd /EnumDirectoryPartitions
```

This command will execute and display all the directory partitions in which this server is enlisted.

The following command will display the information related to the specified directory partition. This way, you can verify your application directory partition and the enlisted members of the partition.

```
dnscmd (servername) /DirectoryPartitionInfo (FQDN)
```

Remove a DNS Server from an Application Directory Partition

As your network evolves and you add, modify, and remove servers, the situation may arise when you need to remove a server from your application directory partition. Remember that once a DNS server is removed from the partition, it will no longer participate in DNS replication. In other words, make sure you want the server out of the loop before you remove it from your application directory partition. Just like you used the dnscmd tool to create application directory partitions and enlist servers, you will also use dnscmd to remove a DNS server from an application directory partition. You will need DNS Admins or Domain Admins permissions to complete this configuration change.

```
dnscmd (servername) /UnenlistDirectoryPartition (FQDN)
```

Here again, (servername) is the name of the DNS server you want to remove, and (FQDN) is the fully qualified domain name of the application directory partition.

Finally, although you are free to enlist or unenlist DNS servers from application directory partitions that you have built, you *cannot* unenlist DNS servers from the DomainDnsZones or ForestDnsZones application directory partitions.

Change Security for a Directory Integrated Zone

As you saw in Figure 11.8, it is possible to change the security of a directory integrated zone in DNS. Each object in Active Directory has something called a *discretionary access control list* (DACL), which defines the users and groups that have access to the object. You can set the permissions of the DACL to allow specific users or groups access to update your DNS zone database files.

1. Open DNS Manager.
2. Find the zone you are interested in maintaining.
3. Right-click, and choose Properties.
4. Click the Security tab.
5. Edit the permissions as needed, as shown in Figure 11.9.

Remember that this procedure works only for Active Directory integrated zones. If you have a standard primary, standard secondary, or other zone type, this procedure is not available.

Figure 11.9: Changing DACL permissions for a DNS zone

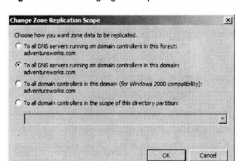

Change Zone Replication

Controlling zone replication allows you to be able to decide the parameters for replication for the DNS zone. These parameters are often called the *replication scope*. When DNS is integrated with Active Directory, it is replicated along with the other AD partitions between domain controllers. Active Directory consists of forest and domain structures, and there are domain controllers at both logical levels of this hierarchy. This structure lends itself to four replication scope options:

- *All DNS servers in the Active Directory forest*: This scope option will replicate DNS zone data to all DNS servers in the Active Directory forest. That's a broad scope, and depending on the size and physical layout of your forest, it could have some significant impact on replication.

- *All DNS servers in the Active Directory domain*: This scope option will replicate DNS zone data to all DNS servers that are running on domain controllers in the Active Directory domain. This seems like a tighter scope than the forest scope, but if you think about the size limitations on a domain (functionally there really aren't any), this could present the same issues as the forest scope, albeit with the limitations of the domain.

- *All domain controllers in the Active Directory domain*: In this scope, you would replicate DNS zone data to all domain controllers whether they were DNS servers or not.

Network Configuration and Communication

PART IV

- *All domain controllers in a specified application directory partition*: This scope allows you to replicate DNS zone data to the domain controllers that you have enlisted in the application directory partition.

Each of the scope options can be used effectively depending on the network environment and DNS implementation in which they are implemented. If you had taken the time to create an application directory partition, it would make sense to change the replication scope to all domain controllers in a specified application directory partition. To make changes in replication scope, you will use the DNS Manager:

1. Open DNS Manager.

2. Locate and right-click the zone, and then choose Properties.

3. On the General tab, locate Replication, and click Change.

4. Select your desired replication scope, as shown in Figure 11.10.

Figure 11.10: Configuring replication scope

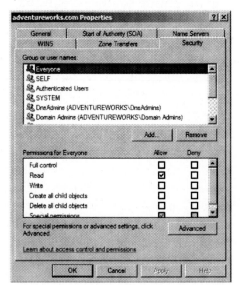

Manage Zone Database Files

When you work with DNS, you have many files to manage. Each DNS server may be responsible for many different DNS zones. Each zone contains its own files and folders that will require some degree of effort in order to create, maintain, update, manage, and secure.

As you work with your DNS environment, you will likely break down your forest into smaller segments that in DNS are referred to as *zones*. If the records in your DNS zone database are designed to allow the resolution of a name to an IP address, you would say the zone is *working forward*, and the zone database type you would create is called a *forward lookup zone*. If your object is to provide an option for the finding of names based on a provided IP address, then you would say your zone is *working in reverse*, or you would create a *reverse lookup zone*. What if you wanted a DNS server that only resolved the names of other authoritative DNS servers in your environment? You would create a *stub zone* to serve your purposes.

Each of the different zone types serves a particular purpose in DNS. You will likely want more than one server for each zone in order to maximize availability to your clients and to add some degree of fault tolerance to your network.

Creating a Forward Lookup Zone

As you learned earlier, when you install DNS as part of Active Directory, the appropriate forward lookup zones for the domain are created automatically. If you choose to add zones or if you are not using DNS as an integrated part of Active Directory, you will use DNS Manager to create and manage forward lookup zones. Not all forward lookup zones are created equally; there are actually three different types, called *primary zones*, *secondary zones*, and *stub zones*.

Primary zones are zones that are created and stored on the local server. They can be updated and maintained directly on the server and can also receive replicated updates from other servers.

Secondary zones are zones that are stored on the local server; however, all of their information comes from updates received from another designated primary server. Secondary servers are a good way to help share the workload that might otherwise be forced onto a standard primary server.

Stub zones create a copy of only the name server records for a given zone. This zone type is useful in helping clients find and query the appropriate internal DNS name server.

To create a new forward lookup zone, follow these steps:

1. Open DNS Manager.

2. Right-click the name of the server.

3. Choose New Zone.

4. Click Next in the Welcome To The New Zone Wizard.

5. Select the type of zone you want to create.

6. Choose whether you want the zone stored in Active Directory by selecting the box at the bottom of the Zone Type screen, as shown in Figure 11.11.

Figure 11.11: Adding a new forward lookup zone

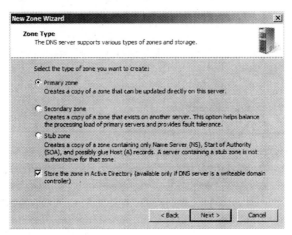

Depending on what type of zone you choose, the wizard will offer you the appropriate options from this point forward, including options for replication, zone name, and the types of updates you will allow.

Changing the Zone Type

One of the nice things about DNS zones is that they are pretty flexible. If you needed, you could actually change a primary zone to a secondary or stub zone, or vice versa. Usually you would do something like this if you were doing maintenance on a server and wanted to limit the effect on DNS or the clients that rely on DNS services. Changing the zone type is a simple procedure:

1. Open DNS Manager.

2. Find the chosen zone, and right-click it.

3. Choose Properties.

4. Next to Type on the General tab, as shown in Figure 11.12, click Change.

5. Select the new zone type, and click OK.

Figure 11.12: Changing the DNS zone type

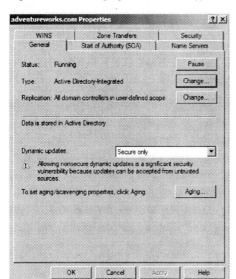

Managing Resource Records

DNS zones contain resource records of various types. These records are created as you create DNS servers, clients, services, and applications. Generally speaking, once a resource record has been created, there is not much you need to do to maintain these records. You may want to change the DACL security permissions if your resource records are part of Active Directory, or you may need to modify a record or even delete one.

You can manage records in the DNS zone using DNS Manager or dnscmd. You simply need to find the resource record in the designated zone.

If you are interested in changing the DACL for a resource record, follow these steps:

1. Open DNS Manger.

2. Locate the zone that contains the resource record.

3. Right-click the resource record.

4. Choose Properties.

5. Select the Security tab.

6. Edit the permission to the resource record, and click OK.

If you want to delete the record, simply right-click the record, and choose Delete. When the message appears asking for confirmation to delete the record, simply click OK.

Configuring Dynamic Update

When you work with DNS servers, it is ideal to have them update one another with their information. Windows Server 2008 R2 allows the use of dynamic updates between configured DNS servers. This really eliminates the need for you to spend your valuable time administering zone databases. Clients who use DHCP can easily get access to an updated DNS server without having to call your help desk. You can configure each of your zones for dynamic updates. If you are using Active Directory integrated zones, you can also specify that the updates are done in a secure fashion and are based on the information in the DACL.

1. Open DNS Manager.

2. Locate the zone where you want to enable dynamic updates.

3. Right-click the zone, and choose Properties.

4. On the General tab, open the Dynamic Updates drop-down list, as shown in Figure 11.13.

5. Choose the type of updates you want to allow, and click OK.

Figure 11.13: Configuring dynamic updates

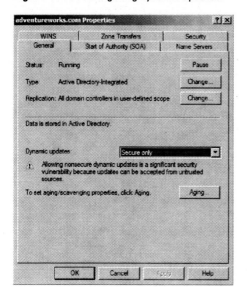

As you probably noticed, dynamic updates can be configured as non-secure and secure. We know some of you are wondering why you would ever consider using nonsecure updates. Imagine if all the DNS servers for the zone were residents of your own private network. You already have tight control over the servers, so you might not choose to enable secure updates only. If your DNS zones are not part of Active Directory, you will not have the option for secure dynamic updates only.

If you are using Active Directory integrated zones, it really does not make sense to use nonsecure updates. Nonsecure updates will provide exposure to your DNS servers to accept updates from unknown, disreputable, or downright malicious sources, and they will open your DNS infrastructure to potential threats. It just doesn't make sense to use anything but secure updates.

Zone Transfer Settings

DNS servers transfer zone data between one another based on a schedule. You can control how the zone is transferred based on the following settings. Each of the settings can be changed or updated, so it is important to note that these settings will be limited if your DNS servers are Active Directory integrated.

- Whether or not the zone is transferred to any other server and to which servers it may be transferred

- The refresh interval, which describes how often the zone files will be transferred

- The retry interval, which describes how long a DNS server will wait to request a transfer after a transfer has failed

- The expire interval, which describes how long the DNS zone data is valid

- The list of servers that are notified when zone data changes

To configure zone transfer settings, follow these steps:

1. Open DNS Manager.

2. Locate the chosen zone.

3. Right-click the zone, and choose Properties.

4. Click the Zone Transfers tab.

5. Select the box to allow zone transfers.

6. Specify the servers that you will allow transfers with, as shown in Figure 11.14.

Figure 11.14: Configuring the zone transfer settings

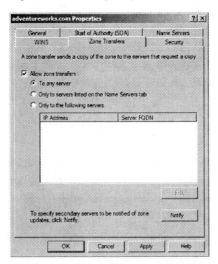

When you configure zone transfers, you can also build something called a *notification list,* which contains a list of servers that will be notified by the master DNS server in your domain when changes are made to the zone. Simply click the Notify button on the Zone Transfers tab to build a notification list.

The settings for Refresh Interval, Retry Interval, Expires After, and Minimum (Default) TTL are on the SOA tab.

1. Open DNS Manager.

2. Locate the chosen zone.

3. Right-click the zone, and choose Properties.

4. Click the Start Of Authority (SOA) tab.

5. Set the values for the selected interval or TTL, as shown in Figure 11.15.

Figure 11.15: Configuring the interval values

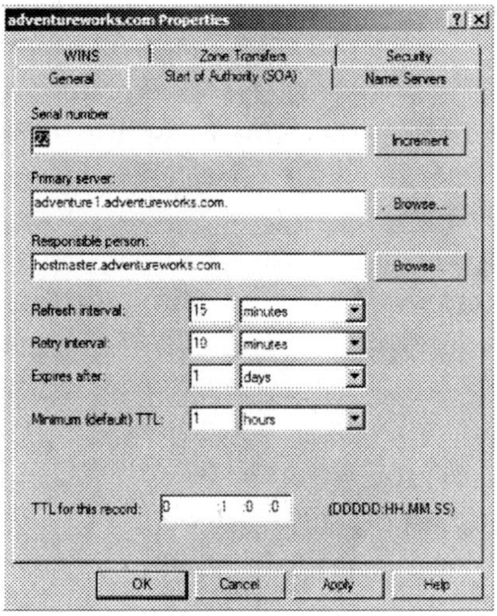

Securing a Zone

DNS provides name resolution services to clients. The information provided by DNS has a direct effect on the functional operation of your network. You want to make sure that you take security into consideration for each of your DNS zones. Generally, DNS has two potential

Network Configuration and Communication

PART IV

security problems that you would worry about. First, you want to make sure that the zone files are secure from unauthorized changes. If an illicit source can update your zone database files, they could really cause problems for your network. Generally, these attacks occur as dynamic updates are pushed to your DNS servers from outside your organization. The easiest way to prevent this type of attack is to enable only secure dynamic updates.

Second, you want to make sure you have taken precautions to prevent unauthorized access to your zone files. Imagine if someone outside your organization set up a secondary server and managed to get updates from your internal primary server. You would effectively be sharing your DNS zone information with an imposter. The easiest way to prevent this type of attack is by configuring a list of servers to which you will allow zone transfers.

If your zones are Active Directory integrated, you can of course use the DACLs associated with the zone to further control access to the files.

Window Server 2008 R2 moves one step further when it comes to protecting the zone database files and adds something called Domain Name System Security Extensions (DNSSEC). DNSSEC allows the DNS zone and all the records in the zone to be cryptographically signed. When a DNS server receives a request for the signed zone files, it returns the files along with the digital signatures. By obtaining a public key, a resolver can verify that the files have not been tampered with.

As you will note, we've discussed each of these topics in earlier sections of this chapter, and we've demonstrated how to do the configurations. Much of securing a DNS infrastructure really comes down to the way it is configured.

Configure Single-Label DNS Resolution

The vast majority of networks use DNS as the primary name resolution system, but there are alternatives. For example, for many years Windows Internet Name Service (WINS) was used as an alternative, and in many networks it still is in use. Unfortunately, as you move forward to the next version of TCP/IP, which is called IPV6, there is no support for WINS. You will need another way to resolve single-label host names besides WINS. If there is no WINS, a DNS client can still resolve a single-label name by appending a *dns* suffix to the name and trying to find it in DNS.

If you are planning on using IPV6, all name resolution will go through DNS. If you still have single-label names in your network, Windows Server 2008 R2 uses a special zone called a *global names zone* (GNZ) to house these records and facilitate the resolution of those names through DNS. GNZ is not a replacement for WINS; instead, it provides an avenue for name resolution while you transition WINS out of your network. The GNZ is created and managed much the same as a standard primary zone. You should not enable dynamic updates for the GNZ to prevent its resource records from being registered into the zone.

Creating the GNZ

The process of creating the GNZ begins with DNS Manager:

1. Open DNS Manager.
2. Right-click the name of the server.
3. Choose New Zone.
4. Click Next in the Welcome To The New Zone Wizard.
5. Select the Primary Zone type, make sure the Store In Active Directory check box is selected, and click Next.
6. Select All DNS servers running on Domain Controllers in this forest.
7. Click Next.
8. Click Forward Lookup Zone.
9. Click Next.
10. Type **GlobalNames** in the Zone Name box, and click Next.
11. Select Do Not Allow Dynamic Updates, and click Next.
12. Click Finish.

It is also possible to enable GNZ from the command line using the dnscmd tool and the following command:

```
DNSCMD /config /enableglobalnamesupport 1
```

Either method will work to enable GNZ, and in both cases you will still need to configure the appropriate records for the zone.

After the forward lookup GNZ has been created, you will need to add the alias resource records (called the *CNAME*), for each of the single-label clients in the network. This can prove to be a daunting task if you have lots of single-label clients and may provide the motivation necessary to quickly upgrade them to traditional DNS clients. To add new CNAME records for the single-label clients, follow these steps:

1. Open DNS Manager.
2. Locate the GNZ.
3. Right-click the zone, and choose New Alias (CNAME).
4. Type in the alias name.
5. Type in the fully qualified domain name.
6. Click OK.

Troubleshoot DNS

DNS is an essential resource for name resolution. When something goes wrong with DNS, it can have far-reaching effects in your network. An understanding of how to troubleshoot DNS can be incredibly valuable. The thing you will love about DNS is that your ability to troubleshoot DNS is directly associated with your understanding of basic DNS operations and the specific DNS configuration you are working with.

TIP   Read the DNS technical reference at http://technet.micro-soft.com/en-us/library/cc732997(WS.10).aspx.

With a good understanding of DNS and a strong understanding of your network, you are well positioned to deal with most of the issues that will crop up in DNS. One of the really good things about DNS is that although there are occasional problems that fall outside the realm of what is considered normal, most of the problems are seen over and over again in networks that are running DNS and are fairly easy to isolate and fix.

When you are trying to troubleshoot a problem in DNS (or anywhere else in your network, for that matter), you should use a root cause analysis approach. What exactly is root cause analysis? It can be described with a single sentence:

Discover the problem before you "fix" anything.

When troubleshooting DNS, you will notice that problems seem to fall into four categories:

- DNS clients
- DNS servers
- Dynamic updates
- Zone problems

As you encounter an issue with DNS, begin by trying to isolate the source of the problem. You will find that the majority of the time the problem will easily fit into one of these four categories. If it doesn't, don't worry—all is not lost. You can keep working to identify the source of the problem.

The most common problems with DNS servers are actually not really problems with the DNS servers at all; they are hardware- or network-related. For example, say your users suddenly flood your help desk with calls indicating they cannot "find" anything on your network. Shares are unavailable, the Internet seems to be down, and some cannot even log in. This sounds like a DNS problem. It is! Where does it fit among the four categories? It sounds like a DNS server problem. At this point, you can begin troubleshooting by checking the physical hardware that supports the DNS server. Is everything actually plugged in and working? You notice that the network cable that connects your DNS server and its network interface card has been laying across a sharp steel beam on top of your server rack, and the weight of the other cables has somehow managed to sever this one. You put in a new cable, and in minutes the network is up and running. Don't just assume that the hardware is fine and move on to other things. Check it out. Many, many times a simple hardware fix is all that is necessary.

If the hardware checks out, then you can start going down your check list of items to identify the problem and then apply the solution. Microsoft maintains a troubleshooting tool specifically for DNS. It is excellent! Not surprisingly, it is broken down into four categories. The vast majority of DNS issues can be solved by using these simple troubleshooting tools. They provide a great level of detail and solutions at each step of the process to help you not only identify the problem but also fix the problem.

TIP   Use the troubleshooting DNS tools at `http://technet.microsoft.com/en-us/library/cc731991.aspx`.

The vast majority of DNS issues will be within your troubleshooting reach if you use the tools discussed in the previous section. If you run into a problem that you cannot solve quickly on your own using the troubleshooting tools, then use other resources at your disposal. The Internet can be a great source of information to help you isolate your problem and find a solution. If you have any kind of support contacts, use them. Support incidents on the phone or in person may make sense if you have exhausted your knowledge without finding a solution. The key is not to give up. Use your root cause analysis skills and your understanding of the environment to find and fix the problem.

12

Troubleshooting TCP/IP

IN THIS CHAPTER, YOU WILL LEARN TO:

Network Configuration and Communication

PART IV

The basis for all network communication is the network protocol, and no other network protocol is more ubiquitous than TCP/IP. It is the core building block for all communication between network servers, clients, routers, switches, and even phones. If you understand how to troubleshoot TCP/IP, you will be able to solve many of the network communication problems that will arise in your networks.

Understand TCP/IP Basics

TCP/IP is a suite of protocols that have been the basis for network communication and traffic control for more than a decade. Although there are other network communication protocol suites, TCP/IP has emerged as the de facto standard in the vast majority of operating systems.

The TCP/IP suite of protocols has undergone a series of revisions. There are currently two versions of TCP/IP: IP version 4 (IPV4) and IP version 6 (IPV6). IPV4 has been popular as a network protocol since the early versions of Windows NT. It has a simple 32-bit addressing scheme and provides a relatively easily routed protocol for inter-network accessibility. The 32-bit address space offers a total of 2^{32}, or 4,294,967,296, addresses. Although that seems like a pretty large number, when you think about the number of client computers connected to the Internet, add the number of networked appliances like switches and routers, then add the websites and web servers of the world, and finally add the servers of the world's businesses, it becomes glaringly apparent that just over 4 billion addresses is not nearly enough to meet the demand. The shortfall of IPV4 addresses was addressed (no pun intended) in the mid-1990s and resulted in the formation of a new suite of protocols called IPV6.

First supported in Windows NT 4, IPV6 offers some significant upgrades to IPV4, including but not limited to a much larger 128-bit address space. This means that the number of potential addresses in IPV6 is 2^{128}, an astonishing 340,282,366,920,938,463,463,374,607, 431,768,211,456 addresses. If you are wondering how you would succinctly express that number, you would say "340 undecillion," but we think it is much easier to understand the full impact and potential of the address space to see it listed in all its base-10, comma-separated, 39-digit glory. Now, 340 undecillion addresses should at least tide the world's IP address appetite over for a little while. That is a big number!

Even though IPV6 has been supported since the Windows NT days, few networks have adopted this new version of IP despite its potential benefits. Like the old proverb states, the network world seems to believe "Better the devil you know than the devil you don't." Choosing between IPV4 and IPV6 is a topic that has engendered debate and even arguments in networking channels worldwide.

The question still remains, "Which IP version should you use?"

While Microsoft was developing the Windows Vista and Windows Server 2008 operating systems, its Windows Core Networking product team had a revolutionary idea. What if there were a protocol that understood both IPV4 and IPV6 natively? This idea resulted in the development of a protocol suite called the Next Generation TCP/IP stack. This stack represents a complete redesign of TCP/IP in both IPV4 and IPV6 and provides needed functionality to meet the communication, connectivity, and performance requirements of the modern network. This means you can have all of the well-known benefits of IPV4 and get all the cool new functions and features of IPV6. You don't have to choose one or the other. You can have both!

Be careful what you wish for, though! Before you begin the process of troubleshooting TCP/IP, it is a good idea to read one of the many books currently available on the inner workings of TCP/IP. The volume of information needed to fully understand TCP/IP will simply not fit into a single chapter, unless of course the chapter was 400 to 500 pages in length. The focus here is on troubleshooting TCP/IP. *Troubleshooting* is a broad term and could also cover hundreds of pages if we tried to cover every possible situation. Instead, this chapter will give you a good methodology to use to discover many of the standard issues associated with TCP/IP troubleshooting and point you to additional tools and resources to help you solve more isolated problems as well.

Troubleshoot TCP/IP

To effectively troubleshoot TCP/IP, it is necessary that you have an approach to troubleshooting that will allow you to systematically identify the source of a problem and then, once the source is identified, allow you to take corrective action that will rectify the problem. This approach to troubleshooting is called *root cause analysis*. Do not simply "try something" to fix the problem. Often you will mask the problem with attempts to fix it and create a more complex environment for future troubleshooting scenarios. The old saying "If it ain't broke, don't fix it!" applies to troubleshooting.

Network Configuration and Communication

PART IV

You will want to employ a step-by-step approach to troubleshooting TCP/IP problems and utilize a number of different tools to help you in your quest for problems and the solutions to resolve those problems. These are some common questions you might ask:

- What are the symptoms of the problem?

- What could cause these symptoms?

- What stuff is working?

- What stuff is not working?

- Is there any kind of relationship between the things that don't work?

- Is this a new problem or one that has been persistently around for a long period of time?

- Have any recent changes been made to the network or systems involved?

- What were the changes?

- What is the scope of the problem?

- Is one machine, a group of machines, or the whole network having problems?

- What do the machines that are having problems have in common?

Often if you can ask the right questions, the answers will lead you to the right place to start troubleshooting, or at very least they can help you narrow the possible problems to a manageable set of issues that you can begin testing in order to identify the culprit.

Understand Troubleshooting Tools

One of the best things about running Windows Server 2008 R2 is that you have a full complement of tools that are included or freely available to you to help you troubleshoot TCP/IP. These tools are included with the installation of Windows Server or can be downloaded from the `http://technet.microsoft.com` website.

> **Event Viewer**   The Event Viewer is found in the Control Panel and is likely the most valuable of the troubleshooting tools. Using the Event Viewer, you will find informational, warning, and error events that will help you identify system problems and their associated causes. Remember that Event Viewer can display information

and events about other systems in your network through the use of subscriptions and so can be used to monitor not just the local machine but many machines throughout your network. We recommend you begin your troubleshooting efforts with the Event Viewer, and when you have a good idea what you are really dealing with, then you can move to the tools listed next.

Performance The Performance tool lets you configure hundreds of different functions of your systems, including some great information related to TCP/IP and its associated traffic. If you are already capturing IP information in your network, you will likely want to view the results from captures before and after a problem is reported.

Command-line tools There are also several command-line tools you can use, as shown in Table 1.1.

Table 12.1: TCP/IP Troubleshooting Command-Line Tools

Tool	Description	Common Commands
IPCONFIG	This command-line tool is generally the place where your troubleshooting begins. This command will display detailed information about the adapters attached to a system and the addressing information associated with each adapter. This command uses a series of switches that allow you to customize the output you receive and even do some basic address updates.	IPCONFIG /ALL
HOSTNAME	This command-line utility will display the host name of the local system.	HOSTNAME
PING	This command-line utility sends Internet Control Message Packets (ICMP) across an inter-network to verify connectivity. It is commonly used to verify the operation of TCP/IP at different levels of the TCP/IP protocol stack.	PING 127.0.0.1
PATHPING	This command-line tool allows you to see the path that an IP packet takes through an inter-network and will show you information about packet losses and where they occur.	PATHPING xxx.xxx.xxx.xxx where x's represent IP Address
TRACERT	This command-line utility will display information about the network route taken from source to destination.	TRACERT xxx.xxx.xxx.xxx where x's represent destination IP address.

Table 12.1: TCP/IP Troubleshooting Command-Line Tools *(continued)*

Tool	Description	Common Commands
ROUTE	This command-line utility will display and allow the editing of routing table information in IPV4.	ROUTE PRINT
ARP	This command-line utility will let you view the Address Resolution Protocol cache.	ARP -A
NBTSTAT	This command-line utility can be used to display information about packets that running NetBIOS over TCP/IP.	NBTSTAT -C
NETSTAT	This command-line utility will show you information about current connections.	NETSTAT -A
NETSH	This command-line utility is not so much a troubleshooting tool as it is a configuration tool for TCP/IP and a whole bunch of other services. It uses something called a *naming context* and allows the configuration of items within its context. The command has a standard IP context an **IPV$** context and an **IPV6** context that can be used to fix configuration problems in TCP/IP interfaces.	NETSH INTERFACE IPV4
TELNET	This command-line utility will let you establish a TCP connection between two systems on your network.	TELNET

Each of these tools will allow you to identify, diagnose, change, or update the TCP/IP environment of your network. As you use the tools, you will find a methodology that works for you and, more important, gives you the right information about the critical segments of your TCP/IP configuration and management.

Troubleshoot IPV6

As you work with TCP/IP networks, you will probably run into some problems. Hardware will fail, users will make changes to their systems that inhibit communication, and applications or updates might install with unintended consequences. Regardless of whether the changes are malicious or unintended, if they impact your TCP/IP infrastructure, you will need to troubleshoot the problems and find solutions quickly and efficiently. There is no one "right" way to do this. There are lots of tools and lots of methods of implementing those tools to help you discover the source of the problem and then craft a solution that will work for your environment. The best advice we can give you regarding your ability to troubleshoot TCP/IP problems doesn't include a troubleshooting methodology. It's this:

"Know your network!"

If you clearly understand the operation of your network, it will be much easier to troubleshoot problems as they arise.

We have used a simple methodology for troubleshooting TCP/IP for a long, long time. We occasionally tweak it a little and add some new tools. Depending on the circumstance, we might change the protocol just a little bit, but the basic operations stay the same. Please keep in mind there is no one "right" way to do this; this just happens to be one of the ways we use.

The vast majority of problems that we have investigated related to TCP/IP have begun with the same complaint: "I can't connect to ..."

Whether it is a network resource, the Internet, a printer, a file share, or any number of other things, when we hear that phrase, the TCP/IP alarm bells sound. If TCP/IP problems are primarily problems of connectivity, then you would be well served to make your primary efforts focus on discovering and resolving connectivity problems.

Verify Connectivity for IPV6

The first thing you will want to do when troubleshooting TCP/IPV6 is to verify that TCP/IP is actually set up and configured correctly. This is generally where you will find the cause and can implement a solution. Consider the following steps when verifying connectivity for TCP/IPV6:

1. Check the physical hardware. Check the network cable. Is it plugged in? Check the connections at switches, hubs, and routers. Don't laugh—you will solve a lot of TCP/IPV6 problems right here in step 1. You might even be well served to simply unplug the cable and plug it back in on the off-chance that the cable somehow became loose even if it looks connected.

2. Verify the function and configuration of the network interface, using the following commands:

ipconfig /all   This will display the status and configuration of the IPV6 interface. Verify that the interface has an address and is in fact enabled. Check the DNS settings for the interfaces to be certain that they are configured correctly.

netsh interface ipv6 show address   This will show you the TCP/IP address of the IPV6 interface, as shown in Figure 12.1.

Figure 12.1: Results of netsh interface ipv6 show address

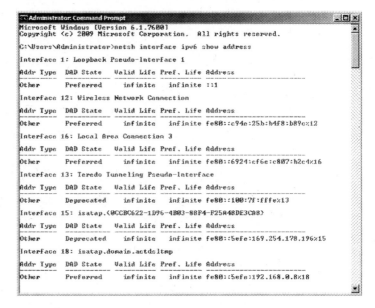

In the event that there is in fact a problem in the TCP/IP configuration, you can change the configuration using the netsh interface ipv6 set command.

We always start here because statistically we have found that many of the problems related to IPV6 have to do with configuration. Once you get the configuration right, TCP/IP works correctly, and your user's connectivity will be restored.

Verify Responsiveness

Of course, not every problem is going to be fixed with a simple check of the hardware and address configuration. Responsiveness is also important. Responsiveness takes into account that communication takes at least two endpoints. If either of the endpoints fails to respond, then the communication cannot take place. If you have checked the local configuration and everything is in order, you should check that the machine is responding.

IPV6 uses something called a *neighbor cache* to store link layer addresses that have been resolved recently. If for some reason the neighbor cache holds incorrect information, it can impede connectivity. You can flush the neighbor cache with no negative effects to TCP/IP:

```
netsh interface ipv6 delete neighbors
```

If you are thinking to yourself, "Hey, that's a lot like the ARP cache from IPV4," you are right!

There is another cache you should also check in conjunction with responsiveness, called the *destination cache*. The destination cache is used to maintain a list of next hop addresses for addresses recently used. As shown in Figure 12.2, you can view the contents of the destination cache using the following command:

```
netsh interface ipv6 show destinationcache
```

Figure 12.2: Results of netsh interface ipv6 show destinationcache

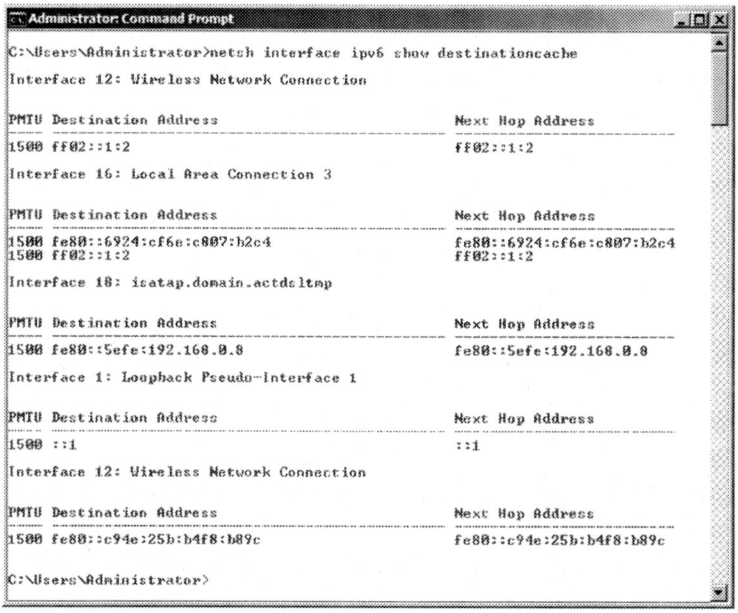

As shown in Figure 12.3, if you decide you want to delete the cache, you can do so with the following command:

```
netsh interface ipv6 delete destinationcache
```

Figure 12.3: Results of netsh interface ipv6 delete destinationcache

Both of the previous steps, deleting the neighbor cache and deleting the destination cache, act as preemptive actions to eliminate the possibility that your machine is being incorrectly directed to a link address that is not going to respond. To truly troubleshoot responsiveness, you will need to start sending packets onto the network and watching for responses. There are a couple of tools that are uniquely suited for this exercise.

PING uses the Internet Control Message Packet to send echo request packets to a host and then measures the response time as the host responds to those echo requests. This tool can be incredibly valuable in verifying responsiveness in IPV6. Traditionally, when you use the PING tool, you begin with the process of pinging the local host address and then move on to the local IP address, then an IP address on the same subnet, next the default gateway of the local router, and finally an address on another network segment. You might have learned that you can skip right to pinging a remote host on another segment; if you get a response, you know everything in the cascade is working. As tempting as that is, in the event that you do not receive a response from the remote host, you really don't know anything about where your problem is located. Start with the local host, and work your way through the list. When you don't receive a response, you have reached the area that is having the problem.

One more very important point concerning PING is that ICMP packets can be considered a security risk, and often network administrators will configure their computers to not accept or respond to ping echo request packets. If you ping a machine and get no response, make certain that the reason you are not getting a response is because there really is no connectivity, not that the system you pinged does not support ping packets. This process of removing or limiting response to specific packet types is often termed *packet filtering*. Packet filtering is a common reason for lack of responsiveness.

If you are confident that TCP/IP has been installed and is configured correctly and you are still not getting connectivity, it may well be an issue of filtering. Consider checking the following:

- Windows Firewall rules
- IPsec policies
- Remote access policies
- IPV6 packet filters
- Router policies

Check the Routing Table for IPV6

If you find yourself unable to connect to remote resources using IPV6, one of the things you will want to check is the routing table. Specifically, you will be looking for routes that have been incorrectly identified or erroneously entered into the routing table. Use ROUTE PRINT, as shown in Figure 12.4.

```
NETSTAT -R
NETSH INTERFACE IPV6 SHOW ROUTE
```

Each of these commands will show you the IPV6 entries on the routing table. To correct or enter a missing route, you will need to use the following:

```
NETSH INTERFACE IPV6 SET ROUTE, ROUTE ADD, or ROUTE CHANGE.
```

It is also possible to remove erroneous or incorrect routes using this:

```
NETSH INTERFACE IPV6 DELETE ROUTE command or ROUTE DELETE.
```

In each of these cases, it is important that you have a clear understanding of what the correct routing table entries should look like and that you are able to recognize entries that are not correct or are simply not there. As we discussed earlier, you really need a good knowledge of the way things are supposed to work in your network infrastructure in order to troubleshoot them effectively.

Network Configuration and Communication

PART IV

Figure 12.4: Routing table displayed using ROUTE PRINT

```
Administrator: Command Prompt                                          _ □ x

C:\Users\Administrator>route print
===========================================================================
Interface List
 16...00 21 86 96 9a 5b ......Local Area Connection - Virtual Network
 12...00 21 5c 7e db 91 ......Intel(R) Wireless WiFi Link 4965AGN
  1...........................Software Loopback Interface 1
 13...00 00 00 00 00 00 00 e0 Teredo Tunneling Pseudo-Interface
 15...00 00 00 00 00 00 00 e0 Microsoft ISATAP Adapter #2
 18...00 00 00 00 00 00 00 e0 Microsoft ISATAP Adapter #3
===========================================================================

IPv4 Route Table
===========================================================================
Active Routes:
Network Destination        Netmask          Gateway        Interface  Metric
          0.0.0.0          0.0.0.0      192.168.0.1      192.168.0.8     25
        127.0.0.0        255.0.0.0         On-link        127.0.0.1    306
        127.0.0.1  255.255.255.255         On-link        127.0.0.1    306
  127.255.255.255  255.255.255.255         On-link        127.0.0.1    306
      169.254.0.0      255.255.0.0         On-link  169.254.178.196    261
  169.254.178.196  255.255.255.255         On-link  169.254.178.196    261
  169.254.255.255  255.255.255.255         On-link  169.254.178.196    261
      192.168.0.0    255.255.255.0         On-link      192.168.0.8    281
      192.168.0.8  255.255.255.255         On-link      192.168.0.8    281
    192.168.0.255  255.255.255.255         On-link      192.168.0.8    281
        224.0.0.0        240.0.0.0         On-link        127.0.0.1    306
        224.0.0.0        240.0.0.0         On-link  169.254.178.196    261
        224.0.0.0        240.0.0.0         On-link      192.168.0.8    281
  255.255.255.255  255.255.255.255         On-link        127.0.0.1    306
  255.255.255.255  255.255.255.255         On-link  169.254.178.196    261
  255.255.255.255  255.255.255.255         On-link      192.168.0.8    281
===========================================================================
Persistent Routes:
  None

IPv6 Route Table
===========================================================================
Active Routes:
 If Metric Network Destination      Gateway
  1    306 ::1/128                  On-link
 16    261 fe80::/64                On-link
 12    281 fe80::/64                On-link
 18    286 fe80::5efe:192.168.0.8/128
                                    On-link
 16    261 fe80::6924:cf6e:c807:b2c4/128
                                    On-link
 12    281 fe80::c94e:25b:b4f8:b89c/128
                                    On-link
  1    306 ff00::/8                 On-link
 16    261 ff00::/8                 On-link
 12    281 ff00::/8                 On-link
===========================================================================
Persistent Routes:
  None

C:\Users\Administrator>
```

Validate DNS Name Resolution for IPV6 Addresses

If the IPV6 addressing configuration and response checks out, you will
want to move up and check on the resolution of host names to TCP/IP
addresses, which means DNS. DNS resolves host names to IP addresses
for both IPV4 and IPV6. You can perform some simple tasks to ensure
that IPV6 host name to IP address resolution is occurring properly.

First verify that your DNS server has been configured to resolve
host names to IPV6 addresses and that it is acting upon name resolution
requests that it receives. To begin, use the HOSTNAME utility to check
the host name of the server and to check the DNS suffix.

Next, open the DNS Manager tool, and verify that all your configured DNS servers appear on the DNS Manager's list of authoritative servers. You can also use the DNS Manager to check the process of forwarding in the event that a host name cannot be resolved to an IP address on the local DNS server. If you need to make changes to the DNS suffix or to connection-specific DNS suffix information, you can do it using DNS Manager.

Flush the DNS Cache

Each IPV6 client maintains a list of recently resolved DNS to IPV6 addresses. This list is called the *DNS resolver cache*. If for some reason a record in the cache had an incorrect address for a given host name, it would limit connectivity. In cases like this, you can flush the contents of the DNS resolver cache using IPCONFIG /FLUSHDNS. See Figure 12.5.

Figure 12.5: Results of IPCONFIG /FLUSHDNS

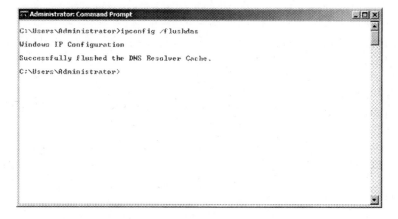

This command will remove all entries from the cache and force the machine to resolve the address with recursive queries sent to the local DNS server hierarchy and get the correct host name to IP address information.

You can quickly check for the function of DNS resolution using the PING tool. PING can be used in conjunction with IP addresses, host names, or FQDNs. For example:

```
PING Computer 1
```

Network Configuration and Communication

PART IV

or

```
PING www.microsoft.com
```

Test IPV6 TCP Connections

So, what if everything works from an IP perspective but you still cannot get a TCP connection to occur between systems? In the majority of cases, this is a problem with packet filtering. You learned earlier in the chapter about packet filtering locations for IP packets. You will need to check the same locations for TCP filtering. Since you will be checking your filters when you are validating IP connectivity, it makes sense to check for TCP filters at the same time. If you didn't check for TCP filtering earlier, it is time to do it now.

One of the easiest ways to check TCP connections is with the TELNET tool. TELNET is a command-line tool that establishes TCP connections between systems. TELNET uses a syntax similar to the PING command; simply use the TELNET command followed by the IPV6 address.

If the connection is possible, TELNET will create it. TELNET connects to a service, so once you connect to a machine, you can execute commands against the machine to test, configure, or view the contents of the remote machine. TELNET is sometimes seen as a potential security risk, so please don't be surprised if the local firewalls or security policies do not allow TELNET packets. If they do not, you may be able to test TCP connectivity with a tool called Test TCP (TTCP). This tool allows you to build TCP connections and also monitor for incoming TCP connection requests. You can configure a computer to "listen" for TCP connections on a specific port, which is good because you can test TCP connections without having any specific services installed or configured.

Troubleshoot IPV4

Troubleshooting IPV4 requires many of the same practices as troubleshooting IPV6. Remember, TCP/IP is a stack of protocols working at different layers of the Open Systems Interconnect (OSI) model for network communication. There is no right way to go about troubleshooting IPV4; you simply need to find a methodology that works for you. We encourage you to take a similar root cause analysis approach to troubleshooting IPV4 as you did with IPV6. The goal of troubleshooting is to identify the reason or reasons preventing connectivity and then make the necessary adjustments to restore connectivity.

Use the Network Connection Repair Tool

When you find a problem with connectivity, it makes sense to begin your troubleshooting in some common areas. The Network Connection Repair Tool will check for some of the most common connectivity problems. If it finds them, it will make the necessary adjustments and reconnect the system.

The Network Connection Repair Tool automates a list of functions including the following:

- Checking that DHCP is enabled and refreshing the IP address lease

- Flushing the ARP cache

- Flushing the DNS cache using IPCONFIG /FLUSHDNS

- Reregistering DNS names using IPCONFIG /REGISTERDNS

- Flushing the NetBIOS name cache

- Reloading the NetBIOS name cache

The really cool thing about the Network Connection Repair Tool is that the whole process is automated, and it can be initiated from the client and requires no administrative intervention. This means you can resolve the most common IPV4 problems with very little administrative effort.

To start the Network Connection Repair Tool, you will need to go to the Network Connections folder. Right-click the connection you want to repair, and choose Repair.

Verify IPV4 Connectivity

If the Network Connection Repair Tool does not fix the connectivity problem, you will need to dig a little deeper to identify and resolve your IP connectivity issues. We recommend you begin at the Event Viewer.

The Event Viewer shows events, warnings, and error messages from the local system or any system to which you have subscribed for event updates. This means the local Event Viewer will collect data about the local system and other systems you choose. You can effectively use the Event Viewer as a central resource to monitor key clients and servers

Network Configuration and Communication

PART IV

throughout your network. The Event Viewer will likely display any related events that are affecting TCP/IP connectivity.

You will want to make sure that the TCP/IP configuration is correct before you do anything else. Does the current configuration match the defined configuration for this network connection? Knowing your network and how the configurations are supposed to be will have tremendous value when you are troubleshooting.

1. Check the physical hardware. Check the network cable. Is it plugged in? Check the connections at switches, hubs, and routers. Don't laugh—you may solve a lot of TCP/IP problems right here in step 1.

2. Verify function and configuration of the network interface.

   Ipconfig /all will display the status and configuration of the IPV4 interface. Verify that the interface has an address and is in fact enabled. Check the DNS settings for the interfaces to be certain that they are configured correctly, as shown in Figure 12.6.

Figure 12.6: Results of IPCONFIG /ALL

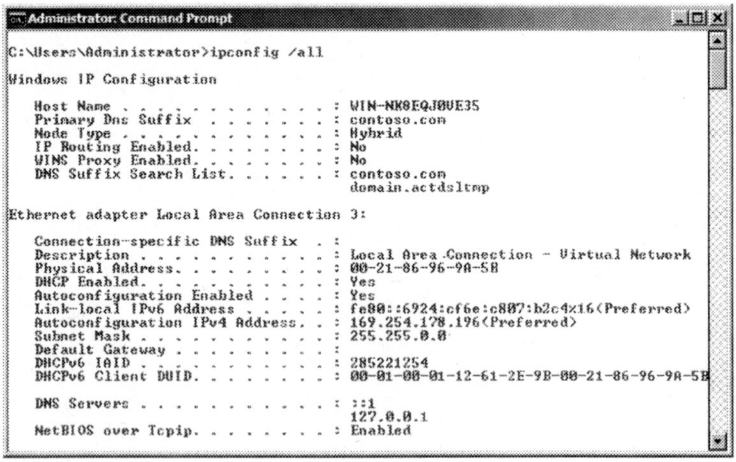

You can use the command-line tool NETSH INTERFACE IP SHOW CONFIG to display the configuration of the IP interfaces and to modify or delete incorrect configuration information.

Verify Responsiveness

Of course, not every problem is going to be fixed with a simple check of the hardware and address configuration. Responsiveness is also important. Responsiveness takes into account that communication takes at least two endpoints. If either of the endpoints fails to respond, then the communication cannot take place. If you have checked the local configuration and everything is in order, you should check that the machine is actually responding to IP requests.

IPV4 uses something called an Address Resolution Protocol (ARP) cache to store IPV4 addresses that have been resolved recently. If for some reason the ARP cache holds incorrect information, it can impede connectivity. You can flush the ARP cache with no negative effects to TCP/IP using this command:

```
ARP -D
```

If you are thinking to yourself, "Hey, that's a lot like the neighbor cache from IPV6," you are right!

The previous step, deleting the ARP cache, acts as a preemptive action to eliminate the possibility that your machine is being incorrectly directed to an IPV4 address that is not going to respond. To truly troubleshoot responsiveness, you will need to start sending packets onto the network and watching for responses. There are a couple of tools that are uniquely suited for this exercise.

PING uses the Internet Control Message Packet (ICMP) to send echo request packets to a host and then measures the response time as the host responds to those echo requests. This tool can be incredibly valuable in verifying responsiveness in IPV4. Traditionally when you use the PING tool, you begin with the process of pinging the local host address and then move on to the local IP address, then an IP address on the same subnet, next the default gateway of the local router, and finally an address on another network segment. You might have learned that you can skip right to pinging a remote host on another segment; if you get a response, you know everything in the cascade is working. As tempting as that is, in the event that you do not receive a response from the remote host, you really don't know anything about where your problem is located. Start with the local host, and work your way through the list. When you don't receive a response, you have reached the area that is having the problem.

Network Configuration and Communication

PART IV

IPV4 has a tool called Trace Route (TRACERT) that allows you to do exactly as its name suggests and trace the route from source to destination in a TCP/IPV4 connection. This tool will help you identify any routing issues that might exist on the route from source to destination computer. Its syntax is as follows:

```
TRACERT -D xxx.xxx.xxx.xxx
```

where x is the IP address of the destination computer.

One more very important point concerning PING and TRACERT is that ICMP packets can be considered a security risk, and often network administrators will configure their computers not to accept or respond to ping echo request packets. If you ping a machine and get no response, make certain that the reason you are not getting a response is because there really is no connectivity, not that the system you pinged does not support ICMP packets. This process of removing or limiting response to specific packet types is often termed *packet filtering*. Packet filtering is a common reason for lack of responsiveness. If you are confident that TCP/IP has been installed and is configured correctly and you are still not getting connectivity, it may well be an issue of filtering. Consider checking the following:

- Windows Firewall rules
- IPsec policies
- Remote access policies
- IPV4 packet filters
- Router policies

Although you are checking for IP filtering issues, you will also want to identify any potential TCP filtering issues. This will save you a troubleshooting step later if you happen to have a problem with TCP connectivity.

Check the Routing Table for IPV4

TCP/IP connectivity issues could be caused by incorrect entries on the IPV4 routing table. You can use the ROUTE PRINT command to show the IPV4 routing table. Here again you will need to be familiar with what the correct routes should look like and then check for any erroneous information on the routing table.

You can add new routes with the ROUTE ADD command. If you find erroneous routes and want to update them with correct information, you can modify the entries with the ROUTE CHANGE command. If you find entries that should just not be there, you can delete routes using the ROUTE DELETE command.

Although you are working with the router and routing table, it makes sense to trace a path through routers from source to destination. You can use the PATHPING xxx.xxx.xxx.xxx command to trace the route. Remember, this tool will display packet losses for each router along the path. Some administrators like to use the -d switch with PATHPING in order to speed up the display of results by preventing the reverse DNS lookup at the internal interface of each router on the path. We like the additional detail provided, and we don't mind waiting. You choose what works best for your situation.

Validate DNS Name Resolution for IPV4 Addresses

If the IPV4 addressing configuration and response checks out, you will want to move up and check on the resolution of host names to TCP/IP addresses, which means DNS. DNS resolves host names to IP addresses for both IPV4 and IPV6. You can perform some simple tasks to ensure that IPV4 host name to IP address resolution is occurring properly.

First verify that your DNS server has been configured to resolve host names to IPV4 addresses and that it is acting upon name resolution requests it receives. To begin, use the HOSTNAME utility to check the host name of the server and to check the DNS suffix.

Next, open the DNS Manager tool, and verify that all of your configured DNS servers appear on the DNS Manager's list of authoritative servers. You can also use the DNS Manager to check the process of forwarding in the event that a host name cannot be resolved to an IP address on the local DNS server. If you need to make changes to the DNS suffix or to connection-specific DNS suffix information, you can do it using DNS Manager.

Flush the DNS Cache

Each IPV4 client maintains a list of recently resolved DNS to IPV4 addresses. This list is called the *DNS resolver cache*. If for some reason a record in the cache had an incorrect address for a given host name, it would limit connectivity. In cases like this, you can flush the contents of the DNS resolver cache using this:

```
IPCONFIG /FLUSHDNS
```

This command will remove all entries from the cache and force the machine to resolve the address with recursive queries sent to the local DNS server hierarchy and get the correct host name to IP address information.

You can quickly check for the function of DNS resolution using the PING tool, as shown in Figure 12.7. PING can be used in conjunction with IP addresses or host name or an FQDN. For example:

```
PING Computer 1
```

or

```
PING www.microsoft.com
```

Figure 12.7: Results of PING www.microsoft.com

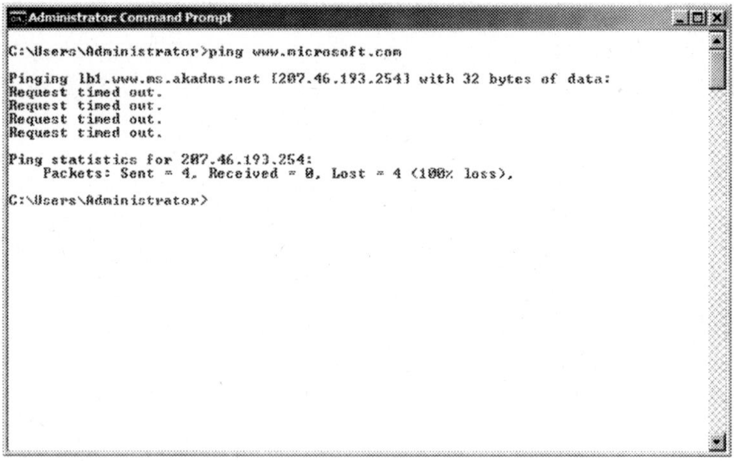

```
Administrator: Command Prompt                                        _□×

C:\Users\Administrator>ping www.microsoft.com

Pinging lb1.www.ms.akadns.net [207.46.193.254] with 32 bytes of data:
Request timed out.
Request timed out.
Request timed out.
Request timed out.

Ping statistics for 207.46.193.254:
    Packets: Sent = 4, Received = 0, Lost = 4 (100% loss),

C:\Users\Administrator>
```

Test IPV4 TCP Connections

What if everything works from an IP perspective but you still cannot get a TCP connection to occur between systems? In the majority of cases, this is a problem with packet filtering. You learned earlier in the chapter about packet filtering locations for IP packets. You will need to check the same locations for TCP filtering. Since you will be checking your filters when you are validating IP connectivity, it makes sense to check for TCP filters at the same time. If you didn't check for TCP filtering earlier, it is time to do it now.

One of the easiest ways to check TCP connections is with the TELNET tool. TELNET is a command-line tool that establishes TCP connections between systems. It uses a syntax similar to the PING command; simply use the TELNET command followed by the IPV4 address.

If the connection is possible, TELNET will create it. TELNET connects to a service, so once you connect to a machine, you can execute commands against the machine to test, configure, or view the contents of the remote machine. TELNET is sometimes seen as a potential security risk, so please don't be surprised if the local firewalls or security policies do not allow TELNET packets.

Network Configuration and Communication

PART IV

PART V

Manage Desktop and Server Virtualization

IN THIS PART ▶

13

Managing Remote Access to Your Server

IN THIS CHAPTER, YOU WILL LEARN TO:

I n this chapter, you will learn how to manage remote access to your server. Often when you think of remote access, you do not think about virtualization. However, remote access is another variation of virtualized access to your servers—whether that comes in the form of a remote desktop or application virtualization. They both factor into you how you grant users on your network access to your servers remotely. You may have heard remote access referred to as Terminal Services in the past. You will see an overview of the new Remote Desktop Services in Windows Server 2008 R2.

You will also see how Windows Server 2008 R2 can offer remote clients the ability to connect via traditional VPNs as well as DirectAccess for Windows 7 clients.

Understand Remote Desktop Services

One of the improved areas in Windows Server 2008 R2 is Remote Desktop Services (RDS). RDS is not fundamentally new; in prior versions of Windows, RDS was known as Terminal Services. Table 13.1 shows the Terminal Services features from Windows Server 2008 with the newly named equivalent services in Windows Server 2008 R2.

Table 13.1: Remote Desktop Services

Windows 2008 Terminal Services	Windows Server 2008 R2 RDS
Terminal Server	Remote Desktop Session Host
Terminal Services Licensing	Remote Desktop Licensing
Terminal Services Session Broker	Remote Desktop Connection Broker
Terminal Services Gateway	Remote Desktop Gateway
Terminal Services Web Access	Remote Desktop Web Access

In addition to these new role services in Windows Server 2008 R2 RDS, Windows Server 2008 R2 also has a new service called Remote Desktop Virtualization Host. This service provides your organization with the ability to create a Virtual Desktop Infrastructure (VDI). VDI is an architectural model where a desktop OS runs in a server-based virtual machine environment. This allows you to connect to the desktop using the Remote Desktop Protocol (RDP) and work with the desktop as if the desktop were locally on the user's physical machine. For an overview of the Remote Desktop Services, see Table 2.1 in Chapter 2.

Understand the Remote Desktop Services Role Services Requirements

After you have determined which RDS role services you want to use on your server, you need to install appropriate prerequisite services for the roles. Table 13.2 lists which RDS role services require additional services.

Table 13.2: Role Services Prerequisites

RDS Role Service	Prerequisites
Remote Desktop Virtualization Host	This new role to Windows Server 2008 R2 requires you have the Hyper-V role installed on your server. In combination with other RDS role services, this service is key to providing your network with a VDI.
Remote Desktop Connection Broker	This role service requires your server be a member of a domain before you can install the service. If the Windows Server 2008 R2 server is not a member of a domain, you will see a message similar to Figure 13.1.
Remote Desktop Gateway	This role service requires the Web Server role, which includes IIS 6 management compatibility for the metabase. Also, this will install IIS security including basic Windows authentication, and client certificate mapping authentication. Additionally, it requires the Network Policy Server and the RPC over HTTP Proxy feature.
Remote Desktop Web Access	This role service requires the Web Server role, which includes common HTTP features (HTTP Redirection) and Windows authentication for security. Additionally, some IIS 6 management compatibilities for the metabase are required.

Figure 13.1: RD Connection Broker error

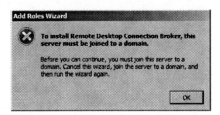

Install Additional Role Services and Prerequisites for Remote Desktop Services

The installation for Remote Desktop Servers can be easy if you are just installing the core Remote Desktop Session Host or can be complicated if you choose to install all the role services. In Chapter 2, you saw some of the basic choices. In this section, you will see some of the additional choices you will have when you install other RDS role services.

1. To open Server Manager, select Start ⇨ Administrative Tools ⇨ Server Manager.

2. Click Roles in the tree menu on the left.

3. Click Add Roles in the details pane on the right to begin installing Remote Desktop Services.

4. On the Add Roles Wizard welcome page, click Next. You can also select "Skip this page by default" to ignore the page for future role installations.

5. On the Select Server Roles page, select Remote Desktop Services. Then click Next.

6. Read the welcome screen, and then click Next.

7. On the Select Roles Services page, select which role services you need to install.

Depending on what role services you have selected, you may see additional choices during your installation. If you choose to install these roles after you have already installed the core Remote Desktop Services, you will need to add role services via Server Manager. Whether you add the role services during your initial install of RDS or after you have installed RDS, the process is similar.

Install Remote Desktop Gateway

Remote Desktop Gateway provides an access mechanism for your Windows Server 2008 R2 Remote Desktop Services via the Internet. The RD Gateway allows your users who are outside your network to securely connect to the RDS server with the SSL protocol over the Internet without having to use a VPN.

When you make the choice to install Remote Desktop Gateway, you may see a screen similar to Figure 13.2 prompting you to install the prerequisite services.

Figure 13.2: Remote Desktop Gateway prerequisites

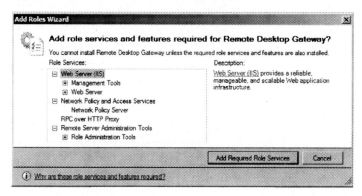

To add the Remote Desktop Gateway service after you have installed RDS, follow these steps:

1. To open Server Manager, select Start ⇨ Administrative Tools ⇨ Server Manager.

2. Expand Roles by clicking the + sign, and click Remote Desktop Services.

3. Right-click Remote Desktop Services, and select Add Role Services.

4. On the Add Role Services screen, select Remote Desktop Gateway.

5. Click Add Required Role Services (if prompted).

6. Click Next in the Add Role Services screen.

7. Select your server certificate required for the SSL communication between clients and the Remote Desktop Gateway server, and click Next.

8. Select Now if you want to configure your connection authorization policy (CAP). The RD Gateway server requires a CAP allowing you to determine which users are allowed to use the gateway. You can configure these later by selecting Later. Select Now, and then click Next.

9. Click Add if you want to add groups allowed to use your RD Gateway server. By default administrators are the only group allowed to connect. After you have added your groups, click Next.

10. Provide a name for your CAP, and you can also choose which authentication mechanism you want to use; by default you will see password and smart card. You can choose one or the other or both. After you have made your selection, click Next.

11. A part of your CAP is also the Resource Authorization Policy (RAP). The RAP allows you to control which computers a user may access via the gateway. You can choose a preconfigured group of computers, or you can choose all computers on the network. Choosing the All option will allow users through the gateway to connect any computer they have permissions to on your network, so you want to use this option with caution. If someone compromises the gateway, they will be able to access any computer on your network. After you have made your selection, click Next.

    If you have installed the prerequisites prior to installing the Remote Desktop Gateway role, you may not see the following steps.

12. On the Introduction to Network Policy and Access Services page, review the information, and then click Next.

13. Review the installed role services, and click Next.

14. On the Introduction to Web Server (IIS) page, review the information, and then click Next.

15. Review the installed role services, and click Next.

16. Review the confirmation screen, and then click Install.

17. Review the summary screen, and click Close.

Install Remote Desktop Web Access

Remote Desktop Web Access provides a way for your users to access your RDS applications via a website on your network. This allows your users to use a browser to connect and leverage RDS.

When you make the choice to install Remote Desktop Web Access, you may see a screen similar to Figure 13.3 prompting you to install the prerequisite services.

Figure 13.3: Remote Desktop Gateway prerequisites

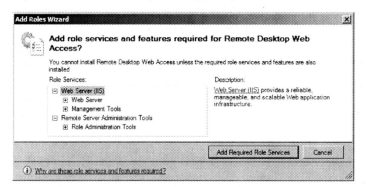

To add the Remote Desktop Gateway service after you have installed RDS, follow these steps:

1. To open Server Manager, select Start ➪ Administrative Tools ➪ Server Manager.
2. Expand Roles by clicking the + sign, and click Remote Desktop Services.
3. Right-click Remote Desktop Services, and select Add Role Services.
4. On the Add Role Services screen, select Remote Desktop Web Access.
5. Click Add Required Role Services (If Prompted).
6. Click Next in the Add Role Services screen.

   If you installed the prerequisites prior to installing the RD Web Access, you may not see the following steps.

7. Review the installed role services, and click Next.
8. On the Introduction to Web Server (IIS) page, review the information, and then click Next.
9. Review the installed role services, and click Next.
10. Review the confirmation screen, and then click Install.
11. Review the summary screen, and click Close.

Manage Remote Desktop Services

In Chapter 2, you saw a brief overview on how to install Remote Desktop Services. In this chapter, you will see a more detailed look at working with the Windows Server 2008 R2 RDS. You will also learn the prerequisites required for each role. Typically, there are a few extra requirements for the services before you can manage them.

Administer Remote Desktop Session Host

The main component you will need to administer when working with RDS is the Remote Desktop Session Host. This is the main component for the services and replaces the core terminal server component from previous versions of Windows Server.

There are two main areas of the licensing server you will configure when working with the Remote Desktop Session Host. You will configure the general settings of the server as well as the connection protocol or protocols users can use on your network to properly connect to the RDS server.

Configure General Settings

When you need to modify settings potentially impacting your entire RDS server, you can find them in the general settings for the RD Session Host on the main page of the administrative tool.

1. Open Remote Desktop Host Session Configuration by selecting Start ⇨ Administrative Tools ⇨ Remote Desktop Services ⇨ Remote Desktop Host Session Configuration. You will see a screen similar to Figure 13.4.

2. To modify any of the settings, double-click any of the settings in the middle task pane, and you will see a screen similar to Figure 13.5.

3. Click the tab of the settings you want to modify. The different settings you can find here are listed in Table 13.3.

4. When you're finished, click Apply if you want to modify other tabs, or click OK to save your settings.

Manage Desktop and Server Virtualization

PART V

Figure 13.4: RD Session Host configuration

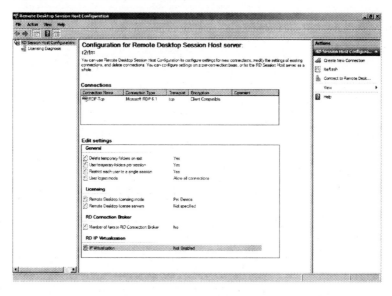

Figure 13.5: Editing RD Session Host settings

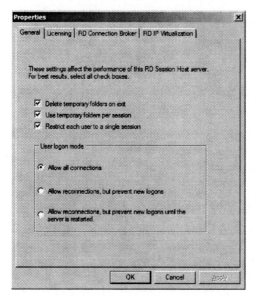

Table 13.3: RD Session Host Configuration Settings

Tab	Setting	Description
General	Delete Temporary Folders On Exit	During an RDS session, temporary folders are created to support applications. To help maintain server drive space, this setting deletes the folders on the RDS server when the session ends. By default, this option is selected.
	Use Temporary Folders Per Session	During an RDS session, temporary folders are created to support applications running properly. By default this option is selected.
	Restrict Each User To A Single Session	This prevents users from logging on to the RDS server with multiple sessions. This will help minimize the amount of resources the RDS server uses.
	User Logon Mode	The settings allow you to perform maintenance or other routine administrative procedures on your RDS server. By preventing new logons, users who are currently connected will be able to reconnect to their RDS session, while any new connections will be denied.
Licensing	Licensing Mode	This allows you to set or change the licensing mode for the server. You can set the licensing mode to Per User or Per Device, and this setting must match the type of RDS CALs you have purchased. This setting can be changed here if you set it during installation of the RDS role.
	Licensing Server	This is where you specify the RDS licensing server for your RDS deployment.
RD Connection Broker	Server Purpose	This determines how your RDS server will work. This setting can be used to join the RDS server to a large number of other RDS servers to create a farm for load balancing. You can also set whether this server will participate in remote desktop virtualization if you want to redirect desktop virtualization.
	Load Balancing	If you have multiple servers in an RDS farm, you can use load balancing settings to control how the servers are best utilized.
	Reconnection	This specifies what adapter and IP will be used for reconnections to the RDS server.

Table 13.3: RD Session Host Configuration Settings *(continued)*

Tab	Setting	Description
RD IP Virtualization	Enable IP Virtualization	These settings are new to Windows Server 2008 R2 and are used to assign IP addresses unique to the session or the application being utilized by the server. In prior versions of Windows Server, every session used the IP address of the server. Now this allows better control for application and session IP-based filtering and security. IP virtualization will require a DHCP server to assign a virtual IP address for the sessions.
	IP Virtualization Mode	Per Session will assign a virtual IP address from a DHCP pool to the session. If you choose Per Program, you will then be able to assign individual IP addresses per application on your RDS server.

Configure Connections for RDS

Configuring connections to your RDS server governs how your clients will connect to the RDS server. When a user connects to RDS, the main protocol used to send information to the client is the Remote Desktop Protocol. RDP essentially consists of screen refreshes sent from the server to the client. The RDP packets travel over TCP protocols, and you can control the communication by modifying or creating new connections. You modify these settings via the following steps:

1. To open Remote Desktop Host Session Configuration, select Start ⇨ Administrative Tools ⇨ Remote Desktop Services ⇨ Remote Desktop Host Session Configuration.

2. To modify any of the settings, double-click any of the settings in the middle task pane.

3. Click the tab of the settings you want to modify. The different settings you can find here are listed in Table 13.4.

4. When you're finished, click Apply if you want to modify other tabs, or click OK to save your settings.

Table 13.4: RD Session Host Configuration Settings

Tab	Setting	Description
General	Security	This determines the security for the communication channel between the client and server. The default value is Negotiate, which will be determined by the capabilities of the client. In most cases, the security layer used will be SSL (TLS 1.0).
	Encryption Level	This setting is also determined by the client and controls the strength of the encryption for the traffic between the client and the server.
	Certificate	You can specify or change the security certificate used to encrypt/decrypt the traffic on your server.
Log On Settings	Client Log On Information	This setting allows you to control how users will authenticate against your server. The default is for the user to specify their credentials; however, you can always specify a certain account to be used by the RDS server.
Sessions	Override User Settings	These settings allow you to control how sessions are disconnected on your RDS server. These settings will free up resources not used on the server for idle sessions, improving the overall performance of your server and other users' sessions.
Environment	Initial Program	This setting will determine what is the program loaded into memory when the user connects to the server.
Remote Control	Remotely View	You can configure these settings if you want to view a user's active session remotely. This will allow you to verify users' connections and use.

Table 13.4: RD Session Host Configuration Settings *(continued)*

Tab	Setting	Description
Client Settings	Color Depth	The settings in client settings control how the RDP session will appear to the user and what the remote desktop interface will look like. You can set the color depth, which will control how the display looks. The better the quality of color, the truer the remote desktop will look to being a native desktop.
	Redirection	This allows you to disable certain aspects of how the remote client is used. The more features you disable, the less functionality and traffic that is sent to the client. The more features you leave enabled, the closer the remote client will look to a real desktop.
Network Adapter	Adapter Settings	This allows you to control which adapter or adapters your RDS server can use, as well as how many connections are limited for the network adapter selected.
Security		This allows you to set which users or groups can connect to the RDS components. When you first open this tab, you will see a warning similar to Figure 13.6. Even though you can modify the users in this option, it is recommended you use the Remote Desktop Users group to control access.

Figure 13.6: RDS security warning

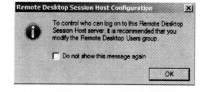

Manage Desktop and Server Virtualization

PART V

Activate Remote Desktop Licensing Server

The RD Licensing component of RDS plays a vital role in your network. This server governs the RDS CALs for your server. If this server is not properly configured or activated, your RDS environment could stop working and prevent connections to your RDS server.

You have two choices for the licensing mode of your RDS server. You can license the server per device or per user. **Per device** allows one device on your network to connect to the RDS server regardless of which user is logged onto the device. This licensing mode is useful when kiosk computers are used heavily in conjunction with RDS for your infrastructure. **Per user** allows you a user to log on to the RDS services from any computer in your network. This mode is useful when you have users who use a variety of workstations to perform their tasks.

One of the key steps you will need to perform on the license server is activating the server. You need to have legitimate RDS CALs you have purchased and then activate your server. To activate the server, you need to go into the RD Licensing Manager tool.

1. To open the RD Licensing Manager, select Start ⇨ Administrative Tools ⇨ Remote Desktop Services ⇨ Remote Desktop Licensing Manager, and you will see a screen similar to Figure 13.7.

2. You will notice your server has an activation status of Not Activated.

3. Right-click your server, and click Activate Server.

4. Review the welcome screen, and click Next.

5. Choose your activation method, which determines how you will verify your RDS CALs. You can connect through the Internet by using a browser or by calling with your telephone. After you have selected your method, click Next.

Figure 13.7: RD Licensing Manager

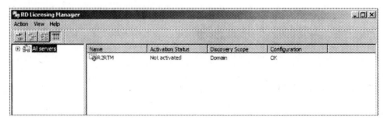

6. No matter which method you choose, you will need your licensing server ID; after you have entered it, click Next.

7. Your server will then be activated.

After your server has been activated, you will then be able to install, configure, and remove your licenses easily. It is just a matter of purchasing the licenses through legitimate sources and having a properly activated server.

Configure Remote Desktop Gateway

The RD Gateway component of Remote Desktop Services provides a tool to allow your users to access the RDS server without using a VPN client. After you have installed the role service, then it is just a matter of working with your Connection Authorization Policy (CAP) and Resource Authorization Policy (RAP) to ensure the security of your server.

The Remote Desktop Gateway Manager will allow you to monitor current connections to the service. You can also modify or create new policies; you just need to open the Remote Desktop Gateway Manager:

1. To open the RD Gateway Manager, select Start ➪ Administrative Tools ➪ Remote Desktop Services ➪ Remote Desktop Gateway Manager.

2. In the RD Gateway Manager, click your server, and you will notice a dashboard screen similar to Figure 13.8. The dashboard allows you an overview picture of what is currently on your server.

3. To view either your CAP or RAP policy, click the + sign next to your server and policies.

4. To modify your existing CAP policies, click Connection Authorization Polices. Click the policy you want to modify and then Properties, located in the right Actions pane.

5. To modify your existing RAP policies, click Resource Authorization Polices. Click the policy you want to modify and then Properties, located in the right Actions pane.

Figure 13.8: Gateway dashboard

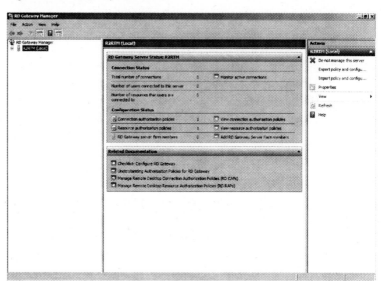

Configure Remote Desktop Connection Broker

Remote Desktop Connection Broker provides a valuable role to your Windows Server 2008 R2 RDS components. This service provides the connection "middle man" between Remote Desktop Web Access and the desktop connection for your remote applications and virtual desktops.

To configure the RD Connection Broker server, you will load the Remote Desktop Connection Manager. The configuration settings you will work with are straightforward after you have loaded the tool. You can do this in Server Manager, or you can use its own dedicated tool. You can find the Remote Desktop Connection Manager by selecting Start ⇨ Administrative Tools ⇨ Remote Desktop Services ⇨ Remote Desktop Connection Manager. You will see a screen similar to Figure 13.9.

One of two major aspects of working with the broker is configuring your RD Web Access servers. The other aspect is configuring Remote Desktop Virtualization Host, which you will see in the next section. To do that, you will need to configure the RD Web Access server. You can add the server manually via the RD Connection Manager tool:

1. To open the RD Connection Manager, select Start ⇨ Administrative Tools ⇨ Remote Desktop Services ⇨ Remote Desktop Connection Manager.

2. Click Add RD Web Access Servers on the Actions pane on the right side of the console window.

3. Enter the FQDN of your RD Web Access server.

4. Click OK.

Figure 13.9: RD Connection Manager

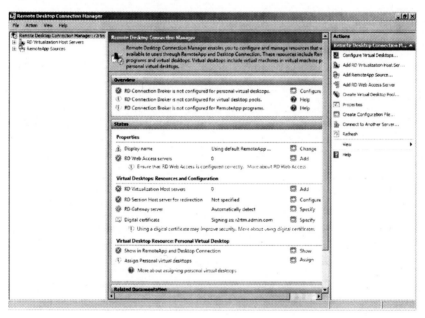

You can also add the RD Web Access server by adding the computer accounts for those servers to the TS Web Access Computers group located in your Active Directory. When you add the servers to the TS Web Access Computers group, they will automatically be displayed in the tool.

You will also need to configure RemoteApp source servers to make sure connections can be brokered by this service:

1. Open the RD Connection Manager by selecting Start ⇨ Administrative Tools ⇨ Remote Desktop Services ⇨ Remote Desktop Connection Manager.

2. Click Add RemoteApp Source on the Actions pane on the right side of the console window.

3. Enter the FQDN of the server that has the RemoteApp tools configured.

4. Click OK.

This will enable RDS components like RD Web Access to provide applications through the RD Connection Broker.

Configure Remote Desktop Web Access

One of the other avenues that your users can access the RDS components on your Windows Server 2008 R2 server is via their local web browser. RD Web Access allows your users to log on to an RDS session via the browser. In RD Web Access, you can let your clients access services from around the world. When you are configuring RD Web Access, you will also need to understand RemoteApp Manager and how you configure applications to run via the RDS components.

What you first need to do to configure RD Web Access is control how the website gets the applications you want to provide. You can choose either a local RemoteApp server or an RD Connection Broker to control your access. Your RDS infrastructure will determine how your users receive applications via the RD Web Access server.

1. Open Remote Desktop Web Access Configuration by selecting Start ⇨ Administrative Tools ⇨ Remote Desktop Services ⇨ Remote Desktop Web Access Configuration.

2. Type in your administrative credentials, and click Sign In. After you are authenticated, you will see a screen similar to Figure 13.10.

3. Select your option, either a Connection Broker server or the RemoteApp server, and enter the FQDN name (usually you will want the full name instead of the NetBIOS name).

4. Click OK, and your server will provide the applications and desktops based on your chosen configuration.

Figure 13.10: RD Web Access configuration

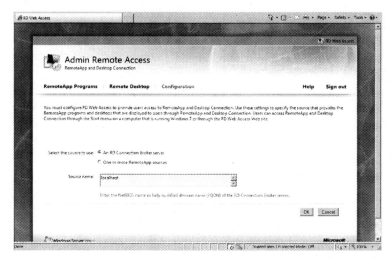

To connect to the RD Web Access server, you need to open the website. By default the website is named RDWeb and is enabled for Secure Sockets Layer (SSL) encryption security. For example, if your server is named R2RTM and your domain is admin, the URL you would type in your browser by default would be https://r2rtm.admin.com/rdweb. After you typed in your authentication, you would see a screen similar to Figure 13.11.

Figure 13.11: RD Web Access

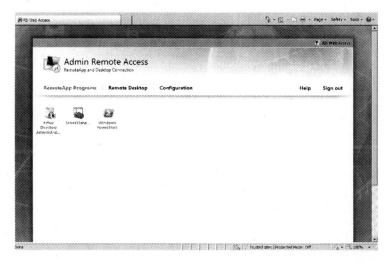

Use the RemoteApp Manager

The RemoteApp Manager is a tool you will use to make applications accessible via RDS. Before you can add applications through RemoteApp, you have to make sure the applications are installed or configured correctly with RDS. Although most applications you will use will work with RDS, other applications, such as Microsoft Office, need to have special installations or licensing done in order for them to work properly on an RDS server. Before installing the applications, you may want to consult the documentation to see whether they will run with RDS, or look for directions for Terminal Services.

To configure applications in RemoteApp, you need to load the RemoteApp Manager either in Server Manager or via its own tool in the administrative tools.

1. Open RemoteApp Manager by selecting Start ⇨ Administrative Tools ⇨ Remote Desktop Services ⇨ RemoteApp Manager. You will see a screen similar to Figure 13.12.

2. To add an application, click Add RemoteApp Programs in the right Actions pane.

3. Read the welcome screen, and click Next.

Figure 13.12: The RemoteApp Manager

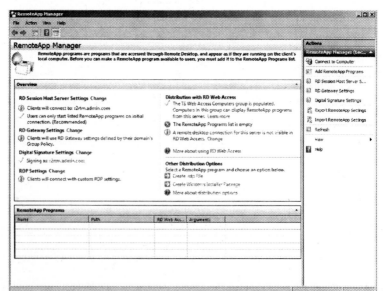

4. Select your applications; you can also browse for your applications if they are not currently listed. You can also modify the properties of a selected application. After you add an application, click Properties, and you will see a screen similar to Figure 13.13.

Figure 13.13: Application properties

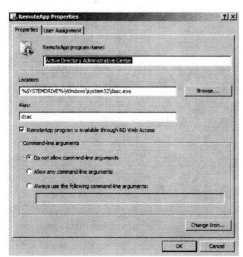

From the properties list you can modify any command-line arguments needed for the program to run or even specify which user accounts or groups can access the particular application. When you are done adding applications, click Next.

5. Review your final settings, and then click Finish.

After you have added remote applications, you can offer the applications to your users. You can make your applications available via the RD Web Access front end, an RDP package, or an .msi package. By default if you have RD Web Access installed, your applications will automatically be available via RD Web Access. If you want to hide the application for RD Web Access, simply click the application and click Hide In RD Web Access in the Actions pane on the right side of the console.

You can create an RDP package and place it on a share or in another location to give it to your users:

1. Open the RemoteApp Manager by selecting Start ⇨ Administrative Tools ⇨ Remote Desktop Services ⇨ RemoteApp Manager.

2. Click the application for which you want to create an RDP package.

3. Click Create .rdp File in the middle details pane or in the right Actions pane.

4. Review the welcome screen, and click Next.

5. Enter the location for the .rdp file (usually a shared folder or some other location your users can gain access to quickly). You can also modify the basic session, gateway, and certificate settings. When you are finished modifying the session settings, click Next.

6. Review the summary screen, and click Finish to create the package.

Creating an .msi package will allow you to create a installation file that will place the remote connection file on the user's Start menu. In the case of applications with files, the .msi package will also set up an extension association. Windows Installer files also offer the flexibility to deploy the applications via scripts.

1. Open the RemoteApp Manager by selecting Start ⇨ Administrative Tools ⇨ Remote Desktop Services ⇨ RemoteApp Manager.

2. Click the application for which you want to create the .msi file.

3. Click Create Windows Installer Package in the middle details pane or in the right Actions pane.

4. Review the welcome screen, and click Next.

5. Enter the location for the .msi file (usually a shared folder or some other location your users can gain access to quickly). You can also modify the basic session, gateway and certificate settings. When you are finished modifying the session settings, click Next.

6. Select where you want the shortcuts created, either on the desktop, in the Start menu, or in the folder you specify. You can also set file extension association, which will automatically launch the RDP session when the user opens a file with the extension.

7. Review the summary screen, and click Finish to create the package.

Connect with Remote Desktop Connection

In addition to using RD Web Access to allow your users to connect to the RDS components, your users also have the ability to connect through programs located on the host computer. In the Microsoft OS, this connection program is called the Remote Desktop Connection and has been typically located in the Accessories group on the Start menu. This connection tool will allow you to connect directly to the RDS components and control many aspects of the connection.

1. Open Remote Desktop Connection by selecting Start ⇨ All Programs ⇨ Accessories ⇨ A Remote Desktop Connection.

2. If you do not want to modify any of the settings, you can fill in the server name and your credentials to log on. However, if you want to modify some of the settings, click Options, and you will see a screen similar to Figure 13.14.

   - *General*: This tab contains the basic connection settings, the server name, and the username. You also have the ability to save these settings to your own RDP file.

   - *Display*: This tab controls the resolution and colors supported for the RDP session.

   - *Local Resources*: This tab allows the RDP session to leverage your existing local resources. Specifically, you can configure audio, keyboard, printers, and the clipboard, as well as other local resources. These were new additions to Windows Server 2008.

   - *Programs*: You can specify which programs will load when the RDP session starts.

   - *Experience*: This is new to Windows Server 2008 R2 and allows you make the RDP session appear very crisp and natural. The goal of these settings is to make the remote connection appear as close to a real desktop as possible.

   - *Advanced*: This tab will allow you to control how server authentication failures are handled and also control the RD Gateway server if configured to allow a secure connection over the gateway.

Figure 13.14: Remote Desktop Connection

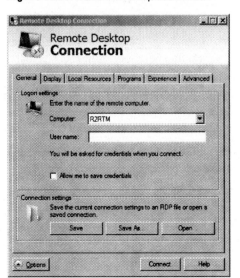

3. When you are done modifying the settings, click Connect, and you will be connected to the RDP services, provided you have permissions and the server is available.

Working with Virtual Desktop Infrastructure

One of the new, key aspects you can take advantage of when using all the RDS components available to your Windows Server 2008 R2 server is the virtual desktop infrastructure. What this allows you to do, in a nutshell, is take a virtual machine created in Hyper-V on your server and enable remote desktop connections to the virtual machine. This provides a flexible desktop access solution for you and your users, as well as giving you centralized management of the desktop sessions. Since the sessions are stored in a virtual machine, you can quickly manage these systems.

What happens under the covers is the user using the VDI to connect to the desktop will initiate the connection with either RD Web Access or a Remote Desktop Connection file. This connection will be routed through the RD Connection Broker, with verification to AD and the RD Session Host, and then the client will be able to access the Remote Desktop Virtualization Host. As you may recall, the Remote

Desktop Virtualization Host role service requires Hyper-V configured on the server. It is the Hyper-V virtual machines loaded on the Remote Desktop Virtualization Host that will provide the desktop to your users. In Figure 13.15, you can see a diagram on how this works.

Figure 13.15: VDI overview

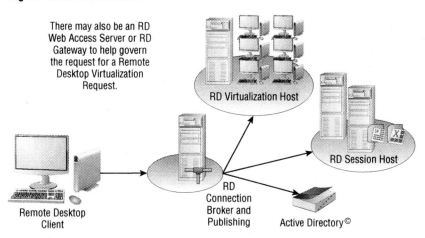

There may also be an RD Web Access Server or RD Gateway to help govern the request for a Remote Desktop Virtualization Request.

RD Virtualization Host

RD Session Host

Remote Desktop Client

RD Connection Broker and Publishing

Active Directory©

There are numerous services to make this work from end to end. However, the RDS tools make this as straightforward as possible. After you have created the virtual client machine to be used for VDI, then you need to configure the various components to properly handle the requests. A majority of your configurations will be completed in the RD Connection Manager.

Configure Virtualization Hosts

One of the first steps is to configure the Remote Desktop Virtualization Host to use the virtual machine you have chosen:

1. To open Connection Manager, select Start ⇨ Administrative Tools ⇨ Remote Desktop Services ⇨ Remote Desktop Connection Manager.

2. In RD Connection Manager, click Add RD Virtualization Host Server in either the middle pane or the Actions pane on the right.

3. Type in the FQDN of the server you installed the Remote Desktop Virtualization Host service on, and click Add; you will see a screen similar to Figure 13.16. You will then need to configure how you will connect to the virtual desktops.

Figure 13.16: RD Virtualization Host Servers

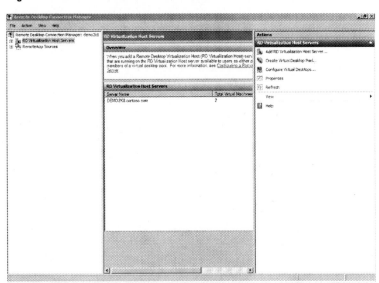

4. Click Configure Virtual Desktops in the right Actions pane.

5. Review the welcome screen, and click Next.

6. You should see the name of your RD Virtualization Host server; if you do not, type in the name, and click Next.

7. You may need to configure your RD Session Host server. This may also already have been configured; if you do not see the RD Session Host server specified, type in the FQDN of the server, and click Next.

8. You may need to configure your RD Web Access Server; this may also already have been configured. If you do not see the RD Web Access server specified, type in the FQDN of the server, and click Next.

9. Review your summary information. You will also notice a check mark in the check box Assign Personal Virtual Desktop. Leave the box selected, and click Finish.

10. To assign a virtual machine, you need to select a user from your AD environment and a virtual machine that exists on the RD Virtualization Host server. It is required that your virtual machines have been named with an FQDN in Hyper-V. If they have not

been, you will see an error message, as shown in Figure 13.17. After you have entered your username and assigned a virtual machine, click Next.

Figure 13.17: RD FQDN error

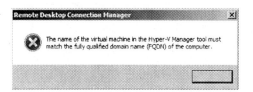

11. Review the confirmation screen, and click Assign.

12. Review the assignment summary; you will also notice a check box if you need to assign another virtual machine that is checked by default; if you need to assign more users or groups, click Continue. Otherwise, clear the check box, and click Finish.

One last configuration you will need to make is to the RD Session Host server. You will need to set the connection broker's server purpose to Virtual Machine Redirection. This is necessary so the server redirects the requests properly to the Remote Desktop Virtualization Host server.

1. To open RD Session Host Configuration, select Start ⇨ Administrative Tools ⇨ Remote Desktop Services ⇨ Remote Desktop Session Host configuration.

2. Double-click the setting under the heading RD Connection Broker.

3. Click Change Settings.

4. Select the radio button Virtual Machine Redirection under the Remote Desktop Virtualization heading.

5. Enter the server name of your RD Connection Broker server. The server will need to be in the Session Broker Computers group in your Active Directory. Your screen should look similar to Figure 13.18.

6. Click OK, and you will see a notification similar to Figure 13.19.

7. Review the message, and if you accept the changes, click Yes.

8. Click OK to exit the settings dialog box.

Figure 13.18: RDS virtualization configuration

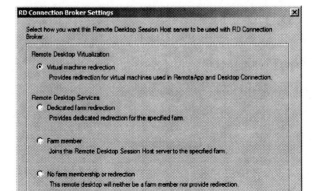

Figure 13.19: RD Session Host changes

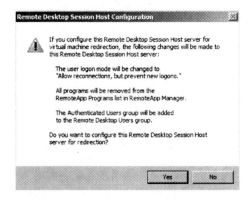

This section gave a brief overview of working with VDI. For more information, visit http://technet.microsoft.com/en-us/library/dd941616(WS.10).aspx.

Work with Remote Clients

In Windows Server 2008 R2, in addition to the RDS components, the server can also be configured to provide powerful capabilities for remote clients to your network. Remote clients like your road warriors, your telecommuters, and other users are not connected to your network on a daily basis. In Windows Server 2008 R2, you still have access to the Routing and Remote Access services that were available in Windows Server 2008. However, you also have a powerful alternative to a normal VPN with a new component to Windows Server 2008 R2 called DirectAccess. You will now get broad overview of working with both solutions.

Install and Configure Windows Server 2008 R2 VPNs

Creating a VPN on your Routing and Remote Access server provides secure remote access to private networks. When you decide to install a VPN and install the Routing and Remote Access role services, you get several capabilities for your network. RRAS can be used in a variety of configurations, as you can see in Table 13.5.

Table 13.5: RRAS Options

Component	Description
VPN Access	This allows clients to connect to your network across the Internet.
Dial-Up Access	This allows clients to connect to your network via a modem or other dial-in equipment.
Demand-Dial Connections	This allows your server to initiate and receive demand-dial connections. Demand-dial connections allow your modem communications to be cost effective by dialing the connections only when needed.
NAT	Network Address Translation allows your users on your network to share a single Internet connection. NAT translates between the public Internet address and your private network IP address scheme.
LAN Routing	This option allows your RRAS server to forward packets from one LAN segment to another.

Understand the Windows Server 2008 R2 Role Services

There are several core services you can choose to configure on your Windows Server 2008 R2 server when you install your VPN for your network. Table 13.6 describes the role services and what their function is.

Table 13.6: Network Policy and Access Role Services

Role Service	Description
Network Policy Server (NPS)	This role service gives you the ability to create access policies governing connection requests for authorization and authentication. This role service also allows you to install a client health enforcement tool called Network Access Protection (NAP).
RRAS Remote Access Service	The core RRAS services provide the VPN capability for your server. The connections can also be made with dial-up connections.
RRAS Routing	This role service will provide LAN and WAN routing services for your network as well as NAT, RIP, and IGMP proxy routers.
Health Registration Authority (HRA)	This is used in conjunction when you roll out your NAP solution. The HRA will validate the health of remote clients connecting to the server by issuing certificates with the health status of the connection client. This role service will require the IIS Management tools, specifically, the IIS 6 WMI and Scripting tools.
Host Credential Authorization Protocol (HCAP)	This is another component for a NAP solution in your network; specifically, the HCAP component is designed to work with the Cisco Network Access Control. This role service will require the IIS Client Certificate Mapping Authentication and Digest Authentication components from the IIS services.

Install Routing and Remote Access Services

You install the Routing and Remote Access Services (RRAS) by adding the role services in Server Manager:

1. Select Start ⇨ Administrative Tools ⇨ Server Manager.

2. Click Roles on the tree menu on the left.

3. Click Add Roles in the details pane on the right.

4. In the list of roles, select Network Policy And Access Services, and click Next.

5. Review the welcome screen for Network Policy And Access Services, and click Next.

6. Select Routing And Remote Access Services; normally you will select both Remote Access Services and Routing. After you have selected the components, click Next.

7. Review the confirmation screen, and click Install.

8. Review the installation results, and click Close.

Configure the VPN

After you have installed the RRAS solutions, you will need to enable and configure the role service. In Windows Server 2008 R2, you will notice there is a wizard drive utility designed to help you configure the VPN.

When you configure RRAS, you will have several choices. Follow these steps:

1. To open Routing And Remote Access, select Start ⇨ Administrative Tools ⇨ Routing And Remote Access.

2. Click your server in the tree on the left. When you first launch the Routing and Remote Access management tools, you will see a screen similar to Figure 13.20.

3. Select Action ⇨ Configure And Enable Routing And Remote Access.

Figure 13.20: Enabling RRAS

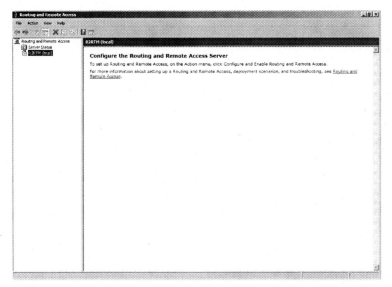

4. Review the welcome screen, and click Next.

5. On the configuration screen, select Remote Access (Dial-Up or VPN), and click Next.

6. How your users will connect and what hardware you have on your server will determine whether you select VPN or Dial-Up. After you have selected your option, click Next.

7. Select the network interface you are using on your Windows Server 2008 R2 server to connect to the Internet. After you have selected your Internet network interface, click Next.

8. Select the internal network adapter in which you want to assign to your remote VPN users.

9. On the IP Address Assignment screen, you can use a DHCP server in your network, or you can create a specific range of IP addresses for the VPN connection. After you make your selection, click Next. If you choose your own range of addresses, you will have an additional step to configure the range.

10. On the next screen, you will see a choice to configure a Remote Authentication Dial-In User Service (RADIUS). You will see a screen similar to Figure 13.21. The RADIUS server is useful if you have several RRAS servers and you want to have a central authentication point. If you have only a single RRAS server, you can click No, as in this walk-through; then click Next.

11. Review the summary screen, and click Finish. You may also receive a few additional warning prompts, which you will need to acknowledge before you can finish your setup. These additional prompts are determined by the other options you may have configured during the setup of these services.

After you have completed enabling and configuring your RRAS server, your Routing and Remote Access management console will look similar to Figure 13.22.

The completed console provides you with the ability to modify any of your VPN settings. Traditionally, once you have configured the VPN, you will not need to perform many day-to-day duties for maintenance. However, the console does provides some nice monitor tools to view server status as well as the ability to see which clients are currently connected via VPN to your server.

Figure 13.21: RADIUS

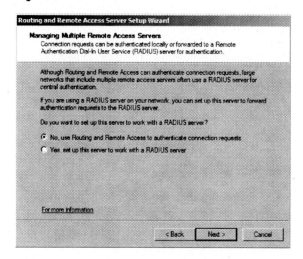

Figure 13.22: RRAS configured

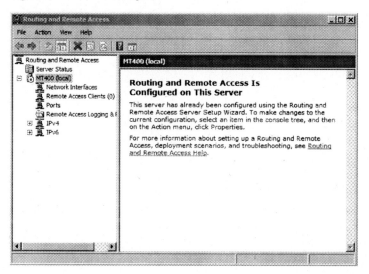

Network Access Protection (NAP)

One of the additional capabilities you have with RRAS is the ability to verify the health of your VPN clients to your network. NAP provides a method for you to quarantine your VPN clients before they are allowed to connect to your server. NAP can also be instrumental in providing remediation for clients not meeting the computer health requirements of your network. To learn more about configuring and working with NAP, please visit http://technet.microsoft.com/en-us/network/bb545879.aspx.

Install and Configure DirectAccess

One of the new features in Windows Server 2008 R2 is DirectAccess. In addition to requiring a Windows Server 2008 R2 server, this feature is available only to Windows 7 clients. This new capability allows you as the IT administrator a great amount of control over your remote clients. DirectAccess will enable your Windows 7 clients the ability to always be connected to your corporate network regardless of how they are connected to the Internet. DirectAccess is a connection solution for Windows Server 2008 R2 servers and Windows 7 clients, surpassing existing VPN solutions. Having your clients always connect provides a consistent management model for you. This provides you with a consistent way to manage, patch, and secure remote workstations that in the past may not have always been connected on a frequent basis. For your users, DirectAccess provides an "always-on" secure connection to corporate networks and resources.

The installation for this tool set can be lengthy and complex, although in the end this work could be worth your time and effort if you have or are planning to have Windows 7 clients in your environment. In this section, you will see an overview of the steps required to configure DirectAccess on your Windows Server 2008 R2 server. There are also numerous prerequisites needed to be configured. Among many other things, DirectAccess requires an understanding of IPv6 (with IPv4 translation), Public Key Infrastructure (PKI), and the use of certificates, as well as a firm understanding of DNS to make this solution work. Microsoft created a nice step-by-step guide located here, which will also include all the necessary prerequisites and client-side configuration: www.microsoft.com/downloads/details.aspx?displaylang=en&FamilyID= 8d47ed5f-d217-4d84-b698-f39360d82fac.

Although the installation can be complex, the tool set on the Windows Server 2008 R2 server, which you will see in this section, is designed to help you through the process. The built-in tools in Windows Server 2008 R2 will make sure you have dotted your *i*'s and crossed your *t*'s for the installation and configuration of DirectAccess.

Install the DirectAccess Management Console

When you need to configure DirectAccess, you will need to install the DirectAccess management console. The management console is a Windows Server 2008 R2 feature and can be installed by adding the feature. The DirectAccess console is a tool designed to step you through the process of properly configuring your server.

1. Open Server Manager by selecting Start ⇨ Administrative Tools ⇨ Server Manager.
2. Click Features on the tree menu on the left.
3. Click Add Features in the details pane on the right.
4. Select DirectAccess Management Console, and click Next.
5. Review the confirmation screen, and click Install.
6. Review the summary screen, and click Close.

After you have installed the console, you can find the tool in the Administrative Tools group, and when you open the tool, you can begin the process of setting up DirectAccess. When you first open the console, you will see a link to help titled Checklist: Before You Configure DirectAccess. This link will take you through all the necessary prerequisite steps.

1. Open the DirectAccess management console by selecting Start ⇨ Administrative Tools ⇨ DirectAccess Management Console.
2. On the tree on the left of the console, click Setup; you may see a screen with some errors like Figure 13.23. If you have errors, take corrective action, and click Retry.
3. After you have fixed any error messages, you will see a screen similar to Figure 13.24.

Figure 13.23: DirectAccess error

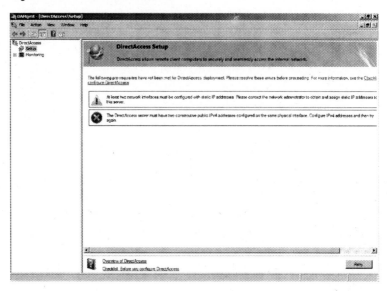

Figure 13.24: DirectAccess setup

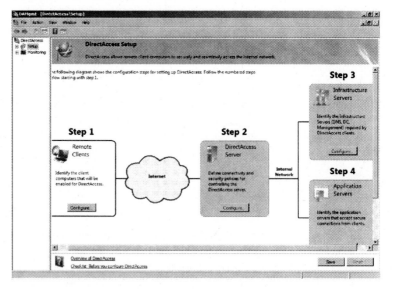

As you can see, the DirectAccess tool provides you a visual step-by-step guidance in properly configuring this powerful connection component. Each configuration step for DirectAccess can be modified after you have done your initial configuration. You also have to complete the steps in order to get a properly configured DirectAccess server:

1. *Remote clients*: In this step, you will configure which clients will be able to use DirectAccess. You will add the appropriate computer groups in your AD infrastructure that contain your preprovisioned DirectAccess systems. Remember, only Windows 7 clients can participate in DirectAccess.

2. *DirectAccess server setup*: In this step, you will configure the connection aspects of your network adapters. You will need to specify which network adapters are used for the Internet and your internal network. You will also have the ability to configure your DirectAccess server to accept logins via smart cards. You will also need to configure your certificate authorities (CAs) for the DirectAccess server used to provide secure communications.

3. *Infrastructure servers*: In this step, you will configure how your clients will access your core infrastructure services such as the AD domain controllers and DNS servers your users will need to access to work with your network infrastructure. You can also configure in this step an internal web server with the ability to provide location services for infrastructure components to your DirectAccess clients.

4. *Application servers*: In this step, you will configure your end-to-end authentication and security for the DirectAccess components. DirectAccess allows you to secure the communication channel from the beginning to the end to keep a safe and secure channel. You also have to ability to control which servers your DirectAccess clients can connect to; you have the ability to restrict communications to certain servers in your network.

As you have seen, this was a brief overview of the configuration for DirectAccess. This is a new solution and provides a secure and fast connection method for your remote clients to connect to your environment in addition to any VPNs you may currently have.

14

Maintaining Virtual Machines

IN THIS CHAPTER, YOU WILL LEARN TO:

Understand Virtualization with Hyper-V

Windows Server 2008 R2 has many opportunities for IT administrators to implement a virtualization strategy. Virtual Server, Application Virtualization, Remote Desktop Gateways, and Remote Desktop all provide opportunities for virtualization. Although all these tools offer something uniquely valuable to the virtual environment, when we think of virtualization with Windows Server 2008 R2, we think of Hyper-V.

Hyper-V enables you to create and host an entire virtualized environment in which you can host client and server operating systems. Hyper-V offers the benefits of running multiple operating systems simultaneously on the same set of physical hardware. The problem of ever-increasing numbers of servers (called *server sprawl*), and its associated costs in both implementation and administration, can be effectively controlled with a Hyper-V environment. There are also benefits related to the testing and development areas of IT because test machine and development environments can be easily built, maintained, and reused. On a system running Hyper-V, the hardware utilization typically goes way up while the hardware and administration costs go way down. These benefits have made Hyper-V a very popular addition to the Windows Server 2008 R2 network.

Install Hyper-V

To install Hyper-V, your system must meet certain requirements:

- It must have an x64-based processor.

- The machine must support hardware-assisted virtualization. The processors must support Intel Virtualization Technology (Intel VT) or AMD Virtualization (AMD-V) enabled through the system BIOS.

- Your system must have hardware-enforced Data Execution Prevention (DEP) via a BIOS-enabled Intel XD bit or AMD NX bit.

- Your system must have Windows Server 2008 R2 Standard edition, Enterprise edition, or Datacenter edition installed.

Hyper-V is installed as a role on Windows Server 2008 R2. You will use Server Manager to install Hyper-V components and the Hyper-V Manager tool:

1. Open Server Manager.

2. Select Roles.

3. Choose Add Roles.

4. Select the box for the Hyper-V role.

5. Click Next.

6. Click Next to verify the informational messages.

7. Select a network adapter to use with your virtual machines. (You can modify this later with the Virtual Network Manager.)

8. Click Next.

9. Click Install.

The server will install the components and services for Hyper-V. See Figure 14.1.

Figure 14.1: Installing Hyper-V

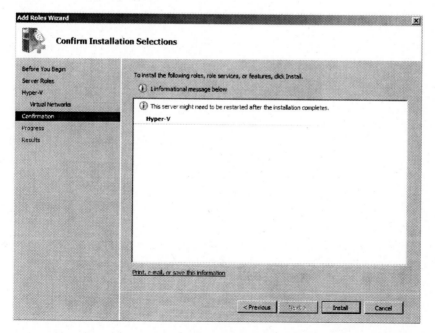

Once the installation of Hyper-V has completed, you will need to restart your computer.

After the restart, you can use a new tool called the Hyper-V Manager to manage your virtual networks and virtual machines. You can open Hyper-V Manager by opening Server Manager, expanding Roles, and selecting Hyper-V. You can also open Hyper-V Manager as a stand-alone tool from the All Programs menu or the Administrative Tools menu depending on how you have configured your Programs menu.

Hyper-V Manager consists of three panes, as you can see in Figure 14.2. The tree pane is on the left side, the details pane is in the center, and the Actions pane is on the right. As you select the server by its name in the tree pane, the options available in the details and Actions panes will update.

Figure 14.2: The Hyper-V Manager

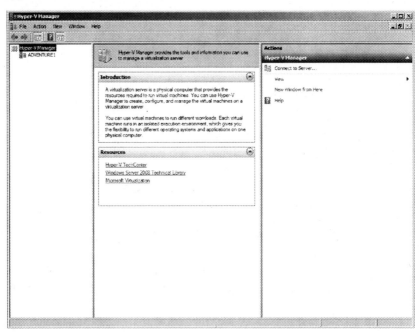

Work with Virtual Networks

The first things you will want to do after installing Hyper-V is to build the virtual network infrastructure you will use to connect your virtual machines to one another and to make them available to the rest of your network, or even the rest of the world.

You can build and manage virtual networks using the Virtual Network Manager tool in the Hyper-V Manager. When the Hyper-V server is selected, you will find the Virtual Network Manager option in the Actions pane, as shown in Figure 14.3.

Figure 14.3: Virtual Network Manager option

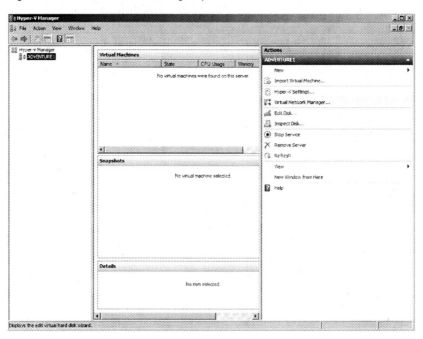

When you click the Virtual Network Manager option, you will see the default network that was created when you installed Hyper-V, and you have the opportunity to create additional virtual networks. Virtual networks come in three distinct types:

External This type of virtual network binds to the physical network adapter so that virtual machines can access the physical network.

Internal This creates a network that can be accessed only by the virtual machines hosted by the local Hyper-V server and the host physical server.

Private This creates a virtual network that can be accessed only by the virtual machines hosted by the local Hyper-V server.

When you are working with virtual machines, you might want to have some machines connected to private virtual networks, such as in a testing environment. Or you might want to have machines connected to the physical network, such as a hosted web server, or a legacy server running as a virtual machine. The cool thing is that Virtual Network Manager does not limit you to creating a single virtual network. You can build multiple virtual networks and link virtual machines to the various virtual networks based on your network needs.

To create a virtual network, follow these steps:

1. Open the Hyper-V Manager.

2. Select the server name in the tree pane.

3. Click Virtual Network Manager in the Actions pane.

4. Select the type of network you want to create (External, Internal, or Private).

5. Click Add.

6. Enter the name of your virtual network, as shown in Figure 14.4.

Figure 14.4: Create Virtual Network Wizard

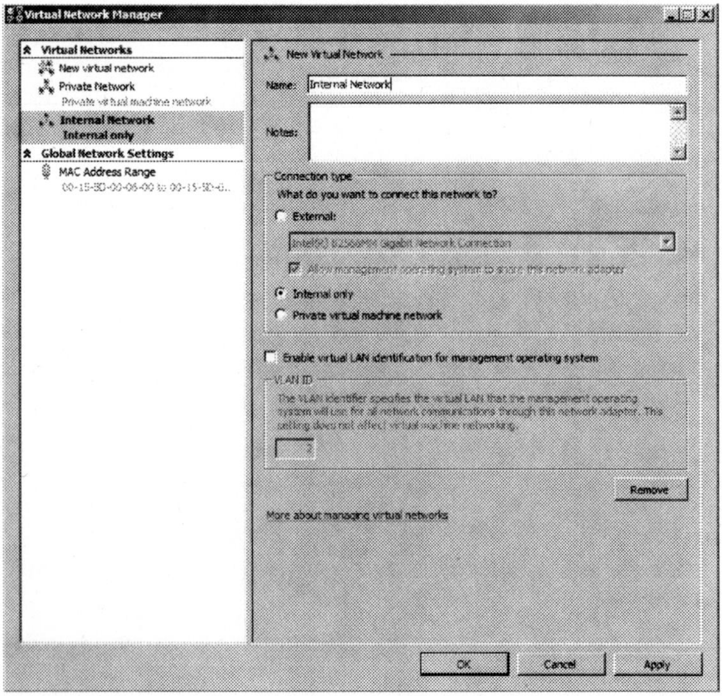

7. Enter any details or notes about the virtual network into the Notes field.

8. Under Connection Type, select the network interface (for an external network), or select the Internal Only or Private Virtual Machine Network radio button.

9. In the event that you are using an external network, you can also enable and use a VLAN ID in conjunction with this virtual network.

10. Click OK.

The nice thing about the Virtual Network Manager tool is that you can easily add new virtual networks and make adjustments or changes to existing networks with relative ease. If you open the Virtual Network Manager, the virtual networks you have already created are visible in the details pane on the left. You can select them by name and make any changes, including removing the entire virtual network, by simply adjusting the settings in the details pane.

Build Virtual Machines

A virtual machine is nothing more than an installed operating system. It is installed, and operates, inside a single special file called a *virtual hard disk* (VHD) file. The VHD file and the specific settings that define the hardware specifications combine to form the overall virtual machine.

Create a Virtual Machine

To create a virtual machine, click the New option in the Actions pane and select Virtual Machine. This will start the New Virtual Machine Wizard. This wizard will guide you through the rest of the process of creating a virtual machine. The process goes as follows:

1. Click Next on the Before You Begin screen.

2. Provide a name for your virtual machine.

3. If you do not want the virtual machine stored in the My Virtual Machines folder, you will need to supply an alternate location.

4. Click Next.

5. Specify how many megabytes of RAM you will allocate to the virtual machine.

6. Click Next.

7. Choose which of your virtual networks you would like to connect to this virtual machine.

8. Click Next.

9. Specify the virtual hard disk. You can create a new one, use an existing one, or defer and attach a hard drive later.

10. Click Next.

11. Choose to install an operating system later, install from a DVD/CD, install from a boot floppy, or install an operating system from a network installation server. This option is available only if you choose to create a new VHD. If you choose another option, you would be taken directly to step 13.

12. Click Next.

13. Read the summary information, and if it is correct, hit Finish (see Figure 14.5).

Figure 14.5: Creating a virtual machine

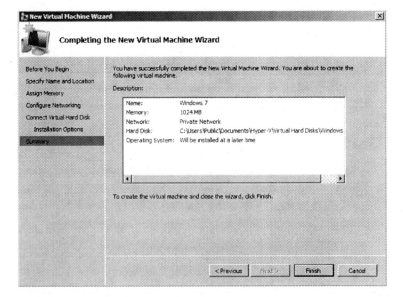

Create Virtual Hard Disks

You undoubtedly noticed when you created a virtual machine that it is possible to create a virtual machine and create the VHD later. The virtual hard disk is the storage component for the virtual machine. It is the location you will install the files for the operating system and applications.

Virtual hard disks have some degree of portability. It is possible to import and export VHD files using Hyper-V and "move" them from one server to another.

All VHDs are not created equal. There are actually three different types. When you build a VHD, you will choose which type to create:

Dynamically expanding VHD   Dynamically expanding VHDs do exactly what the name suggests. The VHD starts relatively small and then dynamically increases in size to accommodate the storage needs of the virtual machine. It is important to note that although the disk automatically increases in size as new data is added to the VHD, it does not automatically shrink in size if data is deleted from the VHD. To resize the VHD file, you will need to run the Edit VHD Wizard.

Fixed VHD   A fixed virtual hard disk provides a specific amount of storage space that is defined at the time the hard disk is created. The size of the VHD will remain fixed regardless of how much data is added to the VHD. It is possible to use the Edit Virtual Hard Disk Wizard to increase or decrease the size of the fixed VHD should the need arise for additional storage space.

Differencing VHD   A differencing virtual hard disk provides storage to enable you to make changes to a parent virtual hard disk without altering the parent disk. The changes are actually made to the differencing disk while maintaining the original integrity of the parent disk.

Create a Virtual Hard Disk

To create a new VHD, follow these steps:

1. Open the Hyper-V Manager.

2. Click New in the Actions pane.

3. Select Hard Disk.

4. Click Next on the Before You Begin page.

5. Select the type of VHD you want to create.

6. Click Next.

7. Name the VHD.

8. Click Next.

9. Specify the size of the disk, or copy the contents of a physical disk.

10. Review the settings you have made, as shown in Figure 14.6, and click Finish.

Figure 14.6: Creating a VHD

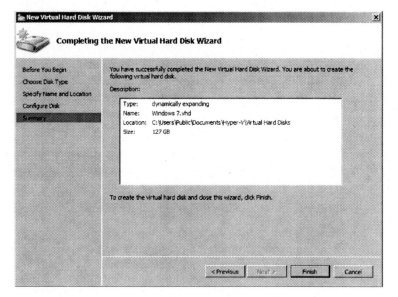

It should be noted here that these steps reflect the process of creating a virtual hard disk with either the fixed or dynamically increasing types. If you were to create a differencing disk to use in conjunction with an existing fixed or dynamically increasing disk, the process would be slightly different.

Use an Existing VHD

The nature of the VHD makes it relatively portable. As of this writing, Microsoft is providing VHD files that can be used by individuals to evaluate Windows Server and other associated platform products. These VHD files can be downloaded and used as the base of a virtual machine. You might create your own virtual machine files complete with operating system and applications and then export the VHD file and use it on another Hyper-V server. The portability and versatility of the VHD file make it very desirable. In fact, it is actually possible to deploy physical copies of Windows Server 2008 R2 and Windows 7 from a VHD file.

You will remember that when you created a virtual machine, you were presented with the option of creating a virtual hard disk to go along with the virtual machine or waiting until later to associate a VHD with the virtual machine. If you selected to associate the VHD file later, you will need to modify the settings of the virtual machine you created.

To add a VHD file to a virtual machine, do the following:

1. Open the Hyper-V Manager.

2. Select the virtual machine to which you want to connect the VHD.

3. Click Settings in the Actions pane.

4. Select Controller IDE 0 or IDE 1, and select Hard Drive, as shown in Figure 14.7.

5. Click Add.

6. Click the Browse button, and locate the VHD file.

7. Click OK.

Figure 14.7: Associating a VHD to a virtual machine

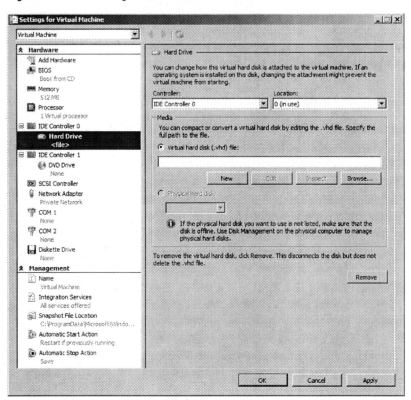

Work with Virtual Machine Settings

Every virtual machine consists of two components: a virtual hard disk and the virtual machine settings. As you saw in the previous example, the settings are what tie the VHD to the virtual machine. They define the operating environment of the virtual machine. You can manage the settings to maximize the performance of both the virtual machines and the physical server that is hosting the virtual machines.

The settings are broken down into two parts, the hardware settings and the management settings.

The hardware settings include the following:

Add Hardware, as shown in Figure 14.8   This setting allows you to add a SCSI controller, a network adapter, or a legacy network adapter.

Figure 14.8: Add Hardware setting

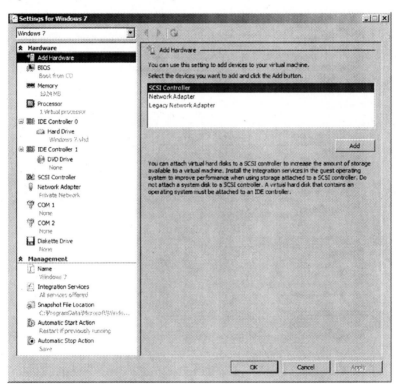

Manage Desktop and Server Virtualization

PART V

BIOS, as shown in Figure 14.9   Using this setting you can modify
the order of the devices in the BIOS start order using the up and
down arrows.

Figure 14.9: BIOS setting

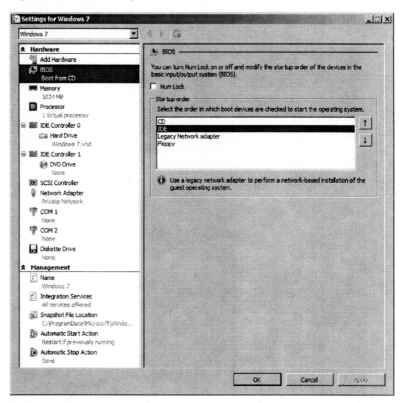

Memory, as shown in Figure 14.10   Memory is critical to the operation of a virtual machine. This setting specifies the amount of physical RAM that is allocated to the virtual machine.

Figure 14.10: Memory

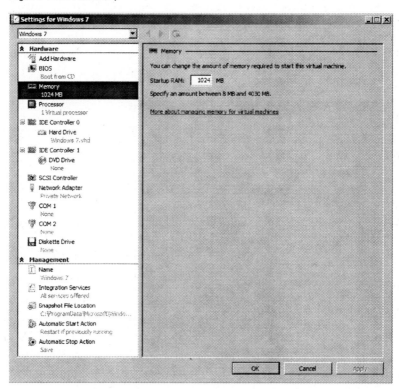

Processor, as shown in Figure 14.11   You can modify the number
of virtual processors assigned to a virtual machine based on the
number of physical processors and cores on each processor. You can
also balance the usage of your processing resources between virtual
machines. In addition, you can limit the processor features that a
virtual machine can use to make it more compatible with different
versions of processors, such as to make a processor more compatible with an older operating system like Windows NT.

Figure 14.11: Processor

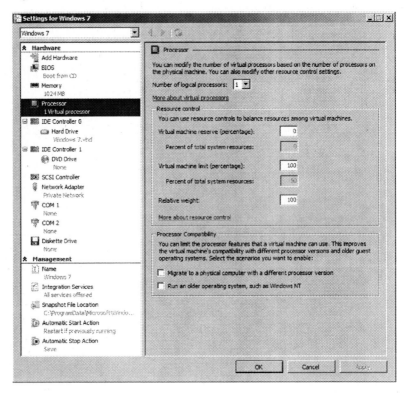

Manage Desktop and Server Virtualization

Controller settings, as shown in Figure 14.12   The Controller settings specify the IDE and SCSI controllers and what they are connected to. Traditionally, IDE 0 is connected to the VHD file that is the base of the operating system. IDE 1 is generally connected to the DVD drive, and you can define exactly what media you want to use with that DVD/CD drive; for example, you may have an ISO image of an operating system and want to install the OS using the image file. You can associate the ISO image with IDE 1.

Figure 14.12: Controller settings

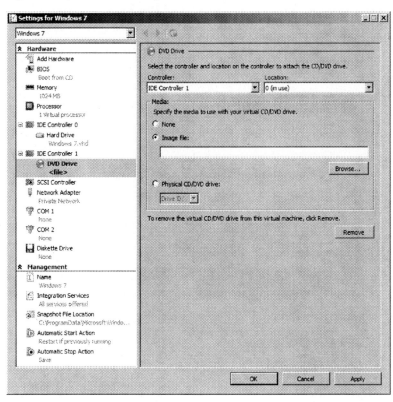

Network Adapter, as shown in Figure 14.13   The Network Adapter setting allows you to define which of the available virtual networks you will connect to.

Figure 14.13: Network Adapter

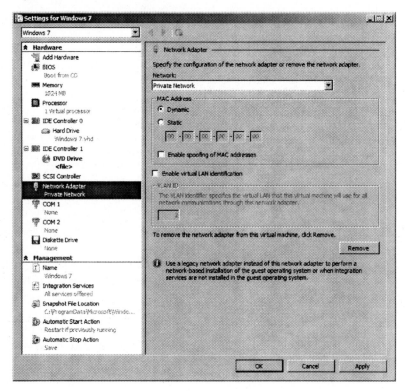

COM settings, as shown in Figure 14.14 The COM settings allow you to configure the virtual machine to communicate with the physical computer through a named pipe.

Figure 14.14: COM settings

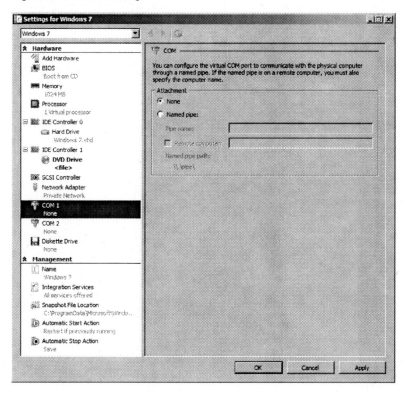

Diskette Drive, as shown in Figure 14.15 Floppy disks are almost nonexistent in modern physical servers. However, they were commonplace in legacy hardware and often were the vehicle for delivering data, applications, and even operating systems. Should you need to use a floppy disk with a virtual machine, you will use this setting. A floppy disk is virtualized by using a virtual floppy disk file (.vfd).

Figure 14.15: Diskette Drive

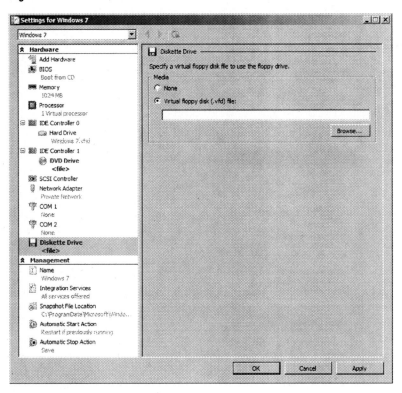

The management settings associated with the virtual machine are as follows:

Name, as shown in Figure 14.16   Each virtual machine has a name. The name can be whatever you choose. It is recommended that you choose a name that allows you to easily recognize your virtual machines. The name of the virtual machine is not permanent. Like any other file, the virtual machine can be renamed.

Figure 14.16: Name setting

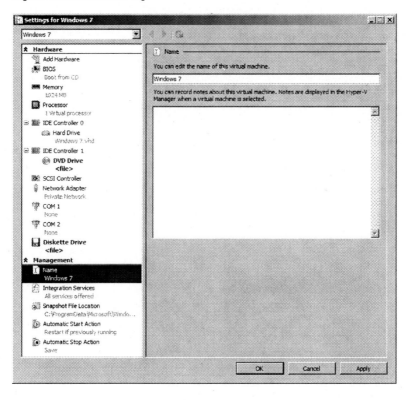

Integration Services, as shown in Figure 14.17 Running a virtual machine can present some interesting challenges and opportunities for interaction between the operating system hosting the Hyper-V server and the virtual machines. These services are called the *integration services*, and you can adjust them based on need. You can also rename the virtual machine with the link in the Actions pane. It will update the value in the settings file.

Figure 14.17: Integration Services setting

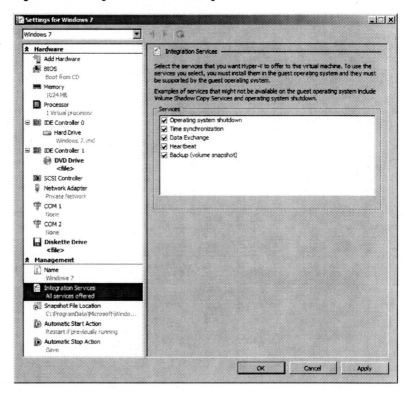

Snapshot File Location, as shown in Figure 14.18 The snapshot
file location defines the physical location where snapshots of virtual
machines will be stored. The snapshot allows the administrator to
make a point-in-time snapshot of a virtual machine, and then if
desired, the administrator can apply the snapshot file to return the
virtual machine to the point in time when the snapshot was taken.
You will learn more about snapshots later in this chapter.

Figure 14.18: Snapshot File Location

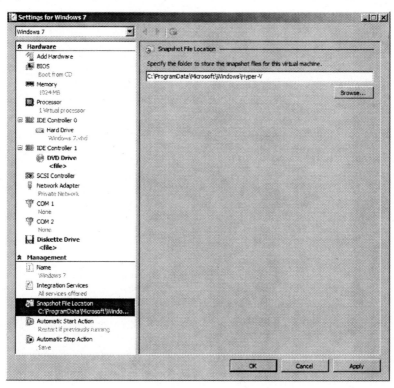

Automatic Start Action, as shown in Figure 14.19   The automatic start action defines what you want the virtual machine to do when the physical machine is started. This setting makes it possible to start a virtual machine automatically each time its associated physical machine is started. You can also configure an automatic start delay so that the virtual machine is not competing with the physical machine for resources necessary to start up.

Figure 14.19: Automatic Start Action

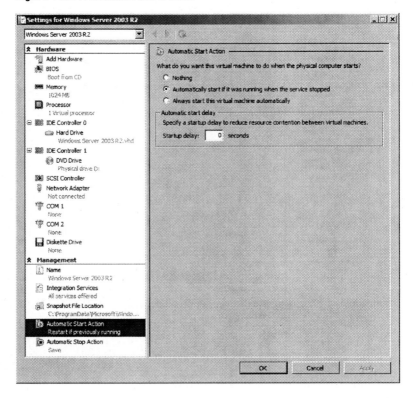

Automatic Stop Action, as shown in Figure 14.20   The Automatic Stop Action setting defines what you want this virtual machine to do when the physical machine that is hosting it shuts down. The default value saves the virtual machines state. You could of course shut down the virtual machine or let it turn off (not recommended since this is the equivalent of pulling the plug).

Figure 14.20: Automatic Stop Action

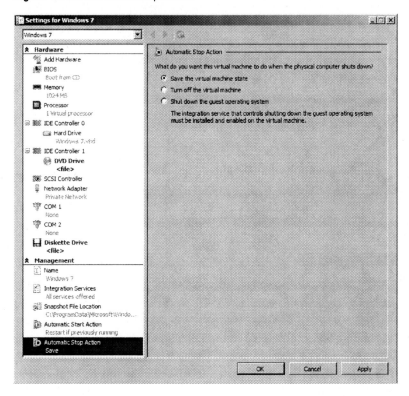

Install an Operating System

The whole point of virtual hard disks, virtual machines, and Hyper-V is to let more than one operating system run on a single set of hardware. When you build the virtual machine and its associated hard disk, the operating system is not included. You will still need to acquire and install the operating system of your choice. Hyper-V is very versatile, allowing you to run Windows operating systems and even SUSE Linux if you so desire. The process of installing an operating system on a virtual machine is very much the same as installing to physical hardware, with a few exceptions.

You will recall from our earlier discussion that a VHD file is an allocation of disk space used to install operating systems and applications and to store data. When you install an operating system, you are actually installing to the VHD.

Install from DVD

One of the most common methods used to install an operating system is to install it directly from the DVD/CD media. Each virtual machine has a setting for the DVD/CD drive. This setting can be configured to capture the physical DVD drive:

1. Set a controller to capture the DVD/CD.

2. Set the boot order to ensure that the DVD/CD is first.

3. Insert the DVD/CD into the physical DVD/CD drive.

4. Start the virtual machine.

5. When prompted, hit a key to boot from DVD/CD.

At this point, the install will proceed as normal.

Install from ISO

DVD/CD is a great methodology for install, but it is certainly not the only option. In fact, many in the IT world have picked up a subscription to TechNet or MSDN that will allow them to download an ISO image of a DVD that can be used to burn a physical DVD. Or, in this case, it can actually be used to install the operating system directly to the virtual machine. The process is similar to a traditional install with one simple setting change:

1. Set a controller to capture the DVD/CD.

2. Select the DVD/CD drive.

3. In the Media section, select the Image File option.

4. Browse to the location of the ISO file, as shown in Figure 14.21.

5. Click OK.

You can get the same effect by using the connection window for the virtual machine. You can use the Media menu, select DVD Drive, and use the Insert Disk option.

When you install an operating system to a virtual machine, remember that all the files are being installed to the virtual hard disk. The operating system is no different from if it were installed to the local hardware. There are not different versions of operating systems for the virtual world. They are the same installs and have the same operational capacity as any other operating system install.

Figure 14.21: Capturing an ISO image

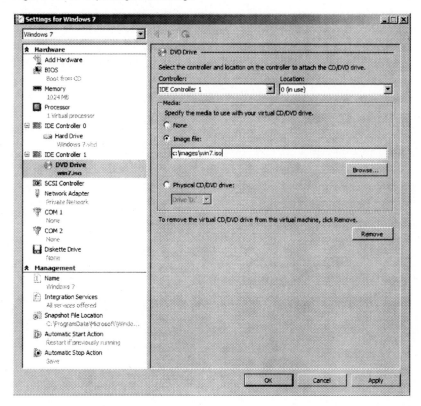

Connect to a Virtual Machine

Once you have a virtual machine created and the operating system is installed and functional, there is one remaining obstacle. The operating system is running in an environment that is essentially invisible to the user. There is no default video output in Hyper-V. You will need to connect an application to the video output of the virtual machine in order to interact with the VM and to see what's going on. The application that you will use to connect to the virtual machine was installed automatically when you installed Hyper-V. The application is called the Virtual Machine Connection tool. Using this tool, you can connect to the virtual machine, control the state of the virtual machine, take snapshots of the virtual machine, and modify some of the settings of the virtual machine.

When you connect to a virtual machine using the Virtual Machine Connection tool, it will automatically use the credentials that you used to log in to the physical machine to establish the connection to the virtual machine. If you want to use other credentials, you can configure those in Hyper-V. By default Administrator permissions are the minimum required permissions necessary to connect to the console. Please note that this does *not* mean that the Virtual Machine Connection tool will log you on to the virtual machine. The credentials supplied are simply used to connect to the virtual machine. You will still need to supply the appropriate credentials to log on to the virtual machine.

To connect to a virtual machine, you can open the Hyper-V Manager and locate the desired virtual machine. Double-click the virtual machine, and the Virtual Machine Connection tool will start. You can also right-click the selected virtual machine and choose Connect, as shown in Figure 14.22.

Figure 14.22: Connecting to a virtual machine

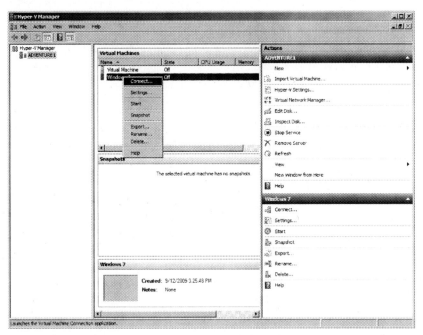

Use Snapshots

The coolest thing about virtual machines is that they are virtual machines. We know you are thinking "Duh!" So, what's the big deal? Virtual machines are really compact. The operating system is located in a VHD file and the settings that go with it. This makes it really easy to take a point-in-time picture of the state of the operating system and the settings associated with the virtual machine. This process is called taking a *snapshot*. The value in this is that you can take a snapshot, work away making changes and updates to the virtual machine, and then (and this really rocks) apply the snapshot to take the virtual machine right back to the state it was in when you took the snapshot.

Virtual machine snapshots are file-based snapshots of the state, disk data, and configuration of the virtual machine. The snapshot creates a file called an AVHD file. You can take multiple snapshots of a single virtual machine, and you can even take a snapshot while the virtual machine is up and running. You can revert or apply snapshots to get to the virtual machine configuration you desire.

You can create snapshots using the Hyper-V Manager or the Virtual Machine Connection tool. Applying snapshots, listing available snapshots, and editing snapshots are tasks available through the Hyper-V Manager only.

Snapshots can help you create specific environments such as those needed in validation and testing. It is easy to reproduce the same environment and settings over and over again. Snapshots are perfect for building a staging server to test hotfixes, patches, and updates before deploying them to your network.

It is important to consider that the things that we love about snapshots can also be the thing that we hate about snapshots. When you take a snapshot, all the data and settings are in the snapshot. Anything you create, delete, save, or install will be reverted to the snapshot state when you revert or apply a snapshot. This means if you create a bunch of documents and then revert to a previous snapshot, all the data created since the snapshot was taken will be gone. If you know this ahead of time, it is not a big deal because you can simply take another snapshot to maintain the current data and state. If you didn't know this ahead of time, it could be really painful.

To make a snapshot of a virtual machine, follow these steps:

1. Open the Hyper-V Manager.

2. Select the virtual machine you want to snapshot.

3. Click Snapshot in the Actions pane, as shown in Figure 14.23.

Figure 14.23: Taking a snapshot

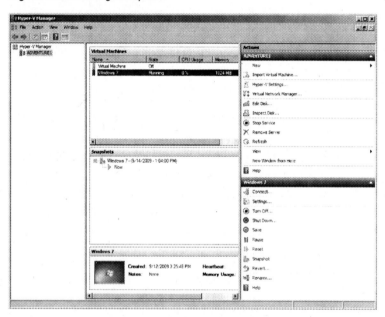

The snapshots will show up in the Snapshots pane in the center of the screen. It is important to note here that when you take a snapshot of a running virtual machine, the performance of the virtual machine will be impacted as the snapshot file is made. Snapshots are stored in a hierarchy. As you create additional snapshots, you will see them show up in the Snapshots pane of the Hyper-V Manager.

After a snapshot is taken, it is labeled with the virtual machine name and a date and timestamp. This is an easy logical way to keep track of snapshots. If for some reason you want to change the name of a snapshot, you can do so using the Rename option in the Actions pane while the snapshot is selected.

To apply a snapshot, you will also use the Actions pane with the snapshot selected. This will allow you to apply the snapshot directly to the virtual machine.

It is possible to export the snapshot for use with a virtual machine using the Export option in the Actions pane.

Finally, it is possible to delete a snapshot, or a snapshot subtree, from the Actions pane with the snapshot selected. When you delete a snapshot, be aware that although the snapshot is no longer listed in the snapshot tree structure, the AVHD file is not deleted until the virtual machine is shut down. When a snapshot is deleted, the data and settings that were stored in the snapshot are merged, and this process can be very time-consuming.

These options, shown in Figure 14.24, provide significant flexibility in working with snapshots.

Figure 14.24: Snapshot options

One final note concerning snapshots is that although snapshots can be used to make a point-in-time picture of a running virtual machine, they do not use the Volume Shadow Copy Service (VSS) and therefore are not a substitute for a permanent backup system. Snapshots can make a great temporary backup. However, you should still configure a backup structure to protect your virtual machines.

Import a Virtual Machine

One of the things you will love about virtual machines is that they are really pretty portable. When it comes right down to it, a virtual machine and a virtual hard disk are easy to move. It is easy to see some of the reasons you might want to import virtual machines. Imagine Microsoft is releasing a new operating system. You decide you would like to try it before you buy it. What if Microsoft made a VHD file available for you to load in Hyper-V so you could try the new operating system? This is actually happening today. Or imagine a situation where you are a software developer, and you have a standard development environment you use for testing. Why not build that environment in Hyper-V, export those files from the machine where they were built, and then import them on other machines throughout your development network?

You can import virtual machines using two different methodologies. The method you choose really depends on what you have to work with to begin with.

If you have a .vhd file and no settings information, you will create a new virtual machine using the Virtual Machine Creation Wizard. When you are given the option for creating a virtual hard disk or using an existing virtual hard disk, simply locate the VHD file and create the virtual machine.

Now if you are lucky, you will have more than just the VHD, and you might have the settings files associated with the virtual machine as well. If this is the case, you don't need to create a new virtual machine. You already have the virtual machine, so you just need to get that virtual machine and its settings associated with Hyper-V Manager and running on this server. It is important to remember that virtual machines can be reused or imported to more than a single Hyper-V server. To import a virtual machine more than once, it is important that when you import, you make a copy of the virtual machine files so that the VM can be imported again elsewhere. To accomplish this task, you use the import tool in the Actions pane.

1. Open the Hyper-V Manager.

2. Click Import Virtual Machine in the Actions pane.

3. In the Import Virtual Machine Wizard, shown in Figure 14.25, browse to the location of the virtual machine.

4. Select the desired import settings.

Figure 14.25: Importing a virtual machine

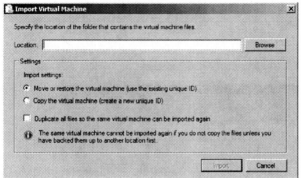

Remember that a virtual machine will stay in the directory from which it is imported. If you want the virtual machine to be housed in a specific location on your server, you need to copy it there before you import it to Hyper-V. Once you have imported the VM, it cannot be moved. Importing a virtual machine is a great way to configure a virtual machine with limited up-front configuration work. What if you had taken the time to build a great virtual machine and wanted to save it so that it could be used again, perhaps on another server in your network? You would want to export that virtual machine.

Export a Virtual Machine

The process of exporting a virtual machine is really the process of saving the name, configuration, VHD, and snapshots associated with a virtual machine. You have already seen how virtual machines are named, how the virtual hard disks are created, and how to make snapshots. The only part of the export process you have not seen is that although each virtual machine has a canonical name that you configured, each virtual machine also has a globally unique identifier (GUID), and each snapshot that you make also has its own unique GUID. Armed with this information, you can begin the process of exporting a virtual machine.

1. Open the Hyper-V Manager.
2. Select the virtual machine you want to export.
3. Click Export in the virtual machine section of the Actions pane.

4. In the dialog box that opens, shown in Figure 14.26, provide a directory location to save the virtual machine.

5. Click Export.

Figure 14.26: Export directory location

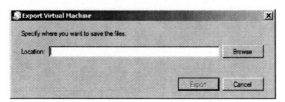

Depending on the size of the virtual machine and its contents, this process can take some time, so be patient. There is no status bar to tell you how much of the export has completed.

During the export process, a new file will be created in the directory you chose for the export directory. The new file will be named with the name of the virtual machine. Inside the new file will be a series of subfolders:

Virtual Machines   This folder will contain an export (.exp) file named for the GUID of the virtual machine. There is also an additional folder here that can be used for an additional .exp file for machines that were exported in their saved state configuration.

Virtual Hard Disks   This folder will contain a copy of each of the virtual hard disks associated with the virtual machine.

Snapshots   This folder will contain an .exp file for each of the snapshots you created in the virtual machine. There are some additional folders here named after the snapshot IDs for any saved state snapshot data and a folder named after the virtual machine ID that will contain the AVHD files for the snapshots.

Once the export has completed, you can use the files in the export directory at will. You can copy them, move them, save them to DVDs (if they are small enough), compress them (if they are not small enough), and of course import them.

While talking about importing, we said that if you want to import a virtual machine more than once, you need to copy all the associated files. The reason for this is that during import Hyper-V will delete the EXP files and replace them with XML files. If there are no EXP files, then the virtual machine cannot be imported. If you plan on using a virtual machine more than once, then you will need to copy the exported virtual machine and its associated EXP files to be certain it can be imported again.

PART VI

Server Tuning and Maintenance

IN THIS PART ▷

Server Tuning
and Maintenance

PART VI

15

Tuning and Monitoring Performance

IN THIS CHAPTER, YOU WILL LEARN TO:

▶ **ANALYZE SERVER ROLES (Pages 496–507)**

- Understand the Best Practices Analyzer (Page 496)
- Use the Best Practices Analyzer (Page 499)
- Use PowerShell with the Best Practices Analyzer (Page 503)

▶ **VIEW SERVER PERFORMANCE DATA (Pages 508–520)**

- Create a System Health Report (Page 508)
- Understand Performance Monitor (Page 512)

▶ **VIEW SERVER EVENTS (Pages 520–529)**

- Work with the Event Viewer (Page 521)

Server Tuning and Maintenance

We all want our servers to run faster and perform at their peak capabilities. However, how do you make your server perform faster without adding hardware? In this chapter, you will see many of the powerful tools designed to help you improve your Windows Server 2008 R2 server. You will see how the built-in Best Practices Analyzer will help you improve the server roles currently installed on your server. You will also learn how the Best Practices Analyzer provides feedback for your environment.

In addition, you will see the Performance Monitor and several of the tools designed to assist you in maintaining and improving the health of your server.

Finally, you'll learn how to read and use the information your Windows Server 2008 R2 server provides you via system-wide events, and you will get an overview of the built-in Event Viewer.

Analyze Server Roles

Installing server roles, with proper planning, on a Windows Server 2008 R2 server can be a fairly straightforward process. But even with the proper planning, sometimes your server roles can be made to run more efficiently. You may also want to make sure your servers and the roles installed on the servers are running properly.

When you install a server, you usually have planned out how it will fit the needs of your business and your network infrastructure. However, what happens when you are not in control and you "inherit" servers from a new customer, from an acquisition, or because you took a new role in your organization? How do you know if the servers and roles are running properly? In the following sections, you will learn about a tool called the Best Practices Analyzer (BPA) that will provide you with guidance to help run your servers more efficiently.

Understand the Best Practices Analyzer

Microsoft has provided the Best Practices Analyzer for several years for the various server platforms currently available. These analyzers were available through a free download from the Microsoft site. With

Windows Server 2008 R2, the Best Practices Analyzer is now built in to the server platform and is available for you to use when you install certain roles on your server. Currently in Windows Server 2008 R2, the BPA is provided only for the following roles:

- Active Directory Certification Services (AD CS)
- Active Directory Domain Services (AD DS)
- DNS
- Remote Desktop Services (RDS)
- Internet Information Services (IIS)

The BPA is like a mini IT consultant running around your Windows Server 2008 R2 server and checking your roles to make sure the ones on your server are running properly. This tool provides you with the ability to manage your servers proactively and get in front of any potential issues or concerns before they happen. The BPA helps you make sure your configurations are good and helps reduce the amount of troubleshooting you have to do when issues do occur.

When you use the BPA, it will analyze your current environment and compare this against common best practices for the particular role. What makes the guidance from the tool unique is that Microsoft is not the only one providing feedback; the feedback comes from IT administrators and customers like yourself, from support professionals, and even from the many folks in the field working for Microsoft.

When you invoke a BPA scanner against one of your server roles, you start the BPA runtime. The runtime is the main process responsible for collecting and comparing the configuration settings on your Windows Server 2008 R2 server. Regardless of which role you are currently scanning, the BPA follows the process illustrated in Figure 15.1.

1. The BPA scans and verifies the current role configuration settings.

2. As the BPA service scans and verifies, the BPA runtime uses a BPA Windows PowerShell script to collect configuration data and store it in an XML document.

3. The BPA runtime then validates the XML document against an XML schema. The schema defines the format and structure of the XML document.

4. The BPA runtime then applies the BPA rules (these are the best-practice configurations) for the environment against the XML document.

5. From there the guidance is used to produce the BPA report. The report is used to help make adjustments to your environment if needed.

Figure 15.1: BPA process flow

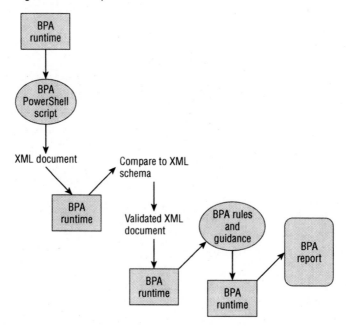

When you first review a report, you may see violations in the report. You do not need to panic when you see violations in your BPA report. These violations do not always indicate a major problem for your server. Remember, the BPA tool is trying to help identify for you server configurations that can result in poor performance, poor reliability, unexpected conflicts, increased security risks, or other potential problems.

Although the guidance in the tool can be a tremendous help in reporting your actual configuration vs. the known best practices, you should always look carefully at the suggestions. The best practices are sound; however, sometimes based on your business rules and the demands of your infrastructure, they may not improve your configuration. So, review the recommendations very carefully.

Use the Best Practices Analyzer

The BPA is located in Server Manager and becomes available after you install the supported roles. You will find the BPA on the role summary screen for the supported roles on your server. The summary screen for the roles provides a wealth of information for your server, and if the role has a BPA available, you will see it there.

1. Open Server Manager by selecting Start ⇨ Administrative Tools and clicking Server Manager.

2. Click the + sign next to Roles in the tree menu on the left to expand the roles.

3. Click the role you want to scan, and you will see a role summary screen similar to Figure 15.2.

Figure 15.2: Role summary screen

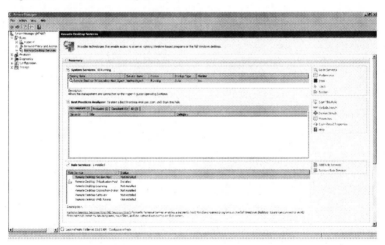

4. Next to Best Practices Analyzer, click Scan This Role, and you will see the BPA process begin to scan your selected role, as shown in Figure 15.3. The scan could take several minutes.

Figure 15.3: BPA scanning

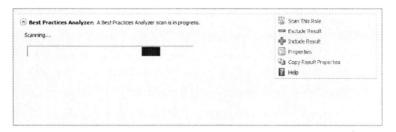

5. After the scan is complete, you will see the BPA report, as shown in Figure 15.4.

Figure 15.4: BPA report

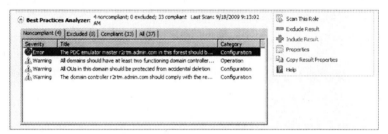

Understand the BPA Report

When you create a BPA report, it considers several factors for your server role. For example, when you run an AD DS BPA scan, the analyzer is checking these aspects of your configuration:

- DNS rules
- Operation master connectivity rules
- Operation master ownership rules
- Number of controllers in the domain
- Required service rules
- Replication configuration rules
- W32time configuration rules
- Virtual machine configuration rules

You can view all the rules scanned for the different roles at http://technet.microsoft.com/en-us/library/dd392255(WS.10).aspx

As you can see, the scan is very thorough. Regardless of what scan you run, you will see several aspects of the report on the summary screen. Your report will have one of three severity levels for each rule. The three levels of severity for the scanned rules are as follows:

Non-Compliant (indicated by an X in a red circle) This means your scanned role is not compliant with the particular BPA rule scanned.

Warning (indicated by an ! in a yellow triangle) This means your current role is compliant, but your current configuration of the role does not meet all the conditions specified by the rule. In general, this means your role will work; however, there may indications the role is not fully functional.

Compliant (indicated by a ✓ in a green circle) This means your scanned role is compliant with the particular BPA rule scanned.

In addition to the severity level, each rule is categorized into one of eight categories. The categories are designed to help you further target and work with the BPA report. In a sense, the categories, as listed in Table 15.1, help you prioritize the tasks you will need to take action on.

Table 15.1: BPA Rule Categories

Category	Definition
Security	These rules help you examine the areas of your server with potential security risks; you'll want to pay close attention to them.
Performance	These rules are designed to help you tune or improve the performance of your servers. These rules help to make sure your server can perform the appointed tasks properly.
Configuration	These rules allow you to verify the configurations of certain roles on your server. These help the role(s) run properly and free of configuration errors.
Policy	These rules identify which areas in the registry or Group Policy need improvements to make sure your role is running in a secure and best-possible fashion.
Operation	These rules will identify whether a role is failing and how to correct the role to get it up and running properly.

Table 15.1: BPA Rule Categories *(continued)*

Category	Definition
Pre-deployment	These rules allow you to identify any issues or possible errors prior to the deployment of a particular role in the enterprise.
Post-deployment	These rules allow you to identify any issues or possible errors after the role has been deployed to the enterprise.
BPA Prerequisites	These rules are for the BPA scanner. In order for certain BPA rules to be included in a report, there may be some prerequisites that need to be met in order for a rule to be scanned. If you have a BPA prerequisite error, this simply means the BPA tool could not scan your role with a particular rule.

Work with the BPA Report

Now that you understand how the report is categorized, you will want to see how to fix any issues the BPA scan detected for you. After the report is processed and you have identified the events you want to view, you will start to see the power behind the BPA reports. Each rule has properties you can view that will tell you what violated the BPA rule. The properties of the report are broken into three sections: what the issue is, what is the impact of the violation, and most important what the resolution is. To see this information, you need to view the properties of the rule:

1. In the BPA report, click the rule you want to view.

2. To view the properties, you can either double-click the rule, right-click the rule and select Properties, or click Properties to the right of the BPA report. After you have done this, you will see a Properties dialog box similar to Figure 15.5.

3. When you are done viewing the information, click Close.

You also have the ability to exclude your BPA rule information from future reports. With a rule highlighted, you can click Exclude This Item, and it will be removed from the report. It will be moved to the Excluded tab of the report.

As you can see, the BPA reports provide some excellent analysis for your server. After you have viewed the error messages and corrected any errors, you should also consider rerunning the BPA for the role to verify the issue has been properly resolved.

Figure 15.5: BPA rule properties

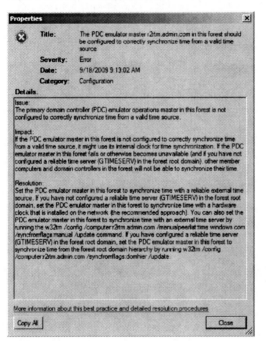

Use PowerShell with the Best Practices Analyzer

The BPA tools also have full PowerShell cmdlet support. You can accomplish the BPA tasks in PowerShell as well. The BPA PowerShell cmdlets are also built in to the server and do not require any additional tools or packages to be installed to use them. The PowerShell tools also provide you with the additional capability to run BPA scans of multiple roles at one time.

To be able to run the BPA PowerShell commands, you need to load both the Server Manager PowerShell module and the Best Practices Analyzer module. You can either load them separately or run Windows PowerShell modules.

1. Load the Windows PowerShell modules by selecting Start ⇨ Administrative Tools and clicking Windows PowerShell Modules.

2. To load the modules separately, after you have opened an administrative PowerShell session, run the following procedure below. If you do not run the BPA commands from an administrative window, you may see a message similar to Figure 15.6 reminding you to run the command in an administrative window.

Figure 15.6: BPA administrator required

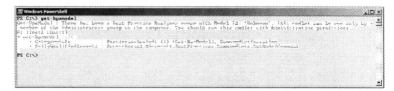

Follow these actions, referenced previously in Step 2:

1. Open administrative PowerShell by selecting Start ⇨ All Programs ⇨ Accessories ⇨ Windows PowerShell.

2. Right-click Windows PowerShell, and select Run As Administrator.

3. If prompted by User Account Control, click Yes.

4. From the PowerShell prompt, type the following, and then hit Enter:

```
Import-Module ServerManager
```

5. From the PowerShell prompt, type the following, and then hit Enter:

```
Import-Module BestPractices
```

There are really four commands you will need to learn, as shown in Table 15.2.

Table 15.2: BPA PowerShell Commands

Command	Usage
Get-BPAModel	This command will allow you to view the roles installed on the server where you can run BPA scans; this tool will also show you when the last scan on a particular role was created.
Get-BPAResult	This command will allow you to view the results for any given BPA scan you have performed.
Invoke-BPAModel	This command will allow you to run a BPA scan on your server for a particular role you want to scan.
Set-BPAResult	This command allows you to filter the BPA report from the Get-BPAResult command to allow you to see only the information you want to view in the report.

BPA PowerShell Examples

To determine which roles are currently installed on the server that you can run a BPA scan against, or to see if a BPA scan has been run, you can use the following command:

Get-BPAModel

You will see results similar to Figure 15.7.

Figure 15.7: Get-BPAModel sample results

The important part of the `Get-BPAModel` command are the model IDs displayed in the results. The model IDs are used in the other BPA commands to perform designated tasks. Currently there are only five IDs you can use to support the five roles currently leveraging the BPA; they're listed in Table 15.3.

Table 15.3: BPA Role IDS

BPA Role ID	Role
Microsoft/Windows/CertificateServices	Active Directory Certification Services (AD CS)
Microsoft/Windows/DirectoryServices	Active Directory Domain Services (AD DS)
Microsoft/Windows/DNSServer	DNS
Microsoft/Windows/TerminalServices	Remote Desktop Services (RDS)
Microsoft/Windows/WebServer	Internet Information Services (IIS)

To scan the Internet Information Services role on your server, run the following command:

```
Invoke-BPAModel -id Microsoft/Windows/WebServer
```

To scan all the roles currently supported by the BPA tool, you could run the following command on your Windows Server 2008 R2 server:

```
Get-BPAModel | Invoke-BPAModel
```

To view the BPA report for the Internet Information Services BPA scan, run the following command, and you will see results similar to Figure 15.8:

```
Get-BPAResult -id Microsoft/Windows/WebServer
```

Figure 15.8: Get-BPAResult sample results

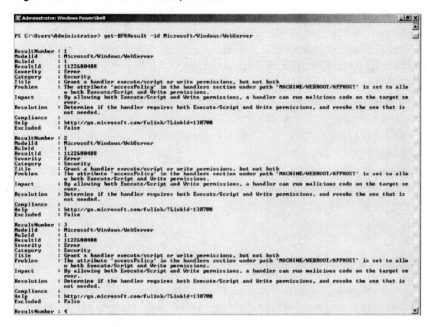

Although you can view the results in the PowerShell window, remember that you can always view the results in the Server Manager interface regardless of where you ran the scan from (the GUI or PowerShell). So if you want to view the full report, we recommend using the Server Manager interface. If you want to filter results, you can do this in PowerShell with the Set-BPAResult command or with the Where clause.

If you want to view a BPA report for Internet Information Services but only with the rules in the Security category, you could run the following command:

```
Get-BPAResult -id Microsoft/Windows/WebServer
| Where { $_.Category -eq "Security" }
```

View Server Performance Data

Working with your performance data is part science and part art. Windows Server 2008 R2 has thousands of performance counters with which you can view, track, and perform analysis. Part of the trick to doing analysis is to understand how the different counters work together to give you an overall picture of the server.

You will see in the following sections some of the new tools in Windows Server 2008 R2, such as the system health report, that will provide you with some excellent pictures of your server from the hardware and software perspectives.

You will also see the basics of how to work with the Performance Monitor and the built-in reliability tools on your server to keep your server running properly.

Create a System Health Report

One of the tools you can use to help troubleshoot problems is the system health report. The system health report includes suggestions to help improve the overall health and performance of the Windows Server 2008 R2 server. The report provides suggestions based on the performance of your server across many aspects:

- Software configuration
- Hardware configuration
- CPU
- Network
- Disk
- Memory

The system health report is also a handy report if you have no knowledge about a server and want to learn more about the server quickly. When you run the report, it will take some time to run to generate information you will be able to use improve the performance. You will need to be a member of the local Administrators group to generate the report. The system health report is located in the Control Panel on your server.

1. Open Control Panel by selecting Start ➪ Control Panel.
2. Click System And Security.

3. Click Generate A System Health Report, which is located in the Administrative Tools section.

After you click Generate A System Health Report, you will see a screen similar to Figure 15.9; the report will take up to 60 seconds to generate.

After the report is generated, you'll see a screen similar to Figure 15.10.

Figure 15.9: Generating a system health report

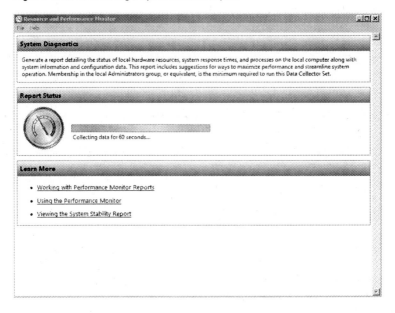

When you start looking at a report, you will notice the several categories and the arrows next to the category headings to allow you to expand the sections to view more information about the report. You may also notice in the middle of each heading bar there is an icon that looks like a three-column table. This icon allows you to open the table of contents for the report. When you click one of the icons, you will see a screen similar to Figure 15.11.

Server Tuning and Maintenance

PART VI

Figure 15.10: System Diagnostics Report

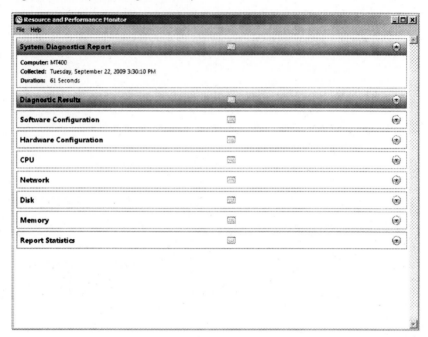

Figure 15.11: System health report contents

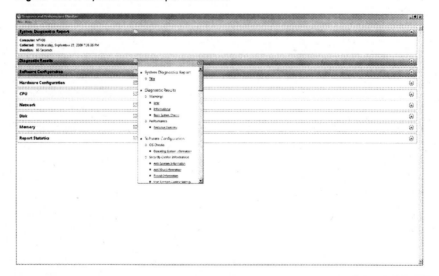

The contents screen will allow you to quickly view any portion of the report. In addition to the individual categories you see in the report, you'll see a wealth of summary information for your server. There is also one area that will provide a quick snapshot of the overall performance of your server. This area is called the *resource overview*, and you can see an example of it in Figure 15.12.

Figure 15.12: Resource overview

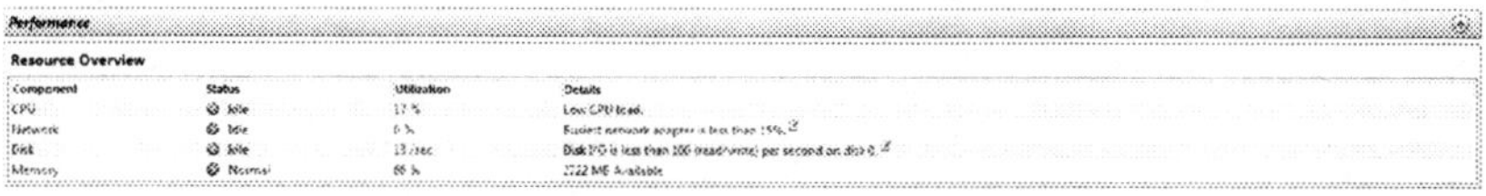

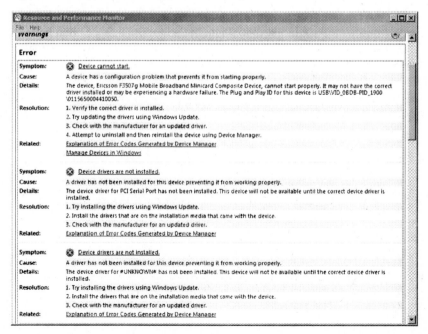

This report not only will give you a general utilization of your server but will also tell you which areas of your server are being the most utilized. For example, when you look at the network utilization, the report will tell you what the most utilized network adapter on your server is.

If the report has warnings, you will see a screen similar to Figure 15.13.

Figure 15.13: System health report with warnings

As you can see, the warnings will tell you the issue and give you steps for resolution. Depending on the nature of the warning, the resolutions may be basic. For example, if you have a hardware warning because of a faulty driver, the system health report will tell you what to do, but the advice is fairly generic:

1. Verify the correct driver is installed.

2. Try updating the drivers using Windows Update.

3. Check with the manufacturer for an updated driver.

4. Attempt to uninstall and then reinstall the device using the Device Manager.

Understand Performance Monitor

When you look at all the tools on your Windows Server 2008 R2 server providing you with performance data, you'll see they are all derived in some fashion from the same data you can generate in the Performance Monitor. As your server's operating systems become more sophisticated, you have many new and useful tools like the system health report allowing you to make sense out of the performance data on your server. This section will give you a brief look at how to leverage the data in the Performance Monitor.

When you look at the reports you can generate, you may want a more detailed picture of what is going on under the hood of your server. This is where the Performance Monitor can help you get into the details of all the data. You can use it to see how many of the different performance data points relate to each other and get the bigger picture. Learning to use the Performance Monitor is a combination of knowing what you are looking for, knowing how to use the tool, and knowing what counters can help you find the areas for improvement.

For example, if you want to monitor memory usage on your system, it is not enough to just look at the counters on the Memory object in the Performance Monitor. You may also want to look at disk I/O. You may be wondering why disk I/O is important. Remember, part of the memory usage on your system is done by the paging file on your system. For example, if you notice memory is not performing optimally, you may decide to add more RAM to your server but then see some of the same issues. Your problem really could have been because of slow reads and writes for the page file because of a slow or faulty hard drive. In other words, you had a false positive test, but you only looked at one portion of the story to determine your issue. The moral is simply that there are many factors to help you determine the performance of your server, and you need to try to do your best to look at as many factors as you can.

You also need to have some historical perspective when you are using the Performance Monitor. What does this mean to you? It offers you a baseline. Sure, you can turn on the Performance Monitor any time you want to peek at the system data. However, factors such as the time of day, the current workload on the server, the number of users logged on, and many other factors could skew your results. Normally, when you run the Performance Monitor, you want to run the counters before, during, and after the workload you are testing on the server. This will give you the most accurate and thorough results. This will also allow you to put your results in context. More important, the Performance Monitor will also allow you to save your results and compare them to a report run several months after you ran the original report.

Work with the Resource Monitor

To begin using the Performance Monitor, you can load the tool via Server Manager and use the Performance Monitor located under the Diagnostics node. You can also load the Performance Monitor in the administrative tools (by selecting Start ⇨ Administrative Tools and clicking Performance Monitor), as shown in Figure 15.14.

Before you start to add your own Performance Monitor counters and build your own data collector sets, you need to look closely at the summary screen when you first load the tool. You have a nice collection of summary information provided for you initially. From the base summary screen, you can gain some nice summary information about the four main resources on your server: memory, CPU, hard drive, and network.

You will also find a tool new to Windows Server 2008 R2 called the Resource Monitor. In the top section of the summary screen you will see a link called Open Resource Monitor. When you click the link, you will see a screen similar to Figure 15.15.

Figure 15.14: The Performance Monitor

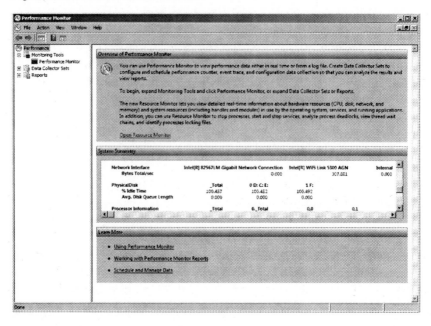

Figure 15.15: The Resource Monitor

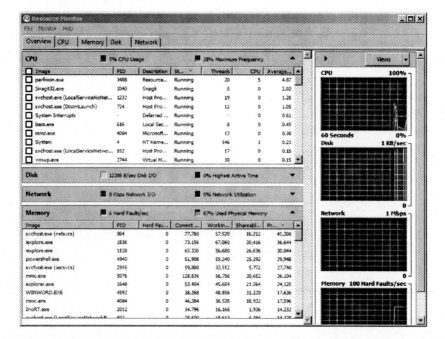

You can also load the Resource Monitor directly. The Resource Monitor is part of your system tools. Select Start ⇨ All Programs ⇨ Accessories ⇨ System Tools, and click Resource Monitor.

The Resource Monitor is similar to Task Manager; however, the Resource Monitor has been greatly enhanced. Just like Task Manager, you get real-time information about what processes, disk resources, network performance, and memory access are currently being used by your server. The Resource Monitor offers much greater detail and access for you to see what is happening under the hood on your server. You will also have the ability to stop processes and start and stop services. You can also get even more valuable information to help the developers in your organization help debug applications. In the Resource Monitor, you get debuggers to diagnose application hangs and deadlocks. One option for working with application problems is by looking at a wait chain. Essentially, a wait chain is the order in which your threads of process execution occur. Each thread in a chain will wait for the additional threads following the initial thread; by analyzing the wait chain, you can potentially discover what is causing your application to have delays or not function.

Run Windows Memory Diagnostics

One of the more frustrating issues you may run into is memory issues. There can be many issues with memory, including poorly written applications, insufficient memory, or even a possible faulty memory chip. How do you know what could be the cause? You generally want to rule out a faulty chip. In Windows Server 2008 R2, you have the ability to run the Windows Memory Diagnostics tool; select Start ⇨ Administrative Tools, and click Windows Memory Diagnostics. You will be presented with a choice to restart your server and check your memory or schedule a memory check for the next time you reboot your system. Whichever choice you make, when your server is rebooted, your physical memory will go through several checks to ensure the integrity of your memory chips.

When your system reboots, you will see a screen similar to Figure 15.16.

Figure 15.16: Windows Memory Diagnostics tool

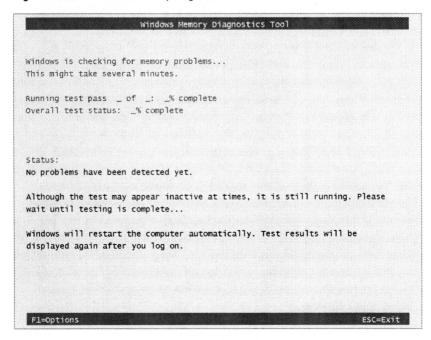

When you press F1, you will be given a choice to perform a basic, standard, or extended test. Each test will perform a series of tests on your server's memory. The more memory you have, the longer the test can take. When the tests are complete, your server will be rebooted automatically. To view the report, you need to open the Event Viewer:

1. Open the Event View by selecting Start ⇨ Administrative Tools and clicking Event Viewer.

2. In the Event Viewer, expand the following tree location applications, and select Services Logs ⇨ Microsoft ⇨ Windows ⇨ MemoryDiagnostics-Results.

3. Click the event to see any errors that may have been reported.

Work with the Performance Monitor

Utilizing the Performance Monitor will allow you to see a variety of system aspects of your server, and when you load the Performance Monitor, your first task will be to load counters to begin measuring and testing your server.

When you add counters to measure, you have a variety of choices to add. First you will be able to choose which systems you want to measure; by default, your local computer is selected. You can also add counters from several main categories. In addition to each counter, there may be several instances you can monitor. For example, when you measure the processor, you will be able to monitor your processor cores, or if you measure physical disk, you will be able to measure the physical drives on your system.

As you look into the sheer volume of counters and instances in the Performance Monitor, this may be a little overwhelming. Try not to get overwhelmed by the data by trying to understand each and every counter. More important, inside the Add Counters dialog box, there is an option to show a description that will explain the counter and, in most cases, explain what values the counter should be if it is running healthy.

1. Open the Performance Monitor by selecting Start ⇨ Administrative Tools and clicking Performance Monitor.

2. Click the + sign next to Monitoring Tools.

3. Click Performance Monitor; by default you will have one counter being measured, your %processor time.

4. Click the green + sign in the Performance Monitor toolbar to add counters you want to measure. You will see a screen similar to Figure 15.17.

5. To add a counter, click the category, click the counter, select the instance you want to monitor, and then click the Add button. Your counter will show in the list to the right, called Added Counters. Likewise, you can also remove a counter by selecting the counter and clicking Remove.

6. When you are done adding your counters, click OK to begin monitoring the selected data. You will see your monitor begin, and your screen may look like Figure 15.18.

Figure 15.17: Performance Monitor's Add Counters dialog box

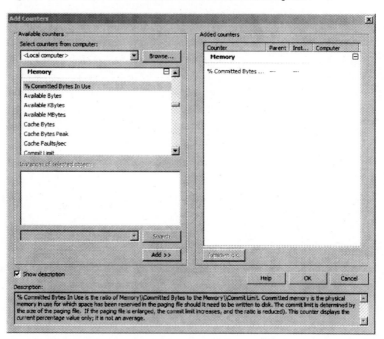

Figure 15.18: Counters in Performance Monitor

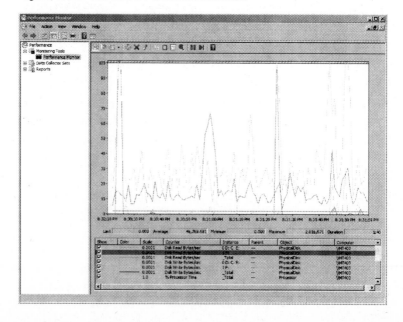

Now you will sit back and wait for the data to populate. You may want to also start your applications you are monitoring here as well to see how certain applications impact your system. You can also save your Performance Monitor counters for future logging use.

1. Inside the Performance Monitor, right-click Performance Monitor in the tree on the left.

2. Select New ⇨ Data Collector Set.

3. Provide a name for your data collector set, and click Next.

4. Select a storage location, and click Next.

5. Verify the creation of the set, and click Finish.

Use Data Collector Sets

Using the Performance Monitor to measure data by adding counters one at a time is a very reactionary way to measure your server's performance. In the Performance Monitor, you can save your existing counters into a *data collector set*. Data collector sets are another built-in feature allowing you some proactive measurement for your server.

Data collector sets allow you to organize multiple performance counters and data collection counters into one logical object. This allows you to easily access and work with frequently used object counters. With data collector sets, you can create log files to track up to three areas for your performance:

Performance Monitor   Allows you to log data about your selected performance counters.

Event Trace Data   Allows you to log data about various service providers on your server. For example, you can track the performance of built-in services.

System configuration information   Allows you to log data to reflect changes to your configuration. For example, you can modify specific registry keys.

Additionally, you can also use data collector sets to proactively measure data by creating Performance Monitor alerts. An alert will fire a set of actions you determine when a counter meets a certain threshold.

1. Inside Performance Monitor, click the + sign to expand data collector sets, and right-click User Defined in the tree on the left.

2. Select New ➪ Data Collector Set.

3. You can use predetermined templates from previous collector sets. Select Create Manually (Advanced), and then click Next. You will see a screen similar to Figure 15.19.

Figure 15.19: New data collector set

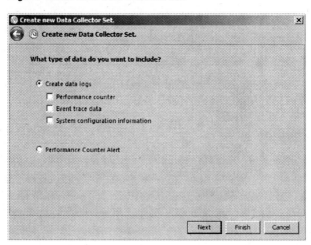

4. Select Performance Counter Alert, and click Next.

5. Add the performance counters you want to set the alert on, set your threshold (either above or below) for the alert, and then click Next.

6. Verify the creation of the set, select Start this Data Collector Set (to start the set), and click Finish.

To view the logs or reports created by the data collector set, you need to look for the name of your data collector set in the Reports section of the Performance Monitor tree.

View Server Events

The ability to look at the events occurring on your server has always provided useful information to help you find the source and resolution for any issues your server may encounter. The Event Viewer is one of the more powerful troubleshooting utilities you can use on your server. More important, this tool has been built in to Windows-based operating systems for years and years. This tool keeps getting more robust and easier to use with each new version of Windows. In the following sections, you will take a brief look at the Event Viewer and how this tool can help manage your environment.

Work with the Event Viewer

The Event Viewer provides you with a wonderful utility to be able to view and track your system-wide events on your server. You can view events from all aspects of your server. You can view the traditional Windows logs (such as Application, Security, Setup, and System). Also, since Windows Server 2008, the Event Viewer provides a method to view events for individual applications and services.

Before you start working with log files in the Event Viewer, you need to know a couple of things. Every log entry and file is stored in an XML format, which will help get the log files small and streamlined. However, log files can take up space on your server, and you need to know how to control how big the log files can become. By default, each log file will take up to 20MB in space. You can also control what happens when the log file reaches the space limit; you have three choices:

Overwrite Events As Needed   This means the oldest events will be overwritten first.

Archive The Log When Full, Do Not Overwrite Events   This will take your full log, save it to disk, and clear the log.

Do Not Overwrite Events Clear The Log Manually   This will force you to clear the log when it becomes full. Before you can see any more events, you will need to clear the log.

You can change the log retention policy by going into the properties of the log file (by right-clicking the log file and selecting Properties) and setting the option for retention. Figure 15.20 shows a picture of the log properties.

Server Tuning and Maintenance

PART VI

Figure 15.20: Log properties

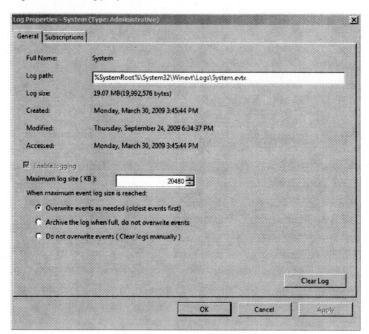

If you choose to clear the log manually, you will want to save the log file. Additionally, saving a log file will also provide you with a way to share data with another administrator or support professional who may be assisting you with your problem. To save the events to a log file, simply right-click the log file and select Save All Events As. This will allow you to save your event log to a file and archive it to a file share or other archival method.

Also, when you look at the many different events located in the log file, they will have one of the following four levels:

Critical Critical events represent a failure of a service and normally result in the service being shut down or crashing.

Error Events result from some application error or other fatal software issue on your server.

Warning This will indicate potential events that can occur on your server.

Information   This includes general events about tasks, normally along the lines of a service turning on successfully or a process starting.

In addition to the four levels, in your Security log, you have two additional event types specific to the security log file: audit success and audit failure. These allow you to see what tasks were audited on your server. For example, the Security log could show you when a person is successful in logging on to your server or accessing an audited file.

To work with the Event Viewer, you need to load the tool and go to the log to review the events for a particular log:

1. Open the Event Viewer by selecting Start ⇨ Administrative Tools and clicking Event Viewer.

2. Click the log you want to view, and you will see events in the pane to the right of the tree; your screen will look similar to Figure 15.21.

Figure 15.21: Event Viewer

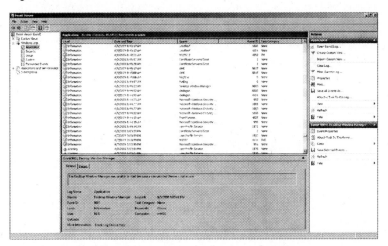

3. To view an event, double-click the event, or right-click and select Properties; you will see a screen similar to Figure 15.22.

Figure 15.22: Event properties

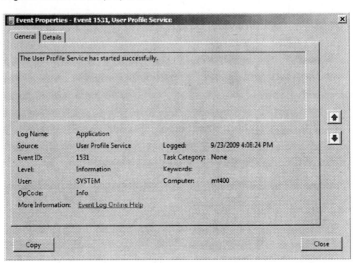

When you view the properties of the event, you can view all the details of the event, the source of the event, the event ID, the classification, and a variety of other information. Looking at the event properties arms you with the information needed to troubleshoot the problem, either by researching help or by performing a search on the Internet.

Filter Events and Creating Custom Views

One of the aspects of the Event Viewer you may have noticed is that there is a lot of server noise. In other words, there are thousands of events, so how do you find the one event or group of events that will be of the most use to you when you are trying to solve a problem? In the Event Viewer there are two ways to do this. You can either filter an existing log or create a custom view for the events.

You can filter on a variety of criteria, date, level, event ID, source, computer, user, keywords, and tasks. This will allow you to reduce the amount of event noise and quickly get to the events you are interested in.

Both of these filter mechanisms utilize very similar steps and procedures. The difference is when you filter a log, you are filtering a specific log. With custom views, you can create a custom filter that will span multiple log files on your server. To filter an event log on your server, perform the following:

1. In the Event Viewer, select the log you want to filter.

2. Click Filter Current Log either in the action pane on the right side of the console or from the menu if you right-click the log. You will see a screen similar to Figure 15.23.

Figure 15.23: Filtering an event log

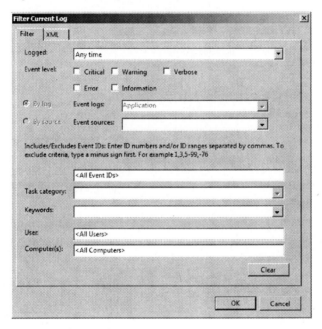

3. Select the criteria you want to filter, and when you are finished, click OK.

Once you create a filter for a log file, the filter will stay on until you turn it off. To turn off the filter on a log file, click Clear Filter in the right Actions pane of the console, or right-click the log you want to clear the filter.

**Server Tuning
and Maintenance**

PART VI

Creating a custom view follows a similar process to filtering a file:

1. In the Event Viewer, click Create Custom View, and you will see a screen similar to when you filtered a log file. The only difference is that a custom view provides you with the capability to span multiple logs. If you select all the log files, you may see an error message informing you that the view could take some time, memory, and processor time to create, as shown in Figure 15.24.

Figure 15.24: Custom view of all logs: error

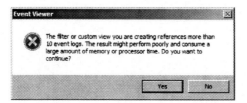

2. After you select your options, click OK.

3. Name your view, choose a location to store the view in your management tree, and click OK.

4. If you want to use your view, click the view in your management tree. By default, the views are stored under the management tree in Custom Views.

Save Event Logs

One other aspect of working with logs is saving them for future performance, analysis, and archival. You can save individual logs or even custom views you have created to files. This allows you to open logs from your own server as well as have another administrator send logs from another server for you to review. To save a log file or a custom view, you just need to right-click the log or the view.

1. In the Event Viewer, right-click your custom view or the log you want to save.

2. Select Save All Events As … when you select a Windows log to save or select Save All Events in Custom View As … when you select one of your custom views.

3. Type in a name, and select a location for the file. After you have named the file and selected a location, click Save.

4. You will see a dialog box asking you to save display information for proper viewing. This is important if you need log files to be viewed in alternate languages from your own. After you have made your selection, click OK.

You can also open saved log files or custom views by right-clicking the custom view or log files in the tree and selecting Open Saved Log.

Subscribe to Events

The Event Viewer also provides you with the ability to subscribe to events on your server or other servers. Subscribing to events allows you to see particular events as they occur. By subscribing to events, you can also view events from multiple servers in one view, since you can have events sent to one central location. Subscribing to events provides you with a similar filter mechanism as you used to create custom views.

To create a subscription on your server, you need to have the Windows Event Collector Service running on your server. The Event Viewer will help turn on this service for you. The first time you click Subscriptions in the Event Viewer management tree, you may see a screen similar to Figure 15.25. You will need to click Yes to take advantage of Event Viewer subscriptions.

Figure 15.25: Event collector server

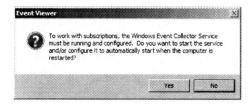

1. In the Event Viewer, click Subscriptions.

2. If prompted to turn on the Windows Event Collector Service, click Yes.

3. Click Create Subscription in the right Actions pane; you can also right-click Subscriptions. You will see a screen similar to Figure 15.26.

4. After you set the computers and filter criteria, click OK; your subscription will be complete.

Figure 15.26: Creating a subscription

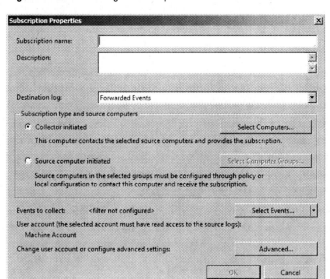

Attach a Task to an Event

One of the more proactive capabilities you can do in the Event Viewer is to attach a task to a particular log or event. Normally you attach tasks to specific events. When you attach a task to an event, you can perform one of the three following actions: start a program, send an email, or display a message. This allows you to be notified if a certain event occurs or run a program that will fix the issue. You can also assign a task to a custom view you may have created.

1. In the Event Viewer, click the event or log you want to create a task for.

2. Give your task a name and description, and when you are done, click Next.

3. Review the event you have selected, and click Next.

4. Select your option; the default is to run a program. Then click Next.

5. Depending on your action you have chosen, you may need to find the program or set up the email or message.

6. When you are done, click Next.

7. Review the summary, and click Finish. You will see a screen informing you that the task was created in Task Scheduler, as shown in Figure 15.27. Click OK to clear the message.

Figure 15.27: Task Scheduler

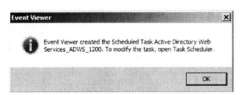

16

Keeping Your Servers Up-to-Date

IN THIS CHAPTER, YOU WILL LEARN TO:

Server Tuning and Maintenance

PART VI

Work with Windows Updates

Windows Servers are interesting from a product evolution standpoint. When a server product is "released," it is really just a point in time where Microsoft burns a DVD with the current operating system files from that designated point in time. In actuality, Windows Server is constantly being monitored through various customer and community tools that provide feedback, and Microsoft is constantly writing new updates, hotfixes, and patches for Windows Server. This process has been going on so long that there is an established rhythm of updates often referred to as Patch Tuesdays, because the updates are released on Tuesday mornings. This ecosystem of regular monitoring and regular updating creates two unique situations.

First, because the Server operating system is being updated at regular intervals, the further removed in time you are from the Windows Server release to manufacturing (RTM) date, the more updates you will need to apply after installation to get that Server up-to-date.

Second, because the Server operating system is being constantly monitored and updates are being released at regular intervals, there is really no such thing as a completed installation of Windows Server. Windows Server 2008 R2 machines are really only as good as the most recent updates you have installed on the servers. This means you will be updating your Windows Server 2008 R2 machine on a regular basis throughout its usable life cycle. There are a couple of methods that you can use to do this and a number of methods to put these updates into production on your Windows Servers.

Find Out What Updates Are

When you consider that Windows Server is constantly being monitored, reviewed, and updated, it is important to consider what exactly is defined as an update. *Updates* are additions to software that can fix or prevent problems, enhance security, or even improve performance. In the help files for Windows Server 2008 R2, Microsoft makes the following recommendation:

> We strongly recommend that you turn on Windows Automatic Updating so that windows can install security and other important or recommended updates for your computer as they become available.

This recommendation provides both insight into the paradigm that Microsoft uses in regard to updates and allows you to see the reality of the frequent changes and updates being made to Windows Server. These updates can be in the form of operating system updates, hotfixes to operating systems or applications, or patches to adjust operations of the operating system or applications.

Use Windows Update

Microsoft has been updating client and server operating systems for the last couple of decades. The company pretty much has the process down to a science. As of this writing, Microsoft makes its updates available publicly at http://update.microsoft.com. You can use this Windows Update site to install a simple application to your server that will review the status of the local server and then compare it to the currently available updates on the website. The administrator can then install the desired updates directly from Windows Update. Each copy of Internet Explorer also has a built-in link to Windows Update, as shown in Figure 16.1. You can access this link in Windows Server 2008 R2 by opening Internet Explorer 8, clicking the Safety menu, and then selecting Windows Update.

Server Tuning and Maintenance

PART VI

Figure 16.1: Accessing Windows Update through Internet Explorer

When you select Windows Update, you will notice that instead of opening a web address, Windows Update is actually a program that

is running in the Control Panel under the system and security tools. As you can see in Figure 16.2, the Windows Update tool allows you to check for updates, change settings for updates, view update history, restore hidden updates, and link to frequently asked questions about updates.

Figure 16.2: Windows Update

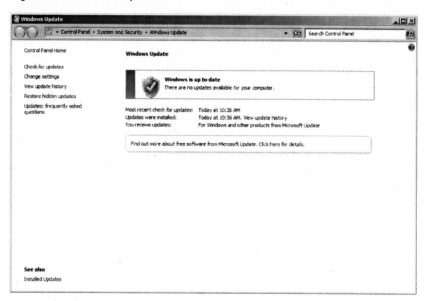

When working with Windows Update, you can specify several settings for your updates. If you click the Change Settings option in Windows Update, you can choose one of the following settings to meet your network needs:

Install Updates Automatically This setting allows the server to download and install updates automatically. This setting removes much of the administrative effort necessary to keep a Windows Server up-to-date. In addition to this setting, you can also define the frequency and time to install new updates. The default setting installs new updates daily at 3 a.m. You will learn about additional options for setting up your automatic update configuration in the next section.

Download Updates But Let Me Choose Whether To Install Them
This option ensures the most current updates are downloaded to the local server but are not actually installed until you choose to allow them. This option is beneficial in an environment where you want to test and validate updates before deploying them to your servers.

Check For Updates But Let Me Choose Whether To Download And Install Them   This option further segments the server from the updates by giving you the opportunity to review the available updates online before downloading or installing the updates.

Never Check For Updates   This option is self-explanatory. It is not recommended for the seemingly obvious reason that if you never check for updates and thus never install updates, your servers will likely be out-of-date. Before you dismiss this setting altogether, though, it might be important to consider that this setting would not necessarily be a bad thing if you were using some other system outside of Windows Update to provide updates to your Windows Server and simply did not want the additional network traffic of having the servers check for updates they should already be receiving them from another source.

It is important to note that the previous settings are only for what Microsoft has deemed "important updates." There are also "recommended updates," which can be configured the same way as important updates. There are also optional updates that will be downloaded and installed based on administrative input. Of course, you can also configure Windows Update to provide updates for additional software running on your Windows Server, such as Office, Exchange, SQL Server, and so on.

Enable Automatic Updates

Windows Update provides a convenient location and process for keeping your Windows Server up-to-date. Windows Update is a great tool, but to make the process even more effective, you can automate it by enabling automatic updates. By using automatic updates, you can eliminate the necessity of going to Windows Update and checking for updates, downloading the updates, and then installing the updates by hand. Depending on the settings you choose, you can download the

Server Tuning and Maintenance

PART VI

updates only or install the updates at a specified time (by default at 3 a.m.), as shown in Figure 16.3. All of this can be configured to be totally automated by using the settings in Windows Update. It is worth noting here that although automatic updates can simplify the process of installing updates to a server, there is also the possibility that as the updates are installed, the server may reboot if the update requires an operating system restart. Consider this implication before you enable automatic updates on your servers.

Figure 16.3: Enabling automatic updates with Windows Update

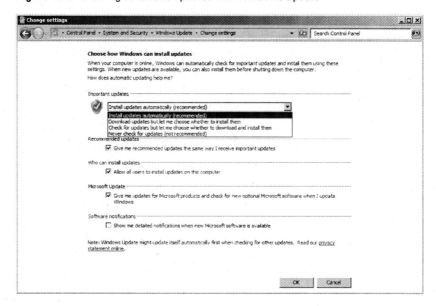

You can also enable automatic updates by using another tool that will automatically be shown after initial installation. When you install Windows Server 2008 R2, you will see a special tool called the Initial Configuration Tasks tool. This tool is broken down into three parts. The first part allows you to provide computer information such as activating windows, setting time zone, and so on. The third part allows you to customize this server by adding roles and features and configuring Remote Desktop and Windows Firewall. The middle area of the Initial

Configuration Tasks tool is the part that you can use to set the update settings for this server, as shown in Figure 16.4.

Figure 16.4: Initial Configuration Tasks tool

When you enable automatic updates, you will be given the opportunity to enable automatic updates or to configure the settings for updates manually. You will also notice that you can download and install updates using this tool.

Whether you choose to configure automatic updates using Windows Update in the Control Panel or during the initial setup of the server using the Initial Configuration Tasks tool, your Windows Server will still check for, download, and install updates using the online Windows Update site. You will not have to go and manually check on which updates are available or which updates have or have not been installed. The updates are installed based on the schedule you define when you set up the automatic updates.

View Installed Updates

With automatic updates enabled, it is easy to forget that the process of updates is occurring in the background. You may want to check periodically which updates have been installed:

1. Select Start ⇨ All Programs ⇨ Control Panel.

2. Select System And Security.

3. Double-click Windows Update.

4. Select View Update History.

As shown in Figure 16.5, when you view the update history, you will see the names of the updates that have been installed, their unique identifiers in parentheses, the status of the install, the importance of the update, and the date each update was installed. Each update can be right-clicked to view its details. One of the cool features of Windows Update in Windows Server 2008 R2 allows you to right-click any update in your update history and copy the details of the update to the Windows clipboard so you can save them to your network log file or print them for your network logbook.

Figure 16.5: Viewing the update history

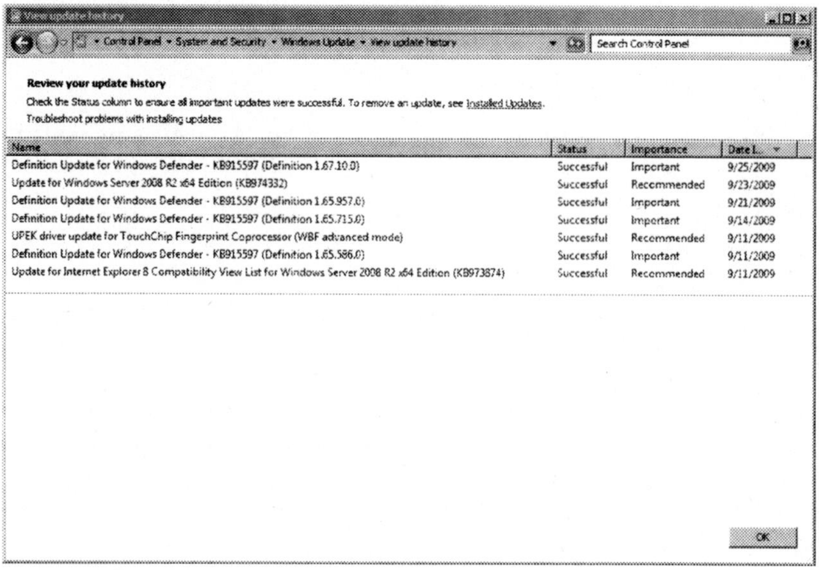

Remove an Update

All updates are not created equally. There are updates for drivers, security, Internet Explorer, Windows Defender, and a whole host of others. Operating system updates for Windows Server 2008 R2 are shown in the Windows Update history; however, they are also shown in another interface utility called simply Installed Updates. This tool not only allows you to see which updates have been installed but also allows you to select any of the installed updates and remove them, as shown in Figure 16.6.

Figure 16.6: Removing updates

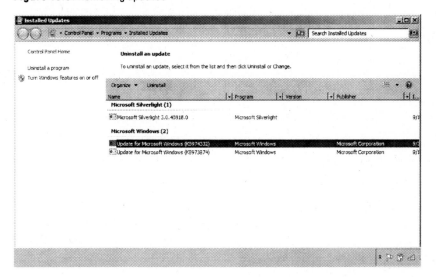

Once you remove an update from your Windows Server, it is highly probable that you will see it on the list of recommended updates again. To avoid this problem, you will need to go to the list of available updates and right-click the update. At this point, you can choose Hide Update so that it will no longer be presented to you as a recommended update.

But what if you were to remove an update and then hide it, only to find out that you actually really do want it installed on your server? The process couldn't be easier, as shown in Figure 16.7:

1. Open Windows Update.

2. Select Restore Hidden Updates.

Figure 16.7: Restoring hidden updates

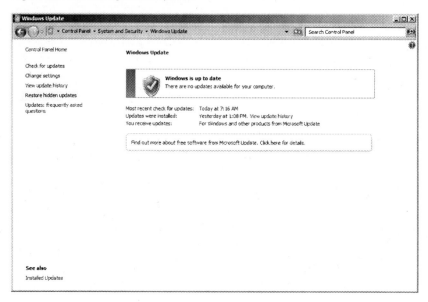

Please keep in mind here that when Microsoft addresses an issue with an update, it may address the same or similar issues again with future updates. Sometimes when you restore updates, you may not see all the updates you had previously hidden, especially if Microsoft since released another more recent update that addresses the same problem. You will only see the new update in the list.

Install Automatic Updates Between Scheduled Times

Automatic updates are great if your computer is up and running all the time. In today's world of green computing and as businesses attempt to save money by minimizing power consumption, it is possible that a scheduled update may occur at a time when your computer is powered off. If this should occur, you have a few options.

When you boot the computer, it will check for available updates and, if configured to do so, will download them. At this point, you will be prompted to install the updates or to postpone the installation to a future time. The updates will automatically be installed with other available updates when the next configured installation time is reached.

If you choose to shut down the computer and updates are waiting to be installed, you will notice a yellow shield on the shutdown button as an indicator. At this point, you can choose to install the updates and then shut down the server.

Use Group Policy to Configure Automatic Updates

Automatic updates are great because you really don't want to go from server to server checking for updates and then installing those updates manually. You probably would much rather have the server take care of that. In addition, you don't need to go to each server in your network to enable the automatic updates on that server in the first place. Group Policy is a great resource for administrators to enforce configurations for automatic updates not only on a single server but on groups of servers and clients in your network.

To configure Group Policy to enable automatic updates, you will need to do the following:

1. Open the Group Policy Management console.

2. Select the policy you will edit (or create a new one).

3. Right-click the policy, and choose Edit.

4. Expand Computer Configuration.

5. Expand Policies.

6. Expand Administrative Templates.

7. Expand Windows Components.

8. Select Windows Update, as shown in Figure 16.8.

9. You will notice that there are 16 options in this policy container having to do with Windows Update. When working with policies, remember that policies have three possible states: enabled, disabled, and not configured. To configure automatic updates using Group Policy, you will need to select the policy called Configure Automatic Updates, as shown in Figure 16.8. Double-click the policy, and then choose Enabled.

Server Tuning and Maintenance

PART VI

Figure 16.8: GPME for Windows Update

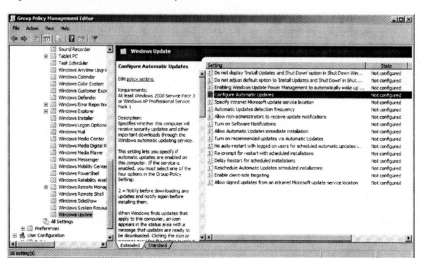

The Configure Automatic Updates policy setting has four different values that you will need to choose from when you enable this policy. They are numbered from 2 through 5, as shown in Figure 16.9:

2 This notifies you before downloading any updates and notifies you again before installing any updates.

3 This is the default setting. This downloads the updates automatically and then notifies you when they are ready to be installed.

4 This automatically downloads the updates and then automatically installs them based on a time scheduled in the Configure Automatic Updates policy setting.

5 This allows local administrators to select the configuration mode for automatic updates. This means the local administrators can choose when the updates will be installed by using their local Windows Update; however, they cannot turn off automatic updates.

Once you have selected one of the four options, you will likely need to establish the scheduled install day and time. There are eight options labeled 0 through 8. Don't ask us where the crazy numbering comes from—first 2 through 5, and now 0 through 8. Just smile and configure the settings.

Figure 16.9: Configure Automatic Updates policy setting's options

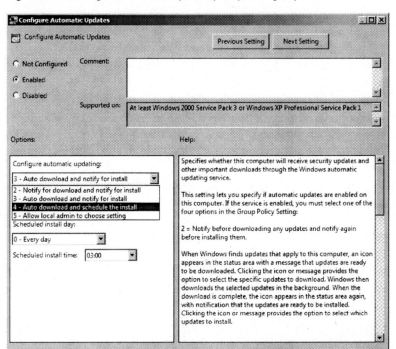

If you want the updates to install every day, choose option 0. If you want the updates to be installed only once a week on a given day, then choose the number representation for the day you want the updates to install:

0 = Every day

1 = Sunday

2 = Monday

3 = Tuesday

4 = Wednesday

5 = Thursday

6 = Friday

7 = Saturday

You will also need to establish a time for the updates to be installed on the scheduled day. The default here is 3 a.m. This setting is made using a 24-hour time setting, so if you wanted to have updates installed in the late evening hours, say at 11 p.m., you would select 23:00. Once this policy is set, you can apply it to servers in your network's sites, domains, or organizational units.

There is an additional setting here that will make automatic updates immediately install. When this setting is configured, it will allow an update to install immediately if the update does not require a restart of the Windows operating system or the interruption of Windows services.

Windows Server 2008 R2 will check for updates using an automatic update detection frequency of 22 hours by default. If you want to change that frequency, you can do so using the policy setting entitled Automatic Updates Detection Frequency. This setting when enabled will specify the number of hours between automatic update checks. The setting is interesting because the server will actually choose a value located somewhere between the actual setting in hours and 20 percent less than its value. This means that if you use a value of 20 hours, the server will check for automatic updates every 16 to 20 hours. This policy works in direct conjunction with Configure Automatic Updates and with Specify Intranet Microsoft Update Service Location.

The policy called Specify Intranet Microsoft Update Service Location is used to enable Windows Update from a server within your corporate network. This means you can provide a central network location to provide updates to your server and client computers inside your network. This can be very desirable in many cases because your server and clients are not getting their updates from an Internet property but rather from an internal network location that can be tightly monitored and controlled.

The desire to move to an even more automated system of updating servers located inside the corporate network and to provide as much automation as possible for Windows Updates will eventually lead you to a group of resources called Windows Server Update Services.

Work with Windows Server Update Services

Windows Server Update Services (WSUS) 3.0 SP2 is a comprehensive resource to help you deploy updates to the servers and clients in your network. This tool is a free download from the Microsoft website. It is incredibly flexible and can be used in very small to very large network environments. WSUS is installed on a server or group of servers in your network and acts as an intranet-based Windows Update server.

Do a Simple WSUS Deployment

In its most basic form, a WSUS deployment consists of a single server on the local intranet inside the DMZ and inside the Internet firewall. This server will be used to connect to Microsoft Update and download available updates in a process that is called *synchronization*. You will synchronize the WSUS server with the Windows Update servers on a regular basis, and the WSUS server will verify that available updates have been synchronized to the WSUS server. The initial synchronization will take an extended period of time if your Internet connection speed is good and longer if it is not. Subsequent synchronizations will be faster because the WSUS server is only synchronizing new updates that have been made available.

WSUS uses standard HTTP ports 80 and 443 to access and download the updates from Microsoft Update. These ports are likely already open on your firewall; if they are not, you will need to open them in order to use the WSUS server. It is possible to change the default communication ports to meet your network's specific needs.

Depending on the size and structure of your network, you may choose to add a WSUS server to your network. These additional servers can be configured to get their updates from the existing WSUS server. This process is called *chaining* servers together. As you chain more and more WSUS servers together, the WSUS deployment can become quite complex.

Automatic Updating is the client-side part of WSUS deployments. The service has to use the port assigned to the WSUS website in IIS. If there are no websites running on the server where you install WSUS, you can choose to use the default website (port 80) or a custom website (ports 8530 or 8531).

Use Computer Groups

One of the coolest things about WSUS deployments is the use of computer groups. Computer groups allow you to target updates to specific groups of computers on your network. There are two default computer groups called All Computers and Unassigned Computers. Each computer that is added to WSUS is added to these two groups. You will

Server Tuning and Maintenance

PART VI

create additional groups to allow WSUS to target updates to specific groups of computers, and you will add computers to your new groups from the Unassigned Computers group. It is important to remember that you cannot remove computers from the All Computers group.

Computer groups allow you to structure your machines in such a way to make it possible to test updates on a small group of machines before deploying those same updates on a broader scale to the rest of your network. If the testing works well, then broad deployment can be easily accomplished. If there is a problem in testing, then you have limited the scope of the problem to a small computer group instead of the whole network.

Use WSUS Server Hierarchy

As mentioned earlier, it is possible to chain WSUS servers together. There are two ways to build those links:

- In *autonomous mode*, the upstream server, or the server connected to Microsoft Update, shares synchronization information with its downstream partner but does not share its computer group information. This way, the available updates are passed from WSUS server to WSUS server while maintaining the integrity of the individual computer groups.

- In *replica mode*, the upstream server shares its synchronization information and its computer group information with its downstream partners. The downstream partners hold the same information and are thus functional replicas of the upstream WSUS server.

It is recommended that you do not create hierarchy beyond three levels deep. At that point, the synchronization lag time introduced to the process becomes prohibitive.

Get WSUS Updates on Disconnected Networks

It is sometimes necessary to operate servers and clients on a network that is not connected to the Internet or to other networks. Servers and clients operating in isolation still need updates. WSUS makes it possible to supply updates to isolated network segments through a simple process:

1. Connect WSUS to Microsoft Update on a connected network.

2. Synchronize the available updates to the WSUS server.

3. Export the updates to media.

4. Hand carry the media to the isolated network segment.

5. Import the updates to the isolated WSUS server.

6. Deploy the updates to the isolated servers and clients.

This method not only makes it possible to deliver updates to isolated or disconnected networks but can also be used to limit the bandwidth in traditional connected WSUS deployments. For example, you might choose to have a single WSUS server synchronize updates with Microsoft Update and then export those updates to DVDs; then you can send the DVDs to be imported to each of your other WSUS servers instead of downloading the same information and slowing performance on the WAN.

Use WSUS with Branch Cache

One of the features of Window Server 2008 R2 is branch cache. This feature can improve WAN performance by caching content on branch servers in order to make that content available to local clients without the need of constant WAN access. If the branch cache feature is installed on Windows Server 2008 R2, it can be used to cache the WSUS synchronization and computer group information. This can really improve the responsiveness of your WSUS servers that are located in branch-office locations.

Choose a Database for WSUS

WSUS requires a database in order to operate; however, you do not need to purchase a database product in order to use WSUS. When you install WSUS 3.0 SP2, it will check for an available database. If it does not find one, it will install one for you. The database it will install by default is called the Windows Internal Database. This is a small-scale version of SQL Server. This version of SQL Server is very simple and does not require hardly any management. (If you want to install full-version SQL Server to host the database for WSUS, you are welcome to do so, but it is not required.) The WSUS database stores the WSUS configuration information, a metadata description of each update, and information about the client computers, updates, and interactions.

Although there is a database that will store information about the updates and the clients that will use the updates, you will not be managing WSUS through the database. There is a built-in management tool called WSUS Manger where you will manage the WSUS servers, updates, clients, and computer groups.

Learn Where to Store the Updates

The ideal place to store the updates from Windows Update is on the local WSUS server. This saves the network bandwidth of clients accessing the WSUS server only to be pointed to another network location to download the updates. There is one caveat here; the updates are going to take up a fair amount of space. Microsoft recommends that you have at least 20GB of local storage at a minimum and actually recommends 30GB. Keep in mind that these numbers are only estimates and could go higher than 30GB depending on your network needs and particular situation.

It is possible to use WSUS to approve updates for your network and then store those updates remotely. The most extreme example of this design would be to use the WSUS server to approve updates for your local clients and then point them to the Internet-based Windows Update servers for the updates. This effectively eliminates the requirement to store updates locally while still allowing you to test and approve the updates coming in to your network.

WSUS uses the Background Intelligent Transfer Service 2.0 (BITS 2.0) protocol for all of its file transfer needs. Each time files are downloaded from servers to clients, they are moved using "spare" bandwidth. This technology also makes it possible to continue downloads, even if the computer is shut down in the middle of a download, once the computer is restarted.

Learn the WSUS Requirements

To run WSUS, your servers must meet the following minimum requirements:

- CPU: 1GHz minimum. 1.5GHz or better is recommended.
- Graphics card: 16MB hardware accelerated or better is recommended.
- RAM: 1GB minimum; 2GB or better is recommended.
- Page file: At least 1.5 times the physical memory is recommended.

- I/O: Fast ATA/IDE 100 hard disk or equivalent SCSI drives are recommended.

- Network adapter: 10MB minimum; 100MB or better is recommended.

- The system partition and the install partition for WSUS must be formatted with the NTFS file system.

- 1GB minimum free space on the system partition is recommended.

- 2GB minimum free space on the volume on which the database files will be stored is recommended.

- 20GB minimum free space on the volume where the content will be stored; 30GB is recommended.

- WSUS cannot be installed on compressed drives.

The current hardware requirements for WSUS should be easily met if you are running Windows Server 2008 R2. If you are not running Windows Server 2008 R2 as your WSUS machine, it is possible to use Windows Server 2003 SP2 or later as your WSUS server and install WSUS 3.0 SP2.

Get More Information on WSUS

WSUS is a great tool for controlling the update process in your network. To understand its true potential and the details associated with deploying and using WSUS, you will want to get the WSUS 3.0 SP2 deployment guide, as well as the WSUS step-by-step guides, available at http://technet.microsoft.com/en-us/wsus/default.aspx.

The information provided there will provide a strong base for using WSUS in your network.

Index

Symbols

$_ variable, 95
| (pipe symbol), 95

A

access
    auditing AD, 168–171
    with IIS role services, 331
    implementing DFS, 243–251
    implementing permissions,
        222–229
    with RD Gateway. *See* Remote
        Desktop Gateway
    with Remote Desktop Web
        Access. *See* Remote Desktop
        Web Access
    shadow copy, 285–286
    share folder, 229–232
    zone security, 389–390
access control entries (ACEs)
    auditing AD with, 169
    defined, 222
access control lists (ACLs), 222
Account Lockout Duration, 135
Account Lockout Threshold, 135
accounts
    creating local user, 118–120
    default local users and groups,
        112–114
    local policies, 130–135
    managing local, 124–127
    permissions. *See* permissions

setting passwords with
    PowerShell commands, 152
ACEs (access control entries)
    auditing AD with, 169
    defined, 222
ACLs (access control lists), 222
activation
    RD Licensing Server, 432–433
    Windows Server Core, 21
Active Directory (AD). *See* AD
    (Active Directory)
Active Directory Administrator
    Center (ADAC), 145–148
Active Directory Service Interfaces
    Editor (ADSI Edit), 172–176
Active Server Pages (ASP), 329
AD (Active Directory)
    adding DNS servers, 364–365
    auditing, 168–171
    automating user and group
        management, 148–155
    Best Practices Analyzer, 497
    creating PSOs, 172–176
    default password
        requirements, 120
    defragmenting directory
        database, 165–168
    fine-grained password policy,
        171–172
    installing on Server Core, 65–68
    joining domain as member, 138
    local groups and, 139–140
    maintaining FSMO roles,
        159–161

Printed in the United States of America
ED-01-07-13